Christ in Men... Today

52 Weeks of Building Spiritual Muscle, One Character Quality at a time

By

Mike Thornton

Bladensburg, MD

Christ in Men... Today

Published by
Inscript Books
a division of Dove Christian Publishers
P.O. Box 611
Bladensburg, MD 20710-0611
www.dovechristianpublishers.com

Cover Design by Mike Thornton

ISBN: 978-1-7348625-7-7

Library of Congress Catalog No. 2020947390

Names: Thornton, Mike, author.
Title: Christ in men... today : 52 weeks of building spiritual muscle, one character quality at a time / Mike Thornton.
Description: Bladensburg, MD : Inscript Books, 2020. | Also available in ebook format.
Identifiers: LCCN 2020947390 (print) | ISBN 978-1-7348625-7-7 (paperback)
Subjects: LCSH: Christian men--Religious life. | Christian men--Prayers and devotions. | Men--Conduct of life. | Prayers. | Devotional exercises. | BISAC: RELIGION / Christian Living / Men's Interests. | RELIGION / Christian Living / Inspirational. | RELIGION / Christian Living / Devotional. | RELIGION / Christian Living / Family & Relationships.
Classification: LCC BV4528.2 .T56 2020 (print) | LCC BV4528.2 (ebook) | DDC 242/.642--dc23.

Published in the United States of America
25 24 23 22 21 20 1 2 3 4 5

I dedicate this book to **Linda**, my wife of 50 years—the woman I love with all my heart—from whom I've learned many of the life lessons shared in this book and who has helped me polish the rough edges of these pages and my life. Thanks, honey; I wouldn't trade one minute. Thanks for 50 years of investing in me. Your reward is great in Heaven,

...and to my daughters **Charlene** and **Jennifer**, both of whom love the Lord and are good models of a Christian wife and mother. They are also a daily reminder that it was all worth it.

To my good friend, **Jim Darst**, who has encouraged me often and without whom, this book probably would not have been finished. Thanks, Jimmy.

To my "adopted" daughter, **Tempest Edwards**, a successful screenwriter and also a flowing fount of encouragement and sometimes necessary prodding to keep me focused and moving forward with this manuscript.

And finally, to my **Lord and Savior, Jesus Christ**, whose Spirit continually gave me subject matter when I sat idle at the keyboard, who has filled me with a love for His Word, and most importantly, has planted in my soul a hope for eternity that grows bigger and bolder each day as I get nearer and nearer to His upward call.

Contents

"For the word of the cross is foolishness to those who are perishing, but to us who are being saved it is the power of God." I Cor. 1:18

Introduction / Invitation

I was an Army Drill Sergeant for Basic Training during Vietnam, a time when you could still be a, well…Drill Sergeant. No political correctness. No feelings to worry about. We were at war, and boys needed to become men in a hurry. One of the things that fed my ego the most was walking into my trainees' barracks and having someone yell, "Atten-shun!" and see everybody scramble to their feet. In many ways, this book shares my journey about God getting *my* attention and turning me from a boy into a man of God.

On this journey, I've been down many rabbit trails that led to disappointment, frustration, and eventually back to forgiveness. I've lost jobs, been cheated out of money, accused wrongly, buried two of my children, and spent almost three years on disability from a motorcycle accident that wasn't my fault.

But through it all, God has been patiently wooing me, correcting my thinking, and slowly putting to death my pride. I say slowly because I fight Him at every turn. I'm comfortable with my pride. And that puts me at odds with surrendering my will to really become the man God intends. I can relate to the Apostle Paul when he talks about doing the things he doesn't want to do (Romans 7:14-25). Don't misunderstand. I'm not there yet, and sometimes it seems more like a forced march with a 50 lb. pack than a Sunday afternoon stroll around the lake, but I am on the right road.

What will it take for God to get *your* attention? I'm not implying that God awaits your wrong turns with glee and a big hammer. Quite the opposite. God's patience is legend. Look at how long he suffered the complaining and insubordination of Israel yet still loved them. But even God's patience has limits. Try to imagine yourself in God's shoes time after time, dealing with the rebellion, grumbling, and disbelief hurled at Him by the Israelites. The thing I'm amazed about is that God didn't zap them sooner. But you and I are the recipients of that same patience and grace. If I got zapped every time I deserved it, there'd be nothing left of me.

The goal of this book is to share with you some of the things I've learned and to point your attention to the only answer—the only anchor—we have in our sin-corrupted world and encourage you that no matter your trials, you have a faithful companion (Deut. 31:6) who will never forsake you. Will you come with me? This book is about character, and I define it this way: "Character is that which is developed through the exercise of my spiritual muscles in trials and prosperity, amid throngs or alone, realizing that growth is a process—not an event—which continues as long as I do; the ultimate measure of which is, How much am I like Jesus?"

"This is the day which the Lord has made; let us rejoice and be glad in it." Psa. 118:24

Today. It's the only day we have. Yesterday is a memory. We can't spend tomorrow. This is about living in the moment, not presuming on the future. That's not to say we shouldn't have a plan if God grants us one more day. But too often, we live in our plan and not in the present. Jesus asks us a pointed question: "*Who of you by being worried can add a single hour to his life?"*[1] Before we are born, God assigns a certain number of days to each of us.[2] Thankfully, we don't know how many. But here's the point. Live each day as if Christ will call you home that day. What will you be doing when He calls? Will He be able to say, "Well done"?

The idea for this book was born over 25 years ago when, for a period of several days, I arose each morning with a new thought about Christ's character qualities. As I jotted them down, I wondered if this could be the making of a daily "devotional." I hesitate to use that word because it smacks of routine drudgery and discipline. But think of the root: *devotion*. Isn't that what God would have of us? Hasn't He said, "You shall have no other gods before Me?"[3] I don't know about you, but I prefer "rubber hits the road" stuff that I can relate to. It's been said, "A message prepared in the mind reaches another mind. A message prepared in the heart reaches another heart." I've tried to share thoughts from my personal journey to a deeper walk with Christ and, in many ways, I've written this book for myself, to be an encouragement on those days I succumb to the temptation to throw myself a pity party. You're welcome to read along. Hopefully, you don't have any of those days.

My prayer as you begin this book is that it will challenge you to draw close to the one true God, creator of heaven and earth, from whom we receive **all** that we need for this world and the next. Please take time to look up the footnotes and read the context.

As we begin our journey together, may I offer you one piece of advice? Say you live in Oregon and want to drive to Florida, but you've never been there. One of the things you'll do is consult an atlas. You'll choose where to stop along the way, whether you want the fastest or most scenic route. The fact is that you *trust* completely in the Mapmaker to get you to your destination. The Christian walk is exactly like that. The Bible is the atlas, and God is the Mapmaker. The question to consider is, "Where do you want to go as your final destination?" The way is clearly marked; Jesus said, "*I am the way and the truth and the life; no one comes to the Father but through Me.*"[4] There are only two final destinations: heaven and hell. Choose wisely; eternity is a long time.

A common denominator for a life of fear, stress, and uncertainty is the need for spiritual peace, to know that your eternal future is secured with a title deed in the right place. There is ONLY ONE way to find that…in Jesus Christ. Each week is a different character quality modeled by Jesus in His life on earth. Each character quality has one week's worth of daily writings intended to encourage a life of righteousness, faithfulness, and purpose.

The reaction to the coronavirus has shown everyone how quickly life on earth can change for the worse. And this isn't even God's (final) judgment yet. But suppose a day, actually a moment, is coming when, like the flip of a light switch, God calls timeout. At that second, everyone will be in one of two camps: those who believed God's warnings

---

1 Matt. 6:27
2 Psa. 139:16
3 Ex. 20:3
4 John 14:6

and prepared, and those who didn't. That day IS coming…soon, and there won't be any additional warnings.

If you're not sure which camp you're in, or if you think that you've "been good enough," then this book is for you. The most important decision you will ever face is how you answer the question when God asks, "What did you do with my Son Jesus?"

Please take time to read these daily words of truth. Your eternal future is at stake. If, after reading, you'd like to learn more about how you can know for sure that you'll be in the right group, turn to page 368 or email us and let us know how we can help. Someone will get back to you right away.

If you'd like prayer for yourself or someone else, email us and give us the prayer request. We welcome your comments. We WILL pray. "*Therefore let us draw near with confidence to the throne of grace, so that we may receive mercy and find grace to help in time of need.*" Heb. 4:16

Mike Thornton
https://needanewplan.com/
MikeThornton2020@gmail.com

Week 1 Sunday

Accountability is telling my children, "Don't do as I say, do as I do."

"Be imitators of me just as I also am of Christ." I Cor. 11:1

It seems exactly the opposite of what a humble person would say: "Do what I do." But that is precisely what Paul says to his Corinthian readers. Keep in mind Paul's goal was not to create little Pauls, but little Christs. Imitating Paul would not result in perfection, but it would increase righteousness, another step in our sanctification.

How are we doing in modeling Christ for our kids? Do they see our emotions (frustration, anger, bitterness, etc.) and do all in their power to avoid us? Or is Christ's love, compassion, and patience visible, drawing them closer to us and Jesus?

Today, be conscious of both audiences; those who live with us and the audience of One.

Father, help me remember that my children are always watching me to see if You're real. May I not abdicate my responsibility or leave it to my wife to model You for them. Help me this week to be the kind of example that, if followed, will bring honor to You. **Amen**.

Accountability is using the Internet in the living room

"Woe to those who deeply hide their plans from the Lord and whose deeds are done in a dark place, and they say, 'Who sees us?' or 'Who knows us?'" Isa. 29:15.

When the things that are unseen are what make up the real world and the things that are seen will all pass away, it's difficult to remember that the all-seeing God is just that – all-seeing. We think if we close our door or turn out the lights or pull the shades, nobody will observe our dark acts.

But don't forget what the Psalmist wrote in 139:12: "*Even the darkness is not dark to You, and the night is as bright as the day. Darkness and light are alike to You.*"

Could Jonah hide from God? No. Has God changed or gotten more lenient? No. So why do we think we can hide (ourselves or our acts) from God? How would our lives change if we were cognizant of the reality that God watches everything? Would we be nicer to our neighbors? Would our expense report be precise? Could we visit all the same websites?

Today, begin the habit of "Practicing God's Presence"[1] and note any changes in your daily activities in a journal.

Father, it's so easy to think that nobody's looking, that just this once won't hurt. Help me be faithful every time. **Amen**.

1 Murray's *Practice of God's Presence*

Accountability is going over my checkbook with my spouse

"You have placed our iniquities before you, our secret sins in the light of your presence." Psalm 90:8

Money can be a temptation whether we have it in abundance or just enough to get by. The secret to its management is realizing that God has given us whatever we have, and He has expectations and guidelines as to its use. Discussing and praying about expenses with your wife is a good way to keep selfish or inappropriate desires at bay.

God has given our wives insight and sensitivity to things that sometimes we gloss over because of our lusts. There is nothing intrinsically wrong with money—even lots of it. Christian organizations need funding. The poor need food. That takes money. But it also takes the right attitude.

If we're giving to be seen or to gain the praise of men, it becomes wood, hay, and stubble. Giving, prompted by the right motive, is always blessed. God even tells us to "put me to the test"[2] regarding our giving. Do it. Take Him at His word. Then expect to see "blessings that overflow."[3]

Lord, You look at money as an indicator of the condition of my heart. Help me to see my heart the way You do and control my spending, so I use whatever finances You bless me with for Your glory. **Amen**.

2 Mal. 3:10
3 ibid

Accountability is letting my spouse dish up my ice cream

"Have you found honey? Eat only what you need that you not have it in excess and vomit it." Prov. 25:16

Is more always better? Jim Rohn, a popular motivational speaker in the '80s and '90s, used to ask his audiences, "Have you heard this—an apple a day…" and then he would add, "it's not a candy bar a day…" Now there's nothing wrong with candy bars (or ice cream) – in moderation. It's a question of who (or what) is in control of God's temple.[4]

When God warns us not to overdo certain things, does that mean He wants to deprive us of good things? Not at all. In fact, it's just the opposite. He wants to give us all things.[5] Do you give your kids as much as they want of everything they want? Of course not. Why? Because you know it wouldn't be good for them.

There are issues of balance, proper nutrition, discipline, etc. Don't you think God, who invented parenting, looks at us the same way? Sometimes, when we have trouble saying no, we need encouragement (a euphemism for a slap on the head) from our wife to help us exercise the right choices. Don't fight it. Remember, she's a gift from "dad."[6]

Father, sometimes my appetites get the best of me, and I know that I'm not taking the best care of Your temple. Teach me to say no when giving in to the desires that could diminish my witness and cause an unbelieving world to sneer. **Amen**.

4 I Cor. 6:19,20
5 Rom 8:32
6 Prov. 19:14

Accountability is leaving my office door open when my secretary is in my office

"To deliver you from the strange woman, from the adulteress who flatters with her words." Prov. 2:16

Pride will whisper in your ear that it won't happen to you, it can't happen to you. You love your wife and family too much. Watch out.[7] With the door closed (or shades pulled, lights out, etc.), it's easy to be misled into thinking nobody will know.

Here's the truth. It doesn't happen the first time you close your door. It's a process that can take months or even years. You get lulled into complacency. You might be able to pull it off for a while. And the excitement and pleasure will seem worth the risk.

But sooner or later, some event or series of "coincidences" will conspire against you, and it's over. You have risked your family, your job, your reputation for a lie. No amount of self-pity or blame ("My wife doesn't understand me.") can undo the disaster.

Keep a picture of your wife and family in a prominent place in your office, a place where you and visitors can see it. You're a businessman. Ask yourself value questions such as: What's the return on investment (of a fling)? What will my shareholders (family) think of it? The solution is easy. Keep your door open when it's just you and another woman.

God, I know you created us male and female with an attraction for each other. Help me to avoid the tree with the forbidden fruit. **Amen**.

7 I Cor. 10:12

Accountability is having a small group that will ask me the tough questions

"Iron sharpens iron, so one man sharpens another." Prov. 27:17

Alpha Male. Top Dog. Leader of the Pack. President. Society likes to hang monikers on its leaders. Sometimes it's for identification purposes, and that's not a bad thing. The bad thing is when we start to think we deserve the title and the respect that leadership accords.

Remember what Jesus told His disciples? "*But it is not this way among you, but whoever wishes to become great among you shall be your servant.*" [8]

One way to avoid the snares of pride, vis-a-vis leadership, is to have a small group of guys who are honest and have earned your trust that you can meet with or call on the phone who will ask you the tough questions. This is difficult for most men because we've bought the lie that we don't need anybody.

You know the old saw, "Power tends to corrupt and absolute power corrupts absolutely."[9] Don't buy what they say about you. You may be a great leader, or you might be a field hand. Flattery is defined as excessive or insincere praise. Its aim is usually selfishly motivated, i.e., what can you do for me?

Even within Jesus' twelve, there were three (Peter, James, and John) that were His inner circle. Do you have anybody (another man) you can really open up to? Make it a priority…today.

Father, sometimes I don't want the honing another godly man can bring. Help me see that as a red flag of my spiritual condition and welcome the teaching, correction, reproof, and counsel for righteous living. **Amen**.

8 Mark 10:43
9 Lord Acton, 1887

Accountability is having specific times for prayer

"And he came to the disciples and found them sleeping and said to Peter, 'So you men could not keep watch with me for one hour? Keep watching and praying that you may not enter into temptation; the spirit is willing, but the flesh is weak.'" Matt. 26:40

How big is your God? Is He too big to be bothered with your insignificant requests? Is He preoccupied with running the universe, and you think, "I can handle this one."?

What's the real reason you don't pray? Pride? Lack of faith? Maybe you just don't understand what prayer is all about? Maybe your biological father left scars that you blame God for, and it's hard to relate to your heavenly father. The world will take your side and say, "that's OK, it's not your fault."

But that doesn't get you closer to the only One who can pierce that protective shield you've built around yourself. If you're having trouble praying, start at the beginning. Ask yourself who God is. Read specific promises about the relationship He wants with you. See Matt. 11:28 "*Come unto me…and I will give you rest,*" and John 15:14,15 "*You are my friends…*" and John 14:2,3 "*I go to prepare a place for you…that where I am, you may be also,*" and many more.

If God didn't want anything to do with you, would He have gone to all the trouble of making the way possible for you to spend eternity with Him? Would He have called you "friend"? Sometimes, the best way to start praying is by thanking God [10] for whatever you're thankful for. "*Every good thing given and every perfect gift is from above, coming down from the Father of lights…*"[11]

How about thanking God for the sun, rain, trees, your senses of sight, hearing, your family, your job, friends, you get the idea. Once you start and allow your heart to overflow with gratitude (you *do* know everything you have God gave to you,[12] don't you?), and you remember that God wants you to talk to Him,[13] and believe that not only *can* God answer, but that He *wants to* answer, you'll want to spend more time with Him.

Also, don't worry about proper phraseology or sentence structure. God looks at your heart and knows your thoughts and desires even without uttering them. Trust Him. Everything He does for you is for your best.

And lastly, pray. Get started. Even if you're not comfortable with it, do it. Try setting a specific time each day and stick with it. One thing that will help is to keep a journal of answered prayer. The more you see God active in your life and on your behalf, the more you'll want to spend time with Him.

Father, if I'm honest with myself and you, I don't know how to pray. I want to have it all together and impress You. Help me remember that You know me, warts and all, and none of that matters. You just want to spend time with me. Drill that into my whole being. **Amen.**

---

10 Eph. 5:20
11 James 1:17
12 I Cor. 4:7
13 I Thess. 5:17

Alertness is the state of mind in which, because of my knowledge of God's truth and standards and my obedience to them, I am able to discern false teaching and actions that are wholly or in part contrary and reject them.

"And do not be conformed to this world, but be transformed by the renewing of your mind, so that you may prove what the will of God is, that which is good and acceptable and perfect." Rom. 12:2

Why do you think con men are so successful? Often, it is because their "con" contains a splinter of truth. The best lies, if you can rank lies, succeed because of partial truths. Where do lies come from? Jesus told us that Satan is a liar and the father of lies.[14] But are we alert enough, do we have enough scripture treasured up in our hearts[15] that we can smell a rat when confronted by a pious-sounding lie?

It's been told that the Feds responsible for detecting counterfeit money don't spend their time studying counterfeit money. They spend time studying the real thing, so when confronted with a counterfeit, no matter how good, they can spot it immediately.

Are you a "Berean"[16] in your Bible study? Can you spot a false teacher? A false religious idea? You don't have to look very far to spot them in the plethora of religious groups available to you today. For a great discussion of false teaching and an accompanying warning, see John MacArthur's book, *The Truth War*.[17]

Your challenge, should you choose to accept it, is to apply the filter of Scripture to the entry portals of your mind. Don't accept "new truth" without testing it against God's finished revelation. If it doesn't line up perfectly, toss it; it's a lie.

Father, Your Word is the only standard of truth. Help me be alert enough to recognize when I'm confronted with lies, no matter how good they sound and how much they appeal to my ego. **Amen.**

14 John 8:44
15 Ps. 119:11
16 Acts 17:11
17 Thomas Nelson Publ., 2007

Alertness is listening to the Holy Spirit's warnings.

"Do not grieve the Holy Spirit of God, by whom you were sealed for the day of redemption." Eph. 4:30

Are you a hunter, a fisherman, a soldier? How do you improve your craft? Don't we want the best tools and weapons at our disposal? Do you realize that one of the best tools we can have is the advice of someone who's been there and done that? Don't we have a better chance of success if we know "where they're biting"?

In the spiritual realm, who has been there and done that better than the Holy Spirit? What does it mean to quench the Spirit? One definition is to put out or extinguish. It's pretty easy in our society of constant noise and clutter to miss the quiet voice of the Lord.[18] Try turning your iPod down, pull out your headphones, listen, meditate.

God wants to communicate with us.[19] But, news flash, God NEVER contradicts His Word with new revelation. How well have we read, memorized, and meditated on our "sword"?[20] Are we continually sharpening it? Don't expect to hear an audible voice, but DO expect the Spirit to speak to your spirit through His Word. Try spending a few minutes of silence after you've read the Word for the day. Don't rush into your day and expect the peace and confidence which only comes from time with God.

Father, I confess that noise is often more comfortable than the quietness I need to hear your spirit. Draw me to you and let me hear only your spirit's voice. **Amen**

18I Kin. 19:11,12
19 Isa. 51:7
20 Eph. 6:17

Week 2 – Tuesday

Alertness is listening to my spouse's warnings.

"Then the Lord God said, "It is not good for the man to be alone. I will make him a helper suitable for him." Gen. 2:18

Ever give much thought to why God said it wasn't good for the man to be alone? Of course, procreation enters the discussion. But what about our tendency to think we know more than we do, especially in the realm of relationships, thoughtfulness, compassion?

God gave us wives as helpers. I believe it was for far more than help with the dishes and laundry. Women, as a rule, are more sensitive to spiritual things. As a rule, they pray more. This is what gives them insight into God's heart. As a result, if we listen to them, we might just make better decisions and avoid some of life's pitfalls. Don't let pride keep you from seeking and heeding your wife's advice.

Lord, help me see all the good and positive things you've given my wife to help me. I know I don't always listen to her, and the humble pie doesn't taste too good. May I see her as your personal gift to me to make life more harmonious. Thank you. **Amen**.

Alertness is watching for changes in attitudes or behavior of those in my care.

"Either make the tree good and its fruit good, or make the tree bad and its fruit bad; for the tree is known by its fruit." Matt. 12:33

Children are God's gift to us.[21] We have an obligation to them and God to model Christ—teach them by words and deeds. What are they watching and listening to? Who are their friends? Where do they hang out? Do they accuse you of being old-fashioned, out of touch with today?

Someday, we'll give account to God for the stewardship we have practiced not only with our finances but also the other talents and our families. The good news is we're not accountable for results, just faithfulness.

Are you too tired when you come home to invest in your kids' lives by talking, listening, challenging them? Then your priorities are out of whack. Make today the day you recommit yourself to your family. Set the bar high. Then monitor progress. Look for small "tells" that indicate rough road ahead. Don't wait to apply course correction. Be vigilant to protect your most important treasure—your family.

God, you created the family and have given me mine. Help me look at them as gifts, not inconveniences. May you empower me to be the kind of example that points them to you and the narrow path to heaven. Thank you for trusting me with them. **Amen**

21 Psa. 127:3

Week 2 – Thursday

Alertness is knowing that I am susceptible to certain temptations and to stay away from circumstances in which those temptations are likely to occur.

"Now flee from youthful lusts and pursue righteousness, faith, love and peace, with those who call on the Lord from a pure heart." II Tim. 2:22

When it comes to physical danger, God has given us a "fight or flight" trigger mechanism. Our heart pounds, the adrenalin flows, and we're on high alert. How do we sense danger in the spiritual realm? Easy as A-B-C.

First, there must be **A**bsolutes. It's always wrong to steal.[22] It's always wrong to cheat on your wife.[23] If you don't know where you're going, any road will take you there. Second, you must be **B**rave enough to stand alone when others taunt you for not "going along to get along."[24] Third, you must make a **C**ommitment to do the right thing even when you think nobody is looking or will know.[25]

What are your specific temptations? Admiration from others? Addictive behavior? Alluring websites? Take some time today to identify specific areas of weakness and ask God (and one or more trusted friends) to help you overcome these temptations.

Father, the way of temptation is a delight to my eyes and other senses, but I know it leads to death. Help me remember and focus on the end of my journey, not just the next step, and keep me on the narrow path. **Amen**.

22 Ex. 20:15
23 Ex. 20:14
24 Ps. 106:23
25 II Chr. 16:9

Week 2 – Friday

Alertness is not letting my guard down because of addictive behavior.

"All things are lawful for me but not all things are profitable. All things are lawful for me, but I will not be mastered by anything." I Cor. 6:12

There are the obvious addictions – drinking, gambling, smoking, pornography – and there's usually an "anonymous" to go along with it. But what about the more subtle activities that can snag us before we realize it? How about work? Eating? Gossiping? Perfectionism? I can hear the rationalizations now: "If I don't work all this overtime, we can't make ends meet." "I need to tell you this about Bob, so you can pray about it with me." "That's just the way God made me."

First of all, to all of us who have addictive behavior patterns – THERE IS HOPE.[26] Second, understand that the enemy is a liar and the father of lies.[27] You'll hear two types of lies. One, "You're too far gone for even God to help; how could he love you like you are?" Two, "You're not really addicted; you just like your __________ and can quit any time you want."

Both lead to the same end—destruction. Remember the old TV show Kojak? Telly Savalas' character would say, "Who loves you, baby?" Ask yourself that question with only two possible answers: A) God; B) Satan. Don't justify your behavior by deluding yourself into believing that you're not hurting anyone. People are watching you, Christian. Man up. Say no to anything that tugs you away from the path of righteousness and invites judgment from others.

Lord, help me to stop justifying my addictive behavior to myself and you. It's wrong, and I seem to be the only one who doesn't see it. Strengthen my resolve and help me remember others are watching, and I don't want to make anyone stumble on their way to you. **Amen.**

26 I Cor. 10:13
27 John 8:44

Week 2 – Saturday

Alertness is knowing that the adversary would destroy me and my family if he could and that he will try to discourage me and make my ministry irrelevant by taking my eyes off the prize.

"For false Christs and false prophets will arise and will show great signs and wonders, so as to mislead, if possible, even the elect." Matt. 24:24

Marathons are mental as well as physical. I'm told there comes a point where your mind wants to quit even though your body is still going. The Christian walk is very much like that. Jesus said, "...In the world you have tribulation, but take courage, I have overcome the world."[28] Expect trials, but trust God's promise to not give us more than we can handle.[29]

What's our best defense against the enemy's lies? The Truth. Store it up. Know it. Refer to it often. In the movie, *A Few Good Men*, Jack Nicholson's character screams the line, "You can't handle the truth." That's how we have to think of Satan. He can't handle the truth. He's been defeated and he knows it. But that doesn't stop him from spreading his propaganda.

Look around at the churches today, especially the large ones with their mega-marketing approach. Beware. Preaching a partial gospel is no gospel at all.[30] Stay the course and avoid listening to slick presentations of half-truths. We're at war and we've already won. But don't let that foster complacency or slackness. The full number isn't in yet or we'd all be home.[31]

Lord, I am continually bombarded with error in attractive packages. Thank you for the truth and accuracy of your Word. Keep my eyes and ears trained to quickly spot and reject the enemy's lie. **Amen**

---

28 John 16:33
29 I Cor. 10:13
30 Gal. 1:6-10
31 Rev. 6:10,11

Week 3 – Sunday

Availability is what leads me to rearrange my priorities and schedule to meet a need in someone else's life.

"But a Samaritan, who was on a journey, came upon him; and when he saw him, he felt compassion, and came to him and bandaged up his wounds, pouring oil and wine on them; and he put him on his own beast, and brought him to an inn and took care of him." Luke 10:33-34

Wouldn't it be great if the only time someone asked for our help was when we had scheduled the time and were just waiting for a phone call? Maybe in a Disney movie. The busy lives we lead rarely leave room for our own family, let alone somebody else. So why does God do it? Why does he pick the worst time (remember Romans 8:28, "*We know that God causes all things...*") for someone to need my help? I suggest our priorities are reversed. We tend to love things and use people.

I believe God uses these interruptions to not only provide a solution to someone else's need, but to teach us value. So what if I can't hook up my new flat screen tonight? So what if I just washed the car and Bob needs a ride...in the rain...on a dirt road? Whose car is it anyway?

What if we could respond like the Samaritan? Don't you think he had a schedule, someplace to be? I'm sure he wasn't just cruising the road to Jericho looking to be a, well you know, a good Samaritan.

What if, when someone calls needing help, I consider it an invitation from God to "walk in one of the good deeds he prepared beforehand"[32] specifically for me? Do you think I'd have a better attitude towards my friend's situation? Do you think I may have put a smile on God's face? God always has a purpose for everything He does. Do we always know it? No. So what? We know and trust that the rest of Romans 8:28 is true, too, "*...to work together for good to those who love God, to those who are called according to his purpose.*"

Today, let's consider it a privilege from God to help a brother in need.

Father, thanks for thinking of me as a resource to help your children. I confess I'm not always excited about it because it inconveniences me. Help me change my thinking and reactions to not only be a blessing, but to receive one as well. **Amen**.

32 Eph. 2:10

Availability is emptying myself of me to make room for God.

"He must increase and I must decrease." John 3:30

Have you ever asked yourself how much of God is enough? There's a great little book, *My Heart Christ's Home*[33] that asks the question a different way. How much of you are you willing to give God?

In the medical world, we get inoculations—a little bit of the real thing—to keep us from getting the real thing. Do we approach God the same way? Just enough to keep us from the real thing. We go to church, pray, say the right things at men's Bible study. But have we really committed to wanting all of God and giving Him all of us?

What are we holding onto that keeps us from total submission? Is it a thing, a person, an attitude? A glass can only be so full. If it's got two inches of oil in it, it can't hold a full glass of water. If my life is full of oil—things that prevent Christ from entering fully—I'm missing out on the relationship God intends for me.

John tells me that "I must decrease."[34] OK, so how? A good place to start is asking yourself, "Do I love God with all my heart, soul, and mind?"[35] Have a trusted friend (or your wife) help you identify those "locked rooms" in your life that need to be unlocked and cleaned out. Then pray and ask the Holy Spirit to guide you into truth.[36] Start today.

Father, you're asking me to leave my comfort zone. I'm scared. Help me to see your way as good and peaceful and to trust you with all areas of my life. **Amen**.

33 R B Munger, InterVarsity Press 1986
34 John 3:30
35 Matt. 22:37
36 John 16:13

Availability is being there when I'm "there" (not letting my mind wander).

"There came a woman of Samaria to draw water. Jesus said to her "Give me a drink." John 4:7

We've all experienced it, as the giver or receiver. We're at a business function or social gathering and someone comes up and starts talking to us. We're polite, but we're scanning the room, not really paying attention. We think, "What opportunities am I missing to talk to "important" people?"

Or, we're on the receiving end of this treatment. You can see it in their roving eyes and hear it in their grunted responses, "uh-huh."

Contrast that with Jesus' attention on the woman at the well. Not only was He talking to her (which was unusual on several levels), but she was His total focus.

We are all busy; we have agendas. We don't like to be interrupted. But God says, "... *look out...for the interests of others.*"[37] Live in whatever moment you're in. Don't let your next agenda item rob the present moment of blessing for you or others.

Lord, often I think more of myself than I should, and it affects how I treat others. Forgive me. Help me see the opportunities to share your love in the interruptions you allow in my agenda. **Amen**.

37 Phil. 2:4

Availability is doing the jobs nobody else wants to do.

"Then He (Jesus) poured water into the basin, and began to wash the disciples' feet..." John 13:5

When you consider jobs that are distasteful, what comes to mind? Following the elephants in a parade? Being an orderly in a nursing home? A paving crew in Phoenix during August? Why are these distasteful? Are you above this type of work?

God has given each of us gift(s) according to His wishes,[38] and they are to be used to edify the body of believers and build up Christ's church. How many of us have prayed for the gift of service? Probably not many. We envy those with public gifts and tend to shun those with the lesser gifts.

Remember God's admonition to associate with the lowly?[39] You want God's blessing? Put to death your pride and realize who your true boss is. If Jesus still walked the earth as a man and asked you to muck out the stalls, would you give Him three reasons why you couldn't? Didn't think so. So, just because you can't see Him doesn't make His requests any less valid. The job has to be done. Don't think, "Here am I, Lord, send somebody else." Focusing on our eternal future[40] helps our perspective on the lowliest of tasks.

Lord, sometimes I forget that I work for You. Give me a good attitude about the chores you assign and help me remember that if You hadn't humbled yourself, I'd still be lost and on my way to hell. Thank you. **Amen**.

38 I Cor. 12:4
39 Rom. 12:16
40 Col. 3:2

Week 3 – Thursday

Availability is sharing my talents where they are needed, not for my glory but because I want to honor God who gave them to me.

"As each one has received a special gift, employ it in serving one another as good stewards of the manifold grace of God." I Pet. 4:10

Are you a one, two, or five talent kind of guy? In the movie *Chariots of Fire*, Eric Liddell ran for God's glory. Do you remember the line? "When I run, I feel His pleasure." Who gave Liddell the ability to run? Did he just wake up one morning and decide today I'm going to be a star Olympic runner?

What talents has God given you? What are you doing with them? Who is benefitting from them? When God parceled out our gifts/talents, He intended us to use them to benefit the body—His body.

Think about how you'll feel when you stand before God and He asks you what you did with what He gave you—if you haven't been faithful.[41] There's still time. Identify your talents. If you need help, ask others who know you well. Then start looking for places to put them to work. If your heart is set on God's glory, you'll have more opportunity than you know what to do with.

Father, thank you for choosing me to work in your vineyard. Help me to not be overwhelmed by the daily grind, but to keep my eyes on the prize and to use the gifts you've given me for your glory. **Amen**.

41 Matt. 25:26

Availability is lending my shoulder to help budge a large object or for a friend to cry on.

"...better is a neighbor who is near than a brother far away." Prov. 27:10

Shoulders are an amazing part of our bodies. On one hand, they do the heavy lifting. Yet they are tender enough to provide comfort and security. Does your church have a "Shoulders" ministry? You'd probably recognize it by different names: Trustees, Deacons, Widows, and Orphans, etc. But they all likely do similar things—help people in need.

If God has blessed you with physical strength and abilities, thank Him for that and show Him your gratitude by signing up for Shoulders. That's step one. Step two is even closer to home. Look around your neighborhood. Is there a widow, an elderly couple, someone with disabilities? Offer your shoulder. Remember the story of the lawyer in Luke 10:25-29? He tried to test Jesus and justify himself by asking the question, "who is my neighbor?" Jesus then told the parable of the Good Samaritan.

The bottom line is, anybody in need is your neighbor. What better way to open a door for the gospel than to let your neighbors know they can count on you for help. Sometimes, you're the only gospel they will read.

God, help me to be more ready to say yes to helping my neighbors than I am to recite three reasons why I can't. **Amen**.

Week 3 – Saturday

Availability is asking God in the morning, "What do you want me to do today?"

"The Lord's lovingkindnesses indeed never cease, for His compassions never fail. They are new every morning; great is Your faithfulness." Lam. 3:22,23

The only ability God asks of us is "avail"-ability. The only day we have is today. Each day is a gift—a blank canvas waiting for our brush strokes. When you look back at the end of the day, what picture will be on the canvas of your life?

Today's history will have been written in the indelible ink of time. Will you have invested your time for the kingdom in the lives of others, or will the book of remembrance[42] have gaps? Will God be pleased with how you spent your day, or will there be regrets? Because each day is new and God's storehouse of compassions is never depleted, forget yesterday[43] and press on.

There's no room for wallowing in self-pity over what you did or didn't do. Confess and leave it at the foot of the cross. Then move forward like your burden was lifted. It was. Remember the cliché, "Today is the first day of the rest of your life." It's never too late to take a stand, make a difference in somebody's life, and store up rewards in heaven.[44]

Father, I know I don't always consider your agenda for me. I rush into my day with ideas and plans that I want to accomplish. Forgive me. Teach me to fit my schedule into yours and not the other way around. Thank you for new beginnings each day. Help me make the most of the opportunities you give me. In Jesus' name, **Amen**.

42 Mal. 3:16
43 Phil. 3:13,14
44 Matt. 6:19-21

Boldness allows me to face and overcome tremendous odds, not because I am clever or strong, but because I am empowered by the Holy Spirit and I know that the results are not my responsibility—only the going.

"But you shall receive power when the Holy Spirit has come upon you; and you shall be My witnesses both in Jerusalem, and in all Judea and Samaria, and even to the remotest part of the earth." Acts 1:8

How different sports would be if the outcome were predetermined. The winning team wouldn't be intimidated by the size of the players, the noise of the crowd, or the pre-game hype. They would run the plays the coach calls with precision and confidence.

Think deeper. What if the winning team were the only ones that knew the outcome? To the opposing fans and team, it might even look like they were winning. They might jeer and taunt, strut and flaunt. But they would still lose in the end.

Isn't the Christian life a lot like that? You've read the Bible; you know how the story ends for believers in Jesus. Is there anywhere in the Bible that tells us we're responsible for the score—the number of converts? No. The world measures us by the numbers. It's always, "what have you done for me today?"

God measures a different way. He doesn't ask, "How did I stack up against Bob?" He asks, "What have you done with what I gave you?"[45] It should be a great comfort to know that God is responsible for the results of our witnessing. And it should also be a great comfort to know our final destination.

But don't get trapped in the "I've—got—my—ticket—punched" rut and stay on the bench. The game (sharing Jesus with a lost world) is exciting. If your game has grown stale, here's the refresher course: remember, repent and return.[46]

Father, the enemy seems overwhelming at times and I seem small and weak. Build my faith and confidence in You so no matter how long the odds, my trust will not waver. Thank you that you've drafted me on the winning team. **Amen.**

45 Matt. 25:19
46 Rev. 2:5

Week 4 – Monday

Boldness is looking beyond my comfort zone into the fires of hell and being motivated to open my mouth to tell others about Jesus.

"And now, Lord, take note of their threats, and grant that Your bond-servants may speak Your word with all confidence." Acts 4:29

Have you ever had a bad burn anywhere on your body? I don't know of anything more painful. Think about spending eternity in a place where the fire is never quenched, thirst is never slaked, and hope for relief is never realized. Jesus gave us a picture of hell by using words like torment and agony. Pretty grim, huh?

Do you know family members and friends or co-workers who haven't been introduced to Jesus? That's the future that awaits them. Have you shared your faith in Christ with them? Once, twice, more? What's holding you back?

Remember how in high school what your friends thought was the most important thing in your world? How many of those people do you still stay in touch with? The point is, there's only one opinion that matters in the scheme of things. When you reach heaven, what will you hear Jesus say? *"Well done, good and faithful slave"* [47] or *"Depart from me, I never knew you."* [48] Don't let fear of what people might think of you keep from sharing the most important truth they will ever hear.

Lord, when I think of the alternative to heaven, it's a scary place. Give me the boldness to get out of my comfort zone and think of those I know and love who haven't met Jesus yet. I long to hear those words from you, "well done." Help me to be faithful in witnessing with my life as well as my words. May I not be a stumbling block to anyone. In Jesus' name, **Amen**.

47 Matt. 25:21
48 Matt. 7:23

Boldness doesn't back down when truth is at stake.

"...and you will know the truth, and the truth will set you free." John 8:32

Have you ever wondered what happens to the freedom that kids have to speak the truth? When my oldest daughter was about four, a neighbor (I'll call her Bobbi) had stopped by to visit. It was summer and she had on shorts. Now, truth be told, there are some things certain people shouldn't wear, and for Bobbi, shorts is one of them. My four-year-old bounces up and, being eye level with Bobbi's thigh, can't help but observe how big this woman is. She looks up and says in that innocent voice, "You sure have big legs, don't you?"

This was one of those times when I was glad to be in the background. I have to confess; I did a fade and left my wife to deal with it. Have you ever been in the place of total freedom since you were a kid? Hopefully, we have learned tact and timing in our conversation skills. But I also hope we haven't diluted the truth to a point where it's either not relevant or maybe not even the truth anymore.

Many people don't want to hear the truth – about themselves or philosophical positions they hold. Why do you think people reject creationism in favor of evolution? Because they don't want the accountability (to a creator) that creationism implies.

I encourage you today to not let the resistance of your audience dictate the content of your message. Freedom always comes at a cost. Christ will steady your wobbly legs. Which would you rather be accused of, telling the truth and possibly keeping someone from hell or not telling the truth because you were uncomfortable?

Lord, I confess sometimes I care too much about what people think and not enough about Your challenge to me to go into all the world. I know You are able to strengthen me both in spirit and body. Let me be bold on Your behalf with those who need to hear the truth. In Jesus' name, **Amen**.

Boldness doesn't wait to see who else is signing up.

"Then I heard the voice of the Lord saying, "Whom shall I send, and who will go for Us?" Then I said, "Here am I, send me!"" Isa. 6:8

You've heard the coach's pep talk, "There's no 'I' in team." And that's a good application of the teamwork principle. But when it comes to doing God's work, often one man is the preferred method. See examples of Abraham,[49] Moses (albeit he made God angry),[50] Jonah,[51] John the Baptist,[52] Stephen[53] and many others, including Jesus himself.

God doesn't call us to do something we're not equipped for, e.g. conduct Billy Graham-like crusades. But He does call us to be ambassadors for Christ.[54]

How many ambassadors to Greece does the United States send? Exactly one. Sure, he has a staff. But he's the voice of America and the President of the United States.

As an ambassador for Christ, we may be called on to speak and act on Christ's behalf in the life of one or many. Yes, we can work with others. In fact, God tells us to.[55] But we must be prepared, individually, to share the hope within[56] whenever the opportunity arises. Look for openings. Salt the conversation with ice breakers like, "Do you know what happens after you die?" or, "Do you think you're good enough to get into heaven?" or the Evangelism Explosion standard, "If you were to die today, do you know where you'd spend eternity?" Know the "Roman Road" way of salvation (Rom. 3:23; 6:23; 8:1; 10:9, 10). Pray, ask the Holy Spirit to open the right doors.

Father, strengthen me today to be Your man at Your time in Your place, even if I'm alone. **Amen**.

49 Gen. 12:1
50 Exod. 4:14
51 Jonah 1:2
52 John 1:6
53 Acts 6:8
54 II Cor. 5:20
55 Heb. 10:24, 25
56 I Pet. 3:15

Boldness is infectious; either pass it to or catch it from others of like mind.

"and let us consider how to stimulate one another to love and good deeds,"
Heb. 10:24

In the medical world, contagion is cause for alarm. Shots are given, masks worn, distance kept. And that's as it should be. But in our walk of faith, two are better than one and three are better than two.[57] Have you noticed how much braver you feel if just one other person goes with you? It's the positive side of mob mentality.

In the Army, we had a saying: "Lead, follow, or get out of the way (expletive deleted)." Either be excited and bold with your faith—it will infect others—or find someone to infect you. There's nothing worse than a glum Christian who is neither bold nor infectious. The body doesn't benefit from your gifts. The root of this is simple; you are focused on yourself and not Christ. Get over it. Get excited. Get back in the game and watch how your boldness will infect others for the kingdom.

Father, forgive me for taking my eyes off Christ. Remind me often that He is the source of both my renewed attitude and my results. Thank you. **Amen**.

57 Eccl. 4:9-12

Week 4 – Friday

Boldness keeps me from being intimidated by the adversary's tactics.

"Be of sober spirit, be on the alert. Your adversary, the devil, prowls around like a roaring lion, seeking someone to devour." I Pet. 5:8

A lion's roar is one of the most intimidating sounds on planet earth; it can make you freeze in place. But he doesn't roar until he already has his prey locked in his sights.

Isn't it great to know that Satan's roar has no effect on believers? He's a master of disguises, and they run the gamut from roaring lion to angel of light.[58] Jesus told us that knowing the truth would set us free.[59] In addition to setting us free from sin and death, truth also sets us free from Satan's power and tricks.

Knowing this is only half the solution. We must boldly resist him, and he'll flee.[60] Don't get cocky and proud at this point. It's not you the devil fears; it's Christ in you—our victor.

Lord, today may I walk humbly with you and not delude myself that by myself I'm somebody for Satan to fear. I ask for boldness to walk by faith and see you work through me. In Christ's name, **Amen**.

58 II Cor. 11:14
59 John 8:32
60 Jas. 4:7

Week 4 – Saturday

Boldness encourages me to stand in the gap for my family.

"But be sure of this, that if the head of the house had known at what time of the night the thief was coming, he would have been on the alert and would not have allowed his house to be broken into." Matt. 24:43

Home security is a multi-billion-dollar business. Think of all the locks and alarm systems sold each year. And, if you believe the spy movies, there isn't a system that can't be hacked. Gun and ammo sales are at an all-time high.

What if we spent as much time and energy preparing for battle with the unseen enemy of our souls? And what would that preparation look like? There are at least three major components. First is intense Bible study. If we know the truth, we won't be as susceptible to the enemy's lies. Second, a life of prayer. Nothing shakes the devil like a praying saint. And third, righteous living. The fewer areas Satan can point to in our lives and say, "yeah, but look at what you're doing over there," the stronger stand we can take.

Set the godly example for your family. Do the right thing even though nobody may be looking. Teach your kids Biblical truth. Prepare them for subtle attacks which will come. Don't give in to peer pressure; keep the standards high. Model Christ for your wife with an attitude of serving. Make your home a stronghold of righteousness, peace, and joy.[61] Keep yourself from (a habit of) sin.[62] Do this and boldness will follow.

Lord Jesus, today, may I not succumb to the temptation of silence when so many around me are lost and I have the only map. **Amen.**

61 Rom. 14:17
62 I Tim. 5:22

Week 5 – Sunday

Brokenness is a gift bestowed on me when my trust in God overcomes my fear of letting go. I cannot receive this gift as long as I retain any sense of my worthiness.

"Though He slay me, I will hope in Him." Job 13:15a

Raise your hand if you admire arrogance in others. It's a huge turn-off. Think of the strutting stars, the bloated businessmen, the affected athletes. We might appreciate their talents, but often their self-centered personalities drive us away.

On the other hand, we're drawn, almost as by a magnet, to those who have little regard for their own self-worth but constantly build others up. I was a drill sergeant in the Army during Vietnam. Boot camp was designed to break the will of the trainees while not discouraging their spirit. The reason was simple. In combat, when an order is given, it needs to be obeyed—now. There's no time to debate when lives are at stake.

God's army is no different. He's our commander-in-chief for the spiritual war we're in. We all bring worldly baggage into the war with us. It weighs us down emotionally, distracts, and slows us from the primary task and causes others to focus on it instead of Jesus. We're not very useful until God breaks our will (remember even Christ prayed "not my will, but Yours")[63] and gets us to see things His way.

There's no discussion or debate. When we're in God's army, we follow orders…period. What are you hanging onto today that keeps you from receiving this gift of brokenness? Why? Do you think your strategy is better than God's? Do you not trust Him enough that you feel the need to hang on to 'just this one thing'? Don't let anything keep you from wearing the uniform.[64]

Father, I can think of all kinds of excuses to postpone surrendering, but they're just that—excuses. I want to be useful in Your kingdom. Grant me the gift of brokenness so that You can rebuild me according to Your plan. **Amen**.

63 Matt. 26:39
64 II Tim. 2:4

Brokenness is the conduit through which God speaks to me.

"Therefore I am well content with weaknesses, with insults, with distresses, with persecutions, with difficulties, for Christ's sake; for when I am weak, then I am strong." II Cor. 12:10

In many places on earth, there is a layer of soil called hardpan. It is so hard that even water cannot penetrate it. Think of that when Paul talks about hardness of heart. Do you know people like that? Are you one?

Remember Ezekiel's encouragement to Israel. God told them He would remove their "heart of stone" and replace it with a "heart of flesh."[65] Many things can contribute to a hard heart. Passed over for a promotion? Worked hard to make the team and at the last minute had a season-ending injury? Loved one taken by death? Sometimes life feels like a conspiracy against us.

How can a God of love allow such things? There are no easy answers. But I do know one thing. If I trust and love God, He causes all things to work together for my good.[66] Sometimes it's hard to give up control and let God have His way in my life. The truth is, He's going to have His way whether I cooperate or not. Why not accept it and watch Him work?[67] Let God amaze you…today.

Father, sometimes life seems unfair, and I guess subconsciously, I blame You. Grow my trust in you so I can let go of the controls and watch you do amazing things in my life—today and every day. **Amen**.

65 Ezek. 36:26
66 Rom. 8:28
67 Jos. 3:5

Brokenness is painful for a moment but yields eternal rewards.

"For momentary, light affliction is producing for us an eternal weight of glory far beyond all comparison." II Cor. 4:17

If only. How full of remorse can two words be? If only I'd left ten minutes earlier, I would have missed the traffic accident, caught my plane, made the sale, been promoted, and lived happily ever after. Instead, I miss my plane, miss the meeting, miss the sale, oh, I miss my job. OK, wake up now.

Seriously, how often do we consider consequences beyond the immediate pinball-like reactions? If only I didn't have to get up Sunday and go to church, I could watch the early game. If only my son hadn't been picked up for substance abuse, I would have been elected to city council.

What is your "if only" today? What do you regret to the point of pain or embarrassment? What if Jesus had said, "If only I didn't have to go to the cross"? Where would we be then? Look, you either believe the Bible or you don't. Either "God causes all things to work together for good"[68] or He doesn't. Don't you think He could have produced a different outcome if He wanted? Of course, He could. That's why we have to ask, "What is God trying to teach me?"

I've ridden motorcycles off and on for over 40 years. It was a Sunday morning. I'd been to early service and was to meet a couple of riding buddies for lunch in the mountains. A woman made a U-turn against a red arrow and took me down. Double compound fracture, emergency surgery, a rod through my tibia and a plate on my fibula. Four months later, my tibia still hadn't mended, and a bone-graft surgery was needed. I had the surgery, and my recovery clock was restarted. Decision time. Do I shake an angry fist at God or do I kick myself (I still have one good leg) for whatever lesson I'm not learning?

I'm probably like a lot of you reading this—a busy "type A" personality. Often, when God wants to speak to me, He has to do something drastic to get my attention and slow me down. Trust me, after four months on crutches with no weight-bearing and the prospect of two to three months more, I'm listening…hard. So it really boils down to this: Do I trust God enough to let go? I'm working on it…today.

God, letting go can be scary because I've built my life on self-dependence. I have no reason to distrust You except that I want the control. Give me the grace today to let go and invite and expect You to take the reins. In Christ's name, **Amen**.

68 Rom. 8:28, emphases added

Week 5 – Wednesday

Brokenness draws others to Christ in me.

"and my message and my preaching were not in persuasive words of wisdom, but in demonstration of the Spirit and of power, so that your faith would not rest on the wisdom of men, but on the power of God." I Cor. 2:4, 5

Public speakers try to get and keep our attention through many techniques. They try humor, shock, change of pace, change of volume, and others. It's the same with advertising. You'll see bright colors, movement, unusual things to grab your attention. The problem with this, especially in advertising, is that if the "interrupt" doesn't closely tie to the product or message, your audience has already tuned out.

It seems Paul had a different approach to spreading his message. He wasn't trying to wow his listeners with his eloquence. He didn't want his listeners attracted to him instead of the message. God, and specifically the Lord Jesus Christ, was always his focus. Paul's goal was to present the simple message of the gospel in humility so that people would be introduced to Jesus and believe in Him and His power to change lives.

This week is about brokenness. My question is, how many of us are able, in humility, to shine the spotlight of truth on Jesus without expecting recognition, fame, even financial reward? We should adopt as our guiding standard John's words, "*He* [Jesus} *must increase but I must decrease.*"[69]

Our proclamation should be like salt in a saltshaker. When we want something salted, we don't care what the shaker looks like. Rebecca Manley Peppert wrote the book *Out of the Salt Shaker & into the World.* Her point is simple. Salt doesn't do any good while it's in the shaker. If we wait until our shaker is polished and shiny before we share the gospel with anyone, our motive is wrong. The truth of the gospel is empowered by the Holy Spirit, not by "persuasive words of wisdom." And it's His job to cause the Word to take root and grow in those who would be saved.

Like the "*alabaster vial of very costly perfume*"[70] that was broken to pour over Jesus' head, we need to be broken so the message we've been called to spread can get out. We may have little cracks from which some of the message occasionally seeps. Not good enough. Jesus told the church at Laodicea, "*because you are lukewarm…I will spit* [lit. vomit] *you out of my mouth.*"[71] I leave you with one question. Are you in or out?

Father, given all the opposing thoughts that bombard me to strive for more and bigger and newer, it's hard to grasp Your mind on this idea of brokenness. Help me to tune my mind only to your station and flood my learning with Your truth—that a broken sinner is your chosen vessel for spreading the gospel. Use me in Your harvest field. **Amen**.

69 John 3:30
70 Mark 14:3
71 Rev. 3:16

Brokenness is the foundation upon which my sanctification is built.

"Therefore everyone who hears these words of mine and acts on them, may be compared to a wise man who built his house on the rock." Matt. 7:24

Growing up in the Los Angeles area in the '50s and '60s, I was relatively poor but never knew it. I always had food and clothes and friends. When I left home at 18 and began to compare, that's when I realized life as I wanted cost more than I had. I was drawn by the sirens of money and position.

Between 18 and 22 (when I met Jesus personally) I made a lot of wrong decisions. I'm not well-traveled, but I have been a few places, Mexico and the Caribbean, to name a couple. And I realized that as an American, how wealthy I really was. I saw Mexicans and islanders living, literally, in cardboard boxes just a couple blocks from the tourist areas. Obviously, their "homes" didn't have any foundation.

So what's my point? Jesus' metaphor in Matthew speaks to building our lives on Him—the only true rock. If we're still building on the foundations of I, me and mine, our structure is no better than those cardboard boxes; it will fall.

If we have invited Jesus to rule our lives, *positionally* we're sanctified. But *practically* we probably have a long way to go. Let's start by making sure we're building on the right foundation.[72]

Father, I know that I can't hide my heart—my motives—from You. Yet often I act as though I can. I long to hear the words "well done" from You. Help me to build my life according to Your plans and only on the foundation of Jesus' atonement. In His name, **Amen**.

72 I Cor. 3:11

Brokenness helps me see me as God sees me.

"For if anyone is a hearer of the word and not a doer, he is like a man who looks at his natural face in a mirror: for once he has looked at himself and gone away, he has immediately forgotten what kind of person he was." Jas. 1:23, 24

I love bumper stickers. My favorite: "God loves you…everybody else thinks you're an idiot." Does God see something in me that others don't? Am I His child and it's just the loving eyes of a parent? Do I represent the name of Christ in a way that draws others to Him, or does my life conflict with my words? As Ethel Waters says, "God don't make no junk."

So how do I get to the point of seeing myself without all my disguises? It starts with a decision. Nike says, "Just do it." God has provided a manual for successful living—the Bible. I start by agreeing what it says about me is true: I'm a sinner,[73] my thoughts are evil,[74] my good deeds are like filthy garments,[75] and I can't do what's right, even though I want to.[76] God sees all that but loves me anyway,[77] and there is nothing in my past that is too big for God's love.[78]

If I don't or can't agree with the Manual, then my pride is what keeps me from seeing and being what God has designed me for. God's plan is that I bear fruit.[79] If my life is not bearing fruit, that's an indicator that a) I'm not wise;[80] and b) I'm not plugged in to the vine.[81]

A friend of mine has a saying that shows our need to be constantly plugged in: "we leak." Think of your life like a cell phone. It's an amazing tool…as long as you're near a tower and your battery's charged.

We're a needy lot. But we know where, more importantly, *who* our food is. Don't be like the person James has in mind; be a doer—let the mirror of scripture show you who you are in Christ (positionally) and how to get there (practically).

Father, it's painful to admit I'm not all that. I confess I've let you down in my sin of pride that often camouflages who I really am. Forgive me and grant me eyes to see me as You do—a sinner, yet covered by Jesus' blood. Thank you in His name. **Amen**.

---

73 Rom. 3:23
74 Matt. 15:19
75 Isa. 64:6
76 Rom. 7:15
77 Rom. 5:8
78 Isa. 1:18
79 John 15:2
80 Prov. 11:30
81 John 15:5

Brokenness delights my Father.

"But the tax collector, standing some distance away, was even unwilling to lift up his eyes to heaven, but was beating his breast, saying, 'God, be merciful to me, the sinner?' I tell you, this man went to his house justified rather than the other for everyone who exalts himself will be humbled, but he who humbles himself will be exalted." Luke 18:13, 14

Are you as tired of politically correct (PC) speech as I am? Apparently, God is too. Malachi says that God is wearied by people calling evil good and (wrongly) saying that God delights in them. What God does delight in is His child who comes to Him in need, broken (of our own abilities) and humble before Him, trusting His goodness and mercy to meet those needs.[82]

Are you a businessman? You can delight God through your honesty.[83] Are you an athlete? Delight God through your disciplined fair play.[84] Are you a parent? Delight God by faithfully teaching your children.[85] When it's all said and done, God delights that we conform to the image of His Son.[86]

Do your words weary God? In your speech, have you become undifferentiated from the world? When my kids were little and I was dropping them off for some event, as they got out of the car, I would remind them that they were a Thornton. I'd get the rolling eyes and the predictable, "Oh, dad." But they knew we had a different standard. The question has been asked, "If you were arrested for being a Christian, would there be enough evidence to convict you?" As you go about your life today, picture God saying to you, "Remember, you're a Christian."

Lord, Your patience with the world and me continues to amaze me. Thank you for second and third and fourth chances. I know You're working in me to help me become like Jesus. I also know that I get in Your way because of my pride and love of men's praise. With Your help today, Lord, let me play my position with renewed commitment and vigor…for Your glory. In Jesus' name, **Amen**.

82 Heb. 11:6
83 Prov. 11:1
84 I Cor. 9:24-26
85 Deut. 6:6, 7
86 Rom. 8:29

Caring motivates me to actively look around with eyes trained to spot unspoken needs then inventory my abilities and assets to see what combination best fits to meet those needs.

"so that there may be no division in the body, but that the members may have the same care for one another." I Cor. 12:25

Nations erect walls on their borders. Neighbors put up fences. Individuals hide behind busyness and happy faces. Isolationism can be found at any level of society. We do this for many reasons, but one is we're scared and hurting. Maybe life has dealt us a hand with lousy cards. Maybe we were the recipient of the playground bully's attention, and it left emotional scars.

It's been said that the Christian community is the only group that punishes its wounded. So it's no wonder we don't share our fears, our needs, our dreams with others. We've been laughed at once too often; we've struck out too many times. I've got great news: There's a God who cares deeply about you.[87]

Knowing that, God's chosen method of delivering His "care" packages often comes in the form of…wait for it…YOU. Sometimes needs are obvious. However, because of the isolationism with which we surround ourselves, we often have to use the eyes of our heart to see the deeper needs. Today, ask God to use you to meet a need in someone's life. Then be on the lookout for your opportunity.

Father, thank you for never being too busy for me. Open the eyes of my heart today to see needs around me and give me wisdom to know what I can do to help. In Jesus' name, **Amen**.

87 I Pet. 5:7

Caring isn't always easy, but it's always required.

"But a Samaritan, who was on a journey, came upon him; and when he saw him, he felt compassion." Luke 10:33

You know the story (in Luke 10). The priest came and went without doing anything. The temple assistant came and went without doing anything. "Religion" had its chance and closed its eyes to the robbed and beaten man's need.

But a despised half-breed saw a need, stopped what he was doing and stooped to help, all at his own inconvenience and cost. Is that why many of us don't get involved? We're too busy, too important, too cheap? Who is it that gave us our resources in the first place?[88] Do you think you did it all by yourself? You have been blessed to bless others.[89] Use your gifts and talents in the service to others…today.

Lord, I'm busy and a lot of it is for You. Don't let me become like the priest and Levite who were too busy to help someone in need. I know that I need your compassion and mercy to survive each day. May I be a conduit of Your blessing by passing it on. **Amen**.

88 I Cor. 4:7
89 Zech. 8:13

Caring is an investment in someone else's eternity.

"Let him know that he who turns a sinner from the error of his way will save his soul from death and will cover a multitude of sins." James 5:20

Fear and intimidation aside, what says "I care" more than concern for someone's eternal destiny? More people are led to Christ by another person than by sitting in a pew. For me, it was a man from Campus Crusade for Christ and the invitation from the mother of a good friend to hear him in a small group setting.

Many of your friends, co-workers and neighbors will not be open to the good news of Jesus. Don't let that discourage you from sharing the hope that's in you.[90] If you have never shared your faith with a non-believer, you're missing one of the greatest privileges on earth. What if the person you share with sees the truth and accepts Jesus as his savior? The feeling of joy that overwhelms you is incomparable.

There are some great materials for building your confidence. *The Way of The Master*[91] is my favorite, and *Dr. Kennedy's Evangelism Explosion*[92] is always a staple. Today, ask yourself, "Who am I watching wend their way to hell, and what am I going to do about it?"

Father, sometimes caring is personally costly. When I'm tempted to think twice about investing in another life, please remind me what caring cost You. **Amen**.

90 I Pet. 3:15
91 www.wayofthemaster.com
92 www.eeinternational.org

Caring proves I know, love and obey Jesus.

"The King will answer and say to them, "Truly I say to you, to the extent that you did it to one of these brothers of Mine, even the least of them, you did it to Me." Matt 25:40

Would you visit Jesus in a hospital or jail? Would you share your food or water with Him? Why? Before you say, "Duh, 'cuz He's Jesus," substitute someone else's name in the questions. Not quite as obvious an answer, is it? Why?

Recently, I was in a motorcycle accident; I suffered a double compound fracture just above my left ankle. One of the highlights of my 2-day stay in the hospital was the visit by a couple of fellow bikers whom I didn't even know. With their leathers and tats, I'm sure the nursing staff was a little concerned. We commiserated, laughed, and before they left, they prayed for me. I was blessed *by* their coming; they were blessed *for* their coming.

Words are important. To say, "I care, I'm sorry you're going through this, I love you" to someone is meaningful. To mow their lawn because they have a broken leg takes it to another level; it proves you care. What will your "cup of water" look like today?

Lord, I know what it feels like to be on the receiving end of someone's care. Give me sensitivity to those around me who hurt, wisdom to meet their need, and commitment to prove that I care in practical ways. In Jesus' name, **Amen**.

Caring sometimes makes me look weak; I need to remember who my audience is.

"When Pilate saw that he was accomplishing nothing, but rather that a riot was starting, he took water and washed his hands in front of the crowd, saying, "I am innocent of this Man's blood; see to that yourselves."" Matt. 27:24

Many top 10 lists of fears include public speaking in front of a large audience. But there are ways to overcome this fear: knowledge, preparation, and practice. Truth also plays a big role in your confidence to speak. If you're right, why do you care what the crowd, irrespective of size, thinks? If you read the previous verses (Matt. 27:11-24), you'll see that Pilate wasn't convinced that Jesus had done anything worthy of the death penalty and he (Pilate) was in a position to do something about it. But he was afraid of the crowd and that word would get back to Caesar.

Many years ago, my family was visiting friends for the evening. The kids, ages 4 – 10, were in the basement playing while the adults were upstairs. All of a sudden, one of the boys came running up the stairs and announced, "They're going to tell on me."

Pilate's choice was based on fear of consequences for not pleasing the crowd. I believe that he cared about Jesus—just not enough to overcome his fear. Do we fear what others think and allow that fear to keep us from doing what's right? Do we stand by while the bully or the crowd picks on the little guy?

God help us today to remember that doing what pleases our heavenly Father is the only thing that matters. Trust Him for the consequences.

Father, I confess that too often, I fear the crowd. I know it's because I don't trust You enough to protect or strengthen me. Forgive me. Help me today to focus on pleasing You, not the crowd. **Amen**.

Caring includes all God's creation.

"A righteous man has regard for the life of his animal" Pro. 12:10

Lions and tigers and bears (oh my).
The rocks the trees that rivers flow by.
In Genesis 1, God made them all,
And told man to care before the fall.

Hug a tree, save a panda, or clean a stream. Nothing wrong with any of those. In fact, God told us to rule over fish, birds, animals, and the earth.[93] Where the problem lies is when environmentalism becomes our religion—our god. God never intended us to worship trees or animals. He created them for us to enjoy and use.

My wife and I tried to teach our kids to always leave a place better than we found it. Carry in, carry out, no trash. You know the drill. Doesn't it just tick you off when you see people throw trash out the window of their car? That's a righteous indignation on behalf of God's creation. The same goes for cruelty to animals. You want to grab some people by the nape of their neck and…I won't go into the details.

If you love God, you'll love His creation and be continually amazed by it. I live in Colorado Springs and love it. With the Rocky Mountains and Pike's Peak for contrast, the sky here is a phenomenal display of God's beauty and creativity. The lightning shows that we get in the summer are a frequent reminder of the awesome power of our God and spawn an attitude of worship…of God, not His creation.

Today, commit yourself afresh to being a good steward of God's creation in a balanced way, not forgetting the God who spoke it all into existence.

Father, I marvel at Your creation—the beauty, the complexity, the majesty. Thank you for a glimpse of what heaven must be like. Remind me that You expect me to use and enjoy it but also to take care of it. **Amen**.

93 Gen. 1:26

Caring can open doors to share the gospel.

"There came a woman of Samaria to draw water. Jesus said to her, 'Give me a drink.'" John 4:7

Homeless people, foreigners, ex-cons—not the type we normally socialize with. Jews didn't socialize with Samaritans either...but Jesus did, and led not only this woman but many of the townsfolk to salvation as well. I don't imagine that Jesus had a "comfort zone" per se, so doing the unexpected was not uncomfortable for Him.

Later in this same passage, Jesus tells His disciples that His food is to do God's will (implied: wherever that takes Him). Why are we out of our comfort zone when an opportunity to talk to somebody different than us presents itself? Is it lack of experience (an excuse) or lack of trust in the One who arranged the meeting?

How do you learn to swim? Obviously, you get in the pool. But something has to happen first—you have to want to learn to swim. It's the same with sharing Jesus with socially undesirable types. It starts with caring for them...perhaps physically at first. This unexpected kindness can open all kinds of doors for the gospel.

Remember, you may be the only Bible someone else reads. Make sure your translation nails it. Putting hands and feet to the gospel starts with caring, progresses by caring, and accomplishes its goal by caring. Today, look around and see if there isn't someone who needs a caring touch...then do something about it.

Jesus, when You walked the earth, there was nobody who was unacceptable to You. I confess, most of the time, I don't want to be bothered by these types and find myself judging them. Forgive me for my piety and selfishness which does nothing to further Your kingdom. Give me another chance, today, to share Your love with someone I normally wouldn't. Thank You. **Amen**.

Week 7 – Sunday

Confidence is knowing, by faith in God's Word, that not only is God able but that He will supply everything I need to accomplish the tasks He has set out for me.

"And my God will supply all your needs according to His riches in glory in Christ Jesus." Phil. 4:19

Ever been to summer camp when you were young? Remember how mom packed way more "stuff" than you needed? Why would anyone need more than one pair of socks—it's only a week?

When Jesus sent His disciples out by twos, He told them to wear sandals and carry a stick,[94] nothing more. Why? He wanted to build their faith that He would provide. We've enlisted in God's army. Some may be officers, most of us are grunts. But we all have the same commanding officer—Jesus Christ—and we're all expected to obey Him.[95]

Think about Paul's comment to the Philippians. He said *all* our needs. If that doesn't build your confidence, I don't know what will. Armies must maintain a certain level of readiness; this includes running, pushups, etc. In God's army, our readiness consists of reading God's Word, memorizing it, meditating on it, prayer, and fellowship with our fellow soldiers. Opportunities for service can come at any time of day or night—we must be ready.

Father, may I remember today that I'm in Your army and that it's Your role to equip me. Grant me the grace to follow orders and keep myself ready. **Amen**.

94 Mark 6:8, 9
95 I Sam. 15:22

Confidence is sharing the gospel truth with someone who doesn't want to hear it because I know they need Jesus.

"And now, Lord, take note of their threats, and grant that your bond-servants may speak your word with all confidence." Acts 4:29

When you think of rowdy crowds, one of the first to come to mind is the Raider Nation and the "black hole" at McAfee Coliseum in Oakland, a place where the rowdiest fans tend to sit.[96] Not a likely venue for spreading the gospel. But haven't you tried to share Christ with a friend or relative and hit the wall there too?

What makes people so hostile to the message of salvation? Why don't they want to hear about God's love and hope for their future? The simple answer is they love sinning[97] and hate the truth. Should we just give up on them? Yes and no. Paul tells Titus to warn a "factious" man twice and then have nothing more to do with him.[98]

Jesus told His disciples not to cast their pearls before swine.[99] These are references to folks who express hatred toward the gospel. On the other hand, we are told to love our enemies and pray for those who persecute us.[100] Don't take it personally. We were warned that the world would hate us.[101] That's actually a good sign—our witness makes it obvious whose team we're on.

Don't give up; you might have to go "undercover" and subtly salt your conversations with icebreakers. As long as there is life in the body, there is hope for deliverance. Don't forget the thief on the cross.[102] It's better to spend eternity in heaven without the rewards of a righteous life than the only other alternative.

Father, I'm forever grateful that you never gave up on me even when I mocked Your children and Your message. May I have the confidence to hang in there knowing that You still specialize in changing hearts. **Amen**.

96 http://sports-venue.info/Fans/Raider_Nation.html
97 II Thes. 2:11, 12
98 Tit. 3:10
99 Matt. 7:6
100 Matt. 5:44
101 John 15:18, 19
102 Luke 23:42, 43

Week 7 – Tuesday

Confidence is stepping into unfamiliar territory because God has prepared my path.

"For the Lord will be your confidence and will keep your foot from being caught." Prov. 3:26

In the movie *Hoosiers*, Gene Hackman takes his team to the Indiana state championship game. It's a big deal for a small-town Midwestern team. Before the game, he has them measure the court because even though they've never played in this arena, he wants them to know it's the exact same size court they play on at home. The basket is only 10 feet high. He does this to help assuage their fear.

God sometimes asks us to step into the unfamiliar because we are exactly the tool He chooses for His purpose. Rather than shake with fear, look at it as a privilege that the God of the Universe picked you out of all the possible candidates. And not only did He pick you, He's going too.[103]

Haven't you found that life as a Christian is a great adventure even though you can't always see much further than a step or two? Trust His Word, trust the Spirit's leading, and take a step of faith. You might just be amazed.

God, it's a challenge to my typical M.O. to step out before I know all the details. Give me wisdom to know it's really You and strengthen my faith to know You're walking with me. In Jesus' name, **Amen**.

---

103 Deut. 31:6

Confidence lets me sleep at night, knowing I'm secure in God's hand.

"It is vain for you to rise up early, to retire late, to eat the bread of painful labors; for He gives to His beloved even in his sleep." Psa. 127:2

The drug counters are filled with all kinds of relaxers and sleep inducers, both prescription and over the counter. Many come with warnings and side effects. There is also sleep therapy if you are averse to meds. It is estimated that the total sleep business is nearly $80 billion.[104]

What if you knew that God has His angels camped out around you for your protection? Would that let you sleep better? He does.[105] Does it surprise you that God cares about your sleep habits? Why? He cares about all aspects of our lives.[106]

Maybe you've tried worry. How'd that work for you? This is one of those "fish or cut bait" issues; either you believe God's Word—in this case about sleep—or you don't. Isn't it great that God gives us choices? Sleep well, friend, God never does.[107]

Father, I want to believe You, but sometimes I just can't turn it off. Help me to internalize Your Word even about something as mundane as sleeping. Thank You for caring about all facets of my life. **Amen**.

104 Figures from 2019
105 Psa. 34:7
106 I Pet. 5:7
107 Psa. 121:4

Week 7 – Thursday

Confidence allows me to use my resources in obedience to God and to bless others.

"The first of all the first fruits of every kind and every contribution of every kind, from all your contributions, shall be for the priests; you shall also give to the priest the first of your dough to cause a blessing to rest on your house." Eze. 44:30

How much of God's Word do you believe? If you're tempted to write that off as a dumb question…don't. God's Word—all of it—is either true or it isn't.

It was about a year after I got saved that one of the adult youth leaders in my church asked me if I tithed. I told him no. He asked, "why not?" I didn't have a good answer. Using logic and scripture, he painted me into a corner by asking if I believed in baptism, the Lord's Supper, and a few other common church doctrines.

It was a huge lesson for me, not just because of the tithing issue, but because scripture was opened to me in a practical, daily life kind of way that I hadn't known before.

Do you know that God doesn't need our money? Then why does the Bible say so much about it? Because God uses it to let us know where our heart (and often our [little 'g'] god) is. Our confidence, with respect to money and other resources, comes from our trust in God's Word.

The psalmist, after a long life, says this, *"I have been young and now I am old, yet I have not seen the righteous forsaken or his descendants begging bread."* [108] Today, God wants to take you to a deeper level of trust in Him and His Word. Let Him.

Father, I want to trust You with my whole heart, but I've got bills to pay, food to buy, and I don't have enough as it is. Help me take Your Word at face value, let You direct my spending and then watch what You do. In Jesus' name, **Amen**.

108 Psa. 37:25

Week 7 – Friday

Confidence allows me to love others unconditionally because God loves me without fail.

"The Lord appeared to him from afar, saying, "I have loved you with an everlasting love; therefore I have drawn you with lovingkindness." Jer. 31:3

Remember the lyrics from the children's song, "Nobody loves me everybody hates me guess I'll go eat worms?" Have you ever felt in your spirit that the song was written for you? How about the '60s Engelbert Humperdinck classic, *Lonely is a Man Without Love*? That sorta says it all. Were you ever picked last for teams? Maybe you were shuffled from home to home as a foster kid and grew up not knowing what real love is. OK, that was then.

As a child of the King—you can get over it; your reality today is that God loves you unconditionally! And it's forever. And it doesn't get depleted by giving some away. Is that good news or what? I know it's often difficult to accept God's love because of the conditions society places on its love. If you're nice enough, pretty enough, rich enough, have an important job, then I'll love you.

Most of us don't measure up to the world's standards. Ask yourself this: "When was the last time the world was right about anything?" God wants us to be a funnel for His love—in one end out the other. The thing about a funnel is the bigger the bottom hole is, the more that can go into the top.

God is looking for "a few good men" whom He can strongly support.[109] Will you be one today by sharing what has freely come to you and cannot be lost, spent or taken away, with others who may still be living an old reality?

Lord, sometimes it's easier to believe the world because of what I see in the mirror. Change my perception to match what You say about me so that I can be Your funnel today. In Jesus' name, **Amen**.

109 II Chron. 16:9

Week 7 – Saturday

Confidence is knowing where I'll spend eternity.

"In the fear of the Lord there is strong confidence and his children will have refuge." Prov.14:26

When the biggest decision you'll ever face is settled, your life will take on a confidence that defies visible reason. You can live your life with the truth of the psalmist, *"The Lord is for me; I will not fear; what can man do to me?"*[110]

In Larry Crabb's book, The Marriage Builder, he addresses the two needs every person on earth has: Security and significance.[111] Unless and until we find the answer to those two issues in a relationship with Jesus, we'll be burdened with...well, insecurity and insignificance.

And the world lies with its answers on how to deal with them. Position, money, popularity, and sex are the typical substitutes offered. But if you've pursued any of them, you know they all lead you down a dead-end alley.

If you have never settled the question of where you will spend eternity, don't delay another day. Trust Jesus' atoning work on the cross to remove your sins.[112] You'll feel your burdens lifted and replaced with confidence that God says what He means and means what He says. If you've already trusted Christ for your salvation, then you know that you're significant and secure in your relationship to Him. No more moping or complaining. If God is for you, what can mere man do to you?[113]

Father, words alone can't express my gratitude for knowing that I'll spend eternity with You. Thank You, thank You. Because of that, let my confidence blossom to be and go and do whatever You tell me and to visibly live my faith for Your glory. In Jesus' name, **Amen**.

110 Psa. 118:6
111 Larry Crabb *The Marriage Builder,* chap. 2 © 1982 The Zondervan Corporation
112Psa. 103:12
113Psa. 56:4

Contentment is recognizing that everything I have—little or much—is a gift from God as part of His sovereign plan for my life. As such, it is exactly the right mix and amount. Lack of contentment, therefore, belies my wimpy faith and betrays my belief in and commitment to the world's system.

"Not that I speak from want; for I have learned to be content in whatever circumstances I am." Phil. 4:11

According to New York-based Kantar Media in a statement on March 17, 2011, over $131 billion was spent by advertisers in 2010 to convince you that you didn't have the right stuff: not enough, too old, passé technology, etc. Is it any wonder we're not satisfied with our lot in life when we're constantly bombarded by sales messages?

How is it possible to be content living in a shack, driving a 10-year-old car, wearing dated fashions, and not having the latest plasma TV technology? Let me put it in perspective. A friend of mine—a solid Christian brother—has been out of work for 30 months. He's an intelligent guy with an electrical engineering degree and an MBA. He had a second interview yesterday and called me last night to say they offered him the job…after two and a half years of looking.

Who knows why God allows some of us to "suffer" trials of this nature? I can assure you of one thing: God NEVER gives us more than we can handle.[114] Maybe we've forgotten where our stuff comes from and think that we're pretty hot (Boy, did I do a great job of landing that contract). Maybe something has replaced God as the object of our worship (Just a few more hours of overtime and that new shiny thing [boat, car, airplane, cabin…whatever] will be mine).

Contentment doesn't come from what we have, but in knowing that what we have comes from God.[115] Are you content today? Praise God. If you find yourself grumpy about your lot in life, my money's on the probability that you've taken your eyes off the prize of Jesus.[116] Confess and turn back. It doesn't mean you'll get new stuff…you may or may not. But you can say with Paul, "I've learned to be content…"

Lord Jesus, I so easily confuse wants and needs. This week let me be satisfied with my portion. **Amen**.

114 I Cor. 10:13
115 Deut. 8:17, 18
116Phil. 3:18-20

Contentment lets me live in the moment.

"If it is disagreeable in your sight to serve the Lord, choose for yourselves today whom you will serve: whether the gods which your fathers served which were beyond the River, or the gods of the Amorites in whose land you are living; but as for me and my house, we will serve the Lord." Joshua 24:15

Old jocks that can't move beyond the glory days and conversations about them are a sad lot. Memories are great; they can motivate us and comfort us. But if that's all we have in life, we're wasting our God-given potential and missing the blessings of "now." If I spend all my time thinking about the past or dreaming about the future, it may mean I'm not happy in the present. You've heard the old saw, "Yesterday is history, tomorrow is a mystery, today is a gift—that's why they call it the present."[117] Each day is a gift from God.

In 2004, I was awakened by a 2:00 A.M. phone call telling me that my 27-year old son had been killed in a motorcycle accident. I don't take today for granted anymore. Life is short, and only God knows the day He'll call us home.[118] So I don't want to miss a single thing that today has to offer: beauty in my surroundings, a new truth shared by a brother, even the trials God has designed specifically for me.[119]

Contentment is mine when I trust God for every aspect of my life and allow Him to decide what's best for me. And isn't it great that not once in history has God missed an appointment or forgotten to schedule my daily blessings?[120]

If you find yourself at one end or the other of the "yesterday – tomorrow" spectrum, take a deep breath and focus on the moment you're in. Memories and dreams are OK, but today is where the action is.

Lord, thank You for another day. Thank You for the blessings You have planned for me today. Thank You that I can trust my future, even the next moment, to You. Help me see that today is all I have and to squeeze the most out of it as my thank offering to You. **Amen.**

117 Origin unknown
118 Psa. 139:16
119 Jas. 1:2-4
120 Lam. 3:22, 23

Contentment doesn't envy my neighbor for his new car.

"The Lord restored the fortunes of Job when he prayed for his friends, and the Lord increased all that Job had twofold." Job 42:10

The above verse is the end of the story and maybe that's all some of Job's neighbors saw and thought, "That lucky dog." But let's go back to the beginning. Have you ever felt like God has invited Satan to put you through the wringer?[121] Anyone have a wife who has counseled them to "curse God and die?"[122]

My guess is that none of us has had the emotional and physical trials that God allowed for Job. There is an American Indian proverb, "Don't criticize a man until you've walked a mile in his moccasins." We would do well to apply that to our lives.

Like Job's neighbors, we don't have any idea what another man has gone through, or how much he gives to charity, or any of his motives. Society may judge us against one another by the size of our bank account, the type of car, how fashion-conscious our wives are, or any of a number of other meaningless standards. Fortunately, God doesn't. He asks one question, "What did you do with my son?"

Once you have the right answer to that question, you can be content with the lot God has provided. You'll know two things for sure: 1) this world is as bad as you'll ever have it, and 2) this world is as good as many of your neighbors will ever have it. Rather than envy their earthly possessions, it should motivate us to share the gospel with them. Think about that…today.

Father, it's so easy to fall into the world's trap of comparing. Help me today to be content with what you deem best for me. In Jesus' name, **Amen**.

121 Job 1:12, 2:6
122 Job 2:9

Contentment lets me be OK with my place at the table.

"They said to Him, "Grant that we may sit, one on Your right and one on Your left, in Your glory." Mark 10:37

Have you ever been embarrassed because you were at the wrong seat, say at a wedding dinner, and the hostess had to ask you to move? It could have been an honest mistake, or it could have been something else. It's the something else we need to think about.

Remember when Jesus exposed the Pharisees for their wrong attitudes and said, "They love the place of honor at banquets..."?[123] The writer of Proverbs had the same thought, "*For it is better that it be said to you, "Come up here," than for you to be placed lower in the presence of the prince...*"[124]

This may be hard for some of us; we want to be where the action is—the important people—not near the wannabes. Why? Because we think more highly of ourselves than we should.[125] Watch out! Pride is lurking and calling you to wrong behavior.

Don't resent an "inferior" place in line or at the table. You'll be fed, and if you have a good attitude, you'll also be blessed. Paul told the Philippians, "*...regard one another as more important than yourselves.*"[126]

You know, if we all did that, we'd fight for the lowliest place. That would be something to watch, wouldn't it? It's like having to get to church early to get a seat...in the back row. *"Man looks at the outward appearance, but the Lord looks at the heart."*[127] Today, ask yourself, "What's more important to me, my heart or my seat?"

God, my pride is alive and well as evidenced by the seat I choose. Forgive me. Help me be content with whatever seat is left and look for Your purpose in placing me there. In Jesus name, **Amen**.

123 Matt. 23:6
124 Prov. 25:7
125 Rom 12:3
126 Phil. 2:3
127 I Sam. 16:7

Contentment can smile even on a cloudy day.

"Yet He commanded the clouds above and opened the doors of heaven;"
Psa. 78:23

Aside from the beauty and variance of clouds, isn't it comforting to know that God controls them too? As a private pilot, one of the things that I used to love to do was fly in and around the bright cumulus clouds—before they became dark and threatening. I am still amazed that a cloud, which has virtually no structural strength, can hold so much water.

But let's talk about clouds as metaphor. Not all our days are sunny. And just like real clouds, which may start as a splash of white against a blue sky, some of our cloudy days can start with clear skies. Then things seem to spiral downward. Traffic is worse than normal, we're late to work, miss an important client meeting, lose the client, reprimand from the boss, our secretary quits, and on and on. We feel like the cartoon character from Li'l Abner: Joe Btfsplk, the world's worst jinx who always had a dark cloud over his head.

So here's the linchpin question: "Do you trust God for the clouds in your life?" Remember, even on what seems the worst day of your life, God promises (present tense) not to give you more than you can handle."[128] We've all heard the humorous saying, "When you can keep your head when everyone around you is losing it, you probably just don't understand the situation." The truth is, when you can keep your head when everyone around you is losing it, you are content in your heavenly Father. Praise Him for that…today.

Father, I love the clouds in the sky, but not so much those in my life. I want to trust you for even the dark days, but so often, I'm paralyzed by the darkness. Help me remember that You're in control and darkness and light are the same to You. **Amen**.

128 I Cor. 10:13

Contentment helps keep my blood pressure down.

"And He said to His disciples, "For this reason I say to you, do not worry about your life, as to what you will eat; nor for your body as to what you will put on." "If then you cannot do even a very little thing, why do you worry about other matters?"" Luke 12:22, 26

Quick, name three things you control the outcome of. There is not one thing I can think of that I totally control. Even of the things I should be able to control—my temper, my attitude, and my response to others—I struggle. I can be the safest driver in the world and still end up in an accident. I can plan an event down to the last detail and even have contingency plans, but I can't guarantee success.

So if all that's true (and it is), why do I fuss and fret when my best plans get derailed? Simple, we live in a sin-cursed world and our enemy delights in messing with us. And, we don't understand all the ramifications, but God allows Satan certain leeway to test us. What we can decide is our diligence, our faithfulness, and whether or not we believe that God controls the outcome.

Is that sounding like a broken record? It should. My goal in these musings is to spark a thought, poke a memory, move you closer in your walk with Jesus. How's it working?

Lord, when I think about the frustrations in my life, I realize it's because I want to be in control, and I can't...that's Your job. Help me today to be content in the knowledge that You can do a better job than I ever could. In Jesus' name, **Amen**.

Contentment trusts God at all times.

"But as for me, I trust in You, O Lord, I say, "You are my God."" Psa. 31:14

"Do you know where you're going to, do you like the things that life is showing you?"[129] If you could be anybody in the world, who would you choose? Movie star? Athlete? Politician? Missionary to a primitive tribe? Are you dissatisfied with your station in life? Why?

Do you know that there is statistical evidence that many people who win the lottery are broke in five years? Is money the root of all evil? No. The *love* of it is.[130] An interesting study by Brickman, Coates, and Janoff-Bulman of UCSF found that 8 weeks after a life-changing event, e.g., win the lottery or major injury, the person returned to their previous level of happiness.

So, as a rule, we adapt pretty well. It starts with a decision—do I allow bitterness and resentment over life's "gifts" to keep me down, or do I say, "Bring it on" and rise above whatever comes? The latter is what, as God's children, is expected of us from our Father.

God is never capricious or vindictive. Everything He does has purpose.[131] And it's for our good.[132] Again, we either believe that and trust Him…or we don't. Don't let negative perspectives on life's events rob you of your contentment. You may not feel content, but if you step out in faith and trust that God has you in mind always, the feelings will follow. Like the hymn writer says, "Trust and obey, there's no other way to be happy in Jesus but to trust and obey."[133]

Father, it's so easy to take my eyes off You and, like Peter, begin to sink. I read the promises in Your Word, but it seems that I have a hard time internalizing them to the point of changing my behavior. Turn the light on for me today so that I can trust you for everything. In Christ's name, **Amen**.

129 Diana Ross, theme from *Mahogany*, 1975
130 I Tim. 6:10
131 II Cor. 5:5
132 Rom. 8:28
133John H. Sammis, 1887

Week 9 – Sunday

Diligence is the attitude of faithfully discharging my duty to my family and employer, always keeping in mind my family's and employer's well-being while remembering that, as a Christian, I am really working for the Lord.

"Whatever you do, do your work heartily, as for the Lord rather than for men, knowing that from the Lord you will receive the reward of the inheritance. It is the Lord Christ whom you serve." Col. 3:23, 24

Work ethic. Sometimes in 21st century America, those two words seem to have all but dropped out of our vocabulary. There seems less and less loyalty on either side of the boss-worker relationship. People are "downsized" to help the bottom line. I know that's the PC way to say it, but when it happened to me, it sure felt exactly like I had been fired.

So how is the Bible relevant in our "modern, enlightened" society? First of all, has God or will God ever change? No.[134] Can we conclude then that God's standards haven't and won't change? Yes.[135] The writer of Proverbs gives us a succinct definition of two paths—two lifestyles—that have ramifications for the workplace: *"The way of a guilty man is crooked, but as for the pure, his conduct is upright."* (Prov. 21:8)

You may not be aware that anyone is watching you. But if you name Christ as your savior and friend, you are constantly under scrutiny. Why? Because Satan will do everything in his power to make your testimony a sham and your witness hollow. Decide today that you will not give the enemy any grist for his mill because you are not a diligent worker. Not so incidentally, your diligence will also cause others to see a difference in you and be drawn to ask why. Get your seeds out; it's planting time.

Father, forgive me for grumbling about the mundane and tedious parts of my life and job, knowing that it is often during these times when You are rebuking the devourer on my behalf. Allow joy to fill my heart this week as I remember that You are my real boss. **Amen**.

134 Heb. 13:8
135 Jas. 1:17

Week 9 – Monday

Diligence keeps me on my knees.

"When the days of feasting had completed their cycle, Job would send and consecrate them [his sons], rising up early in the morning and offering burnt offerings according to the number of them all; for Job said, "Perhaps my sons have sinned and cursed God in their hearts." Thus Job did continually." Job 1:5

How would you like to have "the greatest of all the men of the east"[136] praying and sacrificing to God for you daily? And, on top of that, he's your dad. Wow. We hear too many stories of the other kind of dad; you know the type, verbally or physically abusive, drinks to forget his problems.

As men, we have an awesome responsibility to represent God to our families and stand in the gap for our families before God. How are we doing with it? By the way, it's never too early or too late to start praying for our families. Has your family ever "caught you" on your knees before God? What better example of what you say you believe than to practice it daily.

How about the example of Daniel? He was faithful to pray three times a day[137] even after it was "illegal." What did God think about Daniel's prayers? First, He protected him from the lions. But listen to what the angel Gabriel told Daniel, *"...you are highly esteemed."*[138] Do you think there's a connection between Gabriel's comment and Daniel's prayer habits? Have you been diligent in your prayer time on behalf of your family? If so, praise God. If not, why not start today and watch and trust God to work His work in your family.

Lord God, my family is a gift from You; help me see that more clearly. Give me Your heart for their well-being, wisdom to recognize their needs and the diligence to never give up on them. In Christ's name, **Amen**.

136 Job 1:3
137 Dan. 6:10
138 Dan. 9:23

Diligence doesn't settle for "good enough"; it strives for excellence.

"Finally then, brethren, we request and exhort you in the Lord Jesus, that as you received from us instruction as to how you ought to walk and please God (just as you actually do walk), that you excel still more." I Thess. 4:1

One-hundredth of a second. That's about the time separating Apollo Ohno's 1,500m short track gold medal from whoever took second. At 30 mph, how long does it take the second "nose" to cross the finish line at the Kentucky Derby (the distance by which Charismatic won in 1999)? Do you think silver medal winners who miss gold by the narrowest of margins kick themselves for not reaching deeper, or are they happy with "1st loser"?

Don't send me nasty emails; I'm just trying to make a point. Sometimes second place is as good as we can be—and that's OK…if you've really given your all. Maybe we're only a one-talent guy. That's OK, too, because it's God who doles out the talents. But the issue isn't how well we've done; it's how well we've done compared with how well we could have done if we'd been even a wee bit more diligent—an extra five minutes on our knees, a phone call to a brother I've wronged, time to read Bible stories to our young children, you get my drift.

I don't find anywhere in the Bible where God tells us upon reaching heaven's door, "Good enough, faithful servant." Let's "excel still more"[139] toward a way of life that doesn't settle for less than excellence. I will if you will.

Father, it's so easy to find excuses for not striving for my potential. But You don't want to hear them. Help me focus on the big picture and my future arrival at Your home. I want to hear, "Well done" from You. **Amen**.

139 I Thess. 4:1

Diligence is not something I put on to impress the boss; it's a way of life.

"Watch over your heart with all diligence, for from it flow the springs of life." Prov. 4:23

As you dress for work in the morning (unless you wear a uniform), you probably consider carefully what you'll wear today. Does your tie match? Are your shoes shined? Comb your hair, brush your teeth, and you're out the door. Have you given as much (or any) thought to the attitudes you'll wear today?

Your drive to work is about to reveal what attitude you have. Ever wonder why they call it "rush hour"? I love the poem *The Difference* by Grace L. Naessens. Here's the first stanza which typifies so many of us:

I got up early one morning
And rushed right into the day!
I had so much to accomplish
That I didn't have time to pray.

Take the time to look up the rest of this wonderful poem...and commit it to memory. By the way, diligence will impress your boss, but not if you do it for show. It has to come from the heart. You either are a diligent person or you're not. Remember Jesus' rebuke to the Pharisees? *"For the mouth speaks out of that which fills the heart."* [140] We can't hide what's inside—good or bad—it will come out. Let's start today to make diligence a way of life.

Lord, I'm so foolish to think that I can hide my true self from others, let alone You. Help me to take You seriously and to change my inner man so that it coincides with the outer man that I want others to see. In Christ's name, **Amen**.

140 Matt 12:34

Week 9 – Thursday

Diligence pursues truth and doesn't stop until it's found.

"The plans of the diligent lead surely to advantage, but everyone who is hasty comes surely to poverty." Prov. 21:5

Jack Webb, as Sgt. Joe Friday, a Los Angeles cop in TV's *Dragnet*, which ran (in this iteration) from 1967 – 1970, had a line that worked its way into our vernacular: "Just the facts ma'am." He was looking for the truth and in 30 minutes each week…found it.

I believe part of the reason so many people lose money to scam artists is because they want the easy path to riches and are not willing to complete even a rudimentary level of due diligence to check out "the opportunity." You've heard it, "If it sounds too good to be true…it probably is."

God's Word is truth…all of it, the parts about God's love and mercy but also those that describe His holiness and wrath toward sin. Do you have a particular issue with God that you struggle with say, for example, "How can a loving God send people to hell?" First of all, God doesn't *send* anybody to hell; they *choose* it. Now there's something you might want to dig into further.

With so many churches and doctrines to choose from, how can we know which is true? By comparing it to the standard of truth: God's Word. God can handle our lack of understanding. He can also handle our skepticism, if our goal is to know truth and not just prove somebody (or scripture) wrong. Jesus said we would "know the truth and it would set us free."[141] Make knowing the truth your personal standard…today.

Father, thank You that I can rely on Your Word and build my life on it because it is true. May I not be so lazy that I just accept whatever I hear from a pulpit, but search your Word to see if it lines up. In Jesus' name, **Amen**.

141 John 8:32

Week 9 – Friday

Diligence hangs in there until the job is done.

"Otherwise, when he has laid a foundation and is not able to finish, all who observe it begin to ridicule him, saying, 'This man began to build and was not able to finish.'" Luke 14:29, 30

A football team on offense would be laughed out of the league if they walked off the field at the one-yard line. A term paper would receive a failing grade if all that were turned in was the outline. A surgeon would be sued for malpractice if he didn't stitch up the incision after surgery. Silly examples? Sure. But aren't we tempted sometimes to walk away before we've applied "the second coat?"

Jesus told His audience to price out the job before turning the first shovel. This involves planning, realistic goals, and an honest assessment of our talents and treasure. It's been said that the Christian life is a marathon, not a sprint. What projects have we begun that lie uncompleted? Whose life have we started building into and given up on? How many times have we told ourselves, "This time I'm really going to commit to personal devotions and prayer?"

Believe me; I'm right there with you. Part of it is boredom, but I think most of the time I don't start right. I'm somewhat impulsive (I like to think of it as…spontaneous) and don't plan things from beginning to end. Usually, the final phase of one of my projects becomes tedious and, if I'm not careful (and watched by my wife), I may tend to cut corners.

We need to take Jesus' words seriously. Of course, He's talking about spiritual applications, but there is a very practical side too. If you are prone to start strong and then lose steam before the final lap, ask God to give you the strength to see things through, even today.

Lord, sometimes I have trouble staying focused, especially when the goal line seems to keep moving. Help me honor You by finishing what I start. In Jesus' name, **Amen**.

Diligence will be rewarded in this life and the next.

"His master said to him, 'Well done good and faithful slave. You were faithful with a few things, I will put you in charge of many things; enter into the joy of your master.'" Matt. 25:21

Drive-thru Starbucks, instant mashed potatoes, on-line diploma mills have conditioned us to be the "I want it now, I need it now, I'm going to have it now...generation." As a result, it's hard for us to save part of our paycheck for future needs.

In a recent survey by careerbuilder.com, over 61% surveyed said they lived paycheck to paycheck and didn't put anything away for the future. Contrast that with the wise counsel of Joseph to Pharaoh about preparing Egypt and the rest of the world for the future.[142] The Egyptians were to set aside one-fifth of all their produce—20%. Can you imagine trying to save 20% of your income today? (Not to go down a rabbit trail, but why are we living at or above our means?)

Consider the task Jesus set forth in the above parable. If there hadn't been a sense of reckoning in at least the five- and two-talent guys, and if they didn't have their eyes on that future day, the story would have ended differently.

The marketing pros tell us that we are bombarded with over 3,000 media messages every day. And they all want our money...now. Is it any wonder we can't think about the future?

Well, here's something we can think about. God is interested in what we do with what He gives us. Let me say it again, God is watching how we handle His resources. Can we agree that, as a rule, we can do better in this area? Why not start today and be diligent with whatever God entrusts to you?

Lord, the world offers such attractive packaging. Help me see beyond the glitter to the substance and realize that if it didn't come from You, it's not worth pursuing. Help me also to be faithful to steward Your resources well. In Christ's name, **Amen**.

142 Gen. 41

Week 10 – Sunday

Empathy enables me to communicate to a friend in the valley of trials that I care, I hurt with you. I am at your disposal.

"Blessed be the God and Father of our Lord Jesus Christ, the Father of mercies and God of all comfort, who comforts us in all our affliction so that we will be able to comfort those who are in any affliction with the comfort with which we ourselves are comforted by God." II Cor. 1:3, 4

People mean well when we are grieving, but you know that they don't know the depth of your pain. And when they say, "I know how you feel," you just want to do or say something un-Christian. But, if they have gone through something similar, then their comments and efforts reach deep into your soul and minister to you at a level that really helps.

I've wondered why God allows certain trials in my life. For example, my wife and I have seen God call home our 1-year old daughter and 27-year old son. I know that somehow God has knit these two events into the fabric of our lives to bring glory to Himself. And we have had a few occasions where we really could empathize with others going through the same experience.

There's a phrase in our current vernacular that is supposed to convey sympathy, "I feel your pain." But I think it cheapens the true sentiment and becomes just a glib superficial stab at comfort. Let's look around today and see if God hasn't uniquely prepared us through our trials to be of sincere comfort to someone else.

Jesus, today help me to be sensitive to someone else's needs; to put feet on my faith in Your name. **Amen**.

Week 10 – Monday

Empathy encourages me to go the extra mile.

"Whoever forces you to go one mile, go with him two." Matt. 5:41

In Jesus' day, a Roman soldier could force you to carry his gear one mile. It was a duty of citizenry. But Jesus told His disciples to volunteer freely for the second mile. Many times that act of kindness surprised the soldier and created a seed-planting opportunity.

Think about today's military, fighting in the Middle East, where temperatures can reach over 120 degrees. Their packs can weigh anywhere from 60 to 80 pounds and even more plus boots, fatigues, helmets, weapons...it gets pretty unbearable. Obviously, we can't carry their pack for them. But we can pray for them, individually and as a whole.

Whether we agree with why they're there or not...they are there and need our support. What about their families? Is there something we can do to help them? The point here is simple. There are needs all around us. We just need to look for them and step up to the plate. Can you cook a meal? Mow a lawn? Provide transportation? Can you do it more than once? Thank God that you are able to go one mile. Today, ask yourself, "Am I willing to go two?"

God, thank You for all the resources You have blessed me with. Help me to see needs around me, even when they are not obvious, and to be Your vehicle for delivering the goods beyond the first mile. In Christ's name, **Amen**.

Empathy puts another's short-term needs above my own.

"Treat others the same way you want them to treat you." Luke 6:31

"What goes around comes around" is a modern euphemism for the above verse. You may not be in any particular need at the moment. But wouldn't it be nice to know that when your turn comes, someone will invest in your life. Here's the problem. We can coast through life, often for many years, without serious needs. Thank God for that. But we can get lulled into complacency and think it will always be as it always was.

I've ridden motorcycles off and on for over 45 years, and never had an accident...until March 2011. Had I gotten proud of my record—maybe even a little cocky? Maybe. But I think God allowed it because my zeal for Him had grown lukewarm and my concern for others had, well, slipped would be a nice way to say it.

Throughout my life, I've often been like the jackass you have to hit on the head with a two-by-four just to get his attention. With my broken leg and limited mobility, I've had lots of time to think. God's mercy has overwhelmed me and rekindled my passion for sharing Him. I'm reminded, even as I hobble around on crutches, there are so many worse off than I...physically, but more importantly—spiritually. What can I do in practical ways to put their need above mine? Frankly, not a lot in my present condition. But I can exhibit a positive, grateful attitude. I can smile. I can share the gospel with anyone who will listen.

You'd be amazed how receptive people can be to the saving message of Jesus' death and resurrection when they're down but not quite out. Will you commit with me today to not just "feel their pain" but to actively get involved in a solution?

Father, I get lost in my own self-pity and forget how blessed I am. Forgive me for not keeping my passion for You fired up and help me realize that no matter how bad I think I have it, I still have resources to offer others. In Jesus' name, **Amen**.

Empathy quickly forgives others.

"But if you do not forgive others, then your Father will not forgive your transgressions." Matt. 6:15

Society moves at the speed of superficiality. As we go about our daily agenda, we are programmed to react to external stimuli rather than take time to process and respond in a Godly manner. If we could "count to ten" after a perceived affront, many confrontations would be avoided. If, during our count, we pondered what our "assailant" was going through, we might have a different frame of mind.

Consider the main character—Christian—in John Bunyan's book, Pilgrim's Progress.[143] At one point on his journey, he entered the Slough of Despond, where he was weighed down with his sin and guilt. How many do we meet daily that are similarly weighed down? Do you think that might affect how they think and act toward others, you included?

Jesus warns His followers that forgiveness has to be a way of life. Do I sin? Of course. Do I want my sins forgiven? Of course. Knowing how prone I am to sin helps me have empathy for my fellow travelers and be quick to overlook—forgive—their selfish driving habits, their unfair criticism, and so many other things that I don't deserve. Forgiving others frees me from harboring bitterness, which can lead to all sorts of physical ailments.[144]

Today, before you react, realize two things. First, God is still on His throne, and nothing sneaks up on Him. He allowed this in your life for His purposes. Second, you have no idea what trials others are going through that affect their behavior. Cut them some slack—forgive them—in the power of Jesus living in you.

Lord, help me remember that whatever comes my way today, You have allowed. May I be gracious to others as You are to me and realize that I have no clue what trials others are going through. Use my responses to bring glory to You. In Christ's name, **Amen**.

143*Pilgrim's Progress,* publ. 1678

144 Prov. 17:22

Week 10 – Thursday

Empathy recognizes the log in my own eye.

"Why do you look at the speck that is in your brother's eye, but do not notice the log that is in your own eye?" Matt. 7:3

Fun-house mirrors distort the real us in bizarre and humorous ways, and we're glad we don't really look like that. But seeing ourselves as we really are is an important piece in the puzzle of life. Whether you're a pilot, a surgeon, or a sniper, your job requires keen eyesight. True empathy requires keen insight: the ability to see things as they really are—the need—not the facade we all wear.

And we have to apply the same standard to ourselves too. Jesus called the crowd hypocrites[145] because they were quick to judge others but couldn't see their own depravity. It's only after we have "seen the light" in our own lives that we are free to be truly helpful to others.

My challenge for you today is to look deeply into the mirror of God's Word to see if there's anything at all in your life that blocks you from seeing the truth about yourself. Your spouse or a trusted friend may be able to help. Do this, and your empathy for another will stem from honest assessment and care.

Father, it's not so painful to focus on other people's problems, but I know I need to check my own eyes first. Give me the courage to face the truth about myself…and deal with it. **Amen**.

145 Matt. 7:5

Week 10 – Friday

Empathy looks beyond the warts.

"And a leper came to Jesus, beseeching Him and falling on his knees before Him, and saying, 'If You are willing, You can make me clean.' Moved with compassion, Jesus stretched out His hand and touched him, and said to him, 'I am willing, be cleansed.'" Mark 1:40, 41

In Jesus' day, leprosy was so despised and feared that lepers were required to shout "unclean" whenever someone approached them. They lived apart from society in colonies. According to the World Health Organization, there were 161 new cases of leprosy reported in the United States in 2009. If caught early, common antibiotics are fairly successful in treating the disease. But if not caught, it is a dreadful, crippling disease that can twist bodies into grotesque shapes and disfigurement. And medical science still isn't sure how the disease is transmitted.

Jesus not only talked to this leper, He touched him. I don't know if I could have done that. The leper in Mark's gospel was very real, but let's switch gears and think of leprosy as a metaphor. Who are the "unclean" in your world? Is it the homeless guy who begs by the freeway off-ramp? Is it somebody of a different color? Or language? Or sexual orientation?

Jesus made it very clear; the healthy don't need a doctor.[146] What is it that stops us from reaching out to those who are different than us? God forbid that I think I'm better than them. If I am honest with myself, I have warts too. But I've convinced myself that nobody sees them…hah! Dottie Rambo wrote a song that says it well:

(to the tune of Oh Danny Boy)
Amazing Grace will always be my song of praise.
For it was grace, that brought me liberty,
I do not know, just why He came to love me so.
He looked beyond my faults and saw my need.

Recognizing and admitting our own warts allows us to look beyond the warts of others to their real need…and do something about it.

Lord, how can I expect You to not be turned off by the ugliness of my sin if I can't offer the same to others? Thank You for always seeing my need, not my deceptive facade, and reaching out to touch and heal me. **Amen**.

146 Mark 2:17

Empathy gets off the couch and does something.

"But whoever has the world's goods, and sees his brother in need and closes his heart against him, how does the love of God abide in him?"
I John 3:17

How often do we talk about…Bob? We say things like, "Isn't it terrible what Bob's going through" or "I don't know if I could handle it as well as Bob." The water cooler, the coffee pot, the board room, they're all places where spoken concern can occur. But if the "concern" doesn't leave those venues, it's nothing more than gossip.

What does it take to prod our hearts into action? You can tell how old a tree is by counting the "age rings" in its trunk. I wonder if there is a correlation to how mature a Christian is by how many circles of influence we operate in (1st – family; 2nd – friends; 3rd – co-workers; 4th – neighbors, etc.). John nails it pretty well in the above verse.

Talk is cheap and there's no end of it. Just look at any political pre-election campaign. Blah, blah, blah. I can hear the excuses (because I've made them myself): "But I don't want to embarrass Bob by offering help." "It's too late tonight, maybe I'll call tomorrow." "I've got other commitments." We are busy—sometimes too busy. But if we can't squeeze out some time to help a brother or a stranger, it says volumes about our priorities…and our hearts. If we are unable, that's one thing. But if we are unwilling, watch out. We just might be deceiving ourselves about our salvation. Today, check your heart—your motives—to see if the love of God compels you to get off the couch.

(Just a thought for those of us who are on the receiving end of someone's empathy…let others minister to you. In fact, it's OK to let your needs be known. That's how the body is supposed to work. Don't allow pride to block the blessings God has intended. We can learn a lot by being gracious receivers.)

Father, my life has been very comfortable. Thank You for blessing me with the world's goods. Forgive me for closing my heart to those around me in need. I ask for Your wisdom to discern those lives You would have me invest in. Help me to have the right heart motives and do it in response to You, not because I get points for doing it. In Jesus' name, **Amen**.

Encouragement is what I do when, despite how I'm feeling, I look for the silver lining and share it with others.

"So then let us pursue the things which make for peace and the building up of one another." Rom. 14:19

The miracle of our eyes is beyond amazing. They can interpret colors, focus automatically from close-up to far away, and provide depth perception so we don't run into things. When I look into a mirror, I see myself as I am physically. In a recent survey, people were asked if they would change something about themselves if they could. Over 90% said they would change something.[147] That doesn't speak well to those of us who name Christ as our creator and savior. We're saying that we know better. Don't think so.

But here's the real issue: when we spend so much time focused on ourselves, and become dissatisfied with one or more aspects of our life, how can we ever encourage someone else? If my heart is filled with...me, how is there room for...you? Jesus said, "*...for the mouth speaks out of that which fills the heart.*"[148] If I'm bitter or resentful or angry about my big ears, my short stature, my baldness, where do I go to find something encouraging for my brother—or a stranger? Move away from the mirror and nobody will be hurt. Seriously, we need to spend less time thinking about ourselves and things that we cannot change and more time working on our character. Here's your challenge for today: Find something encouraging to say to everyone you meet...and mean it.

Lord, help me accept myself the way You have created me knowing I'm exactly as You designed me. I really want to be known as an encourager and I can't do that if I spend all my time on me. Thank You for loving and accepting me even with my rough edges. May I do the same with others...for the sake of the kingdom. **Amen**.

147www.harrisinteractive.com
148 Matt. 12:34

Encouragement can start small but have major impact.

"Joshua, the son of Nun, who stands before you, he shall enter there; encourage him, for he will cause Israel to inherit it." Deut. 1:38

Talk about an opportunity. As Moses passed the baton to Joshua, he told the Israelites to encourage him. Joshua had been chosen by God to lead the march into the Promised Land. We know that Joshua's faith was strong because he was one of two spies that came back with a confident report about forging ahead.[149] But the other ten spies were afraid due to the size of the enemy,[150] and it cost Israel another 40 years of wandering.

There are all kinds of things that can shake a leader's confidence: Production problems. Share price problems. Union problems. Scandal among top management. And if there's nobody to represent the other side, it's easy to become discouraged and lose heart.

After 40 years in the desert as a sheepherder, Moses didn't want to be alone "at the top" so badly that he risked God's wrath by negotiating the deal. God graciously gave him Aaron to be Moses' spokesman. But how good was Aaron for Moses? (Just as an aside, have you ever heard a more ludicrous excuse than the one Aaron gave Moses when he returned from Mt. Sinai? "I threw it (the gold) into the fire and out came this calf." [Exod. 32:24])

Moses knew that leaders need encouragement. And he also knew that the Israelites were constant complainers. That's why he told them to encourage Joshua. We may not have the exposure to influence and encourage the next great general or congressman or head of a worldwide ministry. But we can encourage our spouse and kids, our pastor, our boss, and co-workers. We may not affect the outcome of national ideas, but we might help our son pass his algebra test by a positive word of encouragement. Today, just before you walk out the door, make sure you have your encourager's hat on.

Father, my sphere of influence is small, but don't let that stop me from doing what I can where I can when I can to put a smile on someone's face…today. In Jesus' name, **Amen**.

149 Num. 14:6-10
150 Num. 13:32, 33

Week 11 – Tuesday

Encouragement helps keep brothers from sin.

"But encourage one another day after day, as long as it is still called 'Today,' so that none of you will be hardened by the deceitfulness of sin."
Heb 3:13

Have you ever thought that cramping someone's style is a badge of honor, not something to shrink from? Floundering friends and family members, who are trying to run from God, don't want us around reminding them of the light. This is where we have to have thick skin. They will do things and call us names to discourage us and accuse us of "judging" them.

You'll notice the writer of Hebrews encourages us to not lose heart—day after day. Nobody said it's easy being a Christian. But remember, we're in it for the cross-country trip, not the trip to the corner store.

How does encouragement keep someone from sin? First, it lets them know that somebody cares…and is watching. Second, it lifts their spirits; there's nothing like being in a funk to drive a wedge between God and me. Third, sin is deceitful. Using God's truth to encourage a brother turns the spotlight of scripture brightly onto sin's lies. And, just like cockroaches, the lies can't tolerate the light of truth. Which of your brothers needs encouragement today? Do it. Your turn will come.

Lord, help me to stay faithful and close to You so that I can be a light of encouragement to my brothers. **Amen**.

Encouragement that succeeds points the encouragee to God.

"And Jonathan, Saul's son, arose and went to David at Horesh, and encouraged him in God." I Sam. 23:16

"You can do it" "Hang in there" are often empty platitudes which lack substance and miss their intended target. When we're wallowing in self-pity, someone's superficial comments can have the opposite effect on us than what was meant; they are like singing songs to a troubled heart.[151]

On the other hand, we need a certain level of confidence to point others to real solutions, based on the truth of their situation. Is fear the issue that blurs our goal? Maybe it's a nagging sin I can't seem to gain victory over. A pioneer of action-oriented advertising, Claude Hopkins' Tested Advertising Methods, says this, "Platitudes and generalities roll off the human understanding like water off a duck's back. They make no impression whatsoever." That's absolutely true in the marketing and advertising world. Companies that claim things like "the biggest," "the best," etc., are wasting their advertising dollars.

Likewise, when we try to encourage with meaningless words, we're wasting our breath. They tell our intended audience that a) we don't really know or understand the situation, and b) we have nothing of substance to offer them. Pity. We have the truth of God's Word that is "sharper than any two-edged sword"[152] at our disposal. So how do I encourage someone "in God?" First, it requires that I know God personally—His character, His faithfulness, His plan for us. Second, I need to have God's heart for the lost and struggling; my motives for encouraging others must be pure. Third, like Nike, I just need to do it.

Good intentions, it's been said, are the paving material for the road to hell. Today, make sure you're in a right relationship to our Father so that when the opportunity to encourage arises (they're all around us), you'll be prepared.

God, when I consider the responsibility of encouraging someone in You, it makes me realize my need to walk close to You. Thank You that you choose to use me in the lives of my family and friends. Help me stay prepared and sharp so I have more than superficial words to offer. In Christ's name, **Amen.**

151 Prov. 25:20
152 Heb. 4:12

Week 11 – Thursday

Encouragement can be non-verbal.

"Then they sat down on the ground with him for seven days and seven nights with no one speaking a word to him, for they saw that his pain was very great." Job2:13

I've always thought there must be an inverse relationship between the amount of words spoken and their importance. Don't you wish sometimes people would just put a stopper in it? Sometimes, just being there is all a person needs to be encouraged. Your presence says volumes about your feelings for this person. If Job's friends had left after their week of silence…it would have been a good thing. Instead, they lit into him with a barrage of judgments that were totally off base. How'd that strategy work out for them?

We can learn an important lesson from them. They started well but didn't finish well. If we've encouraged someone non-verbally, we should ask (before opening our mouth), do I really need to say anything? Many times the answer will be "no." Just sitting quietly, maybe a hand on a shoulder—just our presence can speak to our friend's heart. Most of us mean well when we try to pump somebody up. But let's take an extra moment or two to assess what our friend really needs. Maybe this is one of those times when being there is enough.

Father, so often I feel at a loss for words. I want to encourage my brothers, but don't want to pour salt into a wound. Help me discern when to speak and when to just be there. In Jesus' name, **Amen**.

Week 11 – Friday

Encouragement from God's Word provides true hope.

"For whatever was written in earlier times was written for our instruction, so that through perseverance and the encouragement of the Scriptures, we might have hope." Rom. 15:4

Perseverance. A word usually associated with trials and long-suffering. Paul tells us that he doesn't consider his present trials even worthy of comparison to the glory that awaits those of us who are in Christ.[153] What would a marathoner be without perseverance? A sprinter. What would a factory worker be without perseverance? Unemployed. So it's not just about trials; perseverance is a way of life.

The verse above tells us that when we add perseverance to the "encouragement of the Scriptures" we have hope. Again, the question arises, "Can I trust what I read in God's book?" Yes, without any reservation. So what kind of hope-producing encouragement does Scripture offer? Good news to the afflicted. Liberty to captives and freedom to prisoners. Comfort for those who mourn. A mantle of praise instead of a spirit of fainting.[154] And many, many more.

Not only are these found in Scripture, they are found in the person of Jesus Christ. That's how we encourage others. We point them to the Jesus of Scripture. Not the Jesus who was just a good teacher, or the Jesus who was just a man. We speak of the One we know, the One who did for us what we are incapable of doing for ourselves—pay for our sin with His blood.

If we don't give encouragement that's tied to eternal hope, what are we really offering? The deception of empty words.[155] Renew your mind[156] so that when you open your mouth, you speak the conviction and hope of Scripture…and do it today.

Father, I know that Your Word is the only real source of truth that I can stake my future on. Give me a love for it that I would read, memorize and meditate on it so that I have more than my opinions to offer someone who's hurting. In Christ's name, **Amen**.

153 Rom. 8:18
154 Isa. 61:1-3
155 Eph. 5:6
156 Rom. 12:2

Encouragement is not about me and comes from pure motives.

"Do nothing from selfishness or empty conceit, but with humility of mind regard one another as more important than yourselves." Phil. 2:3

Many relationships are like a tick and a dog. I'm the tick, you're the dog. I pursue the relationship based on what I can get out of it. The problem arises when you approach me the same way I do you—two ticks, no dog.[157]

That's why Paul tells us to focus on how to give, not get. When we do that, it doesn't matter at all what the other person has to offer. What can a homeless person give you? Gratitude? What can you give a homeless person? You get the picture.

Sometimes I feel closest to God right after a selfless act that has totally been about another person. It's like I hear God saying, "Now you're getting it." If I could only do that more and not be such a "tick." It really boils down to this, "Do I trust God to meet my needs, or do I have to manipulate people and events to make sure I get my share?" I either trust God or I don't. If I do trust Him, it will free me to encourage others without any concern as to when I'll get mine.

Remember what Job said, "*Though He slay me, I will hope in Him.*"[158] Hugh Grant in *Mickey Blue Eyes* has advice for those of us prone to think that it's about me: "fuggidaboudid." Today, put all your needs in the "God basket" and let Him deal with them. Then you can focus on encouraging others, knowing you'll be in better hands than your own.

Father, I know how I blossom under encouragement from others. Let me trust You today to meet my needs, and I'll focus on spreading the sunshine to someone else. **Amen**.

157 Larry Crabb, *The Marriage Builder*, Zondervan Press, © 1982, pg. 32
158 Job 13:15

Week 12 – Sunday

Endurance sees the Christian life as a marathon, not a sprint.

"I have fought the good fight, I have finished the course, I have kept the faith; in the future there is laid up for me the crown of righteousness, which the Lord, the righteous Judge, will award to me on that day." II Tim. 4:7, 8a

What if you knew Jesus would return tomorrow? You could handle anything that came your way, couldn't you? What if He came next week? You could still maintain, couldn't you? So why do we grow weary when it seems like He'll never come?

We have the wrong mindset. First of all, for those of us who live in America, we don't have a long-term perspective...on anything. For example, how many of us can even fathom being involved in a project that would take approximately 180 years to build like the cathedral of Notre Dame? What is that, four generations? Talk about job security.

We're so impatient we get upset if our builder is delayed one or two weeks. How about one or two decades? It just doesn't compute. So for the Christian "race," we need to adjust our mindset. Second, we need to trust God when He says through Peter, "*The Lord is not slow about His promise, as some count slowness, but is patient toward you, not wishing for any to perish but for all to come to repentance.*" (II Pet. 3:9)

It involves focusing not on ourselves but on others who don't know Jesus. When you're trying to finish a project, don't you wish you had more hours in the day? If we consider the fate that awaits the lost, especially our loved ones, that should make us thankful for one more day or year or century. The question is, what are we doing with the time?

Father, it's hard to see time from Your perspective. Help me have the mindset of urgency when it comes to sharing the gospel, knowing that Jesus could return any moment and some in my family aren't in Your family...yet. In Jesus' name, **Amen**.

Endurance keeps your eyes on the prize.

"Do not turn to the right nor to the left; turn your foot from evil." Prov. 4:17

Ever notice when you're driving that if you turn your head left or right and focus on something, you tend to drift in that direction? It's hard to drive straight if we're not looking straight. Worse yet is falling asleep and awaking to the tires in the gravel at the side of the road. Believe me, I've done it and that'll get you focused in a heartbeat.

Our Christian walk is exactly like that. God knew we would be so prone to distractions that He warns us to stay focused. Glancing is one thing. The second or lingering look is what gets us in trouble. Job tells us that he *"made a covenant with his eyes."*[159] The key is how much value we associate with the prize.

When I was about eight or nine years old, one of the local grocery stores had a coloring contest. First prize was a bicycle. My family didn't have a lot of discretionary income, and that bike became an obsession. I painstakingly stayed within the lines, chose appropriate colors, and submitted my entry. I won…second prize—a Lionel electric train. As good a prize as the train was, I valued the bike more highly and was disappointed.

The question each of us needs to answer is this, "How much value do I put on the prize that awaits a life of faithful service?" If the prize of the "upward call of God in Christ Jesus"[160] doesn't excite me and energize me to hang on irrespective of the challenges, I probably should ask, "Am I really part of God's family?" The amazing thing about God's "contest" is everybody can win first prize—the Lord Jesus Christ. Jesus said, "…the one who comes to Me I will certainly not cast out."[161]

Today, evaluate the prize you're chasing, make sure you're in the right race, and get rid of everything that pulls you to the right or left.

Lord, help me realize the value of the prize that's already mine and stay true to Your path. **Amen**.

159 Job 31:1
160 Phil. 3:14
161 John 6:37

Endurance does not listen to mockers.

"Know this first of all, that in the last days mockers will come with their mocking, following after their own lusts, and saying, 'Where is the promise of His coming? For ever since the fathers fell asleep, all continues just as it was from the beginning of creation." II Pet. 3:3, 4

Logic is a beautiful thing…for honest people. Just because something hasn't happened yet doesn't mean it won't ever happen. In 1966, there hadn't been a Super Bowl. On July 4th, 1969 we hadn't put a man on the moon. The missing word in both statements is yet. A comedian did a sketch on Noah in which Noah's neighbors laughed at him and called him Tarzan.

In Noah's conversation with God, Noah said, "Do you know I'm the only one in the neighborhood with an ark?" Well, it had never rained…yet. And we all know how that story turned out. Noah believed God and acted on his belief.

Haven't you found that when you succeed at anything, there are always those trying to bring you down? Ever wonder why? Because your success, your positive attitude, your righteousness silently confronts people who are lazy, negative, and unrighteous.

There is a small, but growing, segment of the population that is labeled "Contrarian." These people believe that if the majority is doing anything, then they will do the opposite and be successful. Interesting philosophy. But we don't have to "test the water" or interpret the polls to know how to act. God has given us specific marching orders that are designed for "*…teaching, reproof, correction, and training in righteousness.*"[162] There have always been mockers of Christianity. The Bible calls them Scribes, Pharisees, whitewashed tombs. But they didn't deter Jesus, or later His disciples, from doing what God had assigned.

Here's a simple test to see if you're doing what God has assigned to you. How often do you encounter mockers? God's love and forgiveness transcend normal logic. That, a good dose of guilt, and wanting to reduce God to how they would deal with sinners keep many from the truth of the gospel. Today, don't let mockers sideline you. Stay in the game. Stay focused. Jesus said, *"I am coming quickly."*[163] You can take that to the bank.

Father, waiting is not my strong suit. Help me stay focused on the truth of Your Word and not listen to the skeptics around me that are challenged by Christ's righteousness in me, who would see me out of the game. In Jesus' name, **Amen**.

162 II Tim. 3:16

163 Rev. 22:20

Week 12 – Wednesday

Endurance keeps me from alluring detours and shortcuts.

"Let no one keep defrauding you of your prize by delighting in self-abasement and the worship of the angels, taking his stand on visions he has seen, inflated without cause by his fleshly mind." Col. 2:18

Who could be against angels? Who wants to call someone a liar because of something he said he's seen? Not me. But I also don't need to hang with people in these camps. Am I saying that in special circumstances, angels and visions don't exist or can't be seen? No. God can allow us to see whatever He chooses.[164] And there is an entire spirit world not visible to us. But seeing into it is not the norm. And when someone seeks to elevate himself because he's seen something over which he had absolutely no control, we are told not to get sucked into their hype (my paraphrase).

God created Satan as a highly intelligent being. He became corrupted through pride, but he didn't forfeit his intelligence. Do you think he would tempt us off the path with grotesque, hideous manifestations of the invisible realm? Of course not. Paul tells us that Satan disguises himself as an angel of light and his demons as servants of righteousness.[165]

God has designed us with an innate desire for Himself and a built-in knowledge of Him through nature.[166] As with everything Satan does, he tries to counterfeit the true, the perfect creation of God and position it as attainable with no effort—the easy path. Remember Jesus' comments about the narrow and broad way?[167] One—the narrow one—is honestly labeled "This Way to Heaven" the other—the broad one—is falsely labeled "This Way to Heaven."

Can you imagine any of the home run greats—Barry Bonds, Hank Aaron, Babe Ruth or Willie Mays—after clearing the fence, deciding they would cut across the pitcher's mound for third to save time? A ludicrous example of a short cut to focus on the path God has outlined for us. There are NO shortcuts, NO detours on the narrow path. Otherwise, it doesn't count.

Stay away from anything that elevates angels to a position of glory or worship. Avoid people and movements that focus on visions and/or experience that "exceed what is written."[168] God is not the author of confusion[169] nor does He mislead any. The road to the Father is clearly marked: Jesus Christ.[170]

Lord, I want to stay on the narrow path, but there are a lot of things that pull me one way or the other. Today, outfit me with spiritual blinders so it's hard for me to look anywhere but to Jesus. In His name, **Amen**.

164 II Kin. 6:17
165 II Cor. 11:14, 15
166 Rom. 1:19
167 Matt. 7:13, 14
168 I Cor. 4:6
169 I Cor. 14:33
170 John 14:6

Endurance sets the example for those around me.

"I can do all things through Him [Christ] who strengthens me." Phil. 4:13

Endurance is as much mental as it is physical. Ask any Navy S.E.A.L. who has earned his trident. Ask a football coach what he means when he says, "We're going to play 60 minutes of football today; not 57 or 58 or 59." It's mental conditioning.

All military, all sports teams, all good sales organizations know if you lose the mental game, you've already lost the physical too. You've heard it said that it's lonely at the top. That comes from being the one who sometimes has to make the tough decisions. It comes from being the one who can't let negative feelings or fears seep into his conscious persona even if everything is falling to pieces around him.

The world has all kinds of tricks to keep us mentally sharp and thinking good thoughts. One of the most widely quoted statements comes from Napoleon Hill: "Whatever the mind of man can conceive and believe it can achieve." The power of positive thinking does have advantages; even the Bible says so.[171] But the danger (to us) comes when we start to think more highly of ourselves than we ought[172] and desire glory that is to be God's alone.

As leaders—and we all lead somebody—we have a responsibility to make sure the example we set points people to our Strength: Jesus Christ. Good leaders are steadfast; they are strong, decisive. Most importantly (even from a worldly sense), they don't take credit for themselves. Everything we have, even our mental toughness and endurance, comes from our Father.[173] We're in the game of life until the final whistle. Get in shape… mentally as well as physically. And above all, let Christ be your strength.

Lord, I don't lead many, but I know many watch me. Help me today to let Christ strengthen my mind to endure to the end. May others be drawn to Jesus because of what they see in me. In His name, **Amen**.

171 Heb. 12:15; Prov. 17:22
172 Rom. 12:3
173 Jas. 1:17; I Cor. 4:7

Endurance doesn't complain when the going gets tough.

"Do all things without grumbling or disputing...holding fast the word of life, so that in the day of Christ I will have reason to glory because I did not run in vain nor toil in vain." Phil. 2:14, 16

A Few Good Men. Army Strong. Military slogans intended to instill pride and esprit de corps. If you've served, you know that the going can get tough...physically and mentally. But it's all about the mission. We either get it done or we don't. Excuses are unacceptable.

The Christian walk is like that. Sure, we still sin. No, we don't always meet God's standard. But that's what the cross is all about—forgiveness. We don't have the luxury of wallowing in it. We pick ourselves up, dust off, and move on. We're soldiers in God's army. He's our Commanding Officer. And, like a finely-honed military unit, we have our mission: *"Go; make disciples; baptize; teach..."*[174]

Is it easy? No. So what? Man up. God has equipped us for everything He asks us to do.[175] Our job each day is to put on the uniform: Truth, righteousness, gospel of peace, faith, salvation, Word of God, prayer[176]...and then stand. You've seen the bumper sticker: "Life is hard...and then you die." There's more than a little truth in that. But where is it written that we coast through life?

Are you grateful to have been born in the greatest country in history? Have you gone without meals, proper clothing, housing, medicine? In less than 100 years, we've gotten soft. It's easy to find a listening ear when we want to complain. Ask yourself this, "Does my complaining do anything for my situation, and does it honor and glorify my C.O?" Of course not. So why do I waste the energy? We've been equipped, trained, and gotten our orders. All we have to do is follow them and move out. Today, slap a hand over your mouth if you realize the next word isn't going to edify.

Father, I find myself complaining more often because things don't go the way I think they should. Forgive me for not just following orders...graciously. May my attitude be a positive influence on those around me. In Christ's name, **Amen**.

174 Matt. 28:19, 20
175 Phil. 4:19
176 Eph. 6:14-17

Endurance is rewarded by my Father.

"His master said to him, 'Well done, good and faithful slave. You were faithful with a few things, I will put you in charge of many things; enter into the joy of your master.'" Matt. 25:21

Finishing a task is often its own reward. The pride of accomplishment, the sense of closure, checking one more thing off our to-do list. Weekends are always too short. Do you have a long-term project? Maybe you love woodworking and you're building an entertainment center. Maybe you're a gear head and you're restoring a '57 Chevy. My hat's off to you. I don't have the patience—or the skills—to do either. I appreciate both finished products but couldn't conceive of tackling either one. You know going in that these are projects that could take a very long time, and you're willing to invest the time because of the end result.

What kind of long-term projects are we working on for the kingdom? In the parable above, how long do you think the master was gone? One year, five years, more? We're just told "a long time."[177] I can see the sign in the master's employment office: "Procrastinators need not apply." We're told that two of the three slaves "immediately went and traded" the talents.[178] They probably didn't know how long their master would be gone and wanted to complete the task before he returned…whenever that was.

Jesus wants us to be like the slaves, faithful. You'll notice in reading the rest of the story that both slaves were rewarded similarly. It wasn't the amount produced that was rewarded. It was their faithfulness. Like the slaves in the parable, we don't know when our Master will return. But we do know that He will; He said so.[179] Are we patiently enduring our Lord's return? Are we about His business? We can't let God's timetable lull us into discouragement or disillusionment. Christ will return. His reward will be with Him.[180] Stay at it and get ready to hear: Well done, good and faithful slave."

Lord, I know your timetable is different than mine and that mine doesn't really count anyway. Don't let me lose sight of the reward that will someday be mine and help me to finish strong. In Christ's name, **Amen**.

177 Matt. 25:19
178 Matt. 25:16
179 John 14:3
180 Rev. 22:12

Even-Tempered allows me to live above, not under, the circumstances.

"For the anger of man does not achieve the righteousness of God." James 1:20

"Road rage" is a term recently added to our lexicon. That's a sorry indictment on the state of our society. How did we get here? Can we ever return to civility? Let's look at a different question. Can we return prayer to schools? Do you think there may be a connection between these questions? A slippery slope is dangerous because we're not even aware we're on it until it's too late and we're gathering speed.

In June 1962, the U.S. Supreme Court banned prayer in public schools. I was in 10th grade, not a Christian, and had a "so what" attitude. You know about the nose of the camel under your tent, right? All decisions have consequences sooner or later. I believe this was a major tipping point in the battle of good vs. evil. Differences were fostered, flames of hatred were fanned. Remember, this was also the time of major racial tensions (e.g. Watts riots – summer '65). All of these things coming together at about the same time was no accident. The result was a society that felt increasingly out of control—and angry. And it's only gotten worse in the last five-plus decades.

One of the most visible expressions comes from drivers who have expectations of "my space" (not to be confused with the social networking web site). They own the road—especially the lane you're in. You've seen 'em. They tool around in the little imports with the noisy tin-can tailpipe. They zip in and out of traffic. If you're like me, praying for them is not the first thing that comes to mind.

James reminds us that our anger takes us in the wrong direction. Is God in control of this "traffic moment"? You bet He is. The question for us today is this, "Can I believe and accept that God has allowed this imposition on my space to hone me and make me more like Christ?"

Lord, I confess, inconsiderate drivers often cause me to lose it. I know it's sin and doesn't achieve the righteousness that I desire. Help me accept your control of my driving circumstances and even smile as I encounter various challenges to stay even-tempered. In Jesus' name, **Amen**.

Week 13 – Monday

Even-Tempered lets me act, not react.

"But I say to you, do not resist an evil person; but whoever slaps you on your right cheek, turn the other to him also." Matt. 5:39

Count to ten…then what, slap him back? We often feel like that, don't we? But that's not quite the picture Jesus paints. How do we get to this level of control without wanting to strike back? I can tell you this: It can't be done in our strength. My flesh hates to let somebody get over on me without wanting to unleash my fury all over their mug.

The degree to which we control our reactions is a good barometer of the degree we trust Christ for this aspect of our lives. Why does it take us so long to realize that our Father is in control of everything? The speed bumps He allows on our road of life are designed to make us like Jesus.[181]

We're not to be like the balls in a pinball machine, bouncing off everything we meet. We should be like the ball in the game Labyrinth. As long as we follow the path, we won't fall into the traps along the way. These traps are everywhere, and they sneak up on us when we're least expecting them.

That's why it's a good practice to start our day with the Lord.[182] It puts our mind in the right frame of reference—focused on God—so that when temptations come, and they will, we'll be armed with the weapons of spiritual battle and not depend on our flesh. Let's make it our goal today to be filled with the Spirit so we don't fulfill the lusts of the flesh.[183]

Father, You know how I struggle with letting others get the better of me. I know it exposes my insecurity and how little I trust You. Today, give me a sense of your protective arms around me. Let me remember the challenges You allow in my life are because You love me and want me to become like Jesus. In His name, **Amen**.

181 Rom. 8:29
182 Psa.5:3
183 Gal. 5:16

Week 13 – Tuesday

Even-Tempered results from choosing right companions.

"Do not associate with a man given to anger; or go with a hot-tempered man, or you will learn his ways and find a snare for yourself." Prov. 22:24, 25

Maybe you grew up in a house where yelling at others was the norm…and I'm not talking about just the kids. Where does anger come from? It's predominately a reaction to disappointment—unmet expectations. We expect our wife to have dinner on the table when we get home. We expect our kids to buckle down and get good grades, be a leader on the team, choose good friends.

These, in and of themselves, are good goals. But maybe your wife has spent her day consoling a friend who's going through a tough time with her marriage. Maybe your kids don't share your goals for their lives. Maybe they're bullied at school. It's OK to set goals…for ourselves. But as husbands and dads, we need to be sensitive to the desires and goals of our family and not set expectations that make *us* feel good.

When we choose friends, we often don't know much about their home life or their upbringing. We select based on today's criteria: Do we like the same football team? Are our kids in soccer together? The same political affiliation? We need to look deeper and discover character. What are the core principles that propel this prospective friend? How does he treat his mother?

Scripture is clear. If we hang with the wrong crowd, we will become like them. Paul tells us, "*Do not be deceived: 'Bad company corrupts good morals.'*" (I Cor. 15:33) Of course, this assumes that you're not the "bad company." If you are one who struggles with anger, try giving people more grace, more space to be who they are. After all, who put you in charge of expectations? Do it today. I trust the results will encourage you to do it tomorrow too.

Lord, I ask for discernment in choosing my friends. Lead me to those that You know can help sharpen me—those with even tempers not easily provoked to anger. In Christ's name, **Amen**.

Even-Tempered does not allow anger to be spawned by jealousy.

"And he said to him, 'Your brother has come, and your father has killed the fattened calf because he has received him back safe and sound.' But he became angry and was not willing to go in; and his father came out and began pleading with him." Luke 15:27, 28

Everybody knows the Prodigal. He's the disrespectful, profligate, wasteful son...whom his father loves. Great lessons in this part of the story. But how often do we consider the older brother (let's call him Bob)? Why did Bob become angry? As we learned yesterday, anger can come from unmet expectations. What did Bob expect? Very simple. Everything else. Little brother took his share of the inheritance and squandered it.

According to custom, Bob would get what was left—twice as much as his brother had gotten. Obviously, Bob thought more of the money than he did of his brother or his dad. His anger came from a confluence of many things: judgmentalism, envy, hatred, greed to name a few.

Are there things bubbling below your surface that are poised to push your buttons? It's time to examine our hearts to see if we have assigned expectations to people or circumstances that we have no right to assign. Are we expecting a promotion? A position on the board? A political appointment? An apology? Forget it. If God wants those things for you, you'll get them...period. If He doesn't, you won't. Can you live with that... without getting angry? If you can, that's a sign of your maturity in the Lord. If you can't, well, scripture is profitable for correction.[184]

Think about "Bob" today and see if there are any parallels in your life. Let the Holy Spirit fill you with peace, so the sine wave of your temper becomes a straight line.

God, I have bought into the world's system and feel cheated when I don't get my way. I rationalize it, but You call it sin. It proves that my trust in You is not where it should be. Help me remember that You are my provider and sustainer...and peace. In Jesus' name, **Amen**.

184 II Tim. 3:16

Week 13 – Thursday

Even-Tempered prevents murder.

"You have heard that the ancients were told, 'YOU SHALL NOT COMMIT MURDER' and 'Whoever commits murder shall be guilty before the court.' But I say to you that everyone who is angry with his brother shall be guilty before the court." Matt. 5:21, 22

Wow. That sounds pretty harsh, doesn't it? Do you know of any instance where Jesus followed a statement like this with, "just kidding"? That probably makes most of us serial killers. I wonder if, when we're tempted to anger, we pictured ourselves aiming a 9mm Glock at the object of our anger, how that would change our words and actions.

We need to take Jesus' comments seriously and think about the consequences of our anger. OK, I can hear the defensive wheels turning. "But it's a righteous anger." I'll grant that the possibility exists, but in reality, it's more likely that we feel one of *our* "rights" was stepped on and we're just out of control—wanting to vent.

How can I get a grip on my anger and the things that trigger it? The answer is easy, but putting it into practice may not be: Trust God. What's one of the most obvious symptoms of an "active" trust in our Father? Isn't it a "peace that passes understanding?"[185]

We need to peel away all the layers of intellectualism, knowledge, and experience and return to a childlike faith that knows God is in control of every moment and every circumstance in the universe. We need to remember that He is our Father, who loves us beyond our comprehension. We may not think that the trials and events that push our buttons are "good gifts,"[186] but we also don't know what's in store for us around the next corner…and He does.

I know faith doesn't seem logical. But when we consider that God made us; God loves us; God saves us, it follows—logically—that He provides for us too. That said, if our focus is on Him and not the anger-producing events that come our way, we will become even-tempered. Don't be discouraged. The cross covers our anger too. But today, let's do whatever we can to incorporate Jesus' warning about murder into our consciousness.

Father, I let so many things push my buttons because I want to be in control. Let me take Your warnings seriously and do what I need to trust You for every moment and every circumstance. In Jesus' name, **Amen**.

185 Phil. 4:7
186 Matt. 7:11

Even-Tempered will let others choose the activity.

"Husbands, love your wives and do not be embittered against them." *Col. 3:19*

You've heard that if two people agree on everything, one of them isn't necessary. And this one: opposites attract. How often do you and your spouse agree on the restaurant, the entertainment, the recreational activity, the vacation destination? Are you easy to live with, as in give and take? Or is your opinion the only one that matters?

Paul doesn't *suggest* that we love our wives; it's a *command.* Why would he add the warning about becoming embittered? Because our wives are sinners...just like us. They were given to us[187] as helpers,[188] not slaves. And they will inevitably do things that irritate us. Our role is to love them sacrificially. How do we do that?

One way is to defer to their choice of activity. Is it really that big a deal to take her for soup and salad instead of the "all you can scarf" buffet? Maybe next time she goes out with the girls, you and a couple of buddies can pig out to your heart's content. The point is this: Instead of harboring bitterness (which will hinder your prayer life),[189] generously go along with her desires, overlook the little things that don't mean a lot in the big picture of life. Don't major on the minors; don't sweat the small stuff. Your blood pressure will be lower, your ego will be in check, and, more importantly, you'll be doing what God wants. Start today and see if you can't turn one day into a habit.

Lord, thank You for my wife. I know You designed her and gave her to me as a helper—a partner. May I not crush her with my demands, but accept her ideas and choices. Bless our marriage and help me set a Godly example that points her to You. In Christ's name, **Amen**.

187 Prov. 19:14
188 Gen. 2:18
189 I Pet. 3:7

Even-Tempered is highly valued by God.

"He who is slow to anger is better than the mighty, and he who rules his spirit, than he who captures a city." Prov. 16:32

You might be a weightlifter able to bench press over 300 lbs. But have you ever been called "mighty"? You might have played "capture the flag" as a kid. But have you ever played "capture a city"? For those of us who can't bench our own weight—and even those who can—God says we're better than the mighty…IF. We're better than the winner of a land grab…IF. These are a couple of big ifs: 1) slow to anger; 2) rule your spirit.

This week we've talked about things and people who can push our buttons. We've looked at ways to mitigate anger's hold on us: Start our day with God; give more grace to those who offend us; be filled with the Holy Spirit. The bottom line—the only way to anger abatement—is to get our arms around the concept that God really is in control. He hasn't forgotten us. On the contrary, He specifically designs trials and circumstances to chip away at our rough edges. Stop fighting it. You won't win…God will just get a bigger hammer.

Counting to ten is intended to slow our anger, and it may work sometimes. But isn't it better to remember that God is in His heaven and still on His throne?[190] Nothing comes our way that hasn't been authorized by a loving Father. Let me say that again. God either designs or approves every circumstance for our good and His glory. We just think that we can deal with it on our own. It's like saying, "I've got this one, God; You go handle the important stuff."

Get it through your head: You *are* important stuff. What other proof do you need than Christ's cancellation of your sin-debt through His death and resurrection? Today, remember that God has called you "better than the mighty," but only if you're slow to anger.

Father, this has been a tough study because I know I have a problem with anger. Help me trust You more to handle the irritations that push my buttons. I realize that my anger doesn't move me toward righteousness. Forgive me. I want that to change so my life reflects the work You're doing. In Christ's name, **Amen**.

190 Psa. 103:19

Excellence doesn't give up until it finds truth.

"Be diligent to present yourself approved to God as a workman who does not need to be ashamed, accurately handling the word of truth." II Tim. 2:15

Recent scandals expose cheating in several areas. If the truth were known, a much different picture emerges than those scandalized want the public to see. In Atlanta, 178 educators, including 38 principals, didn't want the truth of their low scores going public… so they simply altered the scores. Many athletes use performance-enhancing substances because they don't want to be remembered for the numbers achieved by their unaided abilities. And politicians? Are you really surprised?

The world measures differently than God. In the world, it's mano a mano—hand to hand, one on one. But with God, we're measured against ourselves—what did I do with what I was given? How many of us can deal with the truth that we're not likely to be number one…in our jobs, our athletic ability?

Here's another truth: every one of us can be better than we are. For example, we're either known as men of character and integrity or we're not. And in that, we can all be excellent. One thing that may help us is to set a life goal—something really big—like becoming more Christlike. That way, when you set smaller, incremental goals, you have the guideline to ask yourself, "Will this help me attain the bigger goal or will it distract me?"

Without a life goal, many activities, in and of themselves, are OK, but don't facilitate the bigger goal. A life goal helps us stay on the path and off the rabbit trails. It becomes our map for navigating uncharted waters.

What's your truth today? Do you know you could do better, be better, have better family relationships? If the answer is yes, keep going. You don't have to do it alone. God waits for you to ask His help. Don't give up until your truth is something you won't be ashamed to present to God.

Lord God, help me prioritize my days to accomplish those things that move me toward my life goal. In Christ's name, **Amen**.

See also: Psa. 119:160; John 17:17; John 14:6

Week 14 – Monday

Excellence raises the bar and keeps it there.

"So that you may approve the things that are excellent, in order to be sincere and blameless until the day of Christ." Phil. 1:10

In 1962, Chubby Checker recorded *Limbo Rock*, a song about dancing under a limbo bar. One of the phrases was, "how low can you go?" As we look around our society today, that seems an appropriate question to ask also. I've heard someone quip that if God doesn't punish a certain major American city, where public nudity and defecation on the sidewalk is allowed, he'll have to apologize to Sodom and Gomorrah.

Obviously, God is patient, not wanting any to perish.[191] But do we look at our surroundings, shrug our shoulders and say, "what can I do?" What we should do instead is keep inching the bar upward and ask, "How high can I go?" In 1960, Don Bragg (USA) set the men's pole vault record at 4.80 meters (not quite 16 feet). In 2020, Mondo Duplantis holds the record at 6.18 meters (over 20 feet). Before May 6, 1954, nobody thought the 4-minute mile could be broken. But Roger Bannister did it...by less than 1 second. Since that time, over a dozen men have bettered the record.

If you aim for the sun and only reach the moon, haven't you still done well? What form is your quest for excellence taking? Are you setting a "stretch" goal that is attainable (by stretching)? That's great. Reach it then move it again. Don't let anybody tell you that you have no business pursuing your goal, that you're a loser and you'll never make it. Remember why they do that. They're complacent (read: lazy) and don't want their status quo messed with.

The light of righteousness always outshines the darkness. Whether you think you can, or you think you can't...you're right. I had a boss that often said, "The harder you work, the luckier you get." How about a goal of memorizing the Bible? Start with a verse, then two, then a chapter, a book. Before you know it, you'll be able to answer the psalmist's question, *"How can a young man keep his way pure?"*[192] And be able to echo the psalmist's reasoning, *"Your word I have treasured in my heart, that I may not sin against You."* (Psa. 119:11). Today, set a God-honoring goal and don't let anyone deter you from reaching it.

Father, the world reacts negatively when I pursue righteousness. Help me to stay motivated toward that goal because I know it's what You want of me. In Jesus' name, **Amen**.

191 II Pet. 3:9
192 Psa. 119:9

Excellence is when being good isn't good enough.

"Strive to enter through the narrow door; for many, I tell you, will seek to enter and will not be able." Luke 13:24

In our hectic world, we live with deadlines. Product has to ship, newspapers must be printed, mortgages must be paid…on time. Contest entries must be "postmarked by." There are penalties for missing time constraints. Some are financial—a late fee; others result in a lower grade. Some disqualify you from participation. We can usually live with any of these. Sure, it may cost us more or we may miss out on something we really wanted. But it's not life and death.

There is one deadline, however, that we dare not miss. By the way, isn't that an interesting word? Dead…line. An implied line in which one side or one end represents death. Jesus told His listeners to "enter through the narrow door" and "many…will not be able." Some interesting word pictures come to mind. Too fat. Too much luggage. Wrong door.

In life, we all strive for things; we want to "get ahead." And we only have so many days[193] to do it—a deadline, so to speak. The only problem is that we don't know when the dead…line is. One day, God will blow the whistle and call us out of the game.

If we've only been good, we're in trouble. The Bible tells us that our righteous deeds are like a filthy garment (Isa. 64:6). It's a quandary, but there is a solution. However, being good or getting better…isn't it. Jesus told us that He is the way, and nobody gets to God without going through Him.[194] In this case, excellence has nothing to do with deeds, records, or lifestyle; we can't attain it on our own. It has everything to do with Jesus' all-sufficient sacrifice on the cross and our humble and penitent acceptance of God's free gift. If you've never recognized your need for a savior and invited Christ to cleanse your sin, make today your day. You'll not be able to enter the narrow door unless you do.

Holy God, I recognize that no matter how good my deeds, they won't get me through the door. I ask for your mercy and accept Jesus' blood-payment on my behalf. May I strive for righteousness because it pleases You, not because I earn heaven through it. In Christ's name, **Amen**.

193 Psa. 139:16
194 John 14:6

Excellence doesn't wait for the majority.

"And He summoned the crowd with His disciples, and said to them, 'If anyone wishes to come after Me, he must deny himself, and take up his cross and follow Me." Mark 8:34

Though Jesus spoke to a crowd, the invitation was personal. Crowds are almost never right. If you wait for them to embrace your way of thinking, you'll end up in a paralysis of analysis. Think about one of the race riots that took place in Los Angeles (1965 or 1992). If it hadn't been for the crowd—the majority, if you will—how many citizens do you think would have walked down the street with a baseball bat smashing store windows and looting? OK, in L.A., there might have been a few.

Where would the electric light, the telephone, and over 300 uses for the lowly peanut be without Edison, Bell, and Carver pressing on, not only relatively alone but taunted by skepticism for their ideas and patience?

If God is calling you to get out of your comfort zone and do something for Him, don't wait until the idea is mainstream. God often uses just one man who is totally sold out for Him.[195] Don't worry about all the pieces fitting into place. Don't worry if the political winds are blowing favorably. Make sure God is behind it; if He is, it won't—it can't fail.

Set your course, adjust the sail, and…move out. Do it before the enemy sows doubt and second-guessing. Watch for speed bumps, but expect God's blessing. Somebody said that God plus one is a majority. Close, but God is a majority by Himself. He chooses to involve Himself in our lives because that's who He is. He looks for those He can lavish His love on. Will you be one of them today?

Father, sometimes I struggle thinking You even know me, let alone want to bless me. Forgive me for doubting Your Word. Today I pray for great faith to empower me to do great things for You. In my savior's name, **Amen**.

195 II Chron. 16:9

Week 14 – Thursday

Excellence is not an event; it's a way of life.

"For as he thinks within himself, so is he." Prov. 23:7

You've heard the question—usually after you've done something really stupid—what were you thinking? When my kids were little, I taught them this familiar 5-step progression: Thoughts become acts, acts become habits, habits become a way of life, and a way of life becomes your destiny. Aristotle said, "We are what we repeatedly do. Excellence, then, is not an act, but a habit."

It's so simple most people miss it. If you want to change your destiny, change your thinking—that's where it all starts. Do you think any of our great statesmen, athletes, musicians, artists just awakened one day and were great? Of course not. So why should we think it could happen to us?

Nobody would live in a house built without a proper foundation. We may have been blessed by God with talents and skills beyond average. That's cause for gratitude. But to make the most of them, we still have to make a mental commitment as to how far we're willing to push ourselves to go from okay to good to better to excellent. Once we've done that, we have to get off the couch.

It's been said, "You can't steer a ship that's anchored in the harbor." And I would add, barnacles don't grow on a ship at sea. If your way of life isn't all you want it to be—more importantly, if it isn't all God wants it to be—it's not too late. Change your thinking; begin to act; form new habits. You'll be amazed at what can happen. What are you thinking about today?

Lord, my thoughts wander even when I'm praying. Often I feel inadequate and ill-equipped to change my way of life by changing my thinking. Help me to stay focused on You so I can hear when You speak. In Jesus' name, **Amen**.

Week 14 – Friday

Excellence doesn't resort to expediency.

"Therefore, since we have so great a cloud of witnesses surrounding us, let us also lay aside every encumbrance and the sin which so easily entangles us, and let us run with endurance the race that is set before us," Heb. 12:1

Life doesn't allow shortcuts. You pay your dues. Build the foundation first. Little league doesn't supply players to the majors. That's the way it is. For those of us who have tried cutting corners, we've learned—usually the hard way—that any violation of life's rules results in unwanted consequences. Just ask the habitual thief, the one who is unwilling to work an honest job. Sooner or later, he'll do hard time.

There's no shortcut to spiritual maturity either. You want patience? You get trials. You want to get rid of your anger? You get circumstances (and people) that make you mad. Lots of opportunities to practice control. Who said God doesn't have a sense of humor? You want to be a prayer warrior? Pray.

Following the rules takes humility. We have to get rid of pride, which is one of the major encumbrances the writer of Hebrews mentions, and realize that we didn't make life's rules...but we have to obey them. Did you notice that we're *easily* entangled by our sin? And that the race we're in requires endurance? That's why we have to keep our head in the game.

If we spent as much time doing things to improve ourselves—Bible study, memorization, meditation, prayer—as we do on trying to figure out how to beat the game, think how much better off we'd be.

There's a new book about to be released: *Cutting Corners for Dummies.* It's only got one chapter, and that chapter only has one word: DON'T. As followers of Christ, we have a book too; it's filled with instructions from Dad—love letters, poetry, wisdom—all ours without cost. Don't dust it off when company comes; keep it dust-free by daily contact.

Father, I feel like everywhere I look, people are cutting corners, and it seems to work for them. Keep me aware of the fact that You see everything; nothing escapes. I commit to You today that with Your help and strength, I won't take the easy path just because others are. In Christ's name, **Amen**.

Excellence isn't for the lazy or faint of heart.

"Like vinegar to the teeth and smoke to the eyes, so is the lazy one to those who send him." Prov. 10:26

Do you know the opposite of love? It isn't hate. It's apathy—you stop caring. Maybe that's the yardstick by which we measure our love for God—how much we care...for Him and others. Have your prayers gone unanswered? Did that job you expected go to someone else? Have you just...faded away? Maybe you've gotten, well, lazy and apathetic.

God tells us He'd rather we were cold (in our walk with Him) than lukewarm. He says He'll "spit us out."[196] Why do we spit (literally: vomit) something out? Because it's so wretched tasting that the embarrassment of spitting (or throwing up) is easier to bear than continuing to taste it or than getting sick.

Have you ever had vinegar in your mouth? Maybe you've sucked a lemon. You know how it leaves your mouth feeling. And we've all had smoke in our eyes either from a campfire or cigarette. Neither is very pleasant. But that's how we are described by Solomon—if we're lazy.

I love some of the word pictures in Proverbs: *"The way of the lazy is as a hedge of thorns, but the path of the upright is a highway"* (Prov. 15:19). As a kid, we had a huge pyracantha (firethorn) bush right by our front porch. It had small red berries that birds loved and big, stiff thorns. Trimming it was my job, and I learned to respect those thorns. Trying to make your way through a hedge like this would be just about impossible.

So what's the point of all this? Simply this: It boils down to choices—mental commitment. Do you want to be excellent (a choice)? Do you want God to "spit you out" (a choice)? Do you want your path to be a hedge of thorns or a highway (a choice)?"

Your future may seem dim at this point in your life, but, with God, all things are possible.[197] Read God's book and believe it. If you need to change your thinking, do it. It's widely believed that to form or change a habit, it only takes doing something consistently for 30 days. What will your habits look like 30 days from now?

Father, I don't want to be seen as lazy, but sometimes the "hedges" seem impossible. Show me what You want my life to look like and strengthen me through Your Spirit to stay on that path. In Christ's name, **Amen**.

196 Rev. 3:16
197 Mark 10:27

Faithfulness remains true to God's will, regardless of adverse circumstances.

"Do not fear...be faithful unto death, and I will give you the crown of life."
Rev. 2:10

When you think of the word faithful, what comes to mind? A geyser in Yellowstone? The Green Hornet's servant, Kato? Your spouse? Why do we *choose* faithfulness; what are the ingredients; are there consequences for unfaithfulness?

Here's a short list of some of the elements that make up this character trait: love, loyalty, indebtedness, obedience, commitment, and there are others. All of these are good, even essential. But for many of us, isn't reward a big part of it too? And the antithesis: consequences. We go to work each day, we get rewarded. We don't go to work, we get fired. We pay for our purchases, we get to keep and use them. We steal them, well, there are consequences. You get the picture.

These are choices we make daily, often without even a conscious thought. How many of us who aren't military, police, or fire have to consider Jesus' admonition to the church at Smyrna...ever, let alone daily? Do you face choices that could result in death? Have you ever been persecuted for your faith? If you live in America, probably not, at least not to the point of death.

What does faithfulness look like from God's perspective? There are the obvious answers: Don't worship other gods. Don't lie. Don't murder. In fact, I think there's a list of 10. But what about relationship issues: gossip, jealousy, one-upmanship? As with so many other character qualities we've looked at, faithfulness is not an event—it's a way of life. Faithfulness to our Father promises *great* rewards, e.g., a crown of life. But that's icing on the cake—an extra benefit. We are faithful because of our gratitude to our savior for His faithfulness on our behalf. Today, let's remember what Christ's faithfulness cost Him and meditate on it throughout the day.

Father, thank You for being the same yesterday, today, and forever. Thank You that no matter how far I wander, I can depend on Your faithfulness. Help me appreciate more fully the unfathomable price You paid on my behalf. In Jesus' name, **Amen**.

Week 15 – Monday

Faithfulness stays the course in spite of contrary counsel.

"Do not be deceived: 'Bad company corrupts good morals.'" *I Cor. 15:33*

It's hard enough to stay on the narrow path with *good* companions; it's all but impossible with *bad* ones. I can remember periods in my life (high school being one of them) when the most important thing was being part of the "in-crowd." The worst thing, I thought then, was to be on the outside looking in.

I didn't come to Christ until age 22—after my stint in the Army during Vietnam. So I didn't have the Holy Spirit as a filter for choosing the best friends. As a result, the things I was faithful to were self-centered. And the friends I chose had similar values. It wasn't long before I found myself circling the drain.

But God in His mercy had a plan for me. Through a series of events, including a collision with a center divider after drunkenly falling asleep at the wheel, He got my attention…and saved me. I'd like to tell you that from that day to this—over 50 years—I have always been faithful. That would be a lie. But I did begin to surround myself with better friends, ones who will share eternity. And together, we began to grow.

So what's the point? Even though God frequently uses one man to accomplish His purpose, the wisest man who ever lived told us it was better with two or three.[198] If your goal is faithfulness, and it is or you wouldn't be reading this, make sure you choose your companions carefully. They will either encourage you to become more Christlike, or they will be like a backpack of rocks weighing you down.

Men have a propensity to be loners. You know, we think we don't need the touchy-feely relationships that women seem to. But that's a lie from the pit. If you don't have a close friendship with another man, you're missing out on potential blessings. Look around your church, your work, your neighborhood. Maybe you'll need to start by *being* a friend to someone. Don't let any more time slip by thinking this is okay for other guys. You *are* one of the "other" guys.

Lord, I know it's hard to stay on the path, but if I invite someone into my life, they'll see how shallow I am. I recognize that my pride is alive and well in this area too. Thank you for shining your holy light onto this darkness. Show me how to be a friend and lead me to the men You want in my inner circle. In Christ's name, **Amen**.

198 Eccl. 4:9-12

Faithfulness does not depend on onlookers.

"Help, Lord, for the godly man ceases to be, for the faithful disappear from among the sons of men." Psa. 12:1

If truth were told, don't we all love the limelight: The lead in the school play, scoring the winning point, recognition from the boss in front of our peers? The male ego is a fragile thing that can't take too many "hits" without scarring us...sometimes for life.

Did you ever assign an uncomplimentary nickname to someone—perhaps something associated with a body part (Dumbo, Pinocchio, Fat Albert, etc.)—and it stuck? Maybe your nickname is one of those and you've tried to live it down your whole life. Remember the kid's retort: "Sticks and stones will break my bones, but names will never hurt me." Bull. Names can do immense damage.

But here's the great news of Jesus. We can let it all go because we were never created to please the crowd—just the crowd of One. If we remain faithful irrespective of the circumstances or who's watching, we will "delight" our Father.[199]

I don't know your issues today. You may be the rising star of your company. Or you may be barely hanging on. But I do know this: God doesn't experiment with us; He doesn't send a trial our way and then say, "Hey Son, watch this." Sometimes the circumstances of our lives are God's blessing; sometimes they're for correction or reproof. But if our focus is on doing the right thing because it's the right thing to do, not because of who may be in the stands, we can expect God's stamp of approval: "Well done." Do you feel alone? Good. Depend on God who has told us He would never leave or forsake us.[200]

Father, sometimes I feel that in following You, I'm alone. Encourage me through your Spirit to remain faithful to You and what I know to be right regardless of the crowd or lack of. In Jesus' name, **Amen**.

199 Prov. 12:22
200 Heb. 13:5

Faithfulness trumps personal profit.

"And he said to him, 'Well done, good slave, because you have been faithful in a very little thing, you are to be in authority over ten cities." Luke 19:17

Temptations come in all shapes and sizes. Most of them are small and subtle. But don't ever mistake Satan's sinful and evil nature with stupidity. He has been studying human nature for over six millennia. You know the classic "frog in the pot" example. Put a frog in a pot of cool water and slowly bring up the temperature. He'll stay in and boil to death. Toss that same frog into boiling water and he'll be gone in a flash.

We face similar degrees of testing. If you found a bag of money that had been dropped by a Brinks guard, you'd most likely return it. But what do you do when the clerk gives you an extra dollar in change? What about the office supplies that find their way home with you or the few extra minutes of break time?

Jesus talked about "a very little thing." It's not the size of the object; it's our heart attitude—can we be faithful in a very little thing? Is there a size or amount below which it doesn't matter? No. Either our heart is right, or it isn't. Quantity isn't the issue. If you read the rest of the parable in Luke, you'll see that the second slave was only rewarded with half the amount of the first. But Jesus' comment was the same. His reward was based on faithfulness—what he did with what he was given (a common theme in this book).

We are not all "ten talent" guys. The good news is that we're not judged by a ten-talent standard if we're only one or five talent men. Have you committed to always do the right thing, even when it's a very little thing? What's your water temperature today?

Lord God, thank You for the talents You have given me. I re-commit myself to doing the right thing—even if it's a very little thing—because You have trusted me, and I don't want to fail You. Keep me alert to the temptations, especially the subtle ones that find me and grant me victory over them through Jesus, my savior. In His name, **Amen**.

Faithfulness does not fear man's rejection or ridicule.

"O Timothy, guard what has been entrusted to you, avoiding worldly and empty chatter and the opposing arguments of what is falsely called "knowledge..."I Tim. 6:20

Have you ever gone to an away game and worn your team's colors? You can feel the rejection, the condemning glares. But you're there to support your team, and you do it because you're proud and fearless. I remember high school football rivalries that often ended in fights...just because.

Paul has a great word for Timothy: Don't. He tells him to stay away from—don't get sucked into discussions about things that don't matter. Notice Paul doesn't say to avoid the *people* making the arguments. He says to control the topic.

Like Timothy, we've been entrusted with eternal knowledge—the Scriptures. Sometimes, we're anxious to "fly our colors" and prove that we're right. But that approach rarely converts the unsaved to the truth. They dig in and prove their ignorance by defending lies.

We are not to fear man,[201] that's true. And we are confident because we have truth on our side. However, we also need to remember that in discussions of Biblical truth, any rejection is aimed at our Savior, not us. We're only the messenger. Yes, some messengers get shot. But we're in a war with the unseen forces of darkness,[202] and we should consider it an honor to suffer ridicule and rejection for the cause of Christ.[203]

Jesus was giving a pep talk to His disciples just before sending them out, and He told them not to fear physical harm/death, but to fear God.[204] Great advice for us today.

Father, I am grateful to be included in Your family and to be entrusted with the Truth. Grant me wisdom to share it with the right people in the right way and to avoid worthless arguments with those who don't want to hear Your saving message. In Christ's name, **Amen**.

201 Psa. 56:11
202 Eph. 6:12
203 II Tim. 2:3
204 Matt. 10:28

Faithfulness moves me to action.

"Therefore, my beloved brethren, be steadfast, immovable, always abounding in the work of the Lord, knowing that your toil is not in vain in the Lord." I Cor. 15:58

When I hear words like "work" and "toil," I think of a farmer's world. Up before dawn, milk the cows, plant the field, harvest, repair equipment, and fences; it never seems to end. There's too much rain. There's too little rain. There are bugs (and I don't mean Bunny). But thank God for our farmers. I couldn't live that life.

In 2009, I went with a group of guys to Panuco, Mexico to help build a kitchen for a small Baptist church that feeds over 100 kids each day. It was simple concrete block construction, two rooms, two stories, and over 120 90-pound sacks of cement. We hauled and shoveled and mixed and poured and sweat. I don't care if I never see another sack of cement. It was a blessing-filled week, but I couldn't do that kind of work regularly either.

That's the picture of hard work that Paul paints as he encourages the Corinthians (and us) to be faithful in our work for the Lord. The Christian life is not for wimps. How different would it be if we saw our boss—the Lord Jesus—every day. Would we still get discouraged? Still grumble? Although we can't see Him physically, He's as close as prayer. We need to remember that our work, whether "religious" or "secular" (shouldn't be a distinction) is for the Lord.[205] And it's His approval we seek.

If we are "in the Lord," as Paul says, we know our labor is not in vain. Scripture provides a glimpse, a type of dipstick if you will, to measure our "toil" level. Do we need to add a quart or maybe change it completely? Make today the day you commit to being steadfast, immovable, and abounding for the Lord.

Lord, even though I get tired and weary, You still have a place for me to work in Your field. Keep me conscious of Your presence and help me not to grumble or get discouraged as I wait for Christ's return. In His name, **Amen**.

205 Col. 3:23, 24

Faithfulness knows the standard...and accepts it.

"O Lord, who may abide in Your tent?...He who walks with integrity...speaks truth...does not slander...In whose eyes a reprobate is despised... honors those who fear the Lord... swears to his own hurt...does not change... does not put out his money at interest... does not take a bribe against the innocent. He who does these things will never be shaken." Psa. 15:1-5

It's been said, "If you don't know where you're going, any road will get you there." Isn't it great to know that the Bible is very clear in identifying the Road to heaven? And that there is only One?[206]

In every facet of our lives, we have standards that are the minimal acceptable behavior. And we choose which ones to follow. There are consequences for each choice we make—good or bad. The psalmist today lays out a few standards and a fabulous promise. When we don't follow the standard, e.g., we exceed the speed limit, we must be willing to pay the fine...if we're caught. I know I would drive slower if I was caught more often. The cops aren't omnipresent (whew).

But God sees everything His children do[207] and keeps a record of it.[208] There are standards of civic life, standards at work, standards in families. I used to remind my kids that they were Thorntons. The implication being that we had a family standard that may or may not coincide with their peers' families.

If we are striving to be faithful followers of "the way," then it's imperative we know God's standards. Fortunately, they're in the Bible. There's a list of ten starting with "thou shalt and thou shalt not." There's also a list of two. You know, love the Lord your God and love your neighbor.[209] So once we know the standard, we have a choice to follow or not.

Personally, I like the promise of confidence if I follow the rules. As we've discussed many times, it comes down to this: Do I trust God to take care of *me* while I'm doing my best to take care of others? Has it become a way of life, or is it a once-in-a-while event?

Father, thank You for Your clear Word, which lays out the standard You expect. Strengthen me to hold on until the end. In Jesus' name, **Amen**.

206 John 14:6
207 Psa. 33:18
208 Rev. 20:12
209 Matt. 22:37-39

Forgiveness of others guarantees my forgiveness; it's a 2-way street.

"For if you forgive others for their transgressions, your heavenly Father will also forgive you. But if you do not forgive others, then your Father will not forgive your transgressions." Matt. 6:14, 15

I don't know *how* it works, but God's Word says it, so it does. If you're like me, sometimes you don't *feel* like forgiving. We want to roll around in our hurt and anger for a little while because we're justified. Right? We probably spend more than a little time thinking about how to get even.

But Jesus' statement doesn't leave any room for doubt. Another choice to make. I've wrestled with the *need* to be forgiven. I know that sounds like blasphemy, but stay with me. When I observe *others*, I think *I'm* doing pretty well. Why do I need forgiveness? For that matter, why do I even need a savior?

But it's that mindset that keeps a lot of "good" people from coming to Christ. Not until we recognize how far short of God's standard of righteousness we fall, will we realize that our pride and arrogance—trying to take credit for what God alone has done—is one of the ugliest, most deceptive sins around.

The problem comes from adopting the wrong standard. We watch others for our cues instead of internalizing the Bible. We can always find people whose lives are worse than ours and we feel pretty smug. That's when we're in the most danger. At the top of God's "things I hate" list is the sin of pride.[210]

Why do we struggle so hard against God's revealed will? We want the blessings, but we're not always willing to do the "thou shalts" and meet the "if you" conditions. I've written a little software. One of the commands is If…Then. Software is dumb. It does exactly what the programmer told it to. *If* a certain action is taken or condition is met, *then* a pre-programmed response occurs.

God has given us one of the greatest "if—then" promises of all time. *If* we forgive others, *then* He will forgive us. Today, let's consider God's if—thens. *If* we change our input, *then* we can expect the promised blessing.

Father, Your Word has amazing offers that are mine if I meet Your conditions—which are more than fair, given what I *get* vs. what I have to *give*. Thank You for not asking more of me than I can give. Help me realize the value of the forgiveness You offer and quit fighting You. **Amen**.

210 Prov. 6:16, 17

Week 16 – Monday

Forgiveness frees our heart from bitterness.

"See to it that no one comes short of the grace of God; that no root of bitterness springing up causes trouble, and by it many be defiled." Heb. 12:15

I want revenge; I want to strike back and not wait for God's plan and timing, which could include "my enemy" coming to Christ. Then he wouldn't suffer like I have. They wouldn't get "what they deserved." Have you ever felt that way, especially when you think you've been wronged? It's so easy, under my definition of fairness, to gloss over God's claim and right of revenge.[211]

As I write this section on forgiveness, I'm convicted that I haven't forgiven the woman who caused my motorcycle accident. I want to punish her first for the accident itself, but moreover, for her denial and lying about it. Instead of praying for her soul, I'm harboring ill will toward her. That's going to change…soon.

But here's the real issue. If I don't forgive her, I will imagine all sorts of "wrongs" that she has done to me—things I've been cheated out of doing this year—and begin to feel sorry for myself. Do you see how easy it is to justify these feelings? Then, I ponder how unfair God is to let it happen and start to question His goodness and maybe even His awareness of my plight. One thing leads to another, and before I know it, I'm moving in the wrong direction—away from God—and I may not even recognize it. Worse, I may not care. Bitterness comes in quietly and takes root.

Like many of the issues we've discussed, it comes down to this: "Do I trust God or don't I?" The Bible is clear. God is good,[212] and He doesn't change.[213] If I really believe God causes *all things* to work for good...[214] (emphasis mine), then I have no choice but to say with Job, *"Shall we indeed accept good from God and not accept adversity?"*[215]

Are you struggling with not forgiving someone today? It's not worth it; let it go, and God will replace the bitterness with joy.

Lord, this is tough for me. I want what I think is justice and payback, which is really nothing more than revenge. But that's not my right, it's Yours. Renew my total trust in Your goodness and fairness and help me let it go. Fill me with the joy of trusting You today. **Amen**.

---

211 Deut. 32:35
212 Mark 10:18
213 Jas. 1:17
214 Rom. 8:28
215 Job 2:10

Week 16 – Tuesday

Forgiveness was very expensive for God.

"But God demonstrates His own love toward us, in that while we were yet sinners, Christ died for us." Rom. 5:8

Have you ever given someone an expensive gift just because you loved them...without expecting something in return? Do you think God had expectations when He gave His Son? Forgiveness doesn't make sense to me when I juxtapose it with justice. I think, "how does justice get served if I forgive everybody?" Then I think about all the times God forgives me—often for the same thing—when I don't deserve it, and I'm thankful that He doesn't exact justice from me every time I sin.

Forgiveness is the most expensive gift God offers us because it was bought and paid for by Jesus' blood. But He does it gladly, willingly for no other reason than He loves us. How do we even begin to get our arms around that? What does it cost *us* to forgive someone else? A little pride? A slight disruption to our schedule? Why is it sometimes so hard to forgive?

If we look deep, the truth is probably along the lines of revenge or payback. We don't like God's timetable; we want to make sure God doesn't forget to "give them what they deserve," so we offer to "help Him out." How totally like us to want God's mercy and forgiveness for ourselves but not for someone who has wronged us.

Remember, we're all painted with the same brush. Not one of us deserves to be let go. The problem is that we could never do the time to pay our debt of sin. Today, when we struggle with forgiving—either the concept or the act itself—let's not forget that God doesn't give us what we deserve, either. And then, pass it on.

Father, I'm ashamed of my selfishness that profits from Your forgiveness but wants revenge on my enemies. Forgive me...again. Fill me anew with Your Spirit and help me pass on Your love through forgiving and overlooking offenses that come my way. In Jesus' name, **Amen**.

Week 16 – Wednesday

Forgiveness models God's heart for others to see.

"For this reason I say to you, her sins, which are many, have been forgiven, for she loved much; but he who is forgiven little, loves little." Luke 7:47

Examples from our lives are so powerful. I went to see my surgeon to check the progress of my broken leg. He approved 50% weight-bearing and sent me to a medical equipment company that sells braces and prosthetics. The girl who measured my leg for a brace was wearing a prosthetic right leg from the knee down. She's had it since age 18 months. All of a sudden, she had more credibility in discussing my needs than another technician who had two good legs.

Forgiveness is like that. Like the woman in our verse today, she had much to talk about—and be listened to—with respect to God's forgiveness. Jesus said that her "sins are many." What would He say about yours and mine? Does our testimony include the all-encompassing forgiveness so freely given to us by our Father? Do we recognize the enormity and the sheer volume of our sins from which we have been declared pardoned? Has it transformed our selfishness into love—love for God and our fellow alien?[216]

If our conversation isn't filled with references to God's goodness vis-à-vis His forgiveness, we might want to ask ourselves just what did God forgive me of? If I have a hard time coming up with a list, then I'm probably not on the same page as God with respect to defining sin. Today, let's examine our love for others. If it's not what it should be, it's likely we need to revisit our understanding of our own sin to understand the depth of God's love and then mirror it to others.

Father, I am prone to minimize my own sin and quick to point out others'. Forgive me. Help me to see my sin as You do and be quick to confess and abandon it. Empower my witness so others can know the joy of forgiveness and a right relationship with You through Your Son. In His name, **Amen**.

216 Heb. 11:9, 10

Week 16 – Thursday

Forgiveness is an ongoing process.

"Then Peter came and said to Him, 'Lord, how often shall my brother sin against me and I forgive him? Up to seven times?' Jesus said to him, 'I do not say to you, up to seven times, but up to seventy times seven.'" Matt. 18:21-22

The finite number of 490 is not the point. The point is God's absolute promise of forgiveness. As I ponder this topic, I'm reminded of a song from 1959[217] with the lyrics, "Oh oh oh oh over and over I'll be a fool for you." That's how I feel going to God time after time confessing the same sin and vowing to do better next time. But next time, there I am again with the same plea. I guess I'm not alone. Paul must have had the same issue in Romans[218] where he talks about doing the very thing he doesn't want to do.

Aren't you glad that God doesn't keep score on the number of times we sin a particular sin?[219] Having said that, there are two thoughts for our consideration. First, as God forgives us over and over, so we must forgive others over and over. It's not as easy as it sounds. We're more likely to think, "Are you kidding me? You did this again?" and that after only the second time.

It helps to remember how many times God could say the same thing to us. The second aspect of this is to forgive ourselves. The cross was enough to cover *every* sin from *every* person…if they will trust Christ. God didn't add a footnote to exclude your personal habitual sin.

We must believe God when He says, "*Though your sins are as scarlet, they will be white as snow.*" (Isa. 1:18). It's our pride that leads us to think that God won't forgive us over and over, that He has a finite number in mind, and when we exceed it—look out. The reason is that we think God is like us.

We struggle with forgiving the same thing again and again in others (Peter thought he was being magnanimous at seven), and so God must likewise struggle with us. That thought comes from the pit. Reject it and trust God's revealed mercy and compassion. Let it drive you to the sorrow that produces repentance that leads to salvation.[220]

Lord, I feel like such a failure when I have to confess the same things over and over. Help me remember that You are not like me and that You choose to forget how many times I've been down this same road. May I rejoice in my salvation. In Christ's name, **Amen**.

217 Lloyd Price, *(You've Got) Personality*
218 Rom. 7:14-25
219 Jer. 31:34
220 II Cor. 7:10

Week 16 – Friday

Forgiveness is for real men, not for sissies.

"But Jesus was saying, "Father, forgive them; for they do not know what they are doing."" Luke 23:34

Life is filled with hard choices: career direction, college, military, job, spouse, church home, and the list goes on. Forgiveness is on that list too. Have you ever wondered why it's so hard to choose to forgive? I think it's partly because someone has violated our expectations and partly because, in our competitive society, we think we're losing stature when we forgive. You know, something like "real men don't forgive, they get even."

Couldn't be further from the truth. Satan fans the flame of our own fleshly desire to be somebody by feeding us the lies that real men don't do this, or real men don't eat that. Why did God call David a man "after His own heart"?[221] Was it because he killed a lion and a bear?[222] No. David's heart was wholly devoted to God.[223] Did he ever sin? Of course. But even in his weakness, his heart's desire was for the Lord.

It takes a real man to make the hard choices in life…and live with the consequences. Often, it means standing against the crowd. Mob mentality has no room for forgiveness or compassion.[224] The real man thinks on his own and acts on his own. He doesn't need the "security" of the crowd's approval. The real man seeks truth and defends it. The real man is big enough to forgive. Are you a real man today?

Father, I confess that often I look for acceptance in the wrong places; I'm too concerned with public opinion. Grant me strength today to openly stand by my faith in You and be concerned only with what You think of my thoughts, words, and deeds. **Amen**.

221 I Sam. 13:14
222 I Sam 17:36
223I Kin. 15:3
224 Mark 15:11-15

Forgiveness creates opportunities for the gospel.

"As far as the east is from the west, so far has He removed our transgressions from us." Psa. 103:12

Isn't it exciting to grasp new truth? Some call it an aha moment, some an epiphany. Sometimes it's a simple truth: what is 2 plus 2? Sometimes it's earth-changing: God loves me. Have you gotten your arms around the truth of the lyrics from *You Are My King* by Chris Tomlin?

I'm forgiven because You were forsaken.
I'm accepted, You were condemned.
I'm alive and well, Your Spirit lives within me,
because You died and rose again.
Amazing love how can it be
that You my king would die for me?
Amazing love, I know it's true.
It's my joy to honor You,
In all I do, I honor You

I must admit that I usually get teary-eyed when I sing this song because I do know it's true. It's the heart of the gospel message: Christ died in my place to pay the price for my sin that I could never pay. As we forgive others, it often surprises them and opens the door for us to tell them about God's forgiveness. Don't let your pride keep you from forgiving others. That same pride may keep them from the kingdom.

God, thank You for Your amazing love that put Jesus on the cross instead of me. May what You did for me motivate me to pass it on to others. Open my eyes to opportunities to spread the gospel today. In Jesus' name, **Amen**.

Generosity trusts God to supply my needs.

"And my God will supply all your needs according to His riches in glory in Christ Jesus." Phil. 4:19

Most of us have never experienced the demoralizing poverty seen in many parts of the world. Thank God for that. I sometimes think about how my life would be different if I had been born in Europe, Asia, Africa, or even the Caribbean instead of Southern California. But with all the advantages of U.S. citizenship comes one of the most subtle and insidious temptations we could face: materialism.

You've seen, heard, and read them. The clever sales pitch that appeals to our egos, our sense of entitlement, our fear of not keeping up with…whatever. I'm fortunate to have grown up in a family that struggled for income. It taught me the value of work and of a dollar. My dad, though not a good example of godliness, was a great example of doing what was necessary to take care of us.

After I was saved, I became aware of how much I depended on my own abilities and how little I trusted God. Over time, God began to teach me that He was the source of all I had and that He could be trusted to meet my needs. My problem, and the problem we face with materialism, is we confuse wants and needs.

Maybe that's a good place to begin our discussion of generosity—defining needs. Are you eating regularly? Do you have a roof over your head? Clothes to wear? Then your *needs* are met.[225] Anything above that becomes discretionary. I'm not saying God doesn't want us to enjoy life, even some of the luxuries. But beware of what may be on the throne of your heart—usurping God's rightful position.

Someone has said that we should hold possessions loosely so that when God needs them, He doesn't have to pry them out of our hand. If you're stuck in a debt cycle because of materialism, first of all, you're a slave to the lender,[226] but worse, you're not liquid or free to respond to God's invitation to give. Do what it takes to rid yourself of the shackles. You'll experience a sense of freedom, and you'll say to God, "I trust You to meet my needs." Start today.

Father, it's been so easy to believe the sales pitch that tells me I need it. It has caused me to take my eyes off You and diminish my trust that You will provide. Steer me back to the right track so I can recognize opportunities to give. In Jesus' name, **Amen**.

---

225 I Tim. 6:8
226 Prov. 22:7

Week 17 – Monday

Generosity proves God can trust me with true riches.

"Therefore if you have not been faithful in the use of unrighteous wealth, who will entrust the true riches to you?" Luke 16:11

I'll bet not many of us think of our money as unrighteous wealth. But that's what Jesus called it. Pretty harsh indictment to use unfaithful and unrighteous in the same sentence. Do you remember turning 16 and pleading with your dad to borrow the car? Wasn't one of your arguments, "You can trust me, dad"?

Trust is one of those nebulous qualities that can take a long time to earn and an instant to squander. In virtually every walk of life, experience is valued. Proof in the pudding, so to speak. I used to use an illustration with my kids. I'd hold my hands in front of me, palms facing about a foot apart, and tell them that these were walls of trust and responsibility. My job, as their dad, was to move the walls outward in proportion to their proven ability to be trusted. I told them that eventually, I'd remove the walls totally.

Our use of money is God's test of our ability to be trusted. How are we doing? Do the words splurge or impulsive describe you? Then you might want to shuffle your priorities a bit. Look, wealth, in and of itself, is not bad. Jesus told the Pharisees to pay their taxes.[227] It's when we think it's ours to do with what we want that we cross the line of ownership. When we think we have rights to 90% of our income (tithing gets the first 10%), we need to think again—God owns it all and has given us stewardship over it. Someday there will be an accounting, and if you think the IRS is detail-oriented, wait for God's audit.

If you've earned God's trust through faithful stewardship, you get a YDG (ya done good). If not, you still have time. Start considering money an investment by God into you. See if you can improve His Return on that Investment.

Lord, what an awesome concept that You would trust me...with anything. I ask that You help me be faithful with the riches You give that I might look forward to the true riches in heaven. In Christ's name, **Amen**.

227 Matt. 22:21

Generosity includes time and talent as well as treasure.

"...and this, not as we had expected, but they first gave themselves to the Lord and to us by the will of God." II Cor. 8:5

Sometimes, the easiest thing to do is send money. But sometimes money isn't what's needed, laborers are. Sure, money can buy labor. But it can't buy hearts.[228] It can't buy motivation. It can buy someone to sit with an elderly, homebound person. But it can't buy concern for that person's soul.

Do you think God really needs our money? Or our time or talents? Not one bit. Investing in others is for our benefit as well as theirs. We're the ones who get blessed... now and with rewards in heaven.[229] We usually think of being on the giving end of generosity.

But how good are we at receiving it? My sister-in-law, we'll call her Karen ('cuz that's her name), has been generous to me all summer long. Because I've been recovering from a broken leg, she has come to my house every week and mowed my lawn. She likes doing it; it's outside and gives her exercise. But she didn't have to. There were other activities that could have filled that time slot.

What about you? Is there a need in your circle of influence that money alone can't address? Do you have the time and talent to invest, or do you always have an excuse? Think about the Macedonians Paul referred to above. They gave themselves to *the Lord* first. Their generosity was an overflow from that. Maybe it's time for a self-checkup. If our generosity is limited to financial help, perhaps we've withheld some of ourselves from the Lord. Today, let's trust God to meet our needs as we look around to unearth needs of others...then spend some of our time on them.

Lord, I know You don't need my money, or me for that matter. But in Your economy, the more I give, the more I get blessed. Help me not to hoard what I can't take with me but to "send it on ahead" by investing in others. In the Savior's name, **Amen**.

228 John 4:23
229 Matt. 6:20

Generosity is better when it's cheerful.

"Each one must do just as he has purposed in his heart, not grudgingly or under compulsion, for God loves a cheerful giver." II Cor. 9:7

Having once written ads and commercials, my mind frequently goes down some bizarre paths. But as you know, usually the goofier an ad, the better you remember it. And that's the goal of advertising—name recognition. Let's try it here. Picture yourself sitting in church, and the offering plate is coming down the row toward you. When it arrives, you look down, and in the plate, you see a bunch of wee little people laughing and having a good time. These are the cheerful givers. Trust me; you'll never see an offering plate the same way again.

Just before Jesus sent His disciples out on a mission trip, He told them, "Freely you have received, freely give."[230] Cheerfulness results when we acknowledge our role as a funnel. Funnels are not used for storage—it's in the top, out the bottom. How about giving away things that never deplete our supply? A kind word? A smile? Who benefits from hoarding these or metering them? Certainly not you.

It's common lore that it takes fewer muscles to smile than frown, but there's no agreement on the exact numbers. Do you want God to love you when you give? Don't be a grudge. The thing is it comes down to a choice. We're not talking amounts; we're talking heart attitudes. We can cheerfully give things away that we can't keep anyway—time and money—and everybody profits. Or we can disobey Jesus' instruction to His disciples to give freely. Nobody profits and, worse, we miss out on blessing God. When we consider God's daily generosity to us, we know the right choice. Make it happen.

Father, thank You for Your continuous generosity to me. Forgive me for taking it for granted. Today, help me recognize opportunities to give of myself, not just my money, and to do it cheerfully. In Jesus' name, **Amen**.

230 Matt. 10:8

Generosity considers others' needs before my wants.

"Now, brethren, we wish to make known to you the grace of God which has been given in the churches of Macedonia, that in a great ordeal of affliction their abundance of joy and their deep poverty overflowed in the wealth of their liberality. For I testify that according to their ability, and beyond their ability, they gave of their own accord begging us with much urging for the favor of participation in the support of the saints." II Cor. 8:1- 4

Can you imagine the reach of today's church if more of us who claim Christ as our savior had the attitude of the Macedonians? Listen to Paul's description: "ordeal of affliction," "deep poverty," and "begging...to support the saints." We think we're poor if we don't have a 60" flat screen, the latest Apple iWhatever, and membership in the local country club.

Ever wonder why today's church is so anemic and such a turnoff for people who need it the most? It's not a stretch to say that today's materialistic churches are an embarrassment to the cause of Christ. Don't believe me? "The median annual giving for an American Christian is actually $200, just over half a percent of after-tax income. About 5 percent of American Christians provide 60 percent of the money churches and religious groups use to operate."[231] People ask, "Should I tithe on the gross or the net?" My answer is, "Do you want to be blessed on the gross or the net?"

This is not a legalistic argument: What percentage should I give? It's about our heart attitude. When we recognize that God **owns it all**, and He is gracious and generous to allow us to distribute it, our response should be one of humility and awe that He even knows our name,[232] let alone trusts us with His resources. Nothing in our Christian walk says, "I love you, Lord" like a generous heart. Does that describe you today?

Lord God, when I consider Your ownership of everything and Your trust in me to manage it for You, I'm overwhelmed. Help me see giving from Your perspective and continue to earn Your trust for even bigger things. In Christ's name, **Amen**.

231 Christianity Today, Dec. 2008 *Scrooge Lives*
232 Isa. 43:1

Generosity to others is a response to God's generosity to me.

"Give and it will be given to you. They will pour into your lap a good measure—pressed down, shaken together, and running over. For by your standard of measure it will be measured to you in return." Luke 6:38

Expectations based on God's promises are one thing. But demanding that God has to respond a certain way is arrogant, un-Biblical, and God hates it.[233] You've heard them, the so-called "name it and claim it" proponents. Their message is that we can manipulate God so that He's forced to repay us. Do you really want a god that you can control? That wouldn't be much of a god.

What God is looking for is a man who recognizes everything comes from Him, is grateful for it (not like the Israelites, who got their request but incurred God's wrath)[234] and trusts God to replenish exactly the right amount as he gives it away. Are you that man?

It requires humility and faith. Humility says, "*I* didn't do it," and faith says, "I *can* do it with God's help."[235] It also doesn't matter the amount. It's *always* the heart attitude behind the giving. How about this? Try giving to someone you don't like…start with a smile. Jesus gave us the "formula." What standard of measure are you using? Why isn't it bigger? Are you barely making it? God has said He will never leave you or forsake you.[236] Are you trusting Him today? Can He trust you today?

Father, my giving is such a clear picture of my heart, and I don't like what I see. Forgive my selfishness and replace it with gratitude and generosity. In Jesus' name, **Amen**.

233 Prov. 8:13
234 Psa. 106:15
235 Phil. 4:13
236 Heb. 13:5

Generosity is a heart attitude—a way of life.

""Bring the full tithe into the storehouse, so that there may be food in My house, and test Me now in this," says the Lord of hosts, "if I will not open for you the windows of heaven and pour out for you a blessing until it overflows."" Mal. 3:10

Have you ever been called a robber? That's what God called the Israelites.[237] Money is a test. It's spoken of more by Jesus than any other subject. Why? Because God knows our heart and how much we love shiny things—new cars (and motorcycles), boats, guns, electronics, etc. Don't get me wrong; there's nothing wrong with any of those things in and of themselves. Remember that God sees our deepest thoughts and motives.

Are we trying to impress our neighbor? The guys at work? Our wife? Here's the deal. Jesus, quoting Deuteronomy 6:16, said to Satan, "*...you shall not put the Lord your God to the test.*" But God has given us one exception (see today's verse). He commands us to test Him and His integrity with our generosity.

Throughout scripture, we're told to give the first—the best unspotted, unblemished—to God. Does God need our charity? Not at all. But He knows that if we don't put Him at the top of our giving list, the leftovers won't amount to much. Have you set your mind on things above,[238] or are you still trapped in the world's (Satan's) system? Do you trust God enough to be generous with what He's given you?

It's time for a gut check. We either trust God to do what He says—windows of heaven: blessing—or we don't. Can you point to a time in your life or in recorded history that God didn't do what He said He would? Blessings await us, my friend. Let *your* generosity overflow into all areas of your life and then look for God to honor His Word in amazing, overflowing ways.

Father, Your Word is so clear on the subject of money. Today, grant me the confidence in You to trust Your Word and act on it. In Christ's name, **Amen**.

237 Mal. 3:8
238 Col. 3:2

Week 18 – Sunday

Gentleness is not the same as weakness.

"Take My yoke upon you and learn from Me, for I am gentle and humble in heart, and YOU WILL FIND REST FOR YOUR SOULS." Matt. 11:29

Quick, when you think of gentleness, what's the first picture that comes to your mind? Is it a nursing mother? A pair of mourning doves? A 260-pound linebacker? We need to break the stereotypical mold of gentleness. First of all, it is not a synonym for weakness. Gentle does not equal wimp.

In the late '60s, there was a TV series, *Gentle Ben*, about a game warden, played by Dennis Weaver and his "tame" 650 lb. bear. The world would have us believe it's not manly to be gentle. Was Jesus a wimp? Was He not manly? How many of us can "turn the other cheek" as He did so often? How many of us can keep our tongue in check when someone verbally attacks or slanders us?

I find that it takes a lot more control (strength of character) to *not* lash out when I feel my "rights" have been trampled. And, sad to say, I don't always win that battle. But our verse today is not a suggestion; it's a command: Take. Learn. These are both action verbs. And ponder the promise: "You will find rest for your souls." Are you anxious about anything? Are you "soul weary"? Here's the prescription: Take. Learn. What are you waiting for?

Lord, when I listen to the world's thinking, it seems that gentleness is not a manly trait. Today, help me to tune out anything that contradicts Your words to me. **Amen**.

Gentleness is strength, controlled.

"But the fruit of the spirit is…gentleness…" Gal. 5: 22, 23

The human body is amazing. The same combination of muscles that can lift hundreds of pounds can also control a laser to perform delicate eye surgery. The same hand that wields a machete to clear a path in the jungle can precisely control a scalpel to excise a cancerous tumor. Imagine the horrific results of the muscular, athletic surgeon who can't control his scalpel or laser. The gentle touch of the surgeon doesn't mean he can't wield a mean squash racket.

Why is gentleness so hard for us guys? Because we've bought the world's lie that gentleness is for girls. You know, sugar and spice and everything nice… Would you call the God who spoke in thunder[239] gentle? But what did Paul say of himself and his traveling companions? "*We didn't come and exercise authority, but we proved to be gentle among you as a nursing mother.*"[240] If Paul, arguably the most powerful preacher who ever lived, was *gentle*, what standard does that set for us?

It's really a simple matter of what, or more precisely whom, do we trust? Do we trust a world system whose Satanically empowered goal is our destruction?[241] Or do we invest our trust in The One who proves His trustworthiness over and over with a return on our investment—even when we're not watching?

When you're on the winning team, you don't have to be a bully. When you know how the story ends, it should fill you with compassion for those who haven't heard the story. Today, open your mouth—with gentleness, not judgment—to share the greatest story ever told.

Father, it's hard to walk Your path when so many try to point me the other way. Help me, today, to listen for Your voice and not succumb to the clamor of the world. In Jesus' name, **Amen**.

239 Job 40:9
240 I Thess. 2:5-7
241 John 10:10

Gentleness is what Jesus modeled.

"Say to the daughter of Zion, 'behold your king is coming to you gentle, and mounted on a donkey, even on a colt, the foal of a beast of burden." Matt. 21:5

Remember the lyrics of that old Gospel song: Old Time Religion?

Give me that old time religion
give me that old time religion
Give me that old time religion
It's good enough for me.

Let's face it, guys, we don't like humility and gentleness. We like macho. We like big trucks, loud motorcycles, rowdy football games, ice hockey brawls, and MMA fighting. There's no place for "gentle and mounted on a donkey" in our thinking. Ever wonder why? It's simple. We've bought the lie from the father of lies.[242]

Think about this. If Paul could say to the Corinthians, "*Be imitators of me, just as I also am of Christ*"[243] and to the Ephesians, "*Therefore be imitators of God…*"[244] and "*Jesus Christ is the same yesterday and today and forever*",[245] what part of imitating Jesus' gentleness don't we get?

Is the "old time religion" preached and modeled by Jesus *not* good enough for us? I think it's time for those men among us who know Jesus as our savior to answer the question, "Are you in or out?" Time is short. Eternity is just around the corner. Let's decide today that we're tired of sitting in the stands or on the bench. The gospel game needs players[246] who are willing to wear the jersey of gentleness. Will you be one of them?

Lord, forgive me for my pride that can't accept gentleness as a manly thing. Help me today to not look at Christianity as a menu from which to pick and choose but a lifestyle that follows Your example, which includes gentleness. **Amen**.

242 John 8:44
243 I Cor. 11:1
244 Eph. 5:1
245 Heb. 13:8
246 Luke 10:2

Gentleness is contrary to the world's vision of a man, so it must be right.

"But flee from these things, you man of God, and pursue righteousness, godliness, faith, love, perseverance and gentleness." I Tim. 6:11

One definition of a contrarian is "a person who takes up a position opposed to that of the majority, no matter how unpopular." This fits the Christian man perfectly. The Bible is full of "but yous." "*But you shall remember the Lord your God…;*"[247] "*But you, be strong and do not lose courage…*";[248] "*…but you have received a spirit of adoption as sons…;*"[249] and there are many, many more.

The Christian life is one of separation, sacrifice, and sometimes loneliness.[250] But we're not to focus on that; if we do, we lose our joy and contentment. Rather, like in any sport or business venture, we focus on the prize[251]—the goal—and as we do that, the challenges, the impediments fade, and clarity of purpose permeates our existence.

In our verse today, Paul is exhorting Timothy to flee from "disputes about words, envy, strife, abusive language, evil suspicions, the love of money…"[252] and "pursue." That's an action verb that implies it ain't coming without work.

What stands in your way today that keeps you from pursuing gentleness? Is it fear of the crowd; you don't want to be "an outsider?" Hear the words of Jesus to those embarrassed or ashamed to be counted among His followers: *"For whoever is ashamed of Me and My words, the Son of Man will be ashamed of him when He comes in His glory."*[253] If this seems like an impossible challenge, review your goal. God gives us the grace to deal with anything that He allows to cross our paths[254] and He promises that we are *more* than conquerors.[255]

Father, I don't want to be ashamed of You or the path of righteousness that You've called me to. Help me to focus on the goal of pleasing You, knowing that anything else will drag me down. I want to hear You say, "Well done." In Jesus' name, **Amen**.

247 Deut. 8:18
248 II Chron. 15:7
249 Rom. 8:15
250 Matt. 7:13, 14
251 Phil. 3:14
252 I Tim 6:4-10
253 Luke 9:26
254 I Cor. 10:13
255 Rom. 8:37

Gentleness is an unspoken invitation—a sign that says, "I'm open."

"Who among you is wise and understanding? Let him show by his good behavior his deeds in the gentleness of wisdom." James 3:13

Can I see a show of hands? Who among you is wise? James is apparently saying that one "tell" of wisdom is gentleness. Anybody besides me feel busted? One of the greatest compliments someone can pay another person is to seek their advice. My wife is a perfect example of this principle at work. I can't tell you how many hours she spends counseling women, especially younger ones. It's because she is compassionate and gentle and seems to always have time to listen.

Compassionate, gentle, and always has time to listen. I don't know about you, but that doesn't describe me. Here's my dilemma: I know I should be more like my wife, but for decades I lived the antithesis of gentle…and defended it. The good news is that God is so patient with me, and I do want to change.

Writing this book has convicted me over and over that men—specifically me—have the same ability as women to be gentle. Unfortunately, we usually *choose* a different path. To quote Mark Levin, "That's right, I said it." We have a choice of whether or not to be gentle.[256]

And make no mistake, God *is* watching…and so are others in our circle of influence. This may not be a big deal to you, and you may not care that other men aren't beating down your door to ask counsel. But what about your children or grandchildren? Are they afraid of you? Do they freely share what's going on in their lives? How you comport yourself, vis-à-vis gentleness, reveals volumes about your trust that God can and does "have your six."

If it can't be said of you, "He is gentle…" don't wait another day. Make today the day you choose gentleness over machismo. Remember, our goal is to please God, not our buddies.

Father, You have given me so many examples of gentleness in Your dealings with me. Let it finally register that You do it to me so that I will do it to others also. In Christ's name, **Amen**.

256 Col. 3:12

Week 18 – Friday

Gentleness doesn't lash out with the tongue.

"A gentle answer turns away wrath." Prov. 15:1

What do politicians, salesmen, and schoolteachers all have in common? They have to be able to think on their feet. What do most high-school boys have in common? They're good at hurling insults. I can remember in high school having "chop" sessions—times when we would actually practice and hone our skill at "chopping" someone down. Remember the line that started, "Your mother is so ugly…?" Back then, most of it was good-natured and not intentionally hurtful. But today, you're just as likely to be shot for a comment like that.

Ever notice how once the insult trading starts, it always escalates. Our pride is wounded, and we feel justified in lashing out, not really thinking of the consequences. Many times after I've heard a word pass my lips, I've wished it unspoken. But of course, you can't unring the bell. And words that are intended to hurt, hurt. For a very long time. That's why we have to take Solomon's exhortation seriously…*before* we speak.

Do we really want to "turn away wrath"? Or would we just as soon argue because venting feels good at the moment? And we don't consider much beyond the moment. Was Jesus just venting when He said the Pharisees were like "whitewashed tombs"—beautiful on the outside but full of dead men's bones and all uncleanness?[257] Even when Jesus was angry with the money changers and ran them out of the temple,[258] He did not sin with His lips.

Speaking truth, even to shock someone into reality, is not (of itself) sin. It's always the motive behind the words that God weighs. As with so much of what we've talked about in this book, this is another of those opportunities to trust God with our good name—our reputation. We don't have to defend ourselves. Jesus was unfairly accused and didn't say a word.[259]

Sometimes God allows the "fires" in our lives to burn away pride. And, as with Isaiah, who confessed his "unclean lips,"[260] God wants to forgive us of that too. It's not what goes into a man that defiles him (food), but what comes out of his heart.[261] What's yours full of today?

Lord, I confess I am a man of unclean lips (and thoughts). Help me to meditate on Your words today and place them as a filter over my lips, so what I speak will glorify You and point others to You. **Amen**.

257 Matt. 23:27
258 Matt. 21:12
259 Mark 14:53-61
260 Isa. 6:5-7
261 Mark 7:18-23

Gentleness is precious in the sight of God.[262]

"Blessed are the gentle, for they shall inherit the earth." Matt.5:5

Perhaps a fitting final thought for our week-long discussion of gentleness is to consider what God thinks of it. Matthew tells us that the gentle (some translations use "meek") will be the recipients of God's greatest treasure: the earth itself. God could have chosen any adjective He wanted to fill in the blank: blessed are the (fill in the blank). He could have said the righteous or the faithful or the long-suffering. But He didn't. He said the gentle.

Think about Satan's mission. It's to pervert everything God says by getting us to question God. "Did God really say..."[263] is his favorite line. That's why the world's take on masculinity is everything *but* gentle. And by the way, the answer to Satan's question is YES HE DID.

Let's review. Gentleness is strength controlled; it is *not* weakness. It's what Jesus modeled and, when seen in us, invites others to share their hurts. It doesn't lash out with the tongue, and it's the opposite of what the world teaches.

If you consider all that and understand that gentleness is "precious" to God, how can we not fall to our knees in utter shame and humility asking our Father's mercy for perverting His truth in our lives by cavalierly dismissing this character quality because it doesn't fit the mold of how *we* think gentleness should apply?

Maybe reading Job's one-sided conversation with God is an appropriate refresher course as to our role vs. God's role. "Where were you when I...?" Read the rest of the story in Job 38-41. Let's commit to take a stand today and all the rest of our days for gentleness. It's precious in the sight of God.

Father, Your Word is absolutely clear as to what You think of gentleness. Forgive me for, in effect, calling You a liar by conforming both my thinking and actions to the world's definition of manliness. Lord, change my heart that from it may flow the gentleness that You grant me every day. In Jesus's name. **Amen**.

262 I Pet. 3:4
263 Gen. 3:1

Gratitude puts everything in perspective.

"For who regards you as superior? What do you have that you did not receive? And if you did receive it, why do you boast as if you had not received it?" I Cor. 4:7

We love to be recognized—to get credit for things we've done. And that's OK as long as we don't allow pride and its accompanying ugliness to take root. A good habit to cultivate is when someone notices one of our accomplishments and praises us, is to immediately thank God for allowing us to participate in what *He* has done. Do this privately, or your public display of gratitude may be seen as false piety or even hypocrisy.

Paul warns the Corinthians about this very thing by reminding them that *everything* they have—talents, spiritual gifts, etc.—was given to them by God. A gift says more about the giver than the receiver. When we are mature enough to say, "What I *deserve* is eternal condemnation," then we can rightfully appreciate and enjoy whatever lot God has chosen for us and not compare ourselves with others (positively or negatively) or complain that someone has more or better.

Usually, we have just one perspective, ours. It's hard for us to admit that another perspective that differs from ours just may be the correct one. Pride. It affects every area of our life. "Why couldn't John's idea work?" "If we did it Peter's way, we *might* save time."

The key to unlocking our ability to see things from someone else's perspective is gratitude. Do you think your circumstances leave you nothing for which to be grateful? Start at the top and work your way down. There is a God. He's in control. Nothing sneaks up on Him. He loves you. He is merciful and patient. Need more? Maybe it's time to examine ourselves.[264] Memorize today's verse and meditate on it. It will change your life.

Father, when I take time to think about all I have, I see Your hand of blessing in everything. May I consciously develop the habit of attributing any success You grant me to Your working in my life for Your purposes. Thank You for never giving up on me. **Amen**.

264 Lam. 3:40

Gratitude doesn't take anything for granted.

"Give us this day our daily bread." Matt. 6:11

I live in a beautiful part of the country. I can sit on my deck and take in the majesty of Pike's Peak and the Rocky Mountains. The air is clean. Winter is not as cruel as in other places. All in all, a pretty nice place to live. But as with anything we're exposed to on a regular basis, it can become commonplace and mundane. For over 15 years, I also lived within 90 minutes of Yosemite National Park, arguably one of the most beautiful places on earth. People come from all over the world to visit it. For the first few years, I bought an annual pass, and I'd take the family there on a Sunday afternoon for a picnic and hiking. After the first three or four years, I hardly went at all.

As I look back, here's what I think happened: Life. Sometimes we get so bound up in today's activities, we don't stop to smell the roses. We're so busy making a living, we don't make time to enjoy life. Stop right now and look around you. What can you see for which you're grateful? Is there natural beauty? A tree? Clouds? Birds? Are you healthy? Do you have a job? Does God love you in spite of your warts? Think about your feelings the last time you gave a gift to your children. Did they show gratitude? Or did they leave you asking, "Why do I even bother?"

How does your recognition of what God has given you reflect back to Him? Are you grateful, or do you take the daily gifts for granted? A complaining spirit tells the world that you're not grateful for what you have; that you focus on what you *don't* have, or on what others have. Remember God's reaction to the Israelites when they complained during the exodus.[265]

If you find somehow you've lost the ability to be grateful, you've either taken God and His gifts for granted and come to expect them, or you haven't truly considered the source of everything you have (see yesterday's verse). Don't force God to withhold from you because you harbor an ungrateful spirit. Commit, today, to a daily, even verbal spirit of gratitude to the Giver of every perfect gift.[266]

Father, even the good and beautiful that You surround me with can sometimes become common. Remind me daily of Your activity on my behalf as I marvel at Your creation all around me. May I never take You or Your involvement in my life for granted. In Christ's name. **Amen**.

265 Num. 11:1
266 Jas.1:17

Gratitude is a reflection—a measurement—of the amount of sin forgiven.

"...he who is forgiven little, loves little." Luke 7:47

"It's just a drop in the bucket." That saying probably originated from someone who never had to deal with a leaky roof. Those of us who have, know that enough drops and the bucket eventually overflows. There are two ways to deal with a leaky roof. We either repair the source of the problem, or we keep emptying the bucket.

"It's no big deal," we hear people say when justifying bad (sinful) behavior. But, like the leaky roof, if we don't deal with the source of the problem, at some point, it will overflow into habitual sin. When we deny—disagree with God about—our sin, or worse, don't even recognize our thoughts and actions as sin, we can't possibly display the kind of gratitude God deserves.

Sure, we may understand certain overt acts that physically or emotionally harm someone else as sin and even repent and accept God's forgiveness. But until we allow the Holy Spirit free reign in our lives and listen to His soft reminders about our thoughts, our words, our deeds, we will be like the one Jesus spoke of in our verse today: forgiven little.

But is that the reality? Forgiven little? No. We've been forgiven *all*. We may not recognize the amount or severity of our sin, but that doesn't negate the power of Jesus' blood to cleanse us. Today, our challenge is to check our "forgiveness gauge." Jesus said, "...he who is forgiven little, loves little." How much do we love? How much do we love God? Man? Our grouchy neighbor? If you find your love meter isn't registering very high, it's possible you don't recognize the scope of God's forgiveness. Love springs from a grateful heart. A grateful heart comes from knowing your sins—all of them—are forgiven in Christ.

Lord, my pride gets in the way of acknowledging my sin. I think, "it's no big deal." Lift the veil of deceit from my eyes that I may see my sin as You do and call it what it is: sin. Fill me with gratitude for Your complete and total forgiveness in Christ. In His name, **Amen**.

Gratitude recognizes those who have gone before.

"I planted, Apollos watered, but God was causing the growth." I Cor. 3:6

Living in the United States is a wonderful privilege, a blessing from God. But how often do we think on our history and thank God for those who have fought and died for the freedoms we hold so dear? Can you even imagine what life in the Middle East must be like? But here's the conundrum: God loves them too. Not their religion or their rejection of truth, but them. Does that give you cause to be grateful?

You didn't happen here by accident. God had a reason for planting you where He did. Are you blooming where you're planted? In Paul's ministry, he recognized that *all* spiritual growth was from God. He wasn't into numbers; he didn't build mega-churches. He didn't resent Apollos coming along to water the same "garden" after he had sowed. Paul had one thought in mind[267] and that was to "press on toward the goal." And what was that goal? It was the upward call of God in Christ Jesus.[268] And it wasn't just for himself and his traveling buddies. You know, "us four, no more, shut the door." No, Paul's heart was for the lost, and he didn't care who preceded or followed him.

His message was always the same: "Jesus Christ and Him crucified."[269] Can we learn from Paul in this area of being grateful for those who have gone before us and those who will come after? We can if we remember who the harvest belongs to[270] and get our pride of numbers out of the way.

There are very few things in life that don't involve receiving help along the way. Our challenge today is to rejoice over every sinner who repents and accepts Christ as his savior…regardless of whom or what group led him to the Lord. Don't let jealousy rob you of the joy of the Spirit for a brother from another mother.

Father, surely you must be tired of my pride, which wants credit for being allowed to participate in some way in sharing the gospel with a lost world. Remind me of all the people that were involved in my salvation, and bless them with abundant joy. Help me rejoice with each sinner that repents regardless of my involvement. Give me a love for the lost that transcends the desire for personal recognition. In Christ's name, **Amen**.

267 Phil. 3:13
268 Phil. 3:14
269 I Cor. 2:2
270 Matt. 9:38

Gratitude sets our focus on the giver, not the gift.

"...for He Himself is kind to ungrateful and evil men." Luke 6:35

Ever notice a Christmas gift-opening session, especially one where there are three generations? In my family, we go to church on Christmas Eve then come home and open gifts. The kids distribute and we wait until everybody has their pile. It's interesting to observe the focus of each generation. The youngest are all about the number of gifts and the size of the boxes. The parents are focused on the kids and making sure none of the pieces are thrown out with the wrappings. Maybe because I'm in this next group (of two)—the grandparents—I am a little biased. But it seems that my wife and I (aka: Gran and Papa) are more appreciative of the thoughtfulness expressed by our daughters than whatever the gift is.

I'm told that I'm hard to buy for. That's not true...as long as it says Harley-Davidson. How often in our recognition of God's gifts to us do we fall into one of the first categories? James tells us that God is the giver of every "perfect gift."[271] What constitutes a perfect gift? Is it one that has high dollar value? Or maybe one that we've been drooling over but didn't want to buy for ourselves? Maybe. But I think it's one that the Giver has put a lot of thought into: one that fits a specific need or one that challenges us to go deeper with God.

What about the "gift" of a trial designed to trim some sinful habit from our life? Who knows us and our needs better than our heavenly Father? Are we at a point in our walk of faith where we can thank God in all circumstances?[272] What motivates God's gift-giving to us? Isn't it simply that He loves us and wants to give us good things?[273] If God is "kind to ungrateful and evil men," how much more to His children? The real question today is, "Do we love the gift more than the Giver?"

Father, when I take time to reflect on Your gifts, I am amazed that You don't withhold Your mercy, Your grace, or Your love because of my sin. Forgive me for taking You for granted and also for not recognizing Your hand in all that I receive. In Jesus' name, **Amen**.

271 Jas. 1:17
272 Phil. 4:11
273 Matt. 7:11

Gratitude wells up from within and overflows all over our face.

"A joyful heart makes a cheerful face, but when the heart is sad, the spirit is broken." Prov. 15:13

You've seen them. Kids at Disneyland or some other "happy" place. The joy they are experiencing is all over their faces...sometimes literally as ice cream that hasn't quite found the target remains to be cleaned later.

It's impossible to hide what's going on inside us. Luke tells us that our mouth speaks from that which fills our heart.[274] The FBI has made a science of reading body language. For an interesting read, see ex-FBI agent Joe Navarro's book: *What Every Body is Saying*.[275] In it, he describes various "tells"—signs our body gives off frequently belying verbal communication—from feet and hands to eye direction and head position.

Happiness and joy are not the same thing. Happiness depends on circumstances. Joy is a gift of the Holy Spirit.[276] It's also the result of choices we make based on our gratitude. When we are cognizant of all that God has done and continues to do on a moment by moment basis, and we realize we don't deserve any of it, this gratitude-driven joy should light up our face like a beacon. I've occasionally used the line, "Are you as happy as you look?" with someone who seems down.

Advertisers always use smiling people. It conveys a subtle message that happiness is linked to their product. Sourpuss Christians are not a compelling testimony to God's goodness. Today, look in the mirror and ask yourself if what you see displays the goodness of God for which you are eternally grateful.

Lord, when I think about it, Your goodness moves me to gratitude because I know I don't deserve any good thing. Help me to think about it more and make the connection between gift and giver an automatic trigger mechanism which produces joy that others can see and be drawn to You because of. In Christ's name, **Amen**.

274 Luke 6:45
275 ©2008 Harper-Collins Publishers
276 Gal. 5:22

Gratitude sees a silver lining in every storm cloud.

"For His anger is but for a moment, His favor is for a lifetime; Weeping may last for the night, but a shout of joy comes in the morning." Ps. 30:5

A line from an Anne Murray song says, "I can see clearly now, the rain has gone." But faith says, "I can see clearly now because I know who controls the rain." Gratitude reflects our maturity. It allows us to rejoice when others prosper, and it doesn't have to have the best of anything.

I don't know if they still teach an introductory class to mechanical drawing in school, but one of the exercises that I thought was cool was to draw something in perspective. Having an attitude of gratitude helps us to have the same perspective on our life that our Father does. Remember, nothing sneaks up on God.

We can trust that whatever God allows our way is for our good[277] and His glory. As we mature in Christ, we are more able to be grateful for even the storm clouds. If we never had dark clouds, we'd soon take the sun for granted. If we never have trials, we'll soon take the Son for granted.

It's the best illustration I can think of yet falls woefully short of how our Father treats us, but (if you are one) as a parent, don't you want to do more for your kids when they show gratitude? Their gratitude *toward* you opens the door for more blessings *from* you. When our kids (or other people too) show gratitude to us, it encourages us to want to do more.

What if God responds the same way? James tells us we don't have because we don't ask.[278] And we ask and don't receive because of wrong motives.[279] What if an ungrateful, complaining spirit is defrauding us of blessings that God wants to give? Gratitude becomes a way of life. But we have to start. On your mark… get set…

Father, You overwhelm me with Your goodness and mercy in addition to all the material things You bless me with. Heighten my awareness of Your generosity behind all I have. In Jesus' name, **Amen**.

277 Rom. 8:28
278 James 4:2
279 James 4:3

Week 20 – Sunday

Humility is gladly doing even the menial chores.

*"Whatever you do, do your work **heartily**, as for the Lord rather than for men, knowing that from the Lord you will receive the reward of the inheritance. It is the Lord Christ whom you serve." Col. 3:23, 24*

My wife has the gift of hospitality, but I was at the airport when that ship came in. As I write this, it's oh-dark-thirty Easter morning. Today, we celebrate The Resurrection at our house—with nearly 20 people ranging from my youngest grandson at nine to the oldest…me.

So why do I tell you that? Because I'm already convicted by today's topic with regard to the cleanup. Why do I hate it so much? Because my pride whispers things like, "You're the patriarch, let the others do it" or "You've done your part by supplying the house, the main course, etc." It's because my focus is on me rather than on the One we celebrate.

If I believed today's verse and lived it out in my life, it wouldn't matter what task I was called to do. What part of "heartily" does grumbling fall under? I hate pride and what it makes me do, especially today, as I think of what my Savior did for me…without grumbling. He gave all. Let me say that again, He gave ALL.

To the degree my glass is full of pride, humility can't penetrate. They are exact opposites and cannot share the same space. And whether I see it in myself or not, others certainly do. More importantly, God does. And He hates it too.[280] May the gift of The Resurrection penetrate our hearts today and put to death the pride that is so insidious that continually pushes us to be on the throne, and replace it with the humility that honors God and God honors.[281]

Father, as I think about the humility that Your Son displayed and realize that He did it for me, put to death my pride and remind me that whatever task I tackle, I'm doing it to serve my Lord Jesus Christ. In His name, **Amen**.

280 Prov. 6:17
281 I Pet. 5:6

Humility is accepting the way we're made as God's gift.

"I will give thanks to You, for I am fearfully and wonderfully made; wonderful are Your works, and my soul knows it very well." Psa. 139:14

If you ever doubt God's sense of humor, just look in the mirror. Most of us are not Paul Newman or Brad Pitt. But have you ever pondered the fact that *you* are exactly as God designed you? Sure, some of us question whether God knew what He was doing and wish that something could be different, e.g., height, size of ears or nose, or a hundred other things.

A recent survey of teen girls found nearly 100% would change something if they could. The medical "change" industry is a multi-billion dollar a year industry.[282] In *The Journal of Health and Social Behavior,*[283] you'll find many articles that discuss the results of media-driven comparisons. And most comparisons end with negative feelings toward ourselves. If we were honest, we could probably come up with a list of things about ourselves that we'd change if we could. Well, you know what? You *can* change the things that count.

Remember from yesterday's verse Whom it is we serve. Then, even forgetting that He made you exactly the way you are, remember what God told Samuel when he was picking the first king of Israel: "*...man looks at the outward appearance, but the Lord looks at the heart.*"[284] Why are we so preoccupied with the way we look instead of the way we act? Because, again, our focus is on "me" and not the One we need to please.

Hear the Lord's passion and promise to Israel: "*Oh, that they had such a heart in them, that they would fear Me and keep all My commandments always, that it may be well with them and their sons forever.*"[285] Rarely does Scripture even mention appearance, and never does it focus on it as anything of value. The world has distorted God's message of "the heart," and we've fallen for it. Rather than resent our bodies, let's think of ourselves as God does—specifically designed: one of a kind—and rejoice that He knows us by name.[286]

Lord, again I find that I've bought the world's lie about what's really important. Forgive me for not believing You and questioning my design. May I begin to see my uniqueness as Your signature on a one-of-a-kind work of art. Thank You, in Jesus' name, **Amen**.

282 http://www.sleepingswan.com/articles/Plastic_Surgery_Costs.htm
283 http://intl-hsb.sagepub.com
284 I Sam. 16:7
285 Deut. 5:29
286 Isa. 43:1

Humility is part of God's contrarian plan for us.

"Therefore humble yourselves under the mighty hand of God, that He may exalt you at the proper time, casting all your anxiety on Him, because He cares for you." I Pet 5:6,7

How many of us believe that sometimes God could use a little help in moving things toward *our* desired end? Thank you, I see that hand (mine's up too). I'm sure it's not a case of not trusting God, but more a question of timing. Right? Maybe we (subconsciously) think that some small detail of our situation has escaped God's notice, and if we don't do something, well, you know. May I say with all authority, poppycock?

We have been trained to take charge, be in control, lead. Therefore, it goes against our (sinful) nature to take a more passive role. Ah, but therein is the key: we're listening to the wrong "nature." Today's verse begins with "therefore." And as in all good Bible study, the first question to ask is what is therefore there for? Peter has just given a brief job description to the elders, and he wraps it up, saying, "…clothe yourselves with humility toward one another, for God is opposed to the proud, but gives grace to the humble."[287]

So he continues with an exhortation and a promise. Have you ever noticed how many promises God has given us? Can you find one that doesn't have a condition attached? Like any good parent says to their kid, "As long as you live under my roof, my rules apply." C'mon, I know you've even said that yourself. So why should our heavenly Father be different? You want the promise? It's simple. Do it His way.

I'm sure you've found in your Christian walk that most of God's ways are contrarian to the world's ways. Have you forgotten who's in charge of the world…for now? A good rule of thumb is, if most of the people are doing it, do the opposite, and that's probably God's will. Is God taking away our "candy" when He tells us to "humble ourselves"? Absolutely not! Read the last part of the verse again, "…He cares for you." Now you've got a choice. Choose wisely.

Father, I know You care for me. And I also know that Your way is the right way. I get so impatient sometimes because my faith is small, and I want what I want when I want it. Forgive me and help me to trust You for the proper timing in all things. In Christ's name, **Amen**.

287 I Pet. 5:5

Humility is happy when others around us succeed.

"Do nothing from selfishness or empty conceit, but with humility of mind regard one another as more important than yourselves." Phil. 2:3

Competition. In our society, it's generally considered a good thing. It drives athletes, students, and salesmen to be the best they can be. Why? Because of the recognition (and reward) that accompanies it. But what about the feelings of those who miss the top spot? Someone has dubbed second place as "first loser." Believe me, I like to win as much as the next guy. In fact, my family doesn't like to play card or board games because they say I'm *too* competitive. My philosophy is simple: If you're going to play, play to win. (Can I get an amen?)

But here's the truth: God's economy is NOT a "zero-sum" game. It is not a finite pie. Your success doesn't stop me from being successful. So what's the problem? We're lazy. If you're successful and I'm not, while you're basking in the spotlight, it also shines an indirect light on me and exposes my weakness, lack of effort, lack of commitment, etc.

Today's verse gives us the solution. Notice Paul does not say that others *are* more important than ourselves, but we are to *regard* (consider) them as such. If we're secure in our relationship to our Father through the Lord Jesus Christ, nothing or nobody can devalue us; we're free to rejoice with those who rejoice.[288]

Have you ever noticed how many times the Bible tells us to "consider"? James tells us to consider it all joy,[289] Hebrews tells us to consider how to stimulate one another,[290] Paul told the Colossians to consider the members of their body as dead to sin.[291] It boils down to this: we need to renew our minds[292] according to God's Word and dump the world's ways. Today, when others succeed, see if your feelings of resentment aren't the result of pride-based sin. By focusing on others and not me, I can truly be happy for them. It's in God's time, not mine.

Father, Your ways convict me of selfishness and insecurity. It's hard to be happy when others in my sphere of activity are successful because I want the spotlight and the praise of men. Forgive me. Help me today to only focus on what pleases You. In Christ's name, **Amen**.

288 Rom. 12:15
289 Jas. 1:2
290 Heb. 10:24
291 Col. 3:5
292 Rom. 12:2

Humility doesn't take credit for things that belong to God.

"In the wilderness He fed you manna which your fathers did not know, that He might humble you and that He might test you, to do good for you in the end. Otherwise, you may say in your heart, 'My power and the strength of my hand made me this wealth. But you shall remember the Lord your God, for it is He who is giving you power to make wealth, that He may confirm His covenant…'" Deut. 8:16-18

It's been said that if we didn't care who got credit for something, a lot more would get done. Lest you think this is a modern era phenomenon, reread what Moses told the Israelites (above). Man's heart, and his desire to receive recognition from man, has not changed for 6,000 years. Way back in Genesis, God knew that our heart was "only evil continually."[293]

Let's ask ourselves this, "Does it make us mad when we've done something and someone else takes credit for it?" I'll admit my first response is not usually "Praise God" but something far different. Why? It gets back to the same old thing: pride, accompanied by a lack of trust that God really sees everything and will reward me according to His riches in glory in Christ.[294]

I don't know about you, but I get discouraged going to God time after time for the same offenses. (By the way, there's a great book, *Getting To No,* by Dr. Erwin Lutzer that deals with habitual sins.)[295] But if we get mad over someone else taking "our" credit, can you understand how God feels when the results of *everything* we do are determined by Him, and we want to steal His glory? It *is* stealing, by the way: taking something that belongs to someone else.

So how do we break these bonds? Our verse today gives us the answer: Remember the Lord your God. Isn't that really the answer to most of our problems? When we forget God and drift on the sea of self-sufficiency, that's when nothing we touch seems to go right.

Can we believe that God really wants to "do good for us in the end"? Of course we can because He's absolutely trustworthy. Why go one more minute trying to steer our own ship when God waits for us to come to our senses?

Lord God, I struggle so hard with wanting credit for all I do. I know that without your grace and mercy, I wouldn't have anything to take credit for. Help me to live this day knowing it's by Your blessing and only by Your blessing that I accomplish anything. In Christ's name, **Amen**.

---

293 Gen. 6:5

294 Phil. 4:19

295 *Getting To No,* David C Cook Publishing

Humility is accepting that God's grace is sufficient.

"And He has said to me, 'My grace is sufficient for you, for power is perfected in weakness.'" II Cor. 12:9

Everyone who is weak, raise your hand. Didn't think so. We could probably stop right there, and the message would be complete. Instead, let's look at why we have such a hard time doing things God's way. The answer's easy; putting it into practice—not so much. It's our old ugly friend, pride. We argue with God, "If You'd only change (fill in the blank), I'd be so much more effective for You."

Sometimes our "thorn" is another person. It could be a boss that we know we're better than, a peer who is always kissing up, a spouse that hasn't grown like we have, or an extended family that embarrasses us. Sometimes it's a physical trait that keeps us from participating or draws attention. Whatever it is, it's not there by mistake.

Have you ever considered that your boss, peer, spouse, or family is not your competition? You are. What are you doing with what God gave you to become the best "you" you can be? God, who gives gifts as He wills,[296] doesn't judge us against someone else who has different or more gifts. He judges us compared to how we could be according to His design. Sobering thought, isn't it?

In Dr. Lutzer's book,[297] one of the three ground rules he states is, "**As an adult, I am responsible for my actions**." There's no blame game, no excuse that will be acceptable on the other side. We will face God in an examination of our life. Our deeds will either burn up, or they won't.[298] If you haven't already done so, make today the day you stop looking around for someone else to blame and accept God's statement to Paul (and us), "My grace is sufficient for you."

Start each day by looking in the mirror and telling yourself, "I am exactly who God designed me to be." Then, with the clothing of God's grace, go out and pour out your life for the kingdom.

Lord God, I get so discouraged when I compare myself with others who seem smarter, better looking, and more talented. Keep me focused today on the perfect design with which you created me and let me show my thanks by putting You first. In Jesus' name, **Amen**.

296 I Cor. 12:11
297 *Getting To No,* David C Cook Publishing
298 I Cor. 3:11-15

Week 20 – Saturday

Humility does not grow weary in well-doing.

"Let us not lose heart in doing good, for in due time we will reap if we do not grow weary." Gal. 6:9

Today, I'm really talking to myself. Y'all can listen in if you want. The more I observe modern society in its daily habits, the more I'm convinced that the slogan of the '60s, "The Pepsi Generation," should be changed to "The Me Generation." And it's not age-specific. Simple things like manners and respect for persons and property seem to have gone the way of the buggy whip—you still see them now and then, but they're not used much.

So as I apply that in my own life, I find it harder to have the right attitude about doing good to others. "When is it my turn?" I find myself thinking. Doing good is easy when people are grateful and praise you. Not so easy when your good deeds seem to go unnoticed (and unrewarded). I get caught up in thoughts of revenge, hoping for all sorts of negative "blessings" heaped on others.

What's my problem? A short term focus. Our verse says, "in due time," and time is another item on my list of "things I can't control." Additionally, it circles back to the same issue: Do I believe God or not? He promises I will reap if I hang in there. Really? How long? How much? What I've discovered is that I won't have an answer to those questions this side of eternity.

Throughout Scripture, the prophets and martyred saints asked the same question. The best answer I can find is in Rev. 6:11, "*a little while longer.*" Have you noticed how you get a surge of energy when you can see the finish line, and you're willing to expend it all in a final flourish? Let's have that attitude as we finish our life's race, looking for our Savior to say, "Well done."

Father, I know my struggles don't compare to what Jesus went through on my behalf. And, I also know that I brought most of them on myself. But I do get weary and discouraged in the day to day trenches. Help me to focus on the future You have promised and run so as to win and finish strong. In Christ's name, **Amen**.

For additional meditation:

"Whoever exalts himself shall be humbled; and whoever humbles himself shall be exalted." Matt.23:12

"But the humble will inherit the land and will delight themselves in abundant prosperity." Psalms 37:11

Humor is God's safety valve for stress.

A joyful heart is good medicine. Pr. 17:22

If you don't think God has a sense of humor, you've never considered the giraffe. It has the longest neck in the animal kingdom but can't make a sound. When birthing her calf, the mother literally drops the baby from a standing position. What's wrong with the baby giraffe? Oh, he was dropped on his head when he was born.

Sometimes, we tease people by saying something similar about them. But what if God *didn't* have a sense of humor? We'd have no Red Skelton or Bob Hope. We'd take ourselves too seriously…all the time…instead of just most of the time. We've probably all, at one time or another, made fun of someone's anatomy. You know, ears or nose too big, etc.

What we should remember is that God made everything **exactly** as He wanted for His own purpose. I'm sure that if we were honest, we'd all have something to complain about with regard to the way we were made. Something too big or little, too short or tall, brown eyes not blue; there's no end to the list.

How 'bout we stop spending so much time at the mirror and spend more time looking into the mirror of God's Word. There, we find extraordinary promises for each of us, no matter what we look like. By the way, what do *souls and spirits* look like? Do you think your eternal, heavenly body will have any zits? Or be out of proportion? Or be anything less than perfect? Ever consider that God, in His wisdom, gave us just the right body to keep us from becoming puffed up over something we had nothing to do with?[299]

I have a ceramic plaque over the archway in my kitchen. It says: Live Well, Love Much, Laugh Often. One of the surest ways to push my wife's buttons (so I can laugh at her) is to tell her she doesn't have a sense of humor (which she really does). So where am I going with all this? Only to say this: It's OK to laugh at life. It's OK to laugh at yourself. Make sure if you laugh at somebody else, it's because they're funny, not because they're funny looking.

The Bible equates laughter and joyful shouting with thanksgiving.[300] Ask yourself today, can others tell how thankful I am by my laughter and joyful shouting?

Father, thank you for the gifts of humor, laughter, and joyful shouting. Help me today to recognize my "design flaws" as your special mark of ownership and protection on me and to not take myself so seriously. In Christ's name, **Amen**.

---

299 I Cor. 4:7

300 Psa. 126:2

Week 21 – Monday

Humor is God's way of reminding me not to take myself so seriously.

Blessed are you who hunger now, for you shall be satisfied. Blessed are you who weep now, for you shall laugh. Luke 6:21

Focus. That word is in our vocabulary because we don't. You know the applications: tests, sports, sermons. And the list can go on and on. In the early '60s, Pepsi Cola coined the phrase: The Pepsi Generation. There has been the Baby Boomer generation, the Gen Xers, and others. But I submit we are now living in the "Me" generation. It's all about what I want—what feels good to me. It's *my* space, *my* rights, *my* feelings. In other words, we are focused on…wait for it…ME!

In our verse for today, Luke encourages us to not dwell (focus) on our current circumstances, but on the future: "You shall…" Think about this. Is the God who made the promise (you shall…) trustworthy? How many of us, in our flesh, could consider hunger a blessing? How about tears? How could that be a blessing? My answer? I don't know. But here's what I *do* know. God is faithful[301] and cannot lie.[302] If He says my tears shall be turned to laughter, then I can deal with anything He allows.

Based on some of my tears and the circumstances causing them (i.e., burying two of my children), I expect some great belly laughs in heaven. But what's the bigger point here? It's my/our focus. Another word for focus is goals. Bobb Biehl[303] used to say, "Goals are magnets of the future pulling us toward them."

Maybe our focus needs to be on our future and on Him who holds that future rather than on our current situation. Here's today's challenge: Can we have joy in our current circumstances, knowing that our heavenly Father knows what we need[304] before we ask, and trust Him to do what is best for us[305] even if we don't understand or like the answer?

Lord God, You have everything under control, including *my* circumstances. Today, I ask You to grant me greater trust in You even to the point of being able to welcome my trials, knowing that the future You have designed for me includes laughter and my satisfaction. Thank You. In Jesus' name, **Amen**.

301 I John 1:9; I Cor. 10:13
302 Tit. 1:2
303 www.bobbbiehl.com
304 Matt. 6:32
305 Rom. 8:28

Humor has been perverted.

"A time to weep and a time to laugh..." Eccl. 3:4

What makes you laugh? There's a TV show *America's Funniest Videos* that has built an audience on life's foibles. But why do we laugh at grown men and women falling down? What's funny about someone being hurt? I saw a pithy sticker once that said, "Stupid should hurt." And, of course, there's Forrest Gump's famous line: "Stupid is as stupid does."

Ever think that laughing at someone's mistake exposes your pride? We think, "I would never do something that dumb." Really? What if our lives were one long video? Would people think, "How could anybody be so stupid?"

Here's what I think. God created humor and laughter because, as we saw Sunday, "A joyful heart is good medicine."[306] But, as with everything God made, the enemy wants to twist, distort, and morph it into an idol. Think about that. God created beauty—beautiful women, beautiful scenery, beautiful music. What did Satan do? Turned them all into idols.[307]

He's done the same with humor. Where has all the clean humor gone? Oh sure, there are Christian comedians, and I don't mean to denigrate them—they're in the battle. But honestly, what names come to mind when you think of comedians? I have to confess, I laugh at some of them right along with you. But does that kind of humor glorify God? In prayer, could you thank God for the jokes you heard?

Doesn't it hurt your heart that we've fallen so far short of God's standard? And there's no humor in that. But knowing and identifying the problem is half the solution. Make today the day you draw a line in the sand and take a stand for humor that you don't have to hide from God.

Father God, forgive me for not guarding my mind against so much of what the world calls humor. Give me a love for You and Your Word so that I have a filter through which to test everything that comes my way. Grant me courage to stand for You no matter where I am or how few stand with me. In Christ's name, **Amen**.

306 Prov. 17:22
307 Rom. 1:25

Week 21 – Wednesday

Humor does not include coarse jesting.

"and there must be no filthiness and silly talk, or coarse jesting, which are not fitting but rather giving of thanks." Eph. 5:4

To continue on yesterday's theme… One of the major credit card companies has a series of ads touting the memories purchased with their card as "priceless." Maybe. As God's children, we're told to count the cost.[308] What's the cost of laughing at "filthiness, silly talk, and coarse jesting?" Could it be a diminished relationship with our Father?

What could be more priceless than the "pearl of great value"[309] that Jesus compares to heaven? Men, if we're on the path to heaven, we need to stay off the rabbit trails that have hidden costs. What's the value of hearing Jesus say, upon our arrival in heaven, "Well done"?

It's tempting and oh so easy to go along with the crowd to "fit in." But we have to ask ourselves, "Where do I want to fit in?" The Bible tells us to "*come out from their midst and be separate*."[310] Why is it so hard to live a separated life, a life we're called to, a life pleasing to God? Answer this first: How many of Michael Jordan's over 30,000 points would he have made if every time he went to shoot, he looked up into the stands? Answer: not many.

We have the same problem. We take our eyes off the prize.[311] The good news is that we can start today and "forget what lies behind" and focus (Paul says press on) [312] on the right kind of humor—the kind that doesn't get laughs at other people's expense.

Living a separated life can be hard and lonely. But that's because we focus on what we think we're missing out on. Remember, eternity is a long time. Life is short. Thank God often for your salvation, for His daily grace, for the priceless gifts of family and friends. When our heart is filled with God, there's no room for coarse jesting, off-color jokes, or double entendres with sexual overtones. I love a good laugh as much as anyone—and God gave us the ability to laugh. Let's make sure we haven't crossed the line.

Lord, it's so easy to want to fit in with the world. I know it's because I look at the world and not You. Fill me with gratitude for my salvation, your daily grace, and my family and friends. Help me to enjoy life to its fullest, but conscious of Your boundaries. In Jesus' name, **Amen**.

308 Luke 14:33
309 Matt. 13:45, 46
310 II Cor. 6:17
311 Phil. 3:13, 14
312 Ibid.

Humor is not a conversational hit and run.

"Like a madman who throws firebrands, arrows and death, so is the man who deceives his neighbor, and says, "Was I not joking?" Prov. 26:18, 19

We often try to couch truth, or at least our version of it, in humor. Then we pause a beat to see if we get a reaction. If the reaction's negative, we try to spin it by saying, "Just kidding." Or we can use it to divert someone's focus from the real issue.

Reminds me of the girl who called home from college and told her mom, "My boyfriend got me hooked on drugs, and while I was high, I ran over a woman with two babies, and now I'm facing manslaughter charges. I'm not sure I can handle being pregnant in prison." Then, after a couple beats, she said to her mom, "I'm just kidding. But I do have a D in history. I just wanted to put it in perspective for you."

Words mean something. The Bible tells us to "let our yes be yes and our no, no."[313] What if God had finished the 10 commandments, and while Moses was headed down the mountain, He said, "Just kidding?" Humor is not intended to couch deception. [314] You've all heard the joke about how you know when a politician is lying…his lips are moving.

Wouldn't it be wonderful if we could trust every word people speak? Jesus quoted the Old Testament to Satan when He said, "Man shall not live by bread alone, but on every word that proceeds out of the mouth of God."[315] He said it for two reasons. First, we need to know the truth. Second, it's the only word we can trust in all circumstances.

How would our speech be different if we committed today to speak only truth and that which edifies,[316] and also refrain from coarse jesting?[317]

Lord, help me today to guard my speech, first, so it brings honor and not shame to You and second, so it lifts up those around me. In Jesus' name, **Amen**.

313 Matt. 5:37
314 Prov. 26:19
315 Matt. 4:4 (Deut. 8:3)
316 Eph. 4:29
317 Eph. 5:4

Strutting your stuff, when you don't have any, is laughable.

He (God) who sits in the heavens laughs. Psa. 2:4

We've all seen it. The little league baseball game where somebody's pride and joy has all the accouterments—the batting glove, the swagger, the tapping of the cleats with the bat, holding his hand up to "get ready" at the plate—and then strikes out…and blames the ump for a bad call. We'd laugh if it weren't such a sad indicator of what's going on inside the little guy's head.

But aren't we just the same? We puff and strut and expect special recognition and treatment because, after all, we *are* special. But the world just laughs at us. The difference between what I think of myself and what others think of me would probably destroy me if I knew the truth.

I've got good news for all of us. God doesn't *think* we're special. He *knows* we are because He made us special. And He made us *exactly* the way He wanted. Try to wrap your mind around that the next time you don't like the way you are. The flip side is true too. Try to wrap your mind around the truth that all your good points, your looks, physical abilities, intelligence, etc. were given to you[318] by God. We want to take credit for only one side of the coin. Truth is, we can't take credit for either.

We're responsible for what we *do* with what God's given us, but not for its existence. Our inclination is to either become angry or bitter if we think we've been short-changed or to become arrogant and condescending if we perceive ourselves better than others. Neither response is correct. Accept with humility the way you are and focus on glorifying God in all you do.[319] The pressure to meet the world's standards will quickly fade if we do this.

Father, when I compare myself with others, it's easy to either be discouraged or smug. May I remember today that You made me exactly the way I am for *Your* purposes and *Your* glory and keep my pride in check. In Christ's name, **Amen**.

---

318 I Cor. 4:7

319 I Cor. 10:31

No Laughing Matter: The last laugh will be on those who now laugh at God.

The wicked plots against the righteous and gnashes at him with his teeth. The Lord laughs at him, for He sees his day is coming. Psa.37:12, 13

Being on the right side is important. We all want to be on or support a winning team. If Honda beats Ford for best sedan of the year, we puff up a little if we drive the Honda. Let's face it; these "wins" don't amount to a hill of beans in the big picture of life.

But there is one issue, and even though this wraps up the section on humor, that is no laughing matter. If you find yourself on the wrong side of this issue, you will be one about whom the Lord speaks in today's verse. And being laughed at in this world—which we all hate—cannot even be remotely compared with being laughed at by the Lord.

With as much passion as I can put into the written word, **if you don't know the Lord Jesus Christ as your personal savior, do not let the sun go down before you get acquainted**. It means the difference in where you will spend eternity.

You've probably heard someone boast of their rebellion against God by saying something like, "I'll be so busy (in hell) shaking hands and partying with all my friends, I won't have time to regret." The truth, on the other hand, is sobering. The Bible says that hell is a place of torment[320] and weeping and gnashing of teeth.[321]

How many of you like to party in the dark? I mean pitch black where you can't see your hand in front of your face. In addition to the pain and suffering, hell is "outer darkness,"[322] total separation from God and anything good. As Joshua told the rebellious Israelites, "*choose this day whom you will serve.*"[323] While we still have breath, we still have a choice. Choose Jesus. And if you already know the Lord Jesus, someone in your sphere of influence doesn't. Introduce them today.

Father, You are so gracious to us to give us time to come to You in repentance. Open my eyes that I may see the truth of Your Word and understand the eternal consequences of not making the decision to follow Christ before it's too late. In His name, **Amen**.

320 Luke 16:23
321 Matt. 13:41, 42
322 Matt. 8:12
323 Josh.24:15

Integrity is only looking at things your 9-year old daughter can look at with you.

"I have made a covenant with my eyes; how then could I gaze at a virgin?"
Job 31:1

Technology—in many ways it's made our life easier. Living in Colorado where the temperature can drop to single digits and below, I particularly appreciate indoor plumbing. I also prefer HDTV on a big screen for NFL games than the tiny, grainy B&W screen I grew up with. I still shudder when I think of my first "brick" phone in the late '70s. What would we do without today's smartphones? The world at our fingertips.

But is it really a good thing? Jesus said, "*If your right eye makes you stumble, tear it out…*"[324] How easy it is to stumble in the cyberspace of today. Sometimes it can happen innocently. Vile pornography can appear without warning. But here's the test. Do we click off immediately or does our gaze linger?

Here is a good reason why it's important to have a conscious goal of righteousness. Evil can sneak up on us. If we haven't planned and rehearsed how to deal with temptation, it can easily defeat us. It's been said that failing to plan is planning to fail. That's especially true in the spiritual realm.

We have an avowed enemy whose only mission is to "steal, kill and destroy."[325] Are we armored up?[326] Are our "inbound filters" in place as to what we watch on TV, what we search the Web for, what gossip we embrace at work? Job defends his integrity by stating that he had actually made a covenant with his eyes. How many of us can even say we *want* to look away? There's our starting point. May we be sensitive to the Holy Spirit's prompting to "turn away from evil."[327]

Lord, there is so much that draws my eyes away from You and Your plan for my life. Strengthen my desire and conviction to walk in a manner pleasing to you…even if it means I walk alone, knowing that You will never leave me or forsake me and that You will empower me along the way. In Christ's name, **Amen**.

324 Matt. 5:29
325 John 10:10
326 Eph. 6:11-13
327 Prov. 3:7

Integrity keeps its word, regardless of the cost.

"Oh Lord, who may abide in Your tent?...He who walks with integrity...swears to his own hurt and does not change." Psa. 15:1-4

Does it irritate you as much as it does me when professional athletes are one or two years into a longer contract, have an outstanding year, and then want to hold the team hostage while they renegotiate? How would you react if you had signed a 5-year lease on an office building, and because your landlord had a bad year, he comes to you and says, "I'm raising your rent by 20%?"

Don't we have a built-in sense of fairness? Does it still apply when we draw the short straw? Solomon said, "*When you make a vow to God, do not be late in paying it; for He takes no delight in fools. Pay what you vow!*" [328] Pretty strong words to consider.

The idea is to take time and think through the commitment you're about to make... before you make it, not after. Remember the parable of the landowner[329] who hired temporary help throughout the day? He offered the same wage to each of the five groups he hired. When those he hired first—who had borne the heat and burden of the day—saw that the ones who had only worked one hour received the same pay they had agreed to, they thought they would get more. Surprise! They got exactly what they had agreed to.

Now I can certainly relate to the first group. From one viewpoint, it wouldn't seem fair (there's that word again) to do what the landowner did. But what did he do that wasn't fair? He made a contract—a vow if you will—and kept it. The real lesson is about the generosity of the landowner (representative of God) and that in God's kingdom, all receive the same eternal benefits. Let's remember that God watches what we say and expects us to honor our word.

Lord, often my sense of what's fair is tainted by what the world says I deserve. May I live in Your grace today and remember that my eternal future is secure in Christ. Help me to trust Your promise of a future and a hope because You're trustworthy and You've always given me more than I need. In Jesus' name, **Amen**.

328 Ecc. 5:4
329 Matt. 20

Integrity does what's right because it's the right thing to do.

"Therefore, COME OUT FROM THEIR MIDST AND BE SEPARATE," says the Lord. "AND DO NOT TOUCH WHAT IS UNCLEAN; and I will welcome you. II Cor 6:17

"I hear voices telling me what to do." We roll our eyes and say, "Yeah, sure" when a TV cop show portrays the perp as a psycho. But don't we all hear voices telling us what to do? The ads bombard us with what to buy, wear, drive, eat, etc. Our friends would have us think and act like they do. The slippery slope of lack of integrity can start very small—a "white" lie, a tablet from work that finds its way home, a ding in the car next to us in the parking lot with no note from us—all while hearing, "It's OK; it's so little. Don't worry about it."

But what does the voice of God have to say? "Come out…be separate…do not touch." What part of that sounds like "It's OK?" Belonging to something is innate in all of us. We join sports teams, service clubs, churches. Why? Because God created us for fellowship. When we find that with Him, then "It's OK." But, let's face it, we don't like loneliness. We hate to be the last one picked, the odd man out. The PC crowd hasn't hit on the cruelty of musical chairs yet. But it's coming.

How many Biblical characters can you think of who had to take a stand for what God had told them? And do it alone? Here are just a few: Noah, Moses, Joseph, Daniel, Elijah, Jeremiah, John the Baptist, Paul. I'm sure you have your favorites that I didn't list. But you get the point. These men are considered giants of the faith because following God was more important than popularity.

We've all heard, "You've got to go along to get along." My question is, "Why do we want to 'get along' with people whose opinions and lives don't point me to Christ?" God tells us to separate ourselves from the world. Maybe our different lifestyle is just what our neighbor, our co-worker, our spouse needs to come to Christ. Don't focus on what you'll be missing by separating from the world; think about what God has promised: "I will welcome you."

Father, it's only hard to separate myself from the world because I am not focused on You and what You have commanded. Today, bring me back to being "You-centered" so the world's allure fades out of view. In Jesus' name, **Amen**.

Integrity repays others before it indulges itself.

"Owe nothing to anyone except to love one another; for he who loves his neighbor has fulfilled the law." Rom. 13:8

It seems that bankruptcy no longer carries the stigma it once did. Back in the day, men did whatever it took to repay someone's trust in them. But we've heard the commercials for debt elimination companies touting savings of up to 75%. The IRS has programs of a similar nature.

But what of the man of God? Does our word have value? Do we enter agreements thinking in the back of our mind that if it doesn't work, we can always declare BK? Obviously, low credit scores for late pays or collections don't scare us like they once did.

And how about the guy who can't say no to his own desires regarding spending? His club membership, the generous business lunches to impress clients and friends, the credit cards to keep his wife in the latest, all take precedent over repaying outstanding debt. Why? Because if I say no to myself, I might have to explain why I can't play golf with you or go on that fishing trip. My pride is at stake, and I'll protect it no matter what. Beware! God is watching.

And know this: our character is more important to God (and should be to us) than protecting our deadly pride. He will not allow anything to get in His way of molding us into the image of His Son. If you have gotten into a hole with your creditors, stop spending. Deny yourself and take care of your obligations.

We learned Monday how God feels about making promises (to pay) that we don't keep. You don't want to be labeled "fool" by God. Pay what you owe. You'll be relieved of a great burden. God doesn't ever want us to be in debt to others.[330] Why? Because *the borrower becomes the lender's slave.*[331] If we are a slave to debt, we can't be a slave to Christ. It becomes an idol. Commit in your heart before God to repay every dime. Start today.

Father, You have made it clear what you think of those who don't pay what they vow. Your reputation is on the line when I selfishly spend on myself before repaying those who have invested in me. Forgive me. I commit to You today to work out a payment plan that makes my creditors whole before I buy anything more for myself. Thank You for meeting all my needs today and every day. In Jesus' name, **Amen**.

330 Rom. 13:8
331 Prov. 22:7

Integrity includes Intellectual Honesty.

"And you will know the truth and the truth will set you free." John 8:32

In a recent opinion piece in my local newspaper, a "Dr. F" wrote about intellectual integrity in connection with evolution. He called evolution "the first scientific and testable explanation of ... life on earth." Later in the article, he called creationism and intelligent design "wishful thinking."

Now, I'm not a scientist. But I do know that true science never contradicts the Bible. If the "flat earth" folks knew their Old Testament ("*...He inscribed a circle on the face of the deep*," Prov.8:27), they wouldn't have been afraid to sail beyond the horizon.

Real science includes the pillars of observability and repeatability, neither of which applies to evolution. Integrity has an open mind to truth, and all truth is God's truth. Jesus said, "*I am the way and the truth and the life...*"[332] We shouldn't be so dogmatic that we are not open to new ideas even if they conflict with long-held beliefs. The key is to filter everything through the lens of scripture. The Bible was true when it was written, and it's still true today. God *cannot* lie; it's not in His character. And that's why we can stake our eternal future on God's revealed truth: the Bible.

Knowing the truth will set us free from what? Wrong beliefs, wrong decisions, wrong companions. But we have to *know* the truth. Psalm 1 tells us the man who "meditates day and night"[333] will be blessed. My prayer for us today is that God would grant us a new love for His Word and, through that, a new love for Him.[334]

Father, the world around us constantly bombards us with false claims, many purportedly backed by science. Open our eyes to know Your truth and to make it so much a part of our lives that we cannot be led astray. Give us boldness to stand for the truth You have revealed to us in Your Son, Jesus. In His name, **Amen.**

(Author's note: Read and study Psalm 119 for an amazing perspective on God's Word.)

332 John 14:6
333 Psalm 1:1, 2
334 Psalm 119:38

Integrity never weighs your thumb.

"A just balance and scales belong to the Lord; all the weights of the bag are His concern." Prov. 16:11

When butcher shops were more common, it was a frequent practice of unscrupulous butchers to press down on the scale with their thumb, thus charging more than they should have. Proverbs tells us that God is concerned with fair trade practices. Are we? Do our customers get what they think they're getting, at the agreed-upon price? Have you ever sold a car to a private party and not disclosed that nagging engine noise? God saw it.

When my kids were little, I made it clear that punishment for their crimes would be much more severe if they lied about it. Think about that. Why do we remember Ananias and Sapphira?[335] They lied to the Holy Spirit. OK, that was pretty dumb...and they paid immediately with their lives.

But do we lie to God by our deceitful behavior? And just because God doesn't immediately mete out punishment, we're emboldened to think we've gotten away with it. Brothers, do not be deceived.[336] God is patient,[337] waiting for us to come to our senses[338] and return to Him in humility and repentance.

When we name the name of Christ, others—often unseen and unbeknownst to us—are watching everything we do. They may not say anything directly to us, but you can bet they'll pass along any juicy tidbit that reflects negatively on you and on the God you claim to serve. If we understand that God is watching us, not to catch us doing wrong, but to lovingly protect and guide us,[339] we'll live out our integrity so others will see.

From this platform, we earn the right to talk to them about Christ. How embarrassing to share God's love in Christ with someone only to have them question our integrity because of something they've heard. Focus on Christ and His righteousness, and God will take care of everything you need.[340]

Father, with the economy pressing me on all sides, I'm tempted to weigh my thumb at times. I know this doesn't honor You or strengthen my testimony of Christ. Allow my faith in You to be such that I never embarrass You by cutting corners. In Jesus' name, **Amen**.

335 Acts 5:1-11
336 Gal. 6:7
337 II Pet. 3:9
338 Luke 15:17
339 Psalm 32:8
340 Matt. 6:33

Integrity is recognized by all, even our enemies.

"Let your light shine before men in such a way that they may see your good works, and glorify your Father who is in heaven." Matt. 5:16

It's been said that if you don't stand for something, you'll fall for anything. What are *you* standing for today? Is there anything for which you are willing to be mocked, persecuted, killed?

Remember when Jesus was on trial, they couldn't find anything to charge Him with, so they had to trump up charges.[341] I dare say that for most of us, finding something that we're not proud of wouldn't take too long. And, we're not usually aware of it, but our neighbors, co-workers, fellow church members could likely add fuel to that fire.

We are watched and people form opinions. What will the books[342] reveal about our lives? How do you decide what's important and what's not? What are you willing to support emotionally, financially, physically, even if it costs you materially? Here's a good rule of thumb: be determined in your ***principles*** but defer to others for ***preferences***.

Why is it most of us don't like politicians? Because many politicians can be swayed by public opinion. They want to be liked, to be popular, to get re-elected. "Tell 'em what they want to hear" is a familiar mantra in Washington. But you, brothers, are to live differently. The Bible is unambiguous in so many areas. There's no gray area with God.[343] Our words and actions reveal our character.[344]

Decide what principles you will not back down from; make sure they stem from a desire for righteousness in your life and sphere of influence. Your integrity will automatically be a beacon for others to follow.

Lord, You modeled the epitome of integrity and were killed for it. Help me today and each day to move closer to Your example so that when You open the books of my life, I won't be ashamed. In Christ's name, **Amen**.

341 Matt. 26:59
342 Rev. 20:12
343 Matt. 12:30
344 Matt. 12:33-37

Joy comes from knowing our eternal destination.

"Nevertheless do not rejoice in this, that the spirits are subject to you, but rejoice that your names are recorded in heaven." Luke 10:20

Choices. Life is full of them. We make literally hundreds every day...some are conscious, many are not. But one choice that we who know Christ as our savior can make with utmost confidence is to allow joy to penetrate and permeate our lives. Is there a difference between joy and happiness? One is fleeting, one is eternal.[345] One is based largely on circumstances, one is a choice. Happiness is a new puppy. Joy is what you get when he's old and just wants to be with you.

But, you ask, "How can I choose joy in *my* circumstances? You don't understand how bad I have it." I would challenge you that your focus is off. It's on yourself, not on Christ. Let me ask you this. Is God trustworthy? Hasn't He said that He wouldn't give us more than we can handle?[346] Hasn't He said, "I will never desert you nor forsake you?"[347] Hasn't He said, "Cast all your cares on me?"[348] Has He changed His mind? No.

It's the world that pulls us away and down. And who is the ruler of this world?[349] The enemy of our souls: Satan. I am no stranger to the difficulties of this life. But I have learned one thing. Our enemy lies. Why does that surprise us? More importantly, why do we succumb to those lies? Because they appeal to our pride. Just like in the garden when that snake told Eve she could be like God. He hasn't changed his strategy because it still works. So my encouragement to those of us who struggle with lack of joy is this: Read the end of the Bible...we win!

Father, when my focus is on Your Son and what He did for me at the cross, my troubles pale in comparison. Help me today to keep my focus on Him and allow the joy of my salvation to fill me to overflowing. In His name, **Amen**.

345 Psa. 16:11
346 I Cor. 10:13
347 Heb. 13:5
348 I Pet. 5:7
349 John 16:11

Joy comes from focusing on solutions, not problems.

"And He said 'Come!' And Peter got out of the boat, and walked on the water and came toward Jesus. But seeing the wind, he became frightened, and beginning to sink, he cried out, 'Lord save me!'" Matt. 14:29, 30

Can you put yourself in Peter's sandals and imagine his feeling when he got out of that boat? What elation. What joy. But it was short-lived because he changed his focus. He took his eyes off Christ. We often criticize Peter for his lack of faith. But how many of the other disciples left their deck chair? Would we have had the courage to do what he did?

This example is a lesson in focusing. On one hand, if we focus on Peter's failure, he's a slouch. On the other hand, and with a different focus, he's a leader, a trailblazer, a one-of-a-kind. I'm encouraged that even with Peter's impetuousness, he was still a member of Jesus' inner circle.[350]

So how do we learn from Peter? I submit we can learn much from Peter's devotion to Jesus. Yes, he had to be reprimanded on a number of occasions. And yes, he was ashamed and denied Christ. And maybe he wasn't the brightest bulb in the box. But where were the other disciples at Jesus' mock trial? Who else tried to defend Jesus in the garden? Peter's close relationship with Christ gives me great hope because I have been known to need a reprimand or two from my Savior.

But guess what? He always disciplines in love.[351] We've talked a lot about focus. It's really the core of our walk of faith. Paul says it perfectly in his letter to the Philippians. "*More than that, I count all things to be loss in view of the surpassing value of knowing Christ Jesus my Lord, for whom I have suffered the loss of all things, and count them but rubbish so that I may gain Christ...I press on toward the goal for the prize of the upward call of God in Christ Jesus.*"[352] May we be so focused in our walk that the glitter, so tempting, fades into "rubbish" as we become single-minded in following Christ.

Father, Your Word speaks so clearly as to the path You want us to follow. But the world screams at us to turn aside. Keep our focus on the long-range goal of heaven, and don't let us get sidetracked along the way. May we respond quickly to Your discipline, so You don't have to get a bigger stick. In Jesus' name, **Amen**.

350 Matt. 17:1
351 Heb. 12:6
352 Phil. 3:8, 14

Joy is what's left when the tears are done.

"For His anger is but for a moment, His favor is for a lifetime; weeping may last for the night, but a shout of joy comes in the morning." Psa. 30:5

Is there any better feeling than having the sun break through after a dark stormy downpour? The clean air, the vivid colors both remind us that the best is yet to come. Remember when you sat around the table for a family dinner and mom, as she cleared the dishes, said, "Keep your fork." You knew the best—dessert—was yet to come.

That's how it is in the Christian walk. The best is yet to come. Christ has prepared a home in heaven for those who follow Him.[353] And it will be spectacular.[354] What we must face in the meantime is that life will have challenges. Jesus said, *"In the world you will have tribulation..."*[355] He didn't say we ***might*** have tribulation; we can count on it. But, fortunately, He didn't stop there. In the same sentence, He also said, *"...but take courage, I have overcome the world."*

God reiterates His promise that in heaven, He will "wipe away every tear...no mourning, no crying, no pain."[356] In light of our future, can we be anything less than joyful? Think back to our discussion on Sunday. Joy is not dependent on circumstances. Two Christian brothers met on a Sunday morning. One asked the other, "How are you?" The other answered, "Not bad, under the circumstances." The first responded, "What are doing *under* the circumstances?"

James reminds us that we are to *"consider it all joy when we encounter various trials."* [357] The only way we can do that is if we keep our focus on Jesus. Try this bit of cornball poetry; it may help. Rejoice: the choice we voice.

Father, again we're faced with a choice to respond to our circumstances with trust in You. Help us remember all Your promises to be with us. Keep our focus on Jesus and our future with Him in heaven. In His name, **Amen**.

353 John 14:2, 3
354 I Cor. 2:9
355 John 16:33
356 Rev. 21:4
357 James 1:2

Joy is introducing your children to Jesus.

"I have no greater joy than this, to hear of my children walking in the truth." 3 Jn. 1:4

We've all seen the statistics: One in two marriages ends in divorce, even in the church. According to government statistics (in 2012), minority kids are born to unwed mothers 72% of the time. There are all kinds of bad statistics about kids growing up in "fatherless" homes. I couldn't find a single statistic about kids who come to know Christ because of their fathers.

But God keeps statistics too. And He loves it when dads teach their kids about Him.[358] We've talked a lot about focus, and I want to suggest that there's no more important result of our focus on Christ than our kids' perception of the role of Christ in our lives. It's been said that faith is "caught" not "taught."

My dad used to tell me, "Don't do as I do. Do as I say." I hated its hypocrisy. When my kids were little, I told them that if they saw me do it, they could. But here's the point. We're talking about joy. Now that my kids are adults and following the Lord, I couldn't have more joy. But, I'm also selfish. I know that God entrusted them to me when they were little and expected me to teach and set the right example. Now I can expect to hear, "Well done."

No matter how old your children, it's never too late to point them to Christ. It may be a harder road if you've led a non-Christlike life and recently come to know Him yourself. But start with asking forgiveness from your children. Don't expect them to immediately change their feelings. Live your faith. Be consistent. God will open doors to speak to them about what happened to you—about *who* changed your life. When He does, share your testimony with them. Remember how long it took you to come to the truth. They will see the radical change that Christ brought in your life and will be drawn to it. I promise.

Lord Jesus, You were so patient with me when I hated You. Help me to pass that along to those I share Your love with, especially my children. Fill me with Your Spirit today that I may walk in a way that pleases You and points others to You. **Amen**.

358 Deut. 6:6, 7

Joy is a choice in the midst of trials.

"Consider it all joy my brethren when you encounter various trials, knowing that the testing of your faith produces endurance." James 1:2, 3

Wouldn't it be nice if, just before we entered a trial, there was a flashing warning sign: "Trial Ahead?" Then we could stop, pray, and be in a spiritual mindset to do what James encourages us to do—welcome it as God's polishing cloth on our character.

But if you're like me, I'm in it (usually pretty far) before I realize that my initial reaction—let me be kind to myself—could have been better. Why? Because I have expectations of circumstances, of others, of *my* rights. And when *I* am violated, *I* have the right to be mad—to lash out. Don't I? All authority resides with God.[359] We may plan our day, but God chooses our paths.[360]

We don't want to be found shaking our fist at God. I did once. I was on leave from the Army, and, as usual, I was doing stupid things (B.C. days). On a rainy trip from Ft. Ord to Los Angeles, I totaled my car but walked away without a scratch. Instead of being thankful that I was OK, I (figuratively) shook my fist at God and asked, "Why me?" It wasn't audible, but it was clear as a bell. God said back to me, "Why not? There are consequences for (stupid) actions."

That was like hitting the mule with a two-by-four to get his attention. Within a few short weeks after that, I surrendered my life to Christ and received forgiveness and eternal life. I tell you this to point out that, as we've been discussing, my focus was totally wrong. I was my own god, and anything that got in my way was fair game. As God's children, He disciplines us because He loves us.[361] Not only does He *allow* trials in our lives, He carefully tailors them to each of us to work on the areas that are still rough.[362]

I'm not through with my trips to the woodshed, and I'm not saying that all discipline is punishment. But, more and more, the trips (for punishment) are getting less, and I'm more receptive to God's "honing" me for His purposes. Today, we can choose to be joyful…or not.

Father, I don't like pain of any kind, and I don't like my agenda interrupted. But I know I'm not where I need to be in my walk with You. Help me to welcome Your course corrections, knowing that Your discipline comes because You love me. In Jesus' name, **Amen**.

359 Rom. 13:1
360 Prov. 16:9
361 Heb. 12:5, 6
362 Job 1:8, 12

Joy in leading someone to Christ should motivate us to be alert to opportunities to share our faith.

"I tell you that in the same way, there will be more joy in heaven over one sinner who repents than over ninety-nine righteous persons who need no repentance." Luke 15:7

Ever been in a new town and needed directions? I know, as men, we don't need no stinkin' directions. Want to see your wife speechless? Next time you're not quite sure of how to get where you want to be, say, "I think I'll stop here and ask for directions."

Sometimes a map is all we need; a tip from a local is even better. Do you realize that most people around you are not on the path to heaven?[363] Do you also realize that you have the *only* map that can point the way? Jesus said, "*I am **the** way...*"[364] There are many excuses we use for not sharing our map—the gospel—with others. "I don't know enough." "The timing isn't good." "He knows of my life before Christ." But they are all excuses. You don't know enough? *"Be diligent..."*[365] The timing isn't right? *"...be ready in season and out of season;"*[366] He knows me from before. *"Therefore, if anyone is in Christ, he is a new creature;"*[367] You fear criticism? *"Do not fear those who kill the body... but rather fear Him who is able to destroy both soul and body in hell."*[368]

Why is it easier for us to come up with a dozen reasons for not witnessing to our Lord Jesus' saving grace than to just do it? Could it be that we're shackled by the world's system or fear of rejection and ashamed of Christ? I encourage you to examine your motives; *"Test yourselves to see if you are in the faith."*[369] Don't be like those who came on the Day of Judgment and said, "*'Lord, Lord, did we not prophesy in Your name...?' And then I [Christ] will declare to them, 'I never knew you, depart from me.'*"[370] Leading someone to Christ fills you with joy knowing that God would use *me* to further His kingdom.

Father, I know I'm full of excuses about not sharing Your love for sinners. Remind me today of what You did for me when I didn't deserve it, and give me eyes to see the need for a Savior in those around me. Then prod me to open my mouth about You. In Jesus' name, **Amen**.

363 Matt. 7:13, 14
364 John 14:6
365 II Tim. 2:15
366 II Tim.4:2
367 II Cor. 5:17
368 Matt. 10:28
369 II Cor. 13:5
370 Matt. 7:22, 23

Joy is trusting God in the dark.

"Restore to me the joy of Your salvation and sustain me with a willing spirit." Psa. 51:12

Are you in a dark place today? Is it over the loss of a loved one, a job, health, guilt from a sin you can't seem to overcome? Loneliness? If you have a personal relationship with the Lord Jesus, you don't need to stay in the dark.

Hear God speak to you: "*I will never desert you or forsake you.*"[371] Can you think of a darker place, physically or emotionally, than the belly of a big fish? Did God abandon Jonah? Was this just some random fish that happened to be swimming by? God had plans for Jonah just as He has plans for you and me; He tells us that in the verse above.

What does it mean to have plans? It means that God has thought about us and has laid out a path for us. Think about that. The God of all creation *thinks* about us. "*I will instruct you and teach you in the way which you should go; I will counsel you with My eye upon you.*"[372] God's "eye" is never off us. "*...God causes all things to work together for good to those who love God,*"[373]

Sometimes in the dark, we try to focus on our surroundings. Doesn't help much, does it? That's our biggest problem in general—we focus on the wrong things. "*Set your mind on things above, not on the things that are on earth.*"[374]

The material world (things that we see, touch, etc.) is passing away. Heaven is just around the corner. Try focusing on what awaits you soon, and the darkness you're experiencing now will fade and be replaced by the blessed hope of our salvation. "*... weeping may last for the night, but a shout of joy comes in the morning.*"[375]

Father, my darkness sometimes seems pitch black to me. Help me remember that there is no place and no circumstance that can hide me from Your caring eye. Today, may I focus on "things above" and not my problems or *my* plans, but remember Your plans for my future and my hope. In Christ's name, **Amen**.

371 Heb. 13:5
372 Psa. 32:8
373 Rom. 8:28
374 Col. 3:2
375 Psa. 30:5

Kindness is speaking the truth in love.

"And do not let kindness and truth leave you; bind them around your neck, write them on the tablet of your heart." Prov. 3:3

Little Johnny was on his way to his first Junior High dance. His mother's words still rang in his ears, "Find something nice to say to each girl you dance with." Jill was quite overweight and not everybody's first choice, but Johnny found himself on the dance floor with her. He tried and tried and finally hit on what he thought was a sure winner. "You don't sweat much for a fat girl" he said.

Needless to say, that's not the spirit of today's thought. Yes, it's a given that what comes out of our mouth should be the truth. But we don't always have to say everything we think. A good filter is to ask myself *why* I would say it; examine my motive first. Am I truly loving the other person, or am I just venting?

Someone has said that the definition of gossip is truth told with an intent to harm. In today's verse, Solomon encourages us to make kindness and truth (notice the pairing) such a part of our being that they become automatic. One of the fruits of the Spirit is kindness.[376] If we find that we're not being kind, we should probably ask ourselves, "How filled with the Spirit am I?"[377]

Paul reminds us that "*...love is kind.*"[378] It's a pretty good barometer that if I'm not being kind, I'm not walking in the Spirit. My flesh constantly tries to pull me back into my former life of doing what I want—what feels good to me.[379] When we notice this in ourselves, or if we're blessed with a godly mate who "helps" us notice, we should immediately confess it and close the gap on our relationship with Christ. Remember, if you're not feeling close to God, it wasn't He who moved.

Lord God, You always deal kindly with me, and I don't deserve it but have come to expect it. Help me today to treat others the same way. In Christ's name, **Amen**.

376 Gal. 5:22
377 Eph. 5:18
378 I Cor. 13:4
379 Rom. 7:19; Gal. 5:16

Kindness: What goes around comes around.

"Will they not go astray who devise evil? But kindness and truth will be to those who devise good." Prov. 14:22

"Do unto others" is not just a fortune cookie saying. It is a *command* from Jesus Himself.[380] Remember the old playground retort when someone called you a name? "I'm rubber, you're glue; whatever you say bounces off me and sticks on you." The world calls it "karma," but God clearly tells us in today's verse that if we want kindness and truth heading our way, we need to "devise good."

What does that mean? It's simply the law of sowing and reaping at work.[381] I'm not much of a green thumb. Truth be told, I detest gardening. But I know one thing. If I want apricots, I have to plant an apricot tree. It's the law.

Does the same law work in the emotional realm too? Think about the people you like to hang with. What makes them attractive? Chances are, they are positive, upbeat, encouraging souls. Do others think of you that way? If you're in a drought (of positive, encouraging people) lately, take a minute and an honest look in the mirror. Are *you* the kind of guy *you* would want to hang around with? You've heard it said, "To have a friend, be a friend." Why not start today?

Father, I observe so many acts of unkindness that I wonder what will happen to civilization. Help me today to be a model of Your kindness to me so that others may be drawn to You and know the ultimate kindness of eternal life with You. In Jesus' name, **Amen**.

---

380 Luke 6:31
381 Gal.6:7

Kindness in me indicates how much I trust God for daily needs.

"Trust in the Lord with all your heart and do not lean on your own understanding. In all your ways acknowledge Him and He will make your paths straight." Prov. 3:5, 6

Growing up and living in America can be intimidating. We're told that we can do and be whatever we want; we have unlimited paths to choose. At some point—younger is better—we find our groove. Although for some of us who didn't plan well, study hard or have extraordinary talent, we kick around here and there hoping somehow to get out of our mire.

This lifestyle can have very negative effects on our outlook. We blame others, our circumstances, and even God. We're bitter, impatient, unkind. But what's the real root of our problems? Isn't it usually that we "lean on our own understanding?"

Bitterness and unkindness are roommates. We're warned in Hebrews not to miss out on the grace of God, not to let a root of bitterness defile us.[382] The visible things about us that people see are the result of what's going on inside us.[383] If we're kind to those who don't deserve it, that's a good indication we're at peace with God on the inside.

The good news is that it doesn't matter where you are on life's path. As long as you still have breath, you can make right decisions. It begins with having a saving relationship with Jesus Christ. Jesus said, "*...no man comes to the Father but through Me.*"[384]

If you already know Christ, ask yourself this, "Am I trusting in the Lord with all my heart and acknowledging Him in all my ways?" If you're not, why would you expect anything but confusion and dead-end paths?

Remember that God, as a loving Father, disciplines those He loves.[385] Things may not change dramatically overnight, but the peace of God will overwhelm you[386] and external pressures will fade. Don't let anything delay choosing the straight path. "The way of the lazy is as a hedge of thorns, but the path of the upright is a highway." (Prov. 15:19)

Lord, I desire to be on Your highway. I'm tired of the roadblocks and potholes on the paths I've chosen. Today, grant me the humility to acknowledge You in everything and lead me to the straight path. In Christ's name, **Amen**

382 Heb. 12:15
383 Matt. 12:34
384 John 14:6
385 Heb. 12:6
386 Phil. 4:4-7

Kindness from God leads us to repentance; what will kindness from us do for others?

"Or do you think lightly of the riches of His kindness and tolerance and patience, not knowing that the kindness of God leads you to repentance?"
Rom. 2:4

Has anyone ever told you, "I can't hear what you're saying, your actions are screaming too loudly?" How about this one, "Put your money where your mouth is?" People don't take us seriously if our actions don't line up with our words.

Since man's fall in the Garden, our existence has been filled with heartache, pain, and sorrow mixed with an occasional glimpse of happiness. "Life is tough and then you die" just about sums it up. Or how about this word picture? Life is like licking honey from a thorn. Given that this pretty well describes life under the curse for most of us, think about the last time someone showed you a little kindness. It might have been as simple as another driver letting you into his lane. Or a "thinking of you" card from a friend in another state. Whatever it was, can you remember how good you felt?

What does it take to act with kindness instead of anger, putting someone else first? It starts with a *decision* to do it. Put yourself into the story of the two slaves; one owed his master ten thousand talents.[387] The second slave owed the first slave about three months' wages.[388] You know the story. The first slave received mercy and undeserved kindness, then turned around and threw his fellow slave into prison.

Obviously, the story has salvation ramifications vis-à-vis the debt of sin we owe but cannot pay. But for our purposes, you can see what was in the heart of the first slave by his…wait for it…actions. Do you know people like that? You can't believe what they say because their actions belie the contents of their heart. You can only exhibit kindness if you have experienced it and have a desire to reach others for the kingdom.

Lord God, I know that what I deserve from you are Your wrath and eternal condemnation. Thank You for including me in Your kindness. May I remember that when I'm tempted to be unkind to my fellow pilgrims and let Your kindness overflow through me. In Jesus' name, **Amen**.

387 Matt. 18:24 A talent was worth more than 15 years' wages; i.e. an incomprehensible amount of money.
388 Matt. 18:28

Kindness is evangelism's magnet pulling others to Christ.

"Let us not lose heart in doing good, for in due time we will reap if we do not grow weary." Gal. 6:9

Discouragement—losing heart—can be a symptom of wrong expectations. When we are kind or give a gift or offer a service to someone and they don't respond like we think they should, often, disappointment rears its head. That ought to raise a red flag that our motive wasn't pure.

If we can move through life sacrificially and keep doing it though we aren't appreciated or rewarded, we lay up treasures in heaven.[389] This is but another example of our focus being on me rather than on serving Christ. Remember what Paul said to the Corinthians, "*neither the one who plants or the one who waters is anything, but God who causes the growth.*"[390]

What role does the farmer have in the success or failure of his crop? Obviously, he could plant it wrong or water too much or too little, but he has absolutely nothing to do with whether it's one or one hundred bushels per acre.

In our thinking about kindness, it must become a way of life for us—regardless of the response. Can we trust God for the outcome? When we're in the battle for souls, others watch to see if we really believe what we say. What a tragedy to "put on kindness" when we are sharing the gospel and take it off when (we think) nobody's looking.

What quality do you think is at the heart of a person who is described as having a magnetic personality? You wouldn't describe an arrogant or egotistical person that way. No, it's the irresistible draw of kindness. Yesterday's verse (Rom. 2:4) confirms that kindness "leads" us to repentance. Don't give up. The war is (usually) not won in the first skirmish. And yes, there may be casualties. But wouldn't you rather meet Christ doing what He has ordered us to do? He has promised that "in due time," we will reap…if we don't quit.

Father, I'm out of shape for a long battle. I get discouraged so easily. Strengthen me today to focus on the goal of making disciples and leave the results to You. In Christ's name, **Amen**.

389 Matt. 6:20
390 I Cor. 3:7

Kindness is more difficult for the rich.

"What is desirable in a man is his kindness, and it is better to be a poor man than a liar." Prov. 19:22

It is more desirable to be a poor but kind man than a rich liar.[391] Today's thought is simple but profound. Kindness is the outward display of a grateful spirit. How many rich folks do you know who glow in gratitude? Of course, there are some, and often you don't even know they're rich. But the general rule is the opposite. Rich folks believe they deserve what they have—that they've earned it.

Jesus has much to say about the pitfalls of loving money. Notice the word loving. Money is not evil in itself. It only becomes evil when we idolize it. Hear Paul's warning to Timothy: "*But realize this, that in the last days difficult times will come. For men will be lovers of self, lovers of money, boastful, arrogant, revilers, disobedient to parents, ungrateful, unholy, unloving, irreconcilable, malicious gossips, without self-control, brutal, haters of good, treacherous, reckless, conceited, lovers of pleasure rather than lovers of God, holding to a form of godliness, although they have denied its power; Avoid such men as these.*" [392]

Pay attention. Paul doesn't say difficult times *may* come; he says they will come. Jesus said the same thing, "*These things I have spoken to you, so that in Me you may have peace. In the world, you have tribulation, but take courage, I have overcome the world.*"[393]

Kindness grows out of gratitude. Gratitude grows when we have the right focus…on Christ. Try this the next time you're planning a pity party. Take out a pencil and paper and begin listing the things for which you are grateful. There should literally be hundreds you can think of. Before you get too many, your dark cloud of despair should be gone. This book's focus is "Christ in Men." Beware that you don't become one of those in Paul's list above. How can you share the love of Christ that's dwelling in you if are avoided because of your lifestyle?

Jesus, it seems clear from looking at society, that we are living in the days Paul talked about. Forgive me for my pride which motivates much of what I do and help me focus on You and the path You have laid out for me. May my gratitude to You become kindness to others. **Amen**.

391 Commentary note in The MacArthur Study Bible; © 2006 by Thomas Nelson, Inc.
392 II Tim. 3:1-5
393 John 16:33

Kindness is found in Spirit-filled believers.

"The fruit of the Spirit is...kindness" Gal. 5:22

Kindness does not hold grudges. The Lord reminds us, "*Vengeance is mine.*"[394] His Word also tells us, "*But I say, walk by the spirit, and you will not carry out the desire of the flesh.*"[395] When we walk by the spirit (of Christ), our focus is on how to please our commanding officer. It's not on how little comfort or respect or wealth we have. Plotting revenge feeds the monster called bitterness. Bitterness only hurts us. God warns us, *"See to it that no one comes short of the grace of God; that no root of bitterness springing up causes trouble, and by it many be defiled."*[396]

Sometimes the best way to define a word is to look at its opposite meaning. One antonym I think of for kindness is selfishness, self-centeredness. Doesn't an act of kindness require us to do something for someone else? If we're thinking of the welfare of another, we aren't dwelling on our own problems. Jesus told us, "*...your heavenly Father knows that you need all these things. But seek first His kingdom and His righteousness and all these things will be added to you.*"[397]

You know that two things cannot occupy the same space. Likewise, we cannot have two simultaneous thoughts. Paul told the Galatians that walking by the spirit automatically keeps us from carrying out our fleshly desires.

So, it always comes down to focus. What's on your mind today? Is it all the petty grievances the world hurls at us? Or is it the undeserved grace and mercy so freely given by our heavenly Father that should drive us to a life filled with gratitude and kindness? If your daily activities don't display kindness, it may be time to check your spiritual dipstick.

Father, I know that kindness is a barometer that directly links to my gratitude to You for all You do for me. Forgive me for taking Your goodness for granted and thinking I deserve anything. May Your glory be seen in me today through my kindness. In Jesus' name, **Amen**.

394 Deut. 32:35
395 Gal. 5:16
396 Heb. 12:15
397 Matt. 6:32b, 33

Leadership encourages from the front, doesn't push from behind.

"But go now, lead the people where I told you." Ezek.32:34

In the Army, we had a saying, "Lead, follow or get out of the way." Leadership implies many things. It implies you know what you're doing or where you're going. It implies, if you're not the boss, that you're following orders. It implies that you're "qualified" to lead.

An interesting thing about leadership; it also implies that you're a good follower. Let's face it. None of us is the ultimate authority in our sphere of influence. We may be the owner of the company—we have shareholders or investors. We may be a military commander—there's always someone who outranks us.

Ever thought that leadership implies trustworthiness? Who wants to follow a leader that you can't trust? The Bible is full of stories of the men God chose to be leaders. Can you think of one that started out already prominent? Moses? David? Joseph? Daniel? The 12? Leadership is largely a matter of the heart. Think about the great leaders in the Bible. What was the one common thread among them? Wasn't it their utter devotion and commitment to the God who called them?

Think about the years that Joseph spent in prison before God elevated him. Reminds me of Peter: "*Therefore, humble yourselves under the mighty hand of God, that He may exalt you at the proper time.*"[398]

You may not have been called to lead thousands or hundreds or even tens. But you have been called to lead your family. The first question to ask yourself is, "Whom am I following, and where do I get my marching orders?" If you've come this far in this book, your desire is probably to serve well under "the mighty hand of God." It's never too late to grow into the leader God has called you to be.

There's a four-step plan God has outlined: "*Be alert; stand firm; act like men; be strong.*"[399] "*If you have been foolish in exalting yourself or if you have plotted evil, put your hand on your mouth.*"[400] Stop! Be quiet. Turn around and listen for God's soft prompting…leading you in the way of understanding.[401]

Father, sometimes I feel so inadequate to lead myself, let alone others. Open my eyes to the role You have called me to and grant me wisdom to follow the light of Your Word. In Christ's name, **Amen**.

398 I Pet. 5:6
399 I Cor. 16:13
400 Prov. 30:32
401 Prov. 9:6

Leadership assumes responsibility for those it leads.

"What man among you, if he has a hundred sheep and has lost one of them, does not leave the ninety-nine in the open pasture and go after the one which is lost until he finds it?" Luke 15:4

It's been bandied about that during the Vietnam war, the life expectancy of a second lieutenant was only minutes. First of all, that's pure bunk—never supported with hard data. But it raises an interesting point for our discussion on leadership. What makes you want to follow somebody? Isn't part of it that they've "been there, done that, got the tee-shirt"?

What have you done with the faith God gave you that would make others want to follow you? Paul told the Corinthians, "*Be imitators of me, just as I also am of Christ.*"[402] Who are we imitating—the Christ of the Bible or a watered-down version of our own creation? Are we sensitive to the needs of those we lead, or do we have a "get over it" attitude with them?

In our verse above, Jesus uses sheep to make His point. Sheep are some of the dumbest creatures on earth. But we're so much like them. We'd rather follow the crowd than blaze a trail. Did you ever notice that when God wanted something done, He never appointed a committee?

Today, take time to listen in a fresh way to see if God is calling you to a leadership role. Look around our society. Young people emulate the antics and attitudes of rock stars or sports stars. How many of them are worth following? But the reason is clear. We, as parents and social leaders (teachers, politicians, etc.), have abdicated our leadership role. Electronic baby-sitters permeate our young people's minds and activities.

Where are the standards that "everybody knew" from years gone by? Don't throw up your hands and complain, "What can I do?" Draw a three-foot circle on the ground. Step into it. Now pray that God would send a revival inside that circle.

Lord, as I look at society, I fear we're too far down the slippery slope to ever come back. Forgive me for looking the other way and expecting someone else to carry the ball of leadership. Show me the things in my life that make me lethargic, no, make that lazy, and give me the desire and strength to focus on the cross and take up my armor and get dressed for battle. In Jesus' army and in His name, **Amen**.

402 I Cor.11:1

Leadership does what is right(eous) regardless of how lonely it gets.

"Those who have insight will shine brightly like the brightness of the expanse of heaven, and those who lead the many to righteousness, like the stars forever and ever." Dan. 12:3

In April 1521, Martin Luther is quoted as saying (at the Diet of Worms), "I do not accept the authority of popes and councils, for they have contradicted each other—my conscience is captive to the Word of God...God help me! Here I stand." Oh, that we had leaders in our political system, our churches, our homes that had that kind of commitment today.

Are you one of those whom God's eyes are moving to and fro throughout the earth that He might strongly support?[403] Wouldn't that be great, knowing that God had your six? You can. You just have to meet the one qualification: Your heart has to be completely His.

We have so many things pulling us away from that kind of devotion: jobs, families, leisure, friends, good activities. None of these is bad in and of itself. But it's been said that the good gets in the way of the best. You've also heard, "It's lonely at the top." Many of us, I fear, can't handle the loneliness. We want the affirmation of others when what we should be looking for is the affirmation of our heavenly Father. Really, who cares what others think of us?

Isn't the only measurement that counts what God thinks of us? Don't take that wrong and assume a license to be rude or arrogant. We still must be a fragrant aroma[404] to those around us that we not hinder any on their journey to find Christ.

I encourage you today to evaluate your standards. Have you built them on the rock of God's Word, or are they piled precariously on the sands of current opinions and political correctness? As Joshua said in his farewell speech to Israel, "*...choose this day whom you will serve...as for me and my house, we will serve the Lord.*"[405]

Gracious God, You are so patient with me when I fear man's opinion and ridicule instead of fearing You and walking in righteousness. Forgive me and restore me to a close walk with You that others may see Jesus in me and be drawn to Him. In His name, **Amen**.

403 II Chron. 16:9
404 Eph. 5:2
405 Josh. 24:15

Leadership points the way clearly.

"Remember those who led you, who spoke the word of God to you; and considering the result of their conduct, imitate their faith." Heb. 13:7

Have you ever played for a coach that didn't seem to have any kind of game plan? It reminds me of play calling in sandlot football, "everybody go long." Or have you worked for a boss that didn't have a clear mission statement? If you don't know where you're going, any road will get you there.

We probably take it for granted, but the highway system in America is a marvel to behold. We can get on the interstate and go all the way across this land without a map. It's because the road is so well marked.

As leaders, we need to "mark our road" so those who follow us know our destination. Sadly, the Christian church is lacking Biblical direction today. We pander to the "seekers" through rock concert-type worship, watered-down messages that won't offend anyone, and "big tent" style tolerance.

Do you know that Satan is not stupid? If he marked the path to hell with neon lights that actually said "hell," how many followers do you think he'd have? No, he marks it "heaven" and then throws around a few "Christian-sounding" words and uses man's ego to suck us into his trap.

We lack discernment because we don't meditate on the only truth available to us: God's Word. If it feels good—do it. A pop song has a lyric that says, "It can't be wrong when it feels so right."[406]

Generally, the heart is associated with feelings. What does the Bible say about the heart? "*…it is more deceitful than all else and is desperately sick; who can understand it?*"[407] Men, we have to be more discerning about where we find our standards. Who are we going to believe: pop culture which changes with the wind, or God's eternal Word?[408]

Remember in Sunday's message, God commands us to "be alert." It's when we're lulled into complacency that Satan's wiles find their mark. Make sure your "road map" is firmly anchored in the only thing that will survive now and into eternity: God's Word.

Father, I'm so grateful for the unwavering truth of Your word. It's the only source of pure truth on earth. Increase my desire to read, meditate on, and memorize this precious gift so my sword[409] will be sharp for the battle that is coming. In the name of Him who is "the truth," **Amen**.

---

406 Debbie Boone, *You Light Up My Life*
407 Jer. 17:9
408 Matt. 24:35
409 Eph. 6:17

Week 25 – Thursday

Leadership gives credit to the team.

"Let another praise you and not your own mouth; a stranger, and not your own lips." Prov. 27:2

It's been said that you'll get more done if you don't care who gets the credit. Good leaders always make sure their team stands in the spotlight instead of themselves. This is an area where pride is constantly lurking to pounce. "It was my idea; why should I give credit to Bob?" "I was the one who ran 65 yards so Bob could score from the 1-yard line, but Bob gets all the glory. It's just not fair."

Most of us know who Helen Keller is, but how many of us know the story of Anne Sullivan? Where would Keller be without the tireless and unselfish mentoring and friendship given to her by Sullivan? Not many of us, statistically speaking, can be in the spotlight. But every one of us can heroically support and encourage those who are.

When was the last time you called your pastor and said, "Your sermon last week really spoke to me"? Or how about a former neighbor, "Just called to say I miss our friendship"? Or a former boss who taught you a skill to move you up your career path? The list is endless. How often do we tell our wives that we are better men because of them?

But first, we have to "humble yourself"[410] so we can honestly see the value others have deposited into our lives. Pride is so insidious because it "feels" natural. Confidence without arrogance is warm and draws people to us. It gives us a platform from which to share our Savior. Think about it. When was the last time you wanted to hang with someone who was self-centered, egotistical, and thought himself above all?

The Bible tells us "*not to think more highly of (ourselves) than (we) ought to think, but to think so as to have sound judgment.*"[411] The implication is that with sound judgment, we won't "lie" to ourselves. We won't sugarcoat it.

Scripture often reminds us to wait for God's timing to be elevated to the favored seat at the table[412] or the job we've always wanted.[413] God sometimes seems slow[414] according to our timetable. He isn't. And He's never late. Pride is the enemy of trust. Learn to relax in your Father's arms and watch Him work on your behalf.

Lord, slow me down and let me hear Your voice. In Jesus' name, **Amen**.

410 I Pet. 5:6
411 Rom. 12:3
412 Prov. 25:6, 7
413 Gen.41:40:43
414 II Pet. 3:9

Leadership must be ready for opposition.

"The whole congregation of the sons of Israel grumbled against Moses and Aaron in the wilderness." Exodus 16:2

It's one thing to lead a group with a small dissenting faction. But picture yourself in Moses' sandals. The "whole congregation" (estimated at over 2 million) thought he was wrong. Wow. There is a little maxim I try to live by: principle trumps preference. There is much wisdom in those three words. A man of principle—a man of integrity—will make decisions based on principles. However, if principles are not at stake, then he may defer to preferences, specifically other people's preferences.

Imagine standing alone against a mob of 2 million. You'd better be pretty sure of your calling and direction. Moses was. He had spoken to God one on one. Are we sure enough of our direction, based on our time with God in His Word and prayer, that we could stand against opposing opinions? How about from our wives, our co-workers, our fellow church members? Implied in this maxim is the assumption that we have principles. And this is the point for today. What principles guide your decision making, your daily living?

Hopefully, they have their roots in the two-fold summary of all commandments: Love God, love your neighbor.[415] A word of caution is in order. Pride is lurking. When we think we're right, even if we *know* that we're right, we must not think of ourselves as better than those who disagree with us.

Remember that everything we have has been given to us,[416] including our understanding of God's truth. A good leader will patiently and gently persuade others to His (God's) point of view. There will not be hostility, emotional outbursts, or withdrawal. Most people in Jesus' day didn't like His message either. And it eventually led to the cross. But it didn't deter Him from His mission. Thanks be to God for that. He couldn't depart from His message because He knew it was true.

That's our challenge today. When we take our stand, let's make sure it's for Biblical principle and not just our own preference.

Lord God, it's so easy for me to confuse my preferences with Your principles. I ask for wisdom to keep them separate, strength to stand alone when principle is at stake and greater understanding of Your Word that I may have confidence to represent You. Thank You for trusting me with the treasure of Your Word. In Jesus' name, **Amen**.

415 Mark 12:30, 31
416 I Cor. 4:7

Leadership must be accompanied by humility.

"He has told you, O man, what is good; and what does the Lord require of you but to do justice, to love kindness, and to walk humbly with your God."
Micah 6:8

It's easy to believe our own press—good things others say about us—and get puffed up. What God thinks about that can be found in Daniel 4 where the king allowed himself to think that he had built Babylon the great.[417] He forgot his earlier dream and Daniel's interpretation. Verse 31 says, "*While the word was in the king's mouth…*"

God hates pride,[418] especially in those in authority (all authority is from God.)[419] It evokes God's judgment. If you lead others, even if it's just your family, you must take God seriously when it comes to "walking humbly with Him." Really, what do you have to offer those you lead that God didn't bless you with?[420] So when you take credit for what God does, look out. God will not share His glory.[421]

Thirty years ago, I found myself in a position of prominence and authority. I was a marketing executive in a large company. We were on a management retreat in the mountains of Colorado, and I had let my position go to my head. One night at the retreat, my wife had seen the symptoms and was trying to warn me. I still remember my foolish response, "I don't need God." Move over, here comes the lightning.

I wish I could say that the consequences were no big deal. They were. I lost my job and had to sell my house. Like Nebuchadnezzar, I repented and came back to God. It took years before God allowed me enough resources to buy another house. I never did rise to the same level in corporate America. Through it all, my faithful wife never gave up on me.

When God says something in His Word, He means it. There are many promises for those of us who are His children. But there are also warnings. Don't think God won't act just because He doesn't immediately zap us.[422] Take the warnings seriously. The Bible is filled with examples of how God worked in the lives of people to accomplish His will. Don't be one of the examples of not heeding His warnings.

Father, give me grace to believe You for both the good and the warnings. In Christ's name, **Amen**.

417 Dan. 4:30
418 Prov. 6:16, 17
419 Rom. 13:1
420 I Cor. 4:7
421 Isa. 42:8
422 II Pet. 3:9

Loving...Puts others ahead of ourselves

"Do nothing from selfishness or empty conceit, but with humility of mind regard one another as more important than yourselves; do not merely look out for your own personal interests, but also for the interests of others."
Phil. 2:3, 4

What greater example of putting others ahead of ourselves could we have than what Jesus said, "*Greater love has no one than this that one lay down his life for his friends.*"[423] This thought flows well with yesterday's word on humble leadership. Soldiers—brothers in arms—know the meaning of this literally.

But I don't think Jesus was asking His disciples to actually die for Him. Death can be easy compared to a life of humble service, one in which we perhaps don't get the recognition we crave or the credit for what we've done goes to someone else.

I think Jesus was talking about being a servant—a bond slave—to Him. Notice Paul doesn't say others *are* more important than we, but if we *regard* them in that way, we will treat them in the manner God intends. Think about your preparation to meet an important person, say the President of the United States. That's the mindset God wants us to have with others. Sound easy? What about when someone takes "your" space on the freeway? Or when you've come up with a money-saving idea at work and your boss takes credit? Hmmm?

Did you know that love is a choice and not a warm, fuzzy feeling? How else can you explain parental love for a disabled child or a missionary's love for a lost tribe? Many of the things God calls us to do involve choices—and sacrifices—to reach the goal. In today's thought, love must replace selfishness. We have to be outwardly focused, not have a "but what about me" fixation. Choose wisely.

Lord, sometimes the things You ask me to do seem impossible. Then I remember Your Spirit empowers me to do all that You command. Today, may I have an outward focus and not be worried about who gets the credit. In my Savior's name, **Amen**.

423 Jn 15:13

Loving…Is more important than being right.

"Beware of practicing your righteousness before men to be noticed by them; otherwise you have no reward with your Father who is in heaven." Matt. 6:2

What's the good of being right if nobody knows about it? Isn't that the thinking of most of us? When was the last time you let your wife win a discussion (when you *knew* you were right) to avoid it escalating into an argument? I'm seeing a common thread between loving and humility. We are, by nature, selfish beings. We want what we want when we want it. And woe to any who stand in the way.

Am I hitting close to home for some of us? How do you think *I* know about this? Because I've been there…and not that long ago. I venture to say most of us believe we're right in what we think and say. (That goes for our wives too.) So it's natural to defend our position. And we absolutely should when it comes to defending God's truth. But, really, how often are we in that situation? Isn't it more likely we argue for our political persuasion or which car is better or just about anything else we "feel" strongly about?

Peter tells us to "*live with our wives in an understanding way…and show her honor…so that your prayers will not be hindered.*"[424] As we saw yesterday, it's a matter of focus. Our wives need to both see and hear that we love them. Words and actions. How do we show love if we're willing to fight at the drop of a hat to "prove" a point? Do you think you're really proving anything? If you're right, others will eventually see it and come around to your way of thinking. Again, our natural tendency would be to say, "See, I told you so." Don't! Trust God to watch out for your reputation. Trust Him to give you just enough credit that it doesn't go to your head. Love your wife…period. You'll find that quietly knowing you're right is all you need. After all, Jesus said the Pharisees "have their reward in full."[425] Isn't it better to wait for the reward Jesus has planned in eternity?

Father, I confess my pride wants the strokes of men. I feel cheated when I don't get credit for what You've done in my life. How foolish of me to focus on things of earth and not "things above where Christ is."[426] Today, teach me that it's more important to love my wife than to be right. In Christ's name, **Amen**.

424 I Pet. 3:7
425 Matt. 6:5
426 Col. 3:1

Loving…Overlooks wrongs (real or perceived)

"(Love)…does not take into account a wrong suffered…" I Cor. 13:5

Ever eat a big helping of humble pie? Or chicken-fried crow? Where's the Pepto Bismal or Tums? It's a heavy burden being right all the time. But what if we're not? What if we think we've been wronged…and haven't? What if our pride places us on a pedestal, and we think someone is hacking away at it? As Clint Eastwood said, "you're a legend in your own mind."[427]

Have you ever considered how many wrongs you've committed that God forgives and forgets…daily?[428] Remember the story of the slave who owed his master millions of dollars (ten thousand talents)?[429] He was forgiven his tremendous debt, then went out and choked a fellow slave who owed him a hundred bucks. It didn't turn out so well for him. One of my favorite verses is in Lamentations 3:39, "*Why should any living mortal, or any man, offer complaint in view of his sins?*"

Often Jesus would begin an important point by saying, "You have heard…but I say to you." Why do you think Jesus told His disciples to "turn the other cheek" or "go the extra mile"?[430] It's because His followers—we—are different from the world, in thinking and behavior. God has specifically told us that "*vengeance is mine, I will repay.*"[431] It's really a question of do we believe God or not? Can He, will He do what He says…*on my behalf?* Or do I need to take this one? I've heard myself say, "I've got it, God; You can sit this one out." But that's my anger wanting immediate revenge for a perceived wrong against me.

The prophet Nahum had it right when he said, "*…the Lord will by no means leave the guilty unpunished.*"[432] Peter tells us that "*love covers a multitude of sins.*"[433] A short fuse or a sharp, hurtful retort are indicators that our love bucket is low. Can we set aside our pride today and remember how much God has forgiven us in Christ and pass it on?

Lord God, it's beyond our grasp how Your love forgives and forgets the sins of Your children, even when we habitually repeat the same ones over and over. May our gratitude for Your mercy blossom into the fruit of forgiveness to those who offend us. In Jesus' name, **Amen**.

427 Dirty Harry, 1971
428 Heb. 10:17; Ps. 103:11
429 Matt. 18:22-35
430 Matt. 5:38-41
431 Deut. 32:35
432 Nahum 1:3
433 I Pet. 4:8

Loving…Melts the hardest of hearts.

"It is a trustworthy statement, deserving full acceptance, that Christ Jesus came into the world to save sinners, among whom I am foremost of all. Yet for this reason I found mercy, so that in me as the foremost, Jesus Christ might demonstrate His perfect patience as an example for those who would believe in Him for eternal life."
I Tim. 1:15, 16

There's no question that Paul was, arguably, one of the most anti-Christians alive at his time. His hearty approval and participation in torturing and murdering Christians is recorded for us in Acts.[434] But, praise God, the story doesn't stop there. God had other plans for "Saul" that were 180 degrees from where he was heading. You can read the rest of the story about Paul's conversion and empowering in Acts 9.

Do you think Paul qualified as having a "hard heart" toward things of God? Absolutely. So here's the takeaway for us: If God's love can melt the heart of someone committed to killing Christians, think about the impact of our loving someone who doesn't deserve it. Can we love people into the kingdom? Obviously, we don't control who gets saved. But they're more likely to listen to the gospel—God loves them, Jesus died for them and heaven awaits them if they repent, turn from their sin and accept Christ's payment for their sin—if they see God's love alive and active in us.

When was the last time we spent some of God's love on someone we didn't think deserved it? Can you think of someone at work, or in your neighborhood, or even in your church who could use a fresh dose of love? People don't go to the hospital because they're in good health. They go because they're sick. They don't go to church because they're perfect. They go to hear the good news of Christ's victory, get their broken hearts healed, and learn about the liberty and freedom available in Christ.[435]

The world around us is hurting. They are frustrated, angry, lost. They strike out at anyone and anything for temporary relief. Today, let's put on a heart of compassion…and love[436] and see if we can't spot at least one person we can spend some of it on.

Heavenly Father, it hasn't been that long since I was Your enemy. I'm forever grateful You didn't give up on me, but pursued me with Your love until I couldn't resist another day. Help me remember there are many who need what I have and that giving it away doesn't deplete my supply. In my Savior's name, **Amen**.

434 Acts 8:1-3; 9:1, 2
435 Isa. 61:1; Matt. 11:4-6
436 Col. 3:12-14

Loving...Is the right response to all that God has done for us.

"We love because He first loved us." I John 4:19

Has anyone ever thrown you an "Appreciation Day"? When my kids were still at home, and even after they left home, every so often, my wife would put together a special day for one of us. She'd make our favorite meal (including dessert) and serve it on a special plate she had. We'd sit around and take turns affirming the honoree. If it was your turn in the "special" seat, she made you feel like a king. I truly believe that was just one of the things she did that instilled a real love between us as a family.

Love doesn't come automatically. Left alone, we're selfish and greedy. We have to see love modeled for us. Unfortunately, all too often, our role models at home miss the mark. The good news is that it doesn't matter our yesterdays. Our *Heavenly* Father is in the business of todays and tomorrows. For those of us who know Jesus as our Savior and Lord, our heavenly Father has poured out His love within our hearts.[437] He also *proved* His love in that while we were still at war with Him (sinners) Christ died for us.[438]

If our ability to love someone—and by the way, love is a choice not a mushy feeling—is a couple quarts low, we might want to examine ourselves[439] to see if the Spirit of Christ really dwells in us. In today's world of darkness, even the smallest light of truth can seem like a life-saving beacon. When we consider all God has done for us, how can we not love others in kind?

Today, make it your mission to first examine yourself to make sure the love of God is yours. Second, make a conscious effort to single someone out—especially someone to whom you feel superior—and shower them with God's love. You'll be amazed at the results. But be patient, they might not respond immediately. Stay on your mission. Your Commander-In-Chief is watching.[440]

Lord God, I'm overwhelmed when I consider that You love me in spite of me. If I'm honest with You and myself, I'll see that I fall short of Your expectation that I pass Your love to others in my path. Today, may You open my eyes to the hurts around me and grant me courage to get out of my comfort zone and share Your love with someone in need. For the advancement of Christ's kingdom, **Amen**.

437 Rom. 5:5
438 Rom. 5:8
439 II Cor. 13:5
440 Psa. 11:4

Loving God....is the first and greatest commandment

"You shall love the Lord your God with all your heart and with all your soul, and with all your mind. This is the great and foremost commandment." Matt. 22:37, 38

If you're a child of the King, how can you not love Him? Consider just the main points of what He's done for us:

1. Forgiven ALL our sins[441]
2. Empowered us to live righteous lives[442]
3. Secured our future[443]

Whole books could be written to fill in all the sub-points. The qualifier to experiencing this is in the first sentence, "If you're a child of the King." Think about your own parent-child relationship. If you're a parent, you can look in both directions. Children respond to love from their parents. Parents respond to love from their children.

Our earthly love is inferior to God's, but it still gives us a concrete example of the power inherent in love to change people. When God set His affection on us and gave us the indescribable gift[444] of His Son, and we grasp even a portion of the significance of that, we can respond in no other way than to love Him back. That's the easy part. The hard part is to do it "with all your heart, soul, and mind."

It was the custom of Jewish slaves to be freed in the seventh year of their service. If they had grown to love their masters and didn't want to be freed, they would have their ear pierced at the doorway of the master's house, and they would become a "bond-servant."[445] That's the idea of "heart, soul, and mind." We love our Master so much that we don't want to do anything but serve Him. Man, what would our churches and communities look like if we had a few more like that? That's our challenge today. Identify where we are on the bond-servant scale and make adjustments as necessary.

Lord, it's easy to *say* we love You, but much tougher to give up our plans, desires, and wills to *serve* You the way You deserve and command. Today, may You grace us with the desire to serve You instead of ourselves. In Jesus' name, **Amen**.

441 Col. 2:13, 14
442 Eph. 3:16-19
443 John 14:2, 3
444 II Cor. 9:15
445 Tit. 2:9, 10

Loving your neighbor....is the second commandment and puts a bow on all the law and prophets.

"You shall love your neighbor as yourself. On these two commandments depend the whole Law and Prophets." Matt. 22:39, 40

We learned a little about who our neighbor is in Week 6—Caring—when we reviewed the story of the good Samaritan.[446] Have you ever wondered if God knew what He was doing when He gave us this commandment? Haven't you thought (like I have), "But God, you just don't know my neighbor Larry"? If we harbor thoughts like this, we need to examine our own hearts. It's a sure sign that fear, resentment, bitterness, jealousy, or some other sin is lurking there, ready to ensnare us.

Look at the commandment again. It says, "we shall *love*" it doesn't say we have to *like* our neighbor. Remember that love is a choice. Also remember the sorry state you were in when God first loved you.[447] What if God had waited until we cleaned ourselves up before He loved us? We'd have never made it.

How can "the whole Law and Prophets" depend on loving God and loving our neighbor? The simple answer is that love covers a multitude of sins.[448] But it's a lot more than that. When we love God, we see Him as He is, and we realize from what we've been saved (wrong lifestyle, wrong friends, wrong beliefs, and ultimately hell).

From a heart of gratitude, we want to be more like Christ—forgiving and loving. In the proportion that we love God, we can love our neighbor. If you analyze any of the commandments, you'll see that they are fulfilled by responding in love to God or love to our neighbor.

Nobody said it was going to be easy. Jesus told us to deny ourselves and take up our cross *daily.*[449] This covers both the mental and physical aspects of loving our neighbor. If you find this hard, don't forget the power of the Holy Spirit who lives within you. Maybe this is a verse you should add to your arsenal: "*...walk by the spirit and you will not carry out the desire of the flesh.*"[450]

Lord, I admit that sometimes I just don't want to love my neighbor. Show me the log in my own eye and the path to removing it. I want to be obedient and move closer to You. Don't let my pride get in the way. **Amen**.

446 Luke 10
447 Rom. 5:8
448 I Pet. 4:8
449 Luke 9:23
450 Gal. 5:16

Loyalty is a way of life, not a statement on our bio

"Many a man proclaims his own loyalty, but who can find a trustworthy man?" Prov. 20:6

You've probably heard the phrase "I can't hear what you're saying, your actions are too loud." That's the gist of our verse today and a good underpinning of our week on loyalty. There doesn't seem to be a lot of talk about loyalty these days. Could it be that our society has become so enamored with self that the concept of loyalty has fallen on hard times? Some of you will remember that in the working world, loyalty used to be a two-way street. An employee would devote his life to a single company for 30 or 40 years and the company would cherish that commitment and reward the employee with the perks of seniority. Today, it's more likely that a company will look around at the longer-term employees (read: more expensive) and find ways to "down-size" their positions. Then they turn around and hire younger men who might have a degree, but little to no experience, not realizing that you can't put a price tag on commitment and loyalty.

So how does that fit into our study on Christ's character qualities? Solomon seems to equate loyalty to trustworthiness (more on that in Week 41) and implies that it is a quality that's hard to find. When Christ (who is the Living Word) spoke, everything He said was truth.[451] That's why we can have confidence in the Bible—cover to cover. Do you think Christ's disciples would have continued their loyalty to Him and His message if He hadn't proven His loyalty to them before *and* after His death? Would they have endured the harsh treatment and even death for a lie? What are you loyal to today? The guys you work with? Your boss? Your wife? Your church? What if one of them disappoints you and you feel betrayed? Is your loyalty dependent on positive reinforcement? Or do you choose the path that trusts God for your reputation, your daily needs, and your future?

In what's known as *The High Priestly Prayer,*[452] Jesus reminds us that as His followers, we are "not of this world."[453] Wouldn't you expect a visible difference in someone not of this world? Is your difference shining like a beacon or has your battery dimmed the light of your walk to an indistinct glow? More tomorrow…

Lord God, sometimes I feel alone and betrayed by nearly everyone around me. The world has become self-centered to the point of exclusion. Remind me today that I'm not of this world and walk a different path with different standards and a much different reward with You for eternity. In Jesus' name, **Amen**.

451 John 17:17, 19
452 John 17:1-26
453 John 17:16

Loyalty is better than sacrifice and burnt offerings.

"For I delight in loyalty rather than sacrifice and in the knowledge of God rather than burnt offerings." Hosea 6:6

As with so much of what we've discussed, loyalty is a heart attitude. It's placing value on a person not because of what they have done or can do for you, but because they are made in God's image and have intrinsic value regardless of what the exterior looks like. In real estate, it's said that the three most important things are location, location, and location. But there's also something called curb appeal. A house has to look good from the outside for you to want to explore the inside. People don't always have good curb appeal, but that doesn't necessarily take away from what's inside. And, unfortunately, many who have good curb appeal disappoint when we open the door. Remember Jesus called the scribes and Pharisees whitewashed tombs?[454] Why? Because they had good curb appeal but were rotten inside.

There's not always something we can do to change our exterior. Of course, we try. Billions are spent on cosmetics, plastic surgery, the latest fashions. But we can change our heart. It starts with a choice, a commitment to doing things God's way. But, we ask, aren't sacrificing and burnt offerings (modernize it to read religious activity and good deeds) important to God? Only when motivated properly. Consider Paul's warning to the Corinthian believers about what is valuable.[455] The wood, hay, and stubble that get burned up at the Judgment Seat of Christ[456] are activities that have no eternal value. In other words, they're not done with God's glory as the motivation. Could be we want to be seen by others as having it all together. I believe this is especially tempting for those who preach and lead worship. This is not a rebuke to anyone. But it is a warning for all of us to examine our motives. Is our heart attitude right toward being and doing all God has called us to for His glory? Or are we preoccupied with sacrifice and burnt offerings?

Father, I confess that I often seek praise from men rather than You. I can't go back and change anything, and I'm grateful for Your grace that continues to forgive me. But, Lord, I want desperately to have the right motives in doing what You've called me to do…and *only* for Your glory. In Christ's name, **Amen**.

454 Matt. 23:27
455 I Cor. 3:12-15
456 II Cor. 5:10

Loyalty puts others' welfare ahead of our own.

"...He swears to his own hurt and does not change;" Psa. 15: 4c

In the movie *The Transporter,* the Transporter has rules that he lives by. The first rule is, "You don't change the deal." From his perspective, that means neither side can change any of the terms after the deal has been struck. Today's thought is like that. We don't cease putting others' welfare ahead of our own when it gets uncomfortable, or when it gets more expensive than we planned, or when we realize that the deal we made favors the other side.

If we are committed to today's concept, then we operate on the basis that words have meaning. A deal is a deal; a commitment is a commitment. Don't you sometimes wonder if you sold something too cheaply when your price is met without dickering? Were you tempted to let buyers bid up the price? That would not please God.[457] In sports, don't you resent a player that, after a particularly good season, wants to renegotiate his contract? In our verse today, David asks a rhetoric question, "*O Lord, who may abide in Your tent? Who may dwell on Your holy hill?*"[458] Then he answers his own question with a list of eleven prerequisites:

1. He who walks with integrity, and
2. Works righteousness, and
3. Speaks truth in his heart, and
4. Does not slander with his tongue, and
5. Does no evil to his neighbor, and
6. Does not take up a reproach against his friend, and
7. Despises a reprobate, and
8. Honors those who fear the Lord, and
9. Swears to his own hurt and doesn't change, and
10. Does not put out his money at interest, and
11. Does not take a bribe against the innocent.

David then adds the icing, "*He who does these things will never be shaken.*" Here's my question of the day to you. Can God be trusted? He will never change the deal on us. His Word is golden, it's rock-solid, and it stands for eternity.[459] Think about this today. To whom have you committed loyalty? Your wife, your family, your boss, your neighbors? Are you fulfilling your commitment?

Father, it's so easy to walk away when the going gets tough. Thank you for not doing that to me. Help me follow Jesus' example and stay the course regardless of the cost. **Amen**.

457 Num. 30:2
458 Psa. 15:1
459 Matt. 24:35

Loyalty rewards us with life, righteousness and honor.

"He who pursues righteousness and loyalty finds life, righteousness and honor." Prov. 21:21

Trophies. What's so important about trophies? We get them for sports, for acting, for sales superiority, "dad of the year," best motivational speech, biggest fish. There's also the worst this, worst that, etc. Has the intrinsic value of knowing you've done your best been replaced by "no kid left behind…without a trophy"? Honestly, who doesn't like to be recognized for their accomplishments? Who isn't at least a little motivated by some type of reward? Me included. But how many trophies have you ever seen at a funeral or in a hearse?

Timothy tells us, "we have brought nothing into the world, so we cannot take anything out of it either."[460] He goes on to say, "But those who want to get rich fall into temptation and a snare and many foolish and harmful desires which plunge men into ruin and destruction."[461] Pity so many of us, like those hearers of Jesus, were more concerned about the approval of men than the approval of God.[462] We're focusing on loyalty this week. And God has given us a pretty spectacular promise that should appeal to the need for recognition in us: "…pursue…loyalty…find…honor." Is honor a viable goal? I suggest that it's a byproduct of something else.

God's Book tells us that, "*…before honor comes humility*"[463] and "*…a humble spirit will obtain honor.*"[464] Often, we pursue one thing, only to be blessed by God with something entirely different. My belief is that as we pursue loyalty—becoming someone that is trustworthy—God rewards us with eternal "stuff" beyond earthly value. The issue is that many of us won't pay the price of humility. It doesn't make sense. We're taught to compete, to win, to go for the gusto. Well, you might have to rethink that. Although humble people don't clamor for the spotlight, humility and success are not mutually exclusive. Revisit your definition of success and you'll realize that guys like Moses, Abraham, and David (a man after God's own heart)[465]—all great leaders—were also humble followers of God. Take the step. Make the decision. Pursue loyalty. God will honor you.

Lord God, Your way is often just the opposite of what I've learned from the world. Help me to trust *You* and follow *Your* path and then expect the rewards You've promised. In Christ's name, **Amen**.

---

460 I Tim 6:7
461 I Tim 6:9
462 John 12:43
463 Prov. 15:33
464 Prov. 29:23
465 Acts 13:22

Loyalty was modeled for us by Christ Himself.

"A man of too many friends comes to ruin, but there is a friend who sticks closer than a brother." Prov. 18:24

It's been said that you can never be too rich or too thin. Maybe. But today's verse tells us that too many friends can ruin us. I'm guessing that Facebook and Twitter don't know this verse. Perhaps the quandary is in the definition of "friend." Dictionary.com says *friend* is "a person attached to another by feelings of affection or personal regard." I don't know about you, but I'm pretty stingy with my affection.

When I think about being a follower of Christ and becoming more like Him, I observe that He was loyal to His friends[466]...all twelve (not hundreds) of them, even Judas. He had great affection and personal regard for them, even when they abandoned Him in His greatest hour of need. How many of our acquaintances can we say that about? Is it reciprocal? Friendship takes time, energy, commitment. We should know going in that we'll be disappointed from time to time. It's rare that a friendship survives time and distance because it takes work and fellowship to be a friend. We must overlook differences and quirks that otherwise might irritate or offend us. I'm not saying that we should limit our social circles. But I am saying that too many casual relationships can dilute the energy needed by our "inner circle."

Trying to please too many people can result in not pleasing any. A true friend shares your goals, your interests, your faith. A true friend "sharpens" you[467] and doesn't tempt you to "leave the paths of uprightness"[468] but encourages you to "walk in the way of good men."[469] Today, With Christ's help, let's focus on the handful of men that meet these criteria for a "true" friend and become more of a friend to them.

Father, it's tempting to seek approval and friendship from the world. But You've told us that whoever wishes to be a friend of the world makes himself an enemy of God.[470] Don't let us fall into the trap of desiring second best. Help us return to our first love[471] and devote our energy to building our relationship with You. Then, our earthly relationships can have eternal significance. In Christ's name, **Amen**.

466 John 15:15
467 Prov. 27:17
468 Prov. 2:13
469 Prov. 2:20
470 James 4:4
471 Rev. 2:4

Week 27 Friday

Loyalty is what wags its tail at you when you come home.

"Absalom said to Hushai, "Is this your loyalty to your friend? Why did you not go with your friend?" 2 Sam. 16:17

Man's best friend. I don't know about you, but I have (once or twice) thought how nice it would be if my wife and kids were as excited to see me when I come home as is my dog. But, since my kids are grown and my wife of 50 years hasn't done it yet, the likelihood of that happening is about as great as wishing on the "first star I see tonight."

In the Boy Scout Law, Loyalty is #2 in a list of 12; only "trustworthy" ranks higher. You don't hear much about loyalty today. Could it be that in our society, loyalty has become scarce? Zero. That's the number of disciples that stayed with Jesus in His darkest hour.[472] Can you think of ten men who are loyal to you? Five? One? Like many things in life, loyalty is a choice. But if it hasn't been forged in the fires of decisions and trials, it may wane just when you need it most.

Have you ever wondered how you would have reacted in the garden when Jesus was arrested? Why does loyalty fade in battle? Isn't it fear? Has our faith in Jesus Christ matured to the point that we can trust Him to "cover our six" regardless of our circumstances? Perhaps a good verse to store in our memory banks is Hebrews 13:15b, "*I will never desert you, nor will I ever forsake you.*" And another, Psalm 56:3, 4, "*When I am afraid, I will put my trust in You. In God, whose word I praise, In God I have put my trust; I shall not be afraid. What can mere man do to me?"*

Being a follower of Christ, on a daily basis, is not for sissies. Jesus told His disciples to "take up their cross daily."[473] What does it mean in our "modern" society to take up our cross? Are you ridiculed for your faith at work? Do the guys even know you're a Christian? How can you expect to hear, "well done good and faithful servant"[474] if you run and hide when persecuted? We're closer to eternity today than we were yesterday. Borrowing the title from a Charles Dickens' novel, the *Great Expectation* that I have is when I get home to heaven that Jesus will meet me at the gate and be as excited to see me as my dog always is.

Lord Jesus, my spirit is willing to be loyal to *You*, but my flesh is weak. Give me a clearer picture of what *You've* done for me and remind me daily that my cross is nothing compared to Yours. **Amen**.

---

472 Matt. 26:56
473 Luke 9:23
474 Luke 19:17

Loyalty is a foundation stone in the building of relationships or kingdoms.

"Loyalty and truth preserve the king, and he upholds his throne by righteousness."
Prov. 20:28

I confess. I couldn't wait to see the next episode of "24" when the series ran on TV. But I did grow weary of trying to figure out who the mole was; there was always one. And the underlying problem was that loyalties shifted based on the old acronym: WIIFM (what's in it for me). In today's verse, Solomon tells us that loyalty and truth are the 2-pronged preservative that watches over the kingdom. Can you imagine a political environment in which none of the king's (or president's) advisors had hidden agendas? What would that look like? I haven't seen it in my lifetime, nor will I.

Jesus told His followers that they would have tribulation in the world.[475] But He also encouraged them by reminding them (and us) that He has overcome the world. The 1,000-year reign of Christ on earth[476] will be the first time we'll ever see an incorruptible ruler on earth. So, is loyalty blindly following another or overlooking their sin? No. It's finding a kindred spirit—one who shares our values—and coming alongside for the purpose of mutual edification and encouragement. Consider David and Jonathan's[477] friendship. Not only did Jonathan gladly give up his rightful claim to the throne, he actively promoted David to the king. Not only did David prove a good friend to Jonathan while Jonathan was alive, he kept his promise to him after his death.[478]

What does loyalty look like in our lives? Do we commit to someone or some cause until they disappoint or disagree with us? That's not loyalty. That's using. How about loyalty to our wife? Do we allow our eyes to wander, or worse? Remember, you're not the hunk or jock you were when she married you either. If this week's consideration of loyalty has done anything, my prayer is that you take your relationships seriously starting with your wife and kids. They need and deserve your commitment to them. Next, carefully consider your friendships. Do they and can you walk in accountability with each other? Do you share common life goals? Is Christ the focal point of your walk? That doesn't mean you can't be friendly with others. But ask yourself this, "How is this friendship moving me toward Christlikeness?" Think about it.

Holy Spirit, strengthen my inner man to shun the world's way and keep me on the path of righteousness. May I be a loyal husband and friend pointing others to the Savior. In His name, **Amen**.

475 John 16:33
476 Rev. 20:1-6
477 I Sam. 18-20
478 II Sam. 9:3-7

Maturity is required to move from milk to solid food.

"For though by this time you ought to be teachers, you have need again for someone to teach you the elementary principles of the oracles of God, and you have come to need milk and not solid food.." Heb. 5:12

No matter how good chicken fried steak is, you wouldn't feed it to your six-month-old baby. Conversely, you wouldn't feed a bottle of formula to your 16-year old. That's just the way life is. Just as someone would question your judgment by trying to feed inappropriate food to your children, your maturity in Christ should be questioned if, after several or many years in the church, you haven't moved beyond the ABCs of Christianity.

The writer of Hebrews chastises his readers for such non-growth. If you're career military, there is a policy of "up or out." Simply stated, they don't want someone taking up space that isn't pushing for the next stripe, bar, or star. You probably know someone at work that fits that description. Unfortunately, it seems society is training the younger generation to be takers rather than givers, consumers rather than creators. That's why it's all the more important for the man of God to never stop learning and growing in Christ—to become more and more the image of the Savior—in response to God's call.

What NFL team would ever make the Super Bowl if the players never practiced or had coaches who didn't stretch them to their potential? The same is true in any sport or profession. Why should it be different in our walk of faith? We have bosses that push us, customers that demand from us, and family that has needs. All of these compete for our time and energy, and all are important. Just because God is patient and mostly gentle—not giving us what we deserve—wooing us as a loving father, doesn't mean we can ignore His commands such as, "Be diligent to present yourself approved to God... accurately handling the word of truth."[479] And "...grow in grace and knowledge of our Lord and Savior Jesus Christ."[480] There will be an accounting of what God has entrusted to us someday.[481] Let's be eating top sirloin or good ol' homemade chili when He comes... not still drinking mama's milk.

Father, I am truly grateful that You are patient and gentle with me when I so often forget about You or, worse, deny You. Build my desire to know you better and to walk closer to You, not to amass rewards, but because that's what children do to loving fathers. In Jesus' name, **Amen**.

479 2 Tim. 2:15
480 2 Pet. 3:18
481 Matt. 25:19

Maturity results in discernment.

"But solid food is for the mature, who because of practice have their senses trained to discern good and evil." Heb. 5:14

In 1982, Sean Connery starred in the Movie *Wrong is Right.* The plot is full of lies, deception, and hidden agendas, all of which are used to justify the ends of the characters using them. But listen to what Isaiah says, "*Woe to those who call evil good and good evil; who substitute darkness for light and light for darkness…*" Isa. 5:20. Don't you just want to scream when you hear politicians lie and much of the public doesn't seem to get it?

As a child of The King, we are uniquely empowered by the Holy Spirit to discern good and evil. Make no mistake, our adversary "*prowls around like a roaring lion, seeking someone to devour.*"[482] If we are not mature through immersion in the Bible, our senses haven't been trained and we are prime targets of the enemy. Does that mean he can rob us of our salvation? No. "*No one can snatch us out of the Father's hand.*"[483] But if our discernment hasn't been honed by the sword of the Spirit, he can get our eyes to wander from the prize. The devil delights in defeating us in our walk of faith. He knows he can't take our salvation, but he also knows our weaknesses and is crafty in his deceit, using partial truths, outright lies, and alluring circumstances to tarnish our witness and get us to beat ourselves up over repetitive sin which Jesus took care of once and for all on the cross.

So wake up, men. Our salvation is nearer than when we (first) believed.[484] Management 101 teaches that the first step to solving a problem is the recognition that one exists. So let's say we've just realized that our discernment meter's low. Congratulations. You've just finished step one. Now, we have to decide what to do about it. Do we want a closer walk with Christ, one that results in making right choices, shining the light of truth on the world's lies, and hearing "well done" at the end of our journey? The only way to recharge is to plug into God's Word and take it seriously. Remember, we're soldiers in an army. Soldiers don't quit because they're tired, wounded, or lonely. How would you react if the Commander in Chief of an earthly army personally gave you a direct command? That's the attitude of a mature soldier. Keep your eyes on the prize, and the devil's tricks won't suck you in.

Father, sometimes I'm tired, discouraged, and, frankly, lazy. I know the war is not over until Jesus returns. Strengthen my resolve and discipline to stay plugged into the source of power, Your Holy Word, that I won't grow weary before You call me home. In Christ's powerful name, **Amen**.

---

482 I Pet. 5:8
483 John 10:29
484 Rom. 13:11

Maturity: no longer think like a child.

"Brethren, do not be children in your thinking; yet in evil be infants, but in your thinking be mature." I Cor. 14:20

How's your timeline coming? You know, God has given each of us so many days.[485] The life expectancy for a male living in the United States is just over 76 years; for females, just over 81. That aside, we don't know the day or hour God will call us home. We have to be ready at all times. So what does that look like? For one thing, Paul tells us to grow up in our thinking. What does a child think about? Himself…period. How much time do we spend thinking about ourselves? If it's a lot compared to thinking about others, we're still children in our thinking.

What are some things mature thinkers think about? Paul gives us a list in Philippians 4:8 – "*whatever is true, honorable, right, pure, lovely, of good repute, any excellence, anything worthy of praise.*" Of course, we have to think about our family, our job, our place in the community, but do so in the light of our walk with Christ. Yes, we must come to Christ as a "little child"[486] (not chronologically but with pure, childlike faith), but we're not to stay children. Paul says, "*When I was a child, I spoke…thought…reasoned like a child. When I became a man, I did away with childish things.*"[487] What childish things are you still holding on to?

One of the hardest childish things to let go is pride. The child in me still cries out "mine" and I want to control all I see. Maturity moves us closer to the cross and further from self. I keep talking about wanting to hear "well done" from Jesus when I see Him. I guess that's because I can see that average life expectancy heading my way. But I like to think that it's also because I'm allowing Jesus to have more of my heart…sometimes reluctantly, sometimes in tears, but nevertheless more. Can that be our mission today: move toward mature thinking and allow Christ into more corners of our life than yesterday? The best place to start is on our knees, agreeing with God that we've blown it…again. In addition to being our Savior, Jesus is our friend.[488] Talk to Him today. Our timelines are getting shorter every day.

Lord Jesus, I know that time waits for no man. I also know You have numbered my days. Teach us to number our days that we may present to You a heart of wisdom.[489] Help me to do away with childish ways and grow into a mature man intent on Your glory. Thank You. **Amen**

---

485 Psa. 139:16
486 Matt. 19:14
487 I Cor. 13:11
488 John 15:15
489 Psa. 90:12

Week 28 Wednesday

Maturity is a close cousin to Humility.

"When I came to you, brethren, I did not come with superiority of speech or wisdom..."
I Cor. 2:1

Maturity comes by learning. And learning requires humility—an attitude that knows what it knows not but is willing to be taught. Though Paul had the quintessential resume,[490] in today's vernacular, he would have held multiple Ph.D.s, he did not flaunt it.[491] He stayed focused on his mission of spreading the gospel of Christ to a lost world. Remember how much our parents learned between our 15th year and our 22nd birthday? Don't you find it ironic that the more we learn, the more we see how much we don't know? Solomon told us that "*a wise man will hear and increase in learning, and a man of understanding will acquire wise counsel.*"[492] That is the first step to maturity, admitting you don't have all the answers.

Yesterday, we talked about giving up childish things. The common thread here is making a decision…to change. It's been said that a man won't change until the pain (or cost) of not changing becomes unbearable. How dumb is that? Why can't we change just because it's the right thing to do? There have been times in my life when God has really had to shake my tree to get His message through my thick skull. Why do we do that? Life is so much better doing it God's way. More peace. More joy. More intimacy with God. I believe it's because we still have one foot in the world, and our head is on a swivel between Godly living and worldly living. Wanna know what God thinks of that? "*If anyone loves the world, the love of the Father is not in him.*"[493] And, "*So because you are lukewarm, and neither hot nor cold, I will spit you out of My mouth.*"[494]

If we know Jesus as our Savior, the Holy Spirit is coaxing, wooing, prodding us to a closer walk with Him. Remember that our heavenly Father loves and disciplines us as sons.[495] Sometimes, in our immaturity, we force God's hand of discipline…and it hurts. But the writer of Hebrews goes on to say, "*but He disciplines us for our good, so that we may share His holiness.*"[496] That's a worthwhile goal, don't you think? Don't give up.

God, the price of maturity sometimes seems overwhelming and painful and I think, "what does it matter anyway"? Forgive me for forcing You to discipline me because of my hardness of heart. Restore to me the joy of my salvation. In Christ's name, **Amen**.

---

490 Phil. 3:4-6
491 Phil 3:7, 8
492 Prov. 1:5
493 I John 2:15
494 Rev. 3:16
495 Heb. 12:6
496 Heb. 12:10

Maturity grows out of trials

"Consider it all joy my brethren when you encounter various trials, knowing that the testing of your faith produces endurance. And let endurance have its perfect result, so that you may be perfect and complete, lacking in nothing."
James 1:2-4

You ever ask yourself, "What had James been smoking?" when he penned this verse? How can I possibly consider with joy the trials I face? I'm sure some of you have had the same thoughts. The key is to look beyond the immediate to the promise/goal: so that you may be perfect and complete, lacking in nothing. The word James uses for perfect means spiritual maturity. So let me get this straight. If I want to be mature, I can expect trials? Yup. Great plan, huh?

We only have to look to nature to see the value of "trials." Consider how diamonds are made. Carbon minerals under extreme heat and pressure. Or pearls. Irritants inside the oyster. What makes us assign a label of mature to one person and immature to another? It's not just chronological age. If we interviewed the mature man, we'd surely find a history of challenges that were overcome.

Throughout this book, we talk about focus, goals, mission, etc. and how we either trust God or we don't. Here's another chance for us to opt-in. I confess I'm not always joyful in the midst of a trial. But the time between trial and trust is getting shorter. May I suggest you take some time today to assess where you are on your journey with Christ. Ask the tough questions. Be open to input from your wife. Just getting older doesn't guarantee maturity. You've seen the t-shirt that says, "I may be getting older, but I refuse to grow up." Cute, but in the Christian walk, sad. God's plan is for us to be "perfect"—mature—in our relationship with Him. It's crunch time. Are you in the game or content to sit in the stands?

Father, I want to be one of Your first-stringers. But I get discouraged in the midst of trials. Help me keep my focus on You and the goal of maturity so that I begin to see trials as tools in the Master's experienced hands shaping me for specific tasks that You have planned in my future. I choose to trust You. Let me do it sooner than later. **Amen**.

Maturity keeps our boat of doctrine on calm seas

"Until we all attain to the unity of the faith, and of the knowledge of the Son of God, to a mature man, to the measure of the stature which belongs to the fullness of Christ. As a result, we are no longer to be children, tossed here and there by waves and carried about by every wind of doctrine, by the trickery of men, by craftiness in deceitful scheming;" Eph. 4:13, 14

I used to be an avid water skier—not good, just avid. I've skied on lakes of glass and 1-2 foot chop. Trust me; glass is better. The longer I skied, the more I realized that to get the best water, I had to get up early and hit it before the lake got crowded or the wind came up. In our walk with Christ, the waves of trickery, craftiness, and deceitful scheming that we encounter will toss us around in inverse proportion to our maturity. Getting up early and starting our day with Christ in His Word and prayer equip us to more readily identify the enemy's lies and deception. Paul told Timothy, "*evil men... will proceed from bad to worse... You, however, continue in the things you have learned and become convinced of.*"[497]

What things had Timothy learned? Namely, the **truth** of the gospel of Jesus Christ. When we know the truth, everything that doesn't line up with it is...you got it...a lie. Jesus called Satan a liar and the father of lies.[498] What do you think his followers are going to do? Surprise. They lie. If we're tired of the confusing claims of "religious" groups, then we need to work on our *knowledge of the Son of God* to become a mature man. We live in spiritually dangerous times. Persecution is coming for followers of Jesus in America. It's already here in many places in the Middle East. If we're not rock-solid in what we believe, the winds of false doctrine can easily lead us to doubt our salvation and especially our God.

Jesus called Satan a liar;[499] He never said he was stupid. As he did in the garden, Satan wants us to doubt God ("Did God really say?"[500]). Storing scripture in our heart[501] is the best defense we have against falsehood. The Christian life is full of struggles, trials, rejection. You'll lose friends, people will question your sanity. But you'll also get a "get out of hell free" card, paid in full by Jesus' sacrifice on the cross...for YOU. Maturity doesn't guarantee calm sailing. What it does is give us confidence and security in the worst of storms. Put on the life jacket of God's Word and let's set sail.

Father, it seems so simple when I read about it. But as soon as I close the Bible, I'm bombarded with life. Help me transfer it from page to pavement. **Amen**.

497 II Tim. 3:13-17
498 John 8:44
499 John 8:44
500 Gen. 3:1
501 Psa. 119:11

Maturity opens our eyes to God's wisdom

"Yet we do speak wisdom among those who are mature; a wisdom, however, not of this age nor of the rulers of this age, who are passing away; but we speak God's wisdom in a mystery, the hidden wisdom which God predestined before the ages to our glory; the wisdom which none of the rulers of this age has understood; for if they had understood it they would not have crucified the Lord of glory;" I Cor. 2:6-8

By now, I hope you've seen that maturity is a process, not an event. It grows through our knowledge of God and His Word and also through trials and heartaches. Success, if we attribute it to God's blessing, can add to our maturity. In fact, the object of our life focus will determine our path to maturity, whether it's a super-highway or a briar patch.

Solomon commented thus, "*The way of the lazy is as a hedge of thorns, but the path of the upright is a highway.*"[502] The Psalmist tells us that wisdom and maturity go hand in hand. Do you want "to be wiser than your enemies," "have more insight than all your teachers," "understand more than the aged,"[503] then immerse yourself in the Bible.[504]

As I write these final thoughts on maturity, the 2016 presidential election primary season is in full swing with 16 Republican candidates and over two dozen Democrats vying for their party's nomination. If ever our nation needed God's wisdom to lead us into the future (however short that may be), it's now. The signs of spiritual immaturity are everywhere. But, brothers, don't allow what you see around you to cause you to grow weary as you see "the day" drawing near.[505] "Dad" gave us His road map to get us home safely. Let's be like Paul and "*forget what lies behind and press on toward the goal* (of Christlikeness and heaven)."[506] Remember that we started this week off comparing chicken fried steak with mama's milk? Look in the mirror of your accountability partners and ask yourselves, "What's for dinner?"

Lord God, I confess that I do get weary trying to live righteously. But that's probably because I'm doing it in my own strength. Open my eyes to the truth of Your Word that you gave specifically to Your family to lead us safely home to You. Fill me with Your Holy Spirit to energize me for the remaining road ahead, and help me keep my eyes on the prize—eternal life with You. In my Savior's name, **Amen**.

502 Prov. 15:19
503 Psa. 119:98-100
504 Psa. 119:104
505 Heb. 10:25; II Thess. 3:13; Gal. 6:9
506 Phil. 3:13, 14

Mercy is getting what I need, not what I deserve.

"Even though I was formerly a blasphemer and a persecutor and a violent aggressor, yet I was shown mercy because I acted ignorantly and in unbelief." I Tim. 1:13

Can you think of anyone more deserving of condemnation and death than the Apostle Paul? That's what makes him a perfect example to kick off our week on mercy. If we're honest with ourselves, aren't we all a little (or maybe a lot) like Pre-Paul Saul—hunting down, then persecuting and murdering first-century believers? You say you haven't done that. Have you ever been angry at anyone? God says, "...everyone who is angry with his brother shall be guilty (of murder)."[507]

For those of us who are parents, we understand a small example of mercy when our kids misbehave, disrespect us, or ruin our new shiny thing, and we don't kill them on the spot. At best, that is a weak comparison to the mercy our heavenly Father lavishes on us daily. Think about this. We think we're pretty good if we don't steal, take God's name in vain or run someone off the road because they cut us off. But God's measuring stick isn't like ours. On the spectrum of "respectable sins,"[508] we tend to compare ourselves with those who are involved in the society-labeled grosser sins, e.g. adultery, murder, etc. instead of God's standard, some of which are found in a list of things God hates: "…haughty eyes, a lying tongue…a heart that devises wicked plans…one who spreads strife." [509]

When we look in the mirror and see ourselves as God sees us, we should be overwhelmed with gratitude that we don't get what we deserve but rather a daily dose of mercy. May that truth settle over us today and cause us to walk humbly before our God. [510]

Father in heaven, Your mercy is beyond my comprehension, but I'm forever grateful for it because it's what I need, not what I deserve. May it cause me to walk in humility before You. In Jesus' name, **Amen**.

507 Matt. 5:21, 22
508 *Respectable Sins*, Jerry Bridges – Navpress, 2007
509 Prov. 6:16-18
510 Micah 6:8

Mercy overlooks others' offenses because God overlooks mine.

"Should you not also have had mercy on your fellow slave, in the same way that I had mercy on you?" Matt. 18:33

Ever catch yourself thinking or saying, "but God," foolishly implying that God just doesn't understand your situation. Why do we always exempt ourselves from the group we're condemning? It's "those guys" or "that church" that need God's corrective action—not me. Let's remember what Jesus said in the Sermon on the Mount: "*...for in the way you judge, you will be judged.*"[511]

Can you recall the moment you realized God's forgiveness was being offered to you on a *cross-shaped* platter, and how overwhelmed you were because you knew you didn't deserve it? We're called to pass it along, to be ambassadors for Christ.[512] One of the things I love about God's Word is it is so contrarian to the world's ways. Jesus confronted that directly when He said, "*You have heard it said, but **I** say to you...*" [513] (emphasis mine) If you don't get anything else from this book, get this: We are to be totally different from the world. Our thinking, our desires, our relationships, our goals are to be with God's righteousness and glory in mind.

When you take a wife, you no longer strive just to please yourself; your goal is to serve her. The analogy fits our role as the bride of Christ. As new creatures,[514] we are to make Him preeminent in our lives. Sometime when you are looking for a topic to do a Bible study on, consider all of the "but you(s)" in scripture. We are not to repay evil with evil [515] as the world does. You know, their version of the Golden Rule is "do unto others before they do unto you." So as you go about your business today, consider how much mercy God grants you and know that as you pass it along to others who probably don't deserve it either, you can never deplete God's supply. Besides, when you treat others in an unexpected way, you may just open the door to a chance to share what Christ has done for you.

Lord God, I'm reminded today of the debt I could never pay. Yet in Your love and mercy, you canceled it at the cross. May I, in gratitude to you, show that same mercy to those around me. In Christ's name, **Amen**.

511 Matt. 7:2
512 II Cor. 5:20
513 Matt. 5:22, 28, 32, 34, 39, 44
514 II Cor. 5:17
515 I Pet. 3:9

Mercy is a sure way to confound your enemies.

"But you, beloved...have mercy on some who doubt." Jude 20-22

Have you ever felt like you knew something that everyone didn't and it made you smile? Showing mercy to your enemies is like that. They expect you to behave like them in negative circumstances; you know, vengeance, irritation, anger, spite, and the list can go on and on. But what does the Bible say? First, remember that vengeance belongs to God[516] and He will act on our behalf.[517] Also, remember that if we got what *we* deserved instead of God's mercy, we'd be snuffed like a taper candle when the wedding's over.

One thing that God's mercy, working *through* us, does *for* us is give us a heart to pray for our enemies[518] and that results in obedience, which results in reward.[519] Now I like rewards as much as the next guy, but, as in last week's theme: *Maturity* comes through obedience in tough trials. Mercy is another rung in the ladder of maturity. So even if I didn't get a reward, if I want to climb the ladder of Christian growth, mercy is a rung I need.

I have a problem in this area because my flesh wants justice and wants it NOW. But Solomon warns us not to gloat (*rejoice*) when our enemy falls because God *will* see it and be displeased (you don't want God displeased with you, trust me) and turn His anger away from him.[520] Think about your enemy's future if he doesn't know the Lord. That prospect alone should fill you with mercy knowing that this world, this life—no matter how wretched—is as good as it will be, and his eternity will be as black as black can be with "*weeping and gnashing of teeth.*"[521]

So it's decision time again. Do we obey and have mercy on our enemies (doubters *are* enemies of the cross of Christ[522]), or do we try to usurp God's authority and mete out what we think to be justice? On one hand, it's a hard decision, but on the other hand, it's fulfilling to make the right choice...to obey God. No matter how much I think I can play God, I'm not...He IS. And thanks to Him for having mercy on *me* when I forget.

Merciful Father, so many times, I want to take matters into my own hands. Thank you for your mercy that gives what I *need*, not what I deserve. Forgive me for not trusting you to fight for me when *You* know it's the right time and circumstances. May I give mercy to others even though I don't think they deserve it knowing I don't either. In His name, **Amen**

516 Deut. 32:35
517 Ps 18:47
518 Matt. 5:44
519 Matt. 6:6; II Chron. 15:7; Prov. 25:21, 22; Matt. 5:12
520 Prov. 24:17, 18
521 Matt. 8:12; 22:13; 25:30
522 Phil. 3:18

Mercy is patient, kind, forgiving, compassionate

"But the wisdom from above is... ***full of mercy.****" Jas. 3:17*

James gives us insight into God's heart and a clue to whether we're walking according to the Spirit or our flesh. If what we think of as wisdom doesn't contain the elements above, it's very likely—almost a certainty—that it's not from above. If it isn't, where's it from? You know there's no fence to sit, right? Jesus said, "*He who is not with me, is against me.*"[523]

What can we learn from the fact that God's wisdom is "full of mercy?" First of all, since God created us, He knows that we are nothing but dust,[524] and as dust, we are frail, time-limited, and "prone to wander."[525] If not for His mercy, His wisdom would seem harsh, unfair, and impossible to apply. It's mercy that doesn't strike us dead the first (and every) time we sin. Next, consider the word *full.* There are no halfway measures with God.

So many verses tell us of God's more than generous dealings with His children. One of my favorite sections of scripture is in Lamentations 3, where Jeremiah goes on for 18 verses about all the afflictions God has put on Israel. Then in verse 19, he does a quick turn and begins to remember **(*)** all that God is and does for the next 48 verses. I believe the core truth in this section is verses 22 and 23, "*The Lord's* ***lovingkindnesses*** *indeed* ***never cease****, for His* ***compassions never fail****. They are new every morning;* ***great is Your faithfulness.***" (emphasis mine) Another word for compassion is mercy. What if God wasn't faithful? What if He only provided mercy periodically? Our need for mercy is so great, I don't even want to think about God turning off the mercy spigot.

So how should all this impact us today? Let me ask this: Do we want to be considered wise? We can ask for and receive God's wisdom,[526] or we can pursue the wisdom of the world. God calls the latter foolish.[527] But, let's be honest. When we open our mouths, is what comes out pure, peaceable, gentle, reasonable, full of mercy, and good fruits? Is our life marked by unwavering and transparent living? If not, it's time to immerse ourselves in the *only* source of truth that is eternal, never changing, and enables us to know and honor our creator.[528] Aren't you tired of the world's way of doing things? Start today by showing mercy to your family. It will spread.

Father, draw me to Your truth, Your ways, Your example in Jesus and let me be faithful in representing You to my family and sphere of influence. **Amen**

523 Luke 11:23
524 Ps. 103:14
525 Come Thou Fount of Every Blessing
526 Jas. 1:5
527 I Cor. 1:20
528 Ps. 119:38 (*) Remembering God, eliminates self-pity

Mercy is the exemplar of the Golden Rule

"Blessed are the merciful, for they shall receive mercy." Matt.5:7

We've all heard the saying, "what goes around comes around." What does that even mean? It's the idea that what you put out, good or bad vibes or actions, will come back to you. You might know it as The Golden Rule; Treat people the same way you want them to treat you.[529] But, you say, "It doesn't (always) work." Maybe. But today's verse promises if you're merciful to others, you *will* also receive mercy. Here's what it *doesn't* say; "you will receive mercy from everybody you show mercy." You know the author of mercy is God. You also learned yesterday that God is faithful and cannot lie.[530] Wouldn't you rather receive mercy from the "*Giver of every perfect gift* [531]" than the incomplete and inadequate mercy from sinners?

Let's look for a moment at the world's interpretation of the Golden Rule: "Do unto others before they can do unto you." Hasn't life in the 21st century jaded us even a little? Haven't we come to expect scams and deception, even (maybe especially) from our leaders? Aren't you glad you serve a God who doesn't lie to us, tempt us,[532] toy with us (you won't find anywhere in scripture where God "experiments" with us) or abandon us?[533]

We may tend to think that showing mercy to others costs us something. But look at the first word of today's verse: Blessed. There are many possible meanings for the word. One common one is "happy." Another one I like is "endowed with divine favor and protection." Think about what you might be giving up to show mercy to someone. What does it cost to gain happiness? Or God's favor and protection? It's like Master Card's advertising: It's priceless.

Also, consider the word *shall* from our verse. We've already seen that God can't lie. So, if we want or expect to be shown mercy, what's the trigger? Simple. Be merciful. Look at it from the opposite perspective. God has already deposited mercy upon mercy upon mercy into our lives. Doesn't that obligate us even a little to pass it on? Think about that often today, and I guarantee that you'll look forward to opportunities to abound with mercy toward others. Also, think about this: "*For judgment will be merciless to one who has shown no mercy; mercy triumphs over judgment.*"[534]

Father, I focus so much on my needs that I often miss those of people around me. Help me to grasp the knowledge of Your faithfulness to grant mercy to me and let that motivate me to be merciful to all you bring across my path. In the name of Jesus. **Amen**.

529 Matt. 7:12
530 Tit. 1:2
531 Jas. 1:17
532 Jas. 1:13
533 Heb. 13:5
534 Jas. 2:13

Mercy is found at the throne of God

"Therefore let us draw near with confidence to the throne of grace, so that we may receive mercy and find grace to help in time of need." Heb. 4:16

Ever been invited to a party where *you* get the gifts? Me either. But that's exactly what today's verse does. And we don't have to slink in. The King has invited us into His very throne room. We have an engraved invitation. What a picture of the relationship we have with our creator…as long as we have embraced Christ's atoning work on the cross on our behalf. If we haven't, we're just part of the crowd outside the gate being told, "*Depart from me, I never knew you.*"[535]

The writer of Hebrews describes God's throne as a *throne of grace* where we *receive mercy* and *find grace*. Wow. Most kings are depicted as despots, tyrants who, if they were having a bad day, you didn't want to be anywhere around the castle. But our Daddy, the King,[536] welcomes us anytime we come. He's never too busy, never too tired, never irritated because of a bad day. So what's the catch? Well, there's good news and bad news.

First, the bad news. God's mercy and grace are only available and freely given to anyone who comes to Him on His terms. Jesus told His disciples, "*I am **the** way, and **the** truth, and **the** life; no one comes to the Father but through Me.*"[537] ("the" not "a"- emphasis mine) No matter what any person or any religion tells you that differs from this simple truth, i.e. we must come to the Father ONLY through Jesus' sacrificial death on our behalf, they are lying. It's not Jesus plus good deeds, or Jesus plus going to church, or Jesus plus…wait for it… ANYTHING! Paul told the church at Ephesus, "*For by grace you have been saved through faith, and that not of yourselves, it is the gift of God, not as a result of works so that no one may boast.*"[538] If you humble yourself, admit that you are a sinner and can't save yourself (the Bible calls that repenting), and believe that Jesus Christ died in your place, you'll be on the A-list. If you don't, the Bible is clear as to your future: "*And if anyone's name was not found written in the book of life, he was thrown into the lake of fire.*"[539] Please don't wait. Tomorrow is not guaranteed to anyone.

Now the good news. There is NO BAD NEWS for those who are in Christ, only an everlasting relationship with the one who bids us COME.

Father, it's such a simple message many of us miss it because of our pride. Open our eyes to Your truth today that the only bad news we hear is "why did you wait so long?" In the name of Him who died for me, **Amen**.

535 Matt. 7:23
536 Rom. 8:15
537 John 14:6
538 Eph. 2:8, 9
539 Rev. 20:15

There is a time when mercy will cease

"And he cried out and said, "Father Abraham, have mercy on me and send Lazarus so that he may dip the tip of his finger in water and cool off my tongue, for I am in agony in this flame." Luke 16:24

Traveling across country, you'll often encounter "last chance" signs before you hit a long stretch of nothing. You probably look at your gas gauge, check your water and snack supply, and decide if your bladder can go the distance. What if life was like that? Okay, Bob, you've got seven days and 4 hours before your ticket is punched. But life isn't like that. The story that Jesus told (full account in Luke 16:19-31) doesn't give a lot of pre-death details; it just says they both died. That's life. But rather than be resigned to "fate", we have been warned over and over in scripture that we are to be alert,[540] be awake,[541] be on guard[542] so that our final day doesn't take us by surprise in the sense of being ready to meet our maker.

We've talked all week about mercy; how it's freely given by our heavenly Father to those in His family. We looked at what it requires (repent and believe in Jesus Christ alone) to be in God's family. We've also looked very briefly at the consequence of not doing being ready. I urge you to not put off this most important of all decisions you'll ever make.

When my 13-month-old daughter died, we had two days from her accident to her death. Even though she was brain dead, we still had hope she could recover. When my 27-year-old son died, we got a call at 2:00 AM and he was already gone. I don't tell you that to elicit sympathy but to tell you I know how quickly our last breath can overtake us. There is a story in II Samuel 12 about King David's son dying. Take a look, "*He said, 'While the child was still alive, I fasted and wept; for I said, 'Who knows, the Lord may be gracious to me, that the child may live.' But now he has died; why should I fast? Can I bring him back again? I will go to him, but he will not return to me.*"[543] One of the great mercies God grants Christian parents is to know that their (saved) children are waiting for them in heaven.

Hope is an amazing gift of God's mercy. Dante's *Divine Comedy* had it right "Abandon Hope All Ye Who Enter Here." Today's verse is a clear statement that God's mercy is limited. As long as you have breath, it's still available...but only on His terms (see Wk. 29, Friday). Don't wait 'til you meet God and He says to you, "You had your chance."

Oh, merciful God, arouse us from our lethargy regarding Your warnings to be ready and prompt us by your Holy Spirit to seek You with urgency. In Christ's name, **Amen**.

540 Mark 13:37; I Pet. 5:8
541 Rom. 13:11; Rev. 16:15
542 Luke 12:15; II Pet. 3:17
543 II Sam. 12:22, 23

Newness of Life Brings Visible Results

"Now there was a man of the Pharisees, named Nicodemus, a ruler of the Jews; this man came to Jesus by night and said to Him, 'Rabbi, we know that You have come from God as a teacher; for no one can do these signs that you do unless God is with him." John 3:1, 2

Inertia. "We've always done it this way." "That won't work." What if guys like Whitney, Ford, Elon Musk had listened to the naysayers of their day? Where would the electric light, the cotton gin, the automobile, the *electric* automobile all be?" Answer: They wouldn't. It takes guts to buck the status quo, to try something no one has ever done. People laugh. They scoff, ridicule, and ostracize. Why? Maybe because they're jealous. Or comfortable. Or lazy.

Why did Nicodemus go to Jesus by night? He was a prominent teacher and leader in Jerusalem and was afraid of what his pals would say if they knew he was interested in Jesus. Let's look at us for a minute. Is there something we're hanging onto keeping us from spiritual growth? Maybe it's fear or reproach of man[544] that binds us. Maybe it's lack of time. Maybe we're content to go to church and act like a Christian, but the struggles of the Christian life aren't worth the effort. Whatever is holding us back from producing the fruit of righteousness,[545] which is **expected** from **every believer** and is for God's glory, not ours, must be dealt with.

Think about the parable of the talents. Do we want to be the guy Jesus called wicked and lazy[546] or do want to hear "well done"?[547] If there's no fruit in our life, we must ask, "Am I truly saved?" Don't misunderstand. I'm not saying we are saved by "fruit" or works,[548] but, like Nicodemus, we must be born again, and that new birth *automatically* produces fruit.[549] (See James 2:14-26 for a good explanation of faith and works.)

Last week we discussed mercy and its various implications. One of the most important points was being ready for death or Christ's return. This discussion touches on things that may be holding us back from a full-on commitment to Jesus. Even if you have to break out of the world's mold to explore Christ's claims, remember, if the majority is doing something (e.g., rejecting Christ), it's probably a good idea to do the opposite.[550]

Lord God, You have made Yourself knowable and available to us in Your Word. Don't let anything stand in our way of coming to You. In Jesus' name, **Amen**.

---

544 Isa. 51:7; Prov. 29:25
545 Heb. 12:11; Phil. 1:11
546 Matt. 25:26
547 Matt. 25:21, 23
548 Eph. 2:8, 9
549 Eph. 2:10
550 Matt. 7:13, 14

Week 30 Monday

Newness of Citizenship Changes our Eternal Destiny

"For our citizenship is in heaven, from which also we eagerly wait for a Savior, the Lord Jesus Christ." Phil. 3:20

It's 2018, and we have a president that some would say is an alien to politics, an outsider. We have millions of illegal aliens living in our country, some would say to obtain a better way of life, some would say to be granted citizenship. Those of us who know Jesus as our savior are not illegal, but aliens nonetheless. Our citizenship is in heaven. We are like a modern-day Abraham, looking for a *better country.*[551]

So what's the big deal about citizenship anyway? Aren't you who you are regardless of where you live? It depends on your frame of reference. If you're speaking temporally, it probably doesn't matter a whole lot unless you live in a repressed society that doesn't offer any freedoms. But if you're speaking from an eternal perspective, it makes ALL the difference in the world. There are only two "countries" in eternity: heaven and hell. Spoiler alert: You can't wait until you *get* there to decide if you want to *be* there.

The writer of Hebrews is very precise: "A*nd inasmuch as it is appointed for men to die once and after this comes judgment.*"[552] The story of the five wise and five foolish virgins[553] comes to mind. You probably know the story, ten virgins waited for the bridegroom who had been delayed. At midnight when he came, the five wise that were prepared with extra oil for their lamps went into the wedding feast, and THE DOOR WAS SHUT. Later, when the five foolish who tried to buy oil at midnight came back, the bridegroom said: "*I do not know you.*" An even more poignant example is in Jesus' Sermon on the Mount, where He says, "*Not everyone who says to Me, 'Lord, Lord' will enter the kingdom of heaven…I never knew you, depart from Me, you who practice lawlessness.*"[554]

Heavenly Citizenship is freely available to anyone who comes in repentance and faith in Jesus Christ alone for salvation. You don't need a passport, a visa, or any other paperwork. You just need Jesus.

1. All (that includes you and me) have sinned: Rom. 3:23
2. Sin leads to death: Rom. 6:23
3. Jesus paid for your sin through His death on the cross: Rom. 5:8
4. Unless you repent, you will perish: Luke 13:3

Heavenly citizenship carries rights and privileges. "*I have set before you life and death, the blessing and the curse. So **choose life**.*"[555]

Lord, it seems an obvious choice. May I not delay making it. **Amen**

---

551 Heb. 11:16
552 Heb. 9:27
553 Matt. 25:1-13
554 Matt. 7:21-23
555 Deut. 30:19

Week 30 Tuesday

Newness of Thinking Changes Everything

"But whatever things were gain to me, those things I have counted as loss for the sake of Christ. More than that, I count all things to be loss in view of the surpassing value of knowing Christ Jesus my Lord, for whom I have suffered the loss of all things, and count them but rubbish so that I may gain Christ," Phil. 3:7, 8

You've heard the definition of insanity: "Continuing to do the same thing and expecting different results." Today's verse may seem like insanity to the world. Doesn't the world tell us, "Get an education." "Invest wisely." "Get more education." Now don't get me wrong; in and of themselves, these are good things. Here's the problem. When we focus on education or chasing wealth, they become all-consuming. They become our god, and we worship them instead of the true and only God.

To think like Paul, we need a transformation of our thinking. First of all, to determine what is truly important in life and second, how do we attain it. Paul had it down when he told the Roman Christians, "*Do not be conformed to this world but be transformed by the renewing of your mind, so that you may prove what the will of God is, that which is good and acceptable and perfect.*"[556] Though I was saved in my early 20s, the shiny things of the world have always had an allure for me. I felt I was missing out if I didn't travel, have nice cars, nice homes. I was buying—on a long-term payment plan—into the world's system of lies. But, like Adam and Eve, pointing the finger of blame in every direction but at themselves,[557] we are responsible for every decision we make...period.

Aren't you glad God is patient and merciful and doesn't give us what we deserve? What are some of the "everything" that need to change? First, we need to recognize that God is God and I'm not. Job has a great section (chap. 38-41) where God asks Job to explain life. Next, we need to understand that our life should be about glorifying God in all I do.[558] You've seen the WWJD bracelets (What would Jesus Do?). Even though it seems a bit trite, it's not a bad filter through which to process our life choices. Changing actions begins with changed thinking. Here's a progression that determines your life story: A thought produces an action, an action a habit, a habit a way of life, a way of life a destiny. As a new creature in Christ, all things are new...including our thinking.[559]

Lord God, grant me understanding that it's not about me. Help me grasp the truth that Your demands are both justified and in obeying them, my only way to true happiness. In Jesus' name, **Amen**.

556 Rom. 12:2
557 Gen. 3:12, 13
558 Matt. 5:16; I Cor. 6:20; I Cor. 10:31
559 II Cor. 5:17

Newness of purpose follows newness of thinking

"And we know that God causes all things to work together for good to those who love God, to those who are called according to His purpose." Rom. 8:28

Why are you here? What is your purpose? Some of us will say to provide for my family. Others to leave this place better than I found it. Both good purposes. You know good things can get in the way of the best things?

Have we given much thought to God's purpose for us? Remember, "*Go, make disciples ...,*"[560] one of the last things Jesus said to His followers. Oh, you thought that just meant the remaining eleven? There were likely many more than the eleven due to the fact that "*some were doubtful.*"[561] But even beyond that, Jesus intended His command to transcend centuries.[562]

Let's review. Has your citizenship transferred from earth to heaven? Has your thinking morphed into considering all things loss for the purpose of knowing Christ? If it has, praise God. If we're still struggling with it, it's time for some concentrated prayer, confession, and immersion into God's Word. The psalmist prays for God to "*establish Your Word to Your servant as that which produces reverence for You.*"[563] If we lack time in the Word, we must reexamine our thinking and see if there's anything we're holding onto that has replaced God as number one in our lives.

Men, we're in a spiritual war.[564] We need to "*be alert, stand firm in the faith, act like men, be strong.*"[565] "*Your adversary, the Devil, prowls about like a roaring lion seeking someone to devour.*"[566] We are the strong men of our families,[567] and God has stationed us there to resist the Devil[568] and protect them. What higher purpose could there be than to be trusted by the God who created the universe to be responsible for the protection of His children? The other things we do along the way, e.g., earning a living, are secondary to fulfilling this role. We can't let another day go by without making sure our priorities and purposes are in line with God's.

Lord God, Creator of all, I confess that I often want *my* priorities and don't give much thought to what You want of me. Forgive me for making myself god and not submitting to Your purpose. Cleanse me of my sin AND guilt and show me how to get back on the horse and into the battle. Thank You. In Christ's name, **Amen**.

560 Matt. 28:19
561 Matt. 28:17
562 Acts 2:39
563 Ps. 119:38
564 Eph. 6:12
565 I Cor. 16:13
566 I Pet.5:8
567 Matt. 12:29
568 Jas. 4:7

Newness of our environment will come when God is ready

"And He who sits on the throne said, 'Behold, I am making all things new.' And He said, 'Write, for these words are faithful and true.'" Rev. 21:5

For those non-scientists among us, permit a simple definition of the second law of thermodynamics, *entropy:* Everything in a closed system winds down as it moves from order to chaos. We see examples all around us, perhaps in our own flesh. I lay in bed in the morning and think of all the things I'm going to do, then my feet hit the floor and my body says, "Oh no, you won't." Before Adam and Eve sinned, when God created the earth and filled it with all manner of flora and fauna and then his crowning creation: man, He looked it all over and saw that it was "very good."[569] Then sin entered the picture and entropy began. Weeds sprouted up[570] and death became reality. But thank God, the story doesn't end there. On some future day—perhaps in the not too distant future—those of us who trust Christ for forgiveness of sins and salvation, will experience our world being reborn.[571]

When God makes something new, there's nothing to do but be in awe. It's coming. The question is, are we ready for it? Our present world is filled with awe-inspiring sights. So when God tells us that "You ain't seen nothin' yet,"[572] I can't wait. But not all of us will experience the new heavens and new earth. And this has nothing to do with global warming alarmists who want us to believe oceans are rising and will drown us out.

There are two specific reasons not to believe their hype. First, God promised Noah He would never again flood the earth.[573] And second, God "*set for the sea its boundary so that the water would not transgress His command.*"[574] I've never found God's Word to say something that wasn't true. If that weren't the case, how could we believe anything God says?[575] There's a simple reason the ocean and tree crowd think that man can control anything with respect to God's planet. If they had to admit there actually is a God, then logic says they'd have to be accountable to Him. Not something they relish. Same thing for evolutionists. Rather than believe the simple story of a 6-day creation, which requires God, not eons of time, accountability dogs them. News flash: everyone will know the truth sooner or later. Sooner is better.

Father, You must laugh at man's attempt at wisdom which you've called foolishness. Thank you for your patience in bringing sinners to Christ. In His name, **Amen**.

569 Gen. 1:31
570 Gen. 3:17, 18
571 Rev. 21:1
572 I Cor. 2:9
573 Gen. 9:15
574 Prov. 8:29
575 Rom. 3:4

Week 30 Friday

Newness of everything is made possible by Easter

"Blessed be the God and Father of our Lord Jesus Christ, who according to His great mercy has caused us to be born again to a living hope through the resurrection of Jesus Christ from the dead," I Pet. 1:3

In the late 60s, Peggy Lee had a song, ***Is That All There Is,*** that was a cry of desperation years after a catastrophic fire destroyed her family home. With disappointment after disappointment, her life became resigned to being let down by everyone and everything. Here is the sad chorus from that song:

Is that all there is, is that all there is
If that's all there is my friends, then let's keep dancing
Let's break out the booze and have a ball If that's all there is.

Why wasn't there someone to tell her about Easter, resurrection, new life, new hope, new meaning? Easter is on my mind, because as I write this, it's tomorrow. The newspaper is full of ads with Easter sales on everything from food and fashions to plastic eggs and bunnies. How sad. To take the most significant event in human history—Jesus' resurrection from the dead—and turn it into a retail extravaganza. Just another example of how out of sync the world is with God's Word and how easily Christians go along with the crowd because we don't want to stand out.

Like the U.S. Marines, God is looking for a few good men: "*I searched for a man among them who would build up the wall and stand in the gap before Me for the land, so that I would not destroy it; but I found no one.*"[576] How many of us can say with Isaiah, "*Here am I, send me.*"[577] Are we so wrapped up in our own agenda that we can't hear God's battle cry? Men, I don't want to sound like a broken record, but we need to wake up. The enemy never sleeps. Perhaps we don't understand the stakes. Reread today's verse. Focus on "His great mercy," "born again," "living hope," "resurrection of Jesus." What else can we ask for? God has equipped us for battle.[578] We just have to be willing to go.

If the answer to Peggy Lee's question is yes, then *let's break out the booze and have a ball.* But, in Easter, the answer is an emphatic NO; there is so much that awaits us we can't comprehend it this side of heaven.[579] We have a living hope of eternity with Jesus where everything is new.

Father, my heart aches for the lost that are on the path to death. Grant me the boldness and confidence to take the fight to the enemy regardless of rejection, knowing it's not me who is rejected, but You. Thank you for the living hope within that guarantees my future. **Amen**.

576 Ezek. 22:30
577 Isa. 6:8
578 Eph. 6:10-17
579 I Cor. 2:9

Newness is God's glory

"Therefore we have been buried with Him through baptism into death, so that as Christ was raised from the dead through the glory of the Father, so we too might walk in newness of life." Rom. 6:4

A new shirt, golf clubs, boat, car, house. The list goes on. Think about the feeling, however temporary, when you get something new, especially if it's a surprise gift. You might say you glory in the moment. Does it surprise you that God gets glory from making things new? For example after the healing of a paralyzed man, "*They were all struck with astonishment and began glorifying God; and they were filled with fear, saying, 'We have seen remarkable things today.'*"[580]

Unlike our limited, fading glory, God's glory is eternal.[581] And it belongs only to Him.[582] It's actually one of His names: The Glory of Israel.[583] We're on thin ice when we try to take credit (glory) for something that God has done.[584] But God desires that we glorify Him in worship and praise. The longest book in the Bible is filled with both. That should be a clue to help order our priorities. A couple of my favorites are Psalm 19, which starts: "*The heavens are telling of the glory of God and their expanse is declaring the work of His hands.*" Psalm 25: "*To You O Lord, I lift up my soul. O my God, in You I trust.*" Psalm 103: "*Bless the Lord O my soul and all that is within me bless His holy name.*" And so many more.

If you ever feel dry in your private time with God, read through a section of Psalms. You can't do it without coming into contact with His majesty, His power, His mercy. And that, in turn, should prompt your heart to flood with praise for who He is as much as for what He's done. The Bible is filled with the adjective new. Here's just a few: New wine, new moon, new creation, new life, new name, new covenant, new Jerusalem.

It's God's glory to make new stuff that produces praise from our lips. Let me close this section with one of my favorite sections of scripture, Lamentations 3:22-25: "*The Lord's lovingkindnesses indeed **never cease**, for His compassions **never fail**. They are **new every morning**; Great is Your faithfulness. 'The Lord is my portion,' says my soul, 'therefore I have hope in Him.' The Lord is good to those who wait for Him, to the person who seeks Him.*" (emphasis mine)

Almighty God, full of mercy and compassion, all glory belongs to You alone. Thank You for letting me participate in worship and praise to You for Your Word, Your works, and Your future new heavens and new earth. In Christ's name, **Amen**.

580 Luke 5:26
581 John 17:5
582 Isa. 42:8
583 I Sam. 15:29
584 I Cor. 4:7

Obedience, not results, is my measurement

"Has the Lord as much delight in burnt offerings and sacrifices as in obeying the voice of the Lord? Behold, to obey is better than sacrifice and to heed than the fat of rams."
I Sam. 15:22

Nowhere in Scripture can I find a single sentence holding me accountable for results. I find a lot requiring obedience, speaking truth, loving my neighbor. But what if I'm persecuted for the truth, or my neighbor continues his unneighborly ways? So what? God said, through the prophet Micah, "*What do I require of you?*"[585] God's requirements can be summed up in one word: Obedience. We have absolutely no control over the results of our actions. Because of that, God doesn't judge us on whether or not someone got saved because of our testimony. But, and this is important, He does judge us on whether or not we obey His commands. He doesn't judge us sizing us up to others. We are our own measuring stick.

This week, we'll see some really good stuff God has in store for those whose lives are marked by obedience to Him. We'll also see that the opposite is true. One of the biggest hurdles to obedience is wrong counsel from others. We are often encouraged to do what feels right, even though it goes against God's revealed will. For example, putting others ahead of ourselves[586] doesn't come naturally. But God says, "do it." Going the extra mile[587] is beyond the minimum. Many would balk, God says, "do it." So, the bottom line is that we have a choice: Obey—don't obey.

When I was in Jr. and Sr. High School in the 50s and 60s, there was not so much student disobedience and disrespect. It simply wasn't tolerated and was dealt with quickly and decisively…usually with a paddle to your saddle. Even as a Drill Sergeant in the Army (late '60s), physical consequences were a regular occurrence for those trainees who thought they had special privileges. I can only say that those examples of discipline don't compare with God's displeasure over His children's disobedience. Unlike today's social environment where those in authority are afraid to sneeze sideways, God is always thorough, just, and purposeful in His discipline.[588] There's a very simple solution to avoiding God's correction—"*For rulers are not a cause of fear for good behavior, but for evil. Do you want to have no fear of authority? Do what is good and you will have praise from the same.*"[589] Obey—don't obey. What do I require of you?

Father, the concept seems simple: obey, don't obey. But I'm often weak and swayed by those around me to do what *feels* right. Help me to trust Your Word and not my feelings. In Jesus' name, **Amen**.

585 Mic. 6:8
586 Phil. 2:3, 4
587 Matt. 5:41
588 Heb. 12:10
589 Rom. 13:3

Obedience sets the bar

"Do all things without grumbling or disputing; so that you will prove yourselves to be blameless and innocent children of God above reproach in the midst of a crooked and perverse generation, among who you appear as lights in the world." Phil. 2:14, 15

Sometimes, we want the whole world to see us and know our name. Sometimes, and I think this is more often the case, we hope nobody is looking. I remember one time backing my 800 lb. motorcycle out of my garage down an angled driveway. I planned to turn it so I could pull forward into the street. As I was turning while backing, I turned a bit too much, and I reached the tipping point. Fortunately, I had crash bars and was able to lay it down gently. You know the first thing I did? I looked at my neighbors' houses to see if anyone had seen me.

The point in telling on myself is this: we can't control who's watching and when. Paul says in our verse today that we are to be above reproach, to appear as lights in the world. How do we do that? By cultivating a habit of obedience, not because someone is watching but because it's the right thing to do. And, even if nobody sees us, don't forget, God does…always.[590] If we live for the audience of one, it doesn't matter who else is or isn't watching.

As we talked about in Week 29-Monday, everything we do is to be for God's glory.[591] So know this, if we name the name of Jesus Christ, the world is watching, waiting for us to blow it according to their standard or perception of what a Christian should act like. Fair or not, that's the reality we live in. But, we're not alone; God has given us His Holy Spirit[592] to live inside and direct our thinking and our actions. We just have to listen to Him and not all the other voices pulling us away from truth. My question today is this: "How bright is your light?"

Father of Lights, sometimes I really resent the hypocrisy of the world with regard to their expectations of Christians. But then I realize Your standard is *perfection.* May I remember today that as one of Your children, I represent You to a world that loves darkness rather than light, and I'm not responsible for their acceptance or rejection of Your truth. But I am responsible for living above reproach. Empower me to live transparently so others may see Jesus in me. In His name, **Amen**

590 Ps. 32:8; Jer. 16:17
591 I Cor. 10:31
592 John 14:16

Obedience is to Blessing as Disobedience is to Curses

*"Now it shall be, **if** you diligently obey the Lord your God, being careful to do all His commandments which I command you today, the Lord your God will set you high above all the nations of the earth. All these blessings will come upon you and overtake you **if** you obey the Lord your God." Deut. 28:1-14*

*"But it shall come about, **if** you do not obey the Lord your God... that all these curses will come upon you and overtake You." Deut. 28:15-68*

It's hard to visualize the extent of God's blessings and curses without reading all of the above verses, and it's worth the time to look them up and understand that 14 verses describe blessings, but it takes 53 verses to list all the curses, plagues, disasters that accompany disobedience. That, in itself, should be a strong deterrent to disobeying the Lord. But, sadly, it wasn't for Israel and it isn't for most of us.

Fear is considered a primary motivator; you know, fight or flight. And God built into each of us a strong self-preservation instinct to help preserve the human species. It's even used to compare how a husband is to love and care for his wife.[593] Over seventy times in scripture, we are told to fear the Lord, fear God, or fear Him. God's Word can be a great comfort and source of worship and praise for those of us who know Jesus personally. But it can also spawn a terrifying expectation of God's wrath and judgment if we are on the disobedience side of today's equation.[594]

I don't know where you are individually, but God takes obedience seriously. Even when Jesus was on earth, having given up His equality with God (temporarily),[595] He had to "learn" obedience from the things He suffered.[596] If it was important enough to God to school Jesus in obedience, how much more do you think it is for us?

There's probably still a little rebel in each of us. I know it's alive and well in me. It's hard to submit 100% of the time to government authorities, bosses, wives (yes, it's a two-way street) because of pride. But God looks at rebellion as the sin of witchcraft,[597] another of the many sins Jesus died to defang. Let's keep the "long game" in mind today. Life on earth is a vapor.[598] One moment we're here, then we're not. If obedience touts such a list of rewards—and it does—shouldn't we pay attention?

Father, Your Word is very clear that there are only two paths; one is filled with blessings, the other not so much. May I choose rightly. **Amen**

593 Eph. 5:28, 29
594 Heb. 10:26, 27
595 Phil. 2:6
596 Heb. 5:8
597 I Sam. 15:23
598 Jas. 4:14

Obedience is the key to happiness

"He who believes in the Son has eternal life; but he who does not obey the Son will not see life, but the wrath of God abides on him." John 3:36

Buy this. You'll be happy. Go there. You'll be happy. Get rid of wrinkles, lose weight, get whiter teeth, move. Name one product that doesn't promise happiness. Food, cars, clothes, it doesn't matter. They all strut their stuff. So why is there so much anger and hatred if we're happy? We must be buying the econo-brand. Yup, that's gotta be it. Pay extra, get happiness. If you believe that, I've got some property in Florida for you.

Could it be that today's verse holds the key? The biggest question in the universe is answered: "How do I get to heaven?" I'm thinking most people are angry because they haven't dealt with this. Once you have your eternal destination secured, nothing the world throws at you can get you off your game. Robert Frost wrote about a *road less traveled.* Centuries before, Jesus talked about a road less traveled[599] when He pictured the narrow gate and narrow path leading to eternal life. When you realize how long eternity is and compare it to life on earth (a vapor)[600] and its brevity, I can think of nothing producing happiness like obedience to Christ and *knowing* beyond any doubt that I'm not going to experience God's wrath. And it didn't cost *me* anything. It cost Christ plenty—a very painful death on a cross—*for* me.

Here's the rub. Most of us don't have an eternal perspective. We've bought the world's lie that we can have it all…now. I'm reminded of Jack Nicholson's line in the 1992 movie, *A Few Good Men*, "You can't handle the truth." And just what is the truth? One day we will ALL face our creator and have to answer the question, "What did you do with my son?" While we still have breath, it's not too late to jump on the obedience bandwagon. Jesus offers the water of life without cost.[601]

The narrow path, taken by few,[602] can be lonely, challenging, filled with trials, naysayers, and skeptics. But if we "forget what lies behind and press on"[603] to our goal of eternal life with Christ, all of that earthly dross dims in the shadow of the cross. Are you in or out?

Father, the world's lies about how to achieve happiness are everywhere. And, frankly, some of them are pretty attractive. By Your Spirit, help me keep my focus on the prize of eternity with Christ, knowing that the world has nothing that won't burn up in the end. In Christ's name, **Amen**.

599 Matt. 7:13, 14
600 Jas. 4:14
601 Rev. 22:17
602 Matt. 7:14
603 Phil. 3:13, 14

Partial Obedience is no Obedience

"But Peter said, 'Ananias, why has Satan filled your heart to lie to the Holy Spirit and to keep back some of the price of the land?'" Acts 5:3

Grading on a curve was a standard used by some teachers who may have been trying to dodge accountability for poor performance in their classrooms. Standards are what the real world is all about. The US Government's Weights and Measures Division promotes uniformity in... standards to achieve equity between buyers and sellers in the marketplace. Without standards, we'd never know if we really got what we paid for in a gallon of gasoline, a 5-lb. bunch of bananas, or a 10,000 sq. ft. building.

The standard in today's verse was **all of the money** from selling a parcel of land; a sum that was to be donated to the early church. You can read the whole story in Acts 5. Ananias and his wife Sapphira thought they could hold back some of the money, so they lied to Peter. Peter accused them of lying to the Holy Spirit, and God judged them instantly through death.[604] Partial obedience? Hmm.

Suppose Christ had chosen partial obedience in the Garden of Gethsemane?[605] And instead of "drinking the cup" of death, He changed the deal, pulled the plug, walked away. There would be no salvation, no Savior, no future, and "*If we have hoped in Christ in this life only, we are of all men most to be pitied.*"[606]

So you can see from one real example and one what-if example that to not obey completely is the same as not obeying at all. Aren't you glad that Jesus didn't decide that partial was good enough? How about us? Do we sometimes only go part way, thinking that nobody will be the wiser? If you think that, you don't know God very well. Listen to what Ezra said, "*For the eyes of the Lord move to and fro throughout the earth that He may strongly support those whose heart is completely His. You have acted foolishly in this. Indeed, from now on you will surely have wars.*"[607] That's the warning. But look at the promise of "strong support." How would God know whose heart is completely His, if He didn't or couldn't see when we only offered partial obedience? I'm glad that my occasionally partial obedience doesn't limit my salvation; that God doesn't base His gift on my worthiness. Oh, that we could grasp a bigger picture of God's holiness and that would drive us to a more complete obedience.

Lord, I know that You are omniscient and nothing I do escapes Your eye. May I welcome and not fear that because of your support for my wayward heart. Take it and make it completely Yours. **Amen**.

604 Acts 5:3-10
605 Matt. 26:39
606 I Cor. 15:19
607 II Chron. 16:9

Obedience draws a line in the sand

"If anyone does not obey our instruction in this letter, take special note of that person and do not associate with him, so that he will be put to shame." II Thess. 3:14

Exclusivity. The A-list. The in-crowd. Just the name makes us want to be part of the group. I don't ever see a line of folks waiting to get into the "other" groups. Maybe, we're in the other groups by default because we're not cool enough or pretty enough or athletic enough. There's always some qualifier I don't seem to have. But there is one group I have total control over being (or staying) in. The group of obeyers. And it's a pretty select group because the requirement to get in is humility. Obedience requires the humility to say, "I'm not the boss." It requires humility to practice total not partial obedience. Let's be honest, even on our best day, we struggle with obedience.

But here's the good news. Paul's warning in today's verse is clearly for those folks who just don't give a rip. They're gonna do what they're gonna do, and nobody's gonna tell them no. So, unless you're one of "those" people, you can stay in the group. Paul's message is simply that disobedience without repentance should cause shame. When you look at the world's standards today, it's sad that those with manners, those who yield their "rights" to others are so few and far between. And there's no shame.

Scripture warns us that in the last days, "*mockers will come with their mocking, **following after their own lusts.***"[608] And again, "*men will be lovers of self, lovers of money, boastful, arrogant, revilers, disobedient to parents, ungrateful, unholy, unloving, irreconcilable, malicious gossips, without self-control, brutal, haters of good…holding to a form of godliness, although they have denied its power; **Avoid such men as these.***"[609] *(Emphasis mine).*

In God's world, we who obey Him are expected to set a Godly example, a light before men[610] that it causes them to glorify God. What an extraordinary privilege. So, obedience produces glory to God; disobedience results in my shame. Hmmm. Not much of a choice, is it? Isn't it interesting that God never forces us to choose Him, but He is pretty specific about the consequences of making the wrong choice? All those in favor…

Holy God, judge of heaven and earth, sometimes Your ways seem narrow and restrictive. But then I compare obedience and the blessings that come with it to the alternative and I'm overcome with Your goodness. Thank You. **Amen.**

608 II Pet. 3:3
609 II Tim. 3:2-5
610 Matt. 5:16

Obedience displays Christlikeness

"Being found in appearance as a man, He humbled Himself by becoming obedient to the point of death, even death on a cross." Phil. 2:8

Growing up in a rigid household was a mixed bag for me. As all young boys do, I wanted to stretch the boundaries, many of which I didn't like or consider fair. But as I look back with the perspective of being a grandfather, I see the value of obedience in a home and a society. Jesus spoke to His disciples about signs of the end. I'm quoting only one here because it ties to our discussion of obedience. "*Because lawlessness is increased, most people's love will grow cold.*"[611] If you've lived for a few decades, you are seeing it too. Disregard for others' space, property, and preferences has mushroomed into a generation of "me, me, me."

Let's look closer at our role model for all the character qualities in this book: our Lord Jesus Christ. Today's verse is the ultimate definition and standard of obedience. The writer of Hebrews reminds us, "*You have not yet resisted to the point of shedding blood in your striving against sin.*"[612] It is true that some have been martyred for their faith, especially in the Middle East, where Christians are hated. But the reality of the agony suffered by Jesus is beyond our comprehension.[613] Furthermore, what attitude would have to be in place for us to give our life for someone? Paul tells the Romans, "*For one will hardly die for a righteous man, though perhaps for the good man someone would dare even to die.*"[614] That pales by comparison to the next verse, "*But God demonstrates His own love toward us, in that while we were yet sinners, Christ died for us.*"[615]

Before we get discouraged over our failure to measure up to God's standard of obedience—perfection—remember that Christ's act of love covers ALL our sins, including any level of disobedience. The takeaway is that because we're not held guilty, our gratitude, our praise, our motivation to "*walk humbly with our God*"[616] should grow each time we remember our debt that was wiped out at the cross. Persecution is coming. Is our obedience practiced to the point of no return?

Lord Jesus, I can't imagine what You went through for me. Increase my strength, my willingness, my devotion *to* You, so I will be able to stand firm in the hour of trial...*for* You. In Your name, **Amen**.

611 Matt. 24:12
612 Heb. 12:4
613 *A Physician's View of the Crucifixion of Jesus Christ* by Dr. C. Truman Davis
614 Rom. 5:7
615 Rom. 5:8
616 Mic. 6:8

Openness/Transparency puts Christ on display

"You are the light of the world. A city set on a hill cannot be hidden." Matt. 5:14

Years ago, I was on a tour of some underground caverns. Our guide took us deeper and deeper into the amazing formations. Then we were told to stop and grab the rail the lights were about to go out. After a couple minutes of trying to adjust to total darkness without any improvement—I couldn't even see my hand six inches from my nose—the guide lit a single match. That one small match allowed us to see many yards into the distance.

What an example of today's verse. Jesus said that we *are* the light of the world. That's a title we share with Him.[617] He didn't say we could be or would be, we are. As I saw in the darkness of that cavern, one of the properties of light is that it overcomes darkness. Jesus said, "*Men loved the darkness rather than the light for their deeds were evil.*"[618] Like a moth to a flame, the world is drawn to the light in us, even if only out of curiosity or the purpose of mocking. Our job is to make the light attractive. The more our batteries are charged through plugging into God's Word and fellowship with other believers, the brighter our light shines. Does our light sometimes dim or flicker? Sure, especially when we have unconfessed sin or are living in rebellion. But praise God, that's not a permanent condition.

A common theme throughout this book is to be ready for Christ's return to take us home. Knowing that and knowing the world is watching our light, Peter asks a pointed question, *"Since all these things are to be destroyed in this way, what sort of people ought you to be in holy conduct and godliness?"*[619] The answer is simple; open and transparent—nothing hidden. We want others to see Jesus in us, don't we? Aren't we so overjoyed with gratitude for what He's done for us that we bubble over? That's what makes Jesus attractive, the irresistible joy that the world doesn't have. Others *are* watching. Let's give them something to make them want to see the reruns.

Lord God, Your love put Christ on display, and most of the world rejected Him. Don't let us get discouraged when they do the same to us. It's not the messenger they reject, it's the message. May we stay plugged into You so that our light can be seen wherever we go. In Jesus' name, **Amen**.

617 John 8:12; John 9:5
618 John 3:19
619 II Pet. 3:11

Openness/Transparency requires Accountability

"Even the darkness is not dark to You, and the night is as bright as day. Darkness and light are alike to You." Psa. 139:12

There have been several movies and TV shows lately showing our military in a positive way. Amen. One of the things we've seen is the view through night vision goggles (NVGs). I'm sure what we see is not the latest version, but even so, to be able to see in the dark and find the target gives us a big advantage in combat zones. Unlike the greenish aura of NVGs, today's verse gives us a glimpse of what God can see: everything.

If we understand that God not only *sees* everything, He also knows our motives, our *unseen* desires and feelings, then we must also realize that we are open and transparent to Him whether we want it or not. There's a simple but profound children's song that goes like this:

Be careful little hands what you do…
For the Father up above is looking down in love
So be careful little hands what you do.

Why do we resent accountability so strongly? Could it be we're holding onto some "little" sin that we don't want to give up? Could it be that we have a position of leadership that would be in jeopardy if people knew our hearts? Jerry Bridges has a challenging book, *"Respectable Sins-Confronting the Sins We Tolerate,"* [620] that will challenge your walk and make you rethink your current holiness standard. Here are some of the issues he addresses: Anxiety and frustration; Discontentment; Unthankfulness; Pride; Selfishness; Lack of self-control; Impatience and irritability; Anger, and there's more. Get the Bible.

We might as well embrace it. God knows us inside and out; we can't hide anything from Him. Not our thoughts, our actions, our motives. If you don't have another guy that you trust to be open and transparent with, make it a priority to find one. Do it now, I'll wait…

Heavenly Father, I know I'm accountable to You eventually. Help me understand that you've created accountability for my protection now and my holiness, which brings glory to You. I'm so caught up in me that I often miss Your working behind the scenes to transform me into the image of Your Son. Open my eyes. In Christ's name, **Amen.**

620 ©NavPress 2007

Openness/Transparency is not afraid of judgment

"For God will bring every act to judgment, everything which is hidden, whether good or evil." Eccl. 12:14

Last week we talked about fear of authority. And fear is certainly a motivator, short term maybe, but still a motivator. Phobia is another word for fear. We've all heard of phobias. Some of us may have one or two. Just for fun, I looked up a list of the top 100 phobias and found an ironic word that I laughed out loud when I saw it. The fear of long words is called *Hippopotomonstrosesquippedaliophobia*. As silly as it sounds, it's a real condition and appears at number 26. *Arachnophobia,* the fear of spiders, is the most common on this list of 100 and affects women 4 times more than men.

But what is not silly, and what we should have a healthy fear of, is God's judgment. Today's verse says EVERY act (you can also include thoughts and motives)[621] will come under God's judgment. And guess what? God doesn't grade on a curve. His standard is absolute and there's no negotiating. You're either (still) guilty, or you've been born again into God's forever family where Jesus paid the price for your sin and guilt. Here's what I don't understand. Sin and guilt demand payment, punishment for violating a law. And that punishment will be exact,[622] precise, painful,[623] eternal[624]...and avoidable. Jesus paid with His blood to make it avoidable. But many walk away in disbelief, saying things like, "I've done too many bad things" or "That sounds too good to be true" or the dumbest one ever, "I've been pretty good, I'll take my chances." Do you know why Las Vegas has so many fancy, neon-lit buildings? Because the odds favor the house. Always. You want to take your chances? Don't.

The devil won't point out the small print to you. He's at the entrance to the "wide gate"[625] with flashing lights, calling you to "turn in here"[626] while offering pleasure[627] that feels good for the moment.[628] Oh yeah, it feels good. But then comes tomorrow. And remember the one characteristic that defines Satan more than any other: HE'S A LIAR.[629] Don't be naive. Jesus paid your admission to heaven. Repent, become transparent, LIVE.

Lord, open my eyes to Your offer of a "paid in full" ticket to heaven and turn my eyes and mind away from glitzy lies. In Jesus' name, **Amen**.

621 I Chron. 28:9
622 Rev. 20:12
623 Luke 16:24
624 Rev. 20:10, 15
625 Matt. 7:13
626 Prov. 9:16-18
627 Prov. 7:10, 21, 23
628 Job 20:5
629 John 8:44

Openness/Transparency keeps the darkness at bay

"Do not be bound together with unbelievers; for what partnership have righteousness and lawlessness, or what fellowship has light with darkness?" II Cor. 6:14

The boogey man checks under his bed at night for Chuck Norris. (Sorry, couldn't help it.) Many of us are, if not afraid, then at least cautious about the dark. We sleep with nightlights. We have white noise generators. We just don't like it. Physical darkness is one thing. Spiritual darkness is quite another. There are many verses that equate sin and wicked men to darkness. Here are a couple that really nail it. "*The way of the wicked is like darkness; they do not know over what they stumble.*" [630] And, "*For our struggle is not against flesh and blood, but against the rulers, against the powers, against the world forces of this darkness, against the spiritual forces of wickedness in the heavenly places.*" [631]

As we saw earlier, even a very small light dispels darkness. The light of God's Word, the Holy Spirit dwelling in us, and our obedience are obvious to those around us. This open transparency provides a shield of light that darkness cannot penetrate, but, in fact, runs from.[632] As reborn children of God, we walk in the light of understanding.[633] The closer we walk with God, the less power darkness has over us.

So what's the takeaway? The Bible tells us, "*Do not fear those who kill the body but are unable to kill the soul; but rather fear Him who is able to destroy both soul and body in hell.*"[634] What does that mean? As we are pummeled day after day by the craftiness and deceit of men,[635] God promises to have our six. He promises not to allow us to be tempted "*beyond what you are able.*"[636] The Christian walk is one first of all of faith. God is faithful.[637] God cannot lie.[638] Trust Him. And then it's one of action. Sitting on the sidelines because of fear or laziness will only result in Christ's condemnation at His return.[639] Walk in the light. You won't stumble, and others will be drawn to Christ by your life.

Oh God of power, may I walk in Your light, confident and sure of my direction and destination. Make Your pathway clear and help me dump any baggage that hinders my progress. In my Savior's name, **Amen**.

630 Prov. 4:19
631 Eph. 6:12
632 John 1:5
633 Prov. 28:5
634 Matt. 10:28
635 Eph. 4:14
636 I Cor. 10:13
637 Deut. 7:9
638 Tit. 1:2
639 Matt. 25:26

Openness/Transparency...before it's too late

"The night is almost gone, and the day is near. Therefore let us lay aside the deeds of darkness and put on the armor of light." Rom. 13:12

Life is full of warning signs when we approach physical danger; slow, yield, high voltage. And we're taught from childhood to obey them. Ever wonder why we don't take spiritual warnings as seriously? What's the worst that *may* happen if we disregard, say, a high voltage sign? We could get electrocuted. If we know Jesus, that has an upside. What's the worst that *will* happen if we ignore Biblical warnings? Utter darkness, weeping, gnashing of teeth, and burning torment in the lake of fire[640] day and night forever.

Today's verse has an interesting picture: armor of light. What is armor for? Protection. What is light for? Visibility, to see or be seen. In Ephesians, Paul tells us that the "full" armor includes truth, righteousness, the gospel of peace, shield of faith, helmet of salvation, sword of the Spirit, and prayer.[641] Not what we typically think of as armor. So why light? If we have the full armor operating in our life, it *is* the light that points others to Jesus. We're not to hide it.[642] The use of the phrase *put on* tells us it's not optional; it's a command. And, as with all commands, we can choose to obey or suffer the consequences.

But here's what I know. God doesn't give us commands to limit or punish us. He does it for our protection (armor). Remember, He is our "daddy."[643] He loves us with unconditional love.[644] The consequences are not necessarily punishment. This is the point of warning signs. Bad things happen to those who disregard them. Because God loves us, He doesn't want bad things to happen to us. I'm not saying if we obey, we'll never have problems in this life. The rain falls on the righteous and the unrighteous.[645] What I'm saying is God wants to protect us from ourselves, from bad decisions,[646] bad companions,[647] and a bad eternity.

This armor of light is a result of our openness and transparency. When our life is above reproach, open to the toughest scrutiny, we offer the world something they rarely see: a living picture of Jesus Christ. Doesn't that thought fire your jets? If not, you're overdue for a tune-up.

Holy God, help me see that Your commands are meant to protect me, not punish me. May I be in it for the long game—eternity—not today's pleasure. In Jesus' name, **Amen**.

---

640 Rev. 20:10, 15
641 Eph. 6:14-18
642 Matt. 5:14-16
643 Rom. 8:15; Gal. 4:6
644 John 3:16
645 Matt. 5:45
646 Prov. 1:1-7
647 I Cor. 15:33

Openness/Transparency doesn't cover up our sin

"For everyone who does evil hates the Light, and does not come to the Light, for their deeds were evil." Jn. 3:20

How many of us could stand up under the scrutiny currently rampant in Washington and Hollywood? I can't count the recent targets of sexual harassment exposés. We may never know how many are real and how many made it through the creative process. Abraham Lincoln said, "You can fool all the people some of the time, and some of the people all the time, but you cannot fool all the people all the time." And that may be true of mankind. But I guarantee you this, you can't fool God any of the time.

Do you think it's possible to slide so slowly down the slippery slope of sin and darkness that we deny it and become immune to truth? The Bible says, "*The heart is more deceitful than all else and is desperately sick; Who can understand it*?"[648] Have you ever thought or said, "What's the big deal? Everybody's doing it." First of all, everybody's *not* doing "it." Secondly, have you ever heard of lemmings? Sin is subtle. Satan is a master of deception. You know about the frog in the pan of water, right? Turn the heat up slowly and you get boiled frog. Drop him into boiling water, and he's out in a flash. Sin takes hold of us the same way. I doubt if any reading this would wake up one morning and decide today's the day I'm going to cheat on my wife. But it happens slowly step by step, glance by glance, thought by thought. Understand that nobody is immune to temptation. And, temptation, in and of itself, is NOT sin. It's what we do with it that determines.

If we're caught in the snare of sin and think nobody knows, we're deceiving ourselves *and the truth is not in us.*[649] We may attend church, even go to men's groups, but away from the "Christian" crowd, we're...different. Several things will happen. First, your sin will grow in frequency and severity. Second, your lies to cover it will get more elaborate. Third, you will change physically; you'll become tired, get a nervous stomach, and become depressed in the "real" circumstances of your life. Finally, you WILL BE FOUND OUT.[650] Ask Bill Cosby or Harvey Weinstein how it's working out for them.

God is not lurking, waiting to out you at the worst possible moment. But Satan is. He hates you and sets traps everywhere. That's why we need to *walk in the light.*[651] Is your water warming up?

Father, give me strength to get out of the pan and stay on Your path. Forgive me for lying to You and myself. In Christ's name, **Amen**.

648 Jer. 17:9
649 I John 1:8
650 Num. 32:23
651 I John 1:7

Openness/Transparency threatens those who would hide their sin.

"Do not participate in the unfruitful deeds of darkness, but instead even expose them." Eph. 5:11

Have you ever turned over a rock in the forest and seen all the little critters scampering to get away from the light? This week's subject has been about our not living under *a* rock but living in *the* Rock.[652] For much of our lives, we likely have shunned the light which illuminates, exposes, and condemns us. Why? We can't hide anything from an all-seeing God.[653] Let's cut to the chase; walking in the light, openly and transparently, is work. We're tired, even weary. Maybe we don't get the answers to prayer we think we should. Maybe we've been disappointed by those in a position of leadership in the church. Maybe we haven't seen the success we think we deserve. Whatever the reason, I say, so what? God doesn't hold us accountable for the acts of others.[654] We have to answer for our own choices.

Today's verse takes our life one step further. Not only is it our responsibility to obey and (passively?) set an example for those around us, we are called to expose sin openly and aggressively when and where we find it. I'm not saying we become judge, jury, and executioner with our fellow pilgrims. Remember, Jesus warned us about taking the log out of our own eye?[655] But I am saying we can't sit on the sidelines and not speak up for righteousness. *"All that is necessary for evil to prevail is for good men to do nothing."*[656] Look around. This world has lost its way. Politicians no longer lead or do what's best for the country. It seems a fulfillment of prophecy right before our eyes.[657]

We have a choice. We can maintain distance and silence—continue to be part of the problem—or we can boldly become part of the solution. Paul told the Ephesians to *"expose them."* What does that look like? Stealing, swearing, bullying, cheating on IRS returns. There are so many. Paul told Timothy to *"avoid such men."*[658] Examine your relationships. If "friends" aren't pointing you to Christ, they're probably pulling you down to their level. Don't let that keep you from walking in the light. Your actions may even create an opportunity to share Christ with your friends.

Lord, I have become comfortable, even lazy, in my walk with You when there is so much evil around. Grant me boldness to live in the light and to (humbly) call out darkness wherever I find it. For You, **Amen**.

---

652 I Cor. 10:4
653 Job 28:24
654 Deut. 24:16
655 Matt. 7:5
656 Generally attributed to Edmund Burke
657 II Tim. 3:2-5
658 Ibid.

Patience allows God to provide in His time and His way.

"My soul, wait in silence for God only. For my hope is from Him." Ps.62:1

Two vultures sat on a cactus. The first says, "Be patient." The second replies, "Patience nothing. I want to kill something." For "men of action," aren't we more like the second vulture? Waiting (on our wives, on hold, on *anything*) just isn't in our DNA. A common, but wrong, piece of advice goes something like this: "It doesn't matter what you do. Just DO something." That's akin to saying, "It doesn't matter what road you take, just start driving." Neither will move you closer to your goal. You do have goals, don't you? But I digress.

This week will not be an easy trek. One of Satan's most successful strategies is to appeal to our pride (*If* you are the Son of God...[659]) by challenging our knowledge of truth. Remember, he tried this (successfully) in the Garden of Eden when he questioned God's integrity: "Did God *really* say...?"[660] And why would he give up a winning tactic? In this context, he might say, "You don't really need to wait (on God). You're smart and clever. You can make up your own mind. If you don't act now, the opportunity will be gone, and you'll lose out." We should adopt a standard answer to this temptation. Just say, "So what?" The first rule of negotiating is to be willing to walk away (from the deal). That should also be our reaction to pressure to decide. If someone isn't willing to give us time to pray, think, reason, etc. we don't need whatever they're selling. Contrast that with what God said to Isaiah, "Come now, let us *reason* together...[661]"

Think about this. Do we, apart from God's Spirit, possess the resources, the wisdom, the control of circumstances to affect any outcome? So why then wouldn't we give God the chance to "*strongly support*"[662] us? The only reason I can think is we don't meet the criterion of "*whose heart is completely His.*"[663]

Let's start this week by realizing that God *wants* to bless us,[664] He has the resources,[665] and His plan is better than anything we could devise[666]

Father, pour out Your grace on me that I might see a lengthening of my fuse and recognize when I'm under attack by the enemy. **Amen**

659 Matt. 4:3, 6; Matt. 27:40
660 Gen. 3:1
661 Isa. 1:18
662 2 Chr.16:9
663 ibid
664 Lam.3:25
665 Ps. 50:10
666 Isa. 1:19

Patience gives us time to re-think our decisions.

"I waited patiently for the Lord; and He inclined to me and heard my cry." Ps. 40:1

Do I really need this? Do I need it now? If I wait, can I get a better price or more options thrown in? Can I get better quality for the same price? These are good questions to ask ourselves when emotion has us reaching for our wallet. Have I prayed about it? Have I discussed it with my wife? More good questions. Billions of dollars are spent each year by companies trying to get you to buy things you don't need, pay more than you can afford, and convince you that, by all means, you're worth it. Hogwash.

If a salesman won't give you time to ponder, he's not really watching out for your best interest. His eye is on his commission that, nine times out of ten walks out the front door with you. Do you think God doesn't want you to have…fill in the blank? Jesus compared His Father with earthly fathers who "know how to give good gifts.[667] The key is that God gives "what is **good** to those who ask Him.[668] Not everything we want is good for us. But it takes a certain level of maturity to admit that. "I want what I want when I want it" is more likely our mindset.

We've probably all gone grocery shopping when we were hungry. We get home and wonder why we bought this or that. It seemed so appealing just an hour earlier. Patience is a habit that is only acquired over time and practice. Hasty decisions don't *always* have bad consequences, just most of the time. I know a couple who won't make any major (over $200) purchase without sleeping on it. If it still seems right tomorrow after praying and talking it out, then do it. It's good to know specific buying cycles. For example, you can get a better deal on a car during the last 10 days of the month because of dealer reporting requirements.

If you're tempted to decide quickly, go back to the opening questions. In a recent study, more people felt regret than contentment after an impulse purchase (44.5% vs. 42.5%).[669] Are we asking the right questions? Are we asking the right Person? God doesn't want to keep us from good things. But He wants us to seek Him first.[670]

Lord God, help me to keep my focus on You, not shiny objects. In Jesus' name, **Amen**.

667 Matt. 7:11
668 ibid
669 July 2017 www.finder.com
670 Matt.6:33

Patience relinquishes control to God and others

"So then, none of you can be My disciple who does not give up all his possessions."
Luke 14:33

Somebody says you're a "Type A" personality. You respond with, "You say that like it's a bad thing." Leadership (the spiritual gift of administrations)[671] is a big responsibility. One aspect is to develop those in your charge. Because of your experience, age, and presumably wisdom, you likely are a capable leader. But letting others and especially God call the shots is, for you, like watching paint dry. You were probably born with a (pick one) riding crop, bullhorn, conductor's baton in your hand; something to urge others to do things *your* way. You've done things your way for so long, and hopefully successfully, that it's hard for you to not automatically offer advice when you perceive others are struggling and, to you, the answer is obvious.

If we are to grow in patience, we *must* give others the chance to succeed. I know this can be painful, but offer the same grace to others that you like to receive. Remember, the body (of Christ) is supposed to rejoice, not resent, when other members are honored.[672] And as for yielding control to God, rather than say, "I've got this one, God," say something like, "God, show me *Your* plan and give me the humility to follow it." That's right. A key ingredient to growing in patience is...humility. (Told you this week would be hard.) But guess what? This attitude of patience, especially when you've done what's right and suffer for it, finds favor with God.[673]

I used to believe that people (generally) wanted to know when they were doing something in a seemingly less than efficient way, and it was my place to "enlighten" them. After trying out this philosophy, very unsuccessfully, I might add, on my wife, I learned that people (generally) **don't** want to know my opinion. I am trying to learn to keep my mouth shut unless asked for advice. This week is hard for me too.

Since patience is one of the fruits of the Spirit, and I, for one, need much more of it, giving up control of things over which I really have little to no control anyway to God and others will happen as I empty myself of self and allow the Holy Spirit to have more of me. Will you join me this week?

Holy Spirit, today I offer You more say, more control in my life. Help me walk faithfully in Your plans for God's glory. **Amen**.

671 I Cor. 12:28
672 I Cor. 12:26
673 I Pet. 2:19, 20

Patience is not found apart from humility

"Therefore, humble yourselves under the mighty hand of God, that He may exalt you at ***the proper time****." I Pet.5:6 (emphasis added)*

Did you ever wonder what "the proper time" is? The simple answer is, "Whenever God says it is." But more precisely, it's when our preparedness, our readiness, coincides with God's perfect timetable. See if you can see yourself in the following verse:

"Whoever exalts himself shall be humbled and whoever humbles himself shall be exalted." Matt. 23:12

Do you want to be exalted, recognized, praised? Don't jump the gun; become humble. By the way, if we don't humble ourselves, God has infinite ways to do it for us...and He will. The Bible tells us that God *resists* the proud but gives grace to the humble.[674] Being opposed by God on anything is not somewhere you want to be. Start now to kill your pride. This is where you'll need extreme patience; it's not an overnight event; humility often takes years. Pride is so embedded in us, we often don't even recognize it as the motive which drives many of our actions.

Patience and humility are like the chicken and egg question: Which comes first? The answer is Yes. If you work on one, either one, the other can't help but follow. Let's look at today's verse a little deeper. First, it's something that we can **do** ourselves, but not **by** ourselves. It must be "under the mighty hand of God." What does that mean? Simply, don't fight God's dealing in your life. Trials are designed by God to chip away our rough edges and make us more like Christ. When we chafe under God's instruction or correction, it only takes longer and is usually more painful. I remember a note I wrote in the margin of a Bible when I read Psalm 78 and saw how the Israelites continued to demand of God but wouldn't obey. In verse 31, it says, *"The anger of God rose against them and He killed some of their stoutest ones (32) in spite of all this they still sinned and did not believe in His wonderful works."* My note: Repent early.

Because patience and humility are gained through perseverance, don't delay; start now to model Christ's example, who "*humbled Himself to the point of death on a cross.*"[675]

Lord Jesus, your example of patience and humility led You to the cross. Strengthen my resolve to yield anything that stands in my way. **Amen**

674 I Pet. 5:5
675 Phil. 2:8

Patience reduces stress

"The end of a matter is better than its beginning; Patience of spirit is better than haughtiness of spirit." Ecc. 7:8

Seen on a secretary's desk (just before she was fired): "Your failure to plan does not constitute an emergency for me." One executive was fond of saying, "I don't experience stress, I give it to others." Both of these denials of stress can lead to negative consequences. According to the American Psychiatric Association, "*Multiple studies have shown that... sudden emotional stresses — especially anger — can trigger heart attacks, arrhythmia and even sudden death.*"[676] You've probably heard all your life, when you're tempted to respond angrily, count to 10. Some of us probably need to count to 100. Did you know that Chuck Norris counted to infinity...twice? (sorry, couldn't resist) What's a good single-word for patience? Waiting. Waiting gives us precious time to pray quickly, see a bigger picture than the immediate source of irritation, and stop digging.[677]

Impatience belies our inner attitude of superiority. We think we know more or have a better grasp of how to do something than the person causing our irritation. If that's not true, ask yourself why does (whatever's bugging you) bother you so much? You know, the Bible tells us to think about it; "examine ourselves."[678] Two primary reasons. First, to make sure we are "in the faith"[679] and second, not to pass judgment on others.[680]

Deadlines, last-minute changes to our plans, and even our own tempers are just some of the "sandpaper" God uses to polish us for use in His kingdom.[681] In today's verse, Solomon uses the word haughtiness, which implies looking down on others and concludes that patience is better. Can you picture any true servant of God attracting souls for the kingdom with a personality or through an attitude of haughtiness, arrogance, or superiority? You DO want to be used by God for His kingdom, don't you? Listen to Solomon. Patience is the key. Reduction of stress is a by-product.

Heavenly Father, You have blessed me with much. May I not be arrogant because of it and turn people away from You. Fill me anew with Your Holy Spirit to improve my patience and enjoy stress reduction in the process. In Jesus' name, **Amen**.

676 www.apa.org Krantz, D.S., Whittaker, K.S. & Sheps, D.S. (2011). "Psychosocial risk factors for coronary artery disease: Pathophysiologic mechanisms."
677 "*If you find yourself in a hole, stop digging.*" Will Rogers
678 Gal. 6:4
679 II Cor. 13:5
680 Rom. 2:1, 3
681 I Pet. 2:21

Patience builds faith and trust in God

"Therefore do not go on passing judgment ***before the time****, but wait until the Lord comes ... and then each man's praise will come to him from God." I Cor. 4:5 (emphasis added)*

Waiting, without a goal or hope, without a purpose, is like telling your kids, "because I said so." Dante's *Divine Comedy* had it right in the "welcome" sign over the entrance to hell: "Abandon hope all ye who enter here." For those who believe something other than that death ushers us into either heaven (on the blood of Jesus alone) or hell, patience makes absolutely no sense. Patience *has* to be linked to something future. Otherwise, we would let our impulses rule our decision making. Imagine your kids tearing into their Christmas presents on December 19th or dropping out of college or walking away from their marriage and telling you it's because they have no hope for tomorrow. Far-fetched? Maybe. But ask yourself why God doesn't answer every prayer immediately and the way we want it. The simple answer is because, like every good father,[682] He knows that not everything we ask for is good for us. So we can either accept that God is smarter than us or we can build resentment and anger.

Maranatha! Singers wrote the song *In His Time* (1999) in which the lyrics, "*He makes all things beautiful in his time"* are repeated. What a great reminder that we can rest in God and wait, and ALL things will be beautiful in God's timing, not ours. So we wait, with hope, with faith in God's promises knowing that God cannot lie.[683]

So, what future is your patience linked to? Is it a new car, a new job, losing weight, traveling, marrying? There are so many possibilities. As a good friend of mine often says, "That's all going to burn up." What if we focus on something that *can't* burn up? In Matthew 5, Jesus was teaching the crowd through a series of revolutionary ideas and flat out rebukes, e.g., "*Don't worry about what you're going to eat drink or wear* (my paraphrase, things that will burn up), *but seek first God's righteousness...*(something that will last throughout eternity)[684] *and God will provide your temporal needs.*"[685]

If we accept the premise that God *can't* lie, then *everything* He says is true. Let's exercise our patience and see what God will do.

Lord God, You have proven yourself faithful over and over, and still we pause and question and waver in our faith. May today be the day we break out of our rut and trust You fully for our future. For Jesus, **Amen**.

682 Matt. 7:11
683 Titus 1:2
684 Rom. 5:21
685 Matt. 6:31-33

Patience yields insight into God's perspective

"These things you have done and I kept silence; you thought that I was just like you; I will reprove you and state the case in order before your eyes." Ps. 50:21

The long con. The end game. Terms that imply patience, planning, persistence. Peter wrote, "*The Lord is not slow about His promise, as some count slowness, but is patient toward you, not wishing for any to perish but for all to come to repentance.*"[686] In chess, the end game consists of the final moves to place an opponent in checkmate. But it doesn't happen by accident. Likewise, God has been planning His "final moves" regarding us since before creation.[687] We live in an "instant" society. We have instant meals, 1-hour dry cleaning, instant communication via email, Facebook, Twitter, etc. We get our news in 15 second sound bites. All this feeds our impatient nature. But look at what God told His prophet Habakkuk, "*...though it tarries (the vision), wait for it; for it **will certainly come**, it will not delay.*"[688] (emphasis added). We don't view time the same way God does. To Him, "*...with the Lord, one day is like a thousand years, and a thousand years like one day.*"[689]

For those of us who know Jesus, we anxiously await the culmination of God's mercy, namely our final sanctification and glorification.[690] For those who don't know Jesus, be thankful God is giving you more time to wake up,[691] confess your sins,[692] and secure your place in heaven.[693] Don't wait. We can't count on tomorrow. The Bible says, "*...now is the acceptable time, now is the day of salvation.*"[694]

Sometimes, waiting on God's end game seems like it will never happen. Don't despair. It **will** happen just as God said it would.[695]

So what's our takeaway? We are to be busy "laying up treasures **in heaven**."[696] How? Investing in gospel ministries. Praying, with patience, for the lost. Meeting the physical needs of others.[697]

Father, help me to allow your patience to be my example and follow it as an example to others. In Jesus' name, **Amen**.

686 2 Pet. 3:9
687 Eph. 1:4
688 Hab. 2:3
689 2 Pet. 3:8
690 Jude 21
691 Rev. 3:3
692 Rom. 10:9
693 Rom. 10:10
694 2 Cor. 6:2
695 Mark 13:31
696 Matt. 6:19-21
697 Matt. 25:34-40

Perseverance Gets the Job Done

"But the seed in the good soil, these are the ones who have heard the word in an honest and good heart, and hold it fast, and bear fruit with perseverance." Luke 8:15

Perseverance, a working definition: "The willingness to continue even without the catalyst of praise or temporary gratification, and in spite of difficulties, because our eyes are on the prize." Just like seed must persevere to produce fruit (it only happens overnight in fairy tales, e.g., Jack and the Beanstalk), so we must hang in there to "git 'er done." It applies at work, at home, at church, on the athletic field, and especially in marriages. You can't name something worth pursuing that doesn't require us to stick it out. There are so many trite sayings like "winners never quit and quitters never win" that 'cliché' doesn't even begin to describe how the motivation intended by the saying falls flat.

So how does this apply to men who are pursuing *Christ in Men Today?* My first question is this: What is "the job" we're trying to get done? Isn't it to arrive home in heaven and hear Jesus say, "Well done"? [698] Guys, that doesn't happen just sitting in the pew. Knowledge is good,[699] even necessary. But knowledge alone makes arrogant.[700] We have to put that knowledge to work **for the glory of God**.[701] Our life in Christ is a marathon, not a sprint. But, oh, the rewards are worth whatever we have to go through to receive the victor's crown. Paul described it this way, *"Whatever things were gain to me, those things I have counted as loss for the sake of Christ. More than that, I count all things to be loss in view of the surpassing value of knowing Christ Jesus my Lord…"* [702]

This week we'll be looking at endurance, discipline, goal setting, rewards, trials, hardship, and maybe a few more. Don't get weak-kneed on me now. Make it all the way to Saturday and you'll be glad you stuck it out. Hey, there's a new name for us: Stickers. I'll try not to be too hard on us, but men, the time is getting shorter, the kingdom is closer than it's ever been, and God is looking for a few good men whose heart is completely His.[703] And listen to the promise: God wants to **strongly support** them.[704] Can't ask for more than that, can we? Are you in or out?

Lord God, perseverance is not a strong suit for many of us. Forgive our apathy and lethargy when it comes to kingdom work. Strengthen our resolve to follow you more closely in your plan, not ours. In Christ, **Amen**.

698 Luke 19:17
699 Prov. 19:2
700 I Cor. 8:1
701 I Cor. 10:31
702 Phil. 3:7, 8
703 II Chron. 16:9
704 Ibid.

Perseverance is in Good Company

"But flee from these things, you man of God, and pursue righteousness, godliness, faith, love, perseverance and gentleness." I Tim. 6:11

Everybody has a top-10 list of something; cars, software apps, teams, songs, the list goes on. Today's verse gives us a *top-6* list from God. There's also a *bottom-6* list of things God hates (*Prov. 6:16*), but that's for a different discussion. Can any of us read today's list and not know we need more of all of them?

But here's why perseverance stands out from the list: It's a prerequisite for all the others. In our pursuit of Christlikeness, we will encounter all sorts of trials.[705] James says *when* not *if*. The author of Hebrews tells us, "*You have not yet resisted to the point of shedding blood in your striving against sin.*" (*Heb. 12:4*) I'm betting every one of us can, without much delay, think of something or someone providing a hindrance to our (pick one of the six). Perseverance—sticking it out—is what will see us through to victory. Perseverance has its eyes on the prize,[706] not the obstacles. If the prize is valuable enough, and heaven and eternity with Jesus certainly are, we don't often know we're being persecuted because of the joy of knowing and growing in Christ.

The cross clearly was not joyful for Christ, but Hebrews tells us, "*He (Christ)* ***endured*** *the cross, despising the shame...*"[707] (emphasis mine) and He did it for "*the joy set before Him.*"[708] What was the joy that was great enough to enable Jesus to complete His mission? Simply knowing He was perfectly accomplishing His Father's will. Have you ever experienced that kind of joy, of knowing that God was pleased with you?

Without perseverance, it's easy to lose heart, to give up, to quit. But God doesn't want quitters in His army. He wants those who are willing to go the extra mile.[709] If we focus on heaven, trials and yesterdays will only be memories in our rear-view mirrors. Paul tells us to "*forget what lies behind.*"[710] But he doesn't stop there. He goes on, "*...and reaching forward, I press on toward the goal of the prize of the upward call of God in Christ Jesus.*"[711] Just one question as we wrap up today, "What are we pressing on toward?"

Lord Jesus, without Your perseverance, there'd be no salvation, no heaven for me, no future or hope. Thank You for not quitting halfway to the cross. Give me the vision and hope not to quit on You. **Amen**

705 James 1:2
706 I Cor. 9:24; II Tim. 2:5
707 Heb. 12:2
708 Ibid.
709 Matt. 5:41
710 Phil. 3, 13-14
711 Ibid.

Week 34 Tuesday

Perseverance is a Brother of Discipline

"The eyes of the Lord are in every place, watching the evil and the good." Prov. 15:3

It's been said that discipline and character do the right thing, no matter who's watching, just because it's the right thing. If today's verse doesn't convince you, how about this one, "*For the ways of a man are before the eyes of the Lord, and He watches **all** his paths*." (Prov. 5:21, emphasis added). There is a saying, attributed to Abraham Lincoln but probably not original with him: "You can fool some of the people all the time, all of the people some of the time, but you can't fool all the people all the time." It should have added, "You can't fool God any time."

Perseverance requires discipline and vice versa. Neither is easy, nor is the road crowded. We can expect to be mocked, belittled, shunned, and, yes, abused verbally and sometimes physically. So what? As we discussed yesterday, if our focus is on the goal, these nuisances are just that—Satan's attempt to make our eyes wander. And, speaking of goals, now is a good time to paint with a broad brush the discipline of goal setting. If we don't have well-defined goals, one path is as good as any other.

Goals, especially for those of us who aren't used to them, need to be in two parts. First, the ultimate goal and second, intermediate goals. The secret to successful goal achievement is starting with small, somewhat easily attainable goals and keep stretching or moving the goalposts until you can see yourself crossing your ultimate goal line. The beauty of having a big goal is that it points each little goal in the same direction, so everything moves you toward the big finish line. Sound simple? Maybe. Let's think about our big goal for a minute. Yesterday's verse offers some great goals. Unfortunately, since we're all sinners, we won't attain any of them totally until we're called home. But, we can certainly move in their direction as long as we have breath. So, let's get started.

How about godliness? Knowing what God is like comes from only one place: His Word. Let's agree on this: *The final word (on anything) is **The Word**.* So our first mini goal could be to spend time each day in the Word. How much is up to you. Here's a verse that may help, "*Establish Your word to Your servant as that which produces reverence for You.*" (Psalm 119:38) You want to know God and grow in His likeness? This is where you start. Set a goal to spend some quiet time each day—start with 10 minutes or more—and keep a log of each day's reading. Do this for at least a month, and you'll find yourself looking forward to your daily time with God in His Word. Persevere. Don't quit. Get up early. There, that was easy, wasn't it? More tomorrow.

Holy Spirit, fill me with a desire to be in Your Word; guide me in greater understanding and application, and strengthen my resolve to make this a habit each day. Thank you. **Amen**

Perseverance endures hostility

"For consider Him who has endured such hostility by sinners against Himself, so that you will not grow weary and lose heart." Heb. 12:3

It's been said that if we're not experiencing hostility from the world for our faith, we're probably not a very bright light.[712] Jesus knew His disciples were weak (before Pentecost) and needed encouragement.[713] And we're no different. We like to think of ourselves as macho, not needing anyone. But that's a lie from the pit. Solomon, the wisest man to ever live,[714] said this about being an island, "*Two are better than one…woe to the one who falls when there is not another to lift him up…two can resist…a cord of three strands is not quickly torn apart.*"[715]

As we began our focus on goals yesterday, let's add another: *righteousness* (it's OK to have more than one goal to work on). Righteousness is akin to godliness, and both should permeate our entire existence. Our home life, work life, leisure life are all impacted by our choice to follow Jesus. The closer we follow, the more our light shines. The more our light shines, the more darkness we expose and the more people who live in that darkness will resist.[716] But if you don't get any other takeaway from this book, remember this: We only have to please an audience of one! By ourselves, it's easy to slack off, to lose heart, to grow cold in "our first love."[717] That's why it's necessary for us to have at least one accountability partner, a solid believer that we trust with whom we can share our struggles, our victories, and sometimes our doubts; someone that will pray for us, encourage us, keep pointing us to ***The Word***.

I am well aware that it's easy to become a Bible thumper in our zeal to share what Christ has done for us. And in some circumstances, that may be what's needed. But as a rule, two other goals—love and kindness—are generally more effective. Think of how you react when someone bludgeons you with (their perception of) the truth. If you're like me, my reaction is not usually at the peak of godliness. Pray for openings to share your faith. Tell your story of what Christ has done for you. Then leave the results to the Holy Spirit. God never holds us accountable for results—those are His alone—but He does require our faithfulness. The scorekeeping is up to Him.

Father, you know I want to be more like Jesus. But I get discouraged because of my apathy and repetitive sin. Forgive me for allowing that to keep me on the bench and not in the game. In Jesus' name, **Amen**.

712 Matt. 5:14-16
713 Luke 22:31-34
714 I Kings 4:30, 31
715 Eccl. 4:9-12
716 John 3:19
717 Rev. 2:4, 5

Perseverance strengthens faith in the midst of trials

"Therefore we ourselves speak proudly of you among the churches of God for your perseverance and faith in the midst of all your persecutions and afflictions which you endure." II Thes. 1:4

Diamonds are created under great pressure. Gold and silver are refined by extreme heat. People are polished or broken by trials. As believers, we have an ace up our sleeve when it comes to trials. God's Word tells us clearly that "*...I will never desert you, nor will I ever forsake you.*"[718] Remember the trial Daniel's friends underwent? They were thrown into the fire.[719] I can't think of a worse death than being burned alive. But, spoiler alert, they weren't. Nebuchadnezzar saw a fourth "*man...like a son of the gods*!"[720] If God can protect His own in a fiery furnace, don't you think He's powerful enough to keep us through our trials?[721]

It's important to note that God doesn't keep us *from* trials. He keeps us *in* them. In fact, God uses trials to discipline, correct, and perfect us.[722] As parents, don't we correct our children? Why? Because we want them to grow into unselfish, productive adults able to live in and contribute to their society. God's Word assures us that God is a father to us and both corrects us[723] and has compassion on us.[724] And He reminds us that "*All discipline for the moment seems not to be joyful, but sorrowful; yet to those who have been trained by it, afterwards it yields the peaceful fruit of righteousness.*"[725] Remember our goals? Here's another way to attain a little more righteousness.

Keep in mind, discipline has two meanings. One we always associate with negative consequences, and we usually deserve them. The other has positive connotations, for example, military discipline, science disciplines, exercise discipline, etc. Discipline, whether negative or positive, is intended to affect or improve our behavior. In keeping with our goals of godliness and righteousness, we want improvement, don't we? James tells us to welcome trials with joy.[726] Can we do that? Do we trust God enough to do that? Perseverance doesn't give up...no matter what.

Lord, I admit that I don't like many of the trials you allow. Grow my faith so no matter what comes my way, I can welcome it with joy, knowing that You are still on the throne and nothing sneaks up on You. In Christ, **Amen**.

---

718 Heb. 13:5
719 Dan. 3, esp. 24, 25
720 Ibid.
721 I Cor. 10:13
722 James 1:2-4
723 Prov. 3:12
724 Psalm 103:13
725 Heb. 12:11
726 James 1:2

Perseverance Rewards us With Hope

"...tribulation brings about perseverance; and perseverance, proven character; and proven character, hope; and hope does not disappoint, because the love of God has been poured out within our hearts through the Holy Spirit who was given to us."
Rom. 5:3-5

Prisons are filled with people who have lost hope: life sentences without the possibility of parole. Many cancer patients lose hope when they receive the diagnosis. Fans lose hope when their team is on a losing streak. But praise God, we have *eternal* hope because of Jesus. Paul wrote to the Corinthians, "*If we have hoped in Christ* ***in this life only****, we are of all men most to be pitied.*"[727] In other words, "*eat, drink and be merry...for tonight you die.*"[728] This thought—eternal hope—often drives me to thank God for including me in His forever family. Think about it. For those of us who know Jesus as our Lord and Savior, today's verse is a promise to cling to: *Hope does not disappoint.* Sometimes, maybe often, we are disappointed by family, friends, finances, even our own failures. But see the big picture—the end-of-life goal. Does our not getting the job or house or car we want create insurmountable pain? If it does, it's time to adjust our life lens. We've lost sight of the only thing that matters: God's glory in all we do.[729]

Of course, we don't always get our own way. Hallelujah. If we did, how would we grow through trials? When we're tempted to complain about our trials, use that as a reminder that God knows what He's doing, and He doesn't experiment with us. Thank God we don't have wives like Job's, who told him to "*curse God and die.*" [730] But listen to Job's response, "*...shall we indeed accept good from God and not accept adversity?*"[731]

We can't leave out the middle step in today's progression from perseverance to hope, proven character. We've heard a lot lately about how character doesn't matter. Really? A couple questions to put that belief into perspective. Would you hire a thief to run your cash register? Would you hire a registered sex offender to babysit? The answers are obvious. The conclusion? Character *does* matter...especially to God. And He's willing and able to help mold it in us if we're willing. *Hope* ***does not*** *disappoint.*

Lord God, life without hope would be unbearable. Thank You for giving me something to look forward to, to hope in. Heaven will be more than I can imagine, and that keeps me going. **Amen.**

727 I Cor. 15:19 (emphasis added)
728 Luke 12:19, 20
729 I Cor. 10:31
730 Job 2:9
731 Job 2:10

Perseverance Keeps Us Close To God

"Because you have kept the word of My perseverance, I also will keep you from the hour of testing, that hour which is about to come upon the whole world, to test those who dwell on the earth." Rev. 3:10

On Sunday, I promised if you'd walk through this week with me, you'd be glad you did. Here it is. Judgment is coming to the earth. We've seen movies about apocalyptic events, but they don't come close to the destruction that God has planned for those who have rejected His Son. Look at this minor example of the wrath to come. A couple years ago in Texas, a storm dumped softball-sized hail. It smashed through windows, wrecked cars, and caused fear. In a YouTube video, one woman said she'd never been so scared in her life. Another man said, "We were all sitting ducks and there was nothing we could do about it." How much do you think a softball-sized hailstone weighs? Maybe a pound or two? Think about a hundred-pound hailstone[732] and the damage it could do. The good news: for those of us who persevere and keep God's Word, God will "*keep (us) from the hour of testing.*" How's that for something to hope in? A pretty strong motivator to keep us keeping on.

I know, and I'm sure you do, that perseverance is not easy or fun. But really, what's our option? Give up? Stop trusting Christ? As followers of Christ, that's just not an option. So let's consider the value of perseverance. First, our faithfulness pleases God.[733] We all should look forward to hearing, "well done." Second, God promises blessings for our sticking with it: a good reputation,[734] we will bear fruit,[735] we'll be in good company (with our Savior),[736] God will strongly support us,[737] we'll have a hope that doesn't disappoint us,[738] and we'll be spared from God's wrath.[739] Finally, we don't have to do it alone. God promised to "*never desert or forsake us.*"[740] The Holy Spirit lives in us[741] and fills us with hope.[742]

I hope you've gotten as much out of this quick pass through perseverance as I have. May God bless our commitment to stay with it regardless of what the enemy throws at us.

Father, we look forward to Your blessings that far outweigh any trial we encounter as we don't give up following Christ. In Him, **Amen**.

732 Rev. 16:21
733 Matt. 25: 21, 23
734 II Thes. 1:4
735 Luke 8:15
736 Heb. 12:3
737 II Chron. 16:9
738 Rom. 5:3-5
739 Rev. 3:10
740 Heb. 13:5
741 Eph. 1:13
742 Rom. 15:13

Purity is commanded for the family of God

"Draw near to God and He will draw near to you. Cleanse your hands, you sinners; and purify your hearts, you double-minded." Jas. 4:8

Buckle up. This is going to be a tough subject. Scripture has over 150 references to purity and its derivatives. Some apply to inanimate objects such as pure gold (50 verses alone), but most apply to us. Did you ever wonder why, when purity is so hard to attain and maintain, does God demand it of us? There are many reasons, but a couple stand out. First, God is pure, pure love, pure mercy, pure truth, pure righteousness, and many more. Second, because He is pure, He cannot tolerate sin in any form, including impure thoughts and deeds. Third, and this is for us, in His wisdom and knowledge, He knows purity is for our own good. I won't go too far down a rabbit trail, but permit just one example: Ezekiel 23 is a perfect example of some of the things God hates and **will judge.** Listen to just the last verse (49) of Chapter 23: "*Your lewdness will be requited upon you, and you will bear the penalty of worshipping your idols; thus you will know that I am the Lord God.*"

Regardless of what our "progressive" society accepts, God's standard hasn't and **never will** change (more on that Saturday). Read about the flood (Genesis 6-8) in which God destroyed the *entire* world except for 8 people. Read about Sodom and Gomorrah's destruction (Gen.13:12, Gen. 18:20, Gen.19:4, 5, 24, 25). And one more especially applicable today:

(Rom. 1:18-27), men…

…suppress the truth

…without excuse

…knew God – did not honor Him

…abandoned natural function of the woman

…burned with desire…another man

…receiving due penalty of their error

"God is not mocked, whatever a man sows, this he will also reap." [743]

Men, we can't continue to say we know God and not change our behavior. How do you think the front office of the Denver Broncos would act if, while Peyton Manning was the starting quarterback, he wore an Oakland Raiders sweatshirt to the golf course? You're right, not well. Isn't God a little more deserving of our commitment, our loyalty? I warned you this week would be tough. Stay tuned…

Father, Your Word is very clear, but so often I either don't believe you mean it or You're not watching, or I can get by just this once. Open my eyes Lord to Your righteousness and hatred of sin, mine included, and prick my heart to not only desire purity but to live it out. In Jesus' name, **Amen**.

743 Gal. 6:7

Purity starts in the mind and influences our choices

"...like newborn babies, long for the pure milk of the word, so that by it you may grow in respect to salvation..." I Pet. 2:2

React or choose? How often do we find ourselves in the first category? Reactions are good—even necessary—when we are faced with danger. But seriously, how often does that happen? Someone cuts you off in traffic. Your response is a good indicator of which camp you're in. Yesterday, we touched on changing our behavior.

ALL behavior starts with a thought; it may be subconscious, but it still starts in our mind. In the week on Excellence, we discussed the progression from thought to action to habit to way of life to destiny. So, to change our actions, we must first change our thinking. In Romans 12:2, Paul tells us, "*Do not be conformed to this world, but be transformed by the renewing of your mind...*" The best way to do that comes from today's verse ("*long for the pure milk of the word*"). Psalm 119:11 reinforces that: *"Your word I have treasured in my heart that I may not sin against You."*

How are we doing on our time in the Word, reading, memorizing, meditating? You know the definition of insanity: doing the same thing and expecting different results. Think about this: Our loving Father has given us the exact blueprint for life, peace, our future—everything we need to survive in a sin-cursed world. Could it be we have bought into God's love and know nothing of His holiness and intolerance of sin? Or have we let the cares and trials of the world suppress our love of and commitment to the Bible?

We stand at the threshold of eternity—closer than ever before. How can we expect to hear "well done" if we can't get our mind and what we feed it under control? It's not too late to form a new habit (thought, then repeated action) that includes more time in God's Word. We will not change (our actions) until we change our thinking. Proverbs reminds us, "*It is by his **deeds*** (not words) *that a lad distinguishes himself, if his conduct is pure and right.*"[744]

As we ponder today's words, remember, tomorrow isn't guaranteed to anybody.

Lord God, forgive me for letting my agenda squeeze time I spend with You in Your Word. Rekindle in me a love for You and Your Word that I will have a greater repository of Your truth to draw on in my daily battles with the world and the enemy. In Christ's name, **Amen**.

744 Prov. 20:11 emphasis mine

Purity honors and pleases God

"He who loves purity of heart, the king is his friend." Prov. 22:11

Can you even get your head around having *a* king, let alone *the* king as your friend? How about this? Knowing our own sinful thoughts and actions, God still sees us as *new creations* and blesses us with *every* spiritual blessing.[745] How is that possible in light of our sin? That's the good news of grace and mercy showered on those who trust Christ for forgiveness and salvation. As astounding as it sounds, Isaiah says, "*But the Lord was pleased to crush him (Christ)...*"[746] and "*...taste death for everyone...*"[747] "*bringing many sons to glory.*"[748]

When we think deeply about what God did for us in Christ, how can we respond any other way than to offer God a pure heart, cleansed from sin—a gift we did nothing to earn—as an expression of our gratitude?

With that as background, how do we acquire purity of heart? The good news is that *positionally*, if we know Jesus personally, we are already there (new creations), but *practically*, we're somewhere on the path (sanctification) that we'll be on until God calls us home. I believe it begins by recognizing how badly we miss the goal (sin) and often shun correction or reproof,[749] especially if it comes from our wives.

Pride erects a defensive shield around us and blinds us to our sin. So, the first step is to recognize that though we are saved, we still sin...sometimes badly and sometimes repeatedly. Next, remember that Jesus died for ALL our sins—past, present, and future—and "*there is now no condemnation for those who are in Christ Jesus.*"[750]

Now, it's rubber hits the road time. What habits do you want to change to free up more time with "Dad"? They'll be easier to identify if you ask yourself, "Does what I'm doing bring honor and pleasure to God or just me?" I'm not asking you to give up sports-watching or video gaming, or (fill in the blank), just to practice moderation. Paul set a great example when he told the Corinthians, "*All things are lawful for me, but not all things are profitable. All things are lawful for me, but I will not be mastered by anything.*"[751]

Father, I'd like to be Your friend, but I don't feel worthy because of my sin. Drill into me the breadth of Jesus' sacrifice—for me—and give me strength to change my habits to honor You. In Jesus' name, **Amen**.

745 II Cor. 5:17; Eph. 1:3
746 Isa. 53:10
747 Heb. 2:9
748 Heb. 2:10
749II Tim. 3:16
750 Rom. 8:1
751 I Cor. 6:12

Purity has no guilt or regrets

"I have made a covenant with my eyes; how then could I gaze at a virgin?" Job 31:1

Mockers gonna mock, scoffers gonna scoff, haters gonna hate. How's that for a motivational thought for the day? When most people think of purity, they think of female virginity. In the western world's perspective, this concept has lost much of its appeal and there's always been a double standard. Girls who lost their virginity before marriage were thought loose or promiscuous and to be shunned by society. Boys, on the other hand, were given a badge of honor by their peers. Even though the idea of virginity (for men and women) seems outdated by society, hear what God says, "*Let no one look down on your youthfulness, but rather in speech, conduct, love, faith and purity, show yourself an example of those who believe.*"[752]

For those of you old enough to remember the Ivory Soap tag line: "99 44/100% pure", I have a question. Pure *what* and what made up the other 56/100%? So, even secular advertisers give lip-service to the value of purity. Do a Google search on pure water. You'll find pure spring water, pure distilled water, pure spring bottled water, pure spring organic water. Question: What is organic water?

When I was in high school, a girl who got pregnant was treated like she had leprosy. Today, girls bring their babies to school. "*Once a taboo subject, teen parenthood has not only become more accepted among high-schoolers — in some cases, it's become a status symbol.*"[753] Most girls and some guys have severe guilt and/or regrets or both. Violating sexual purity usually has lifelong consequences. The Bible speaks very clearly about pre- or extra-marital sex. Don't. "*How can a young man [or woman] keep his [her] way pure? By keeping it according to Your word.*"[754] With so many (worldly/evil) forces pulling us along with the crowd, it's harder to make a public stand for Biblical purity. Pornography is thought by many to "not hurt anybody." "*Currently, the porn industry makes more money than Major League Baseball, the NBA, and the NFL* combined, *and what do we get for that money? A litany of well-documented problems, including failed relationships, addiction, depression, isolation, impotence, and an STD epidemic.*"[755] As with ALL societal issues, God's Word is the final answer. "*But I say, walk by the Spirit and you will not carry out the desires of the flesh.*"[756]

Lord, lead me not into temptation, in Jesus' name. **Amen**

752 I Tim. 4:12
753 www.businessinsider.com 4/25/19
754 Ps. 119:9
755 January 2012 article on catholicexchange.com
756 Gal. 5:16

Purity means not walking in the gray area

"...for you were formerly darkness, but now you are light in the Lord; walk as children of light." Eph.5:8

What is the main property of light? It dispels darkness, the brighter the light, the less darkness. Shadows appear when something blocks the light. If we are to walk as children of light, and if God's Word is black and white, what color are shadows? Do you know what lurks in shadows? Spiders...and bad people—all sorts of evil. If the Christian life were simply black or white (it is, we just don't like "restrictions"), we'd have no problem turning from evil. If Satan labeled the path to hell, Hell, nobody in their right mind would walk there. But he doesn't; he labels it heaven (remember, who's the father of lies[757]). When my kids were little and a "gray" area about something they wanted to do came up, they would ask, "What's wrong with it?" My response was, "What's right with it?" We have been lied to so long by the world and its influences that we don't realize we're going along because it feels ok.

What harm is there in fibs or "white" lies? I ask the same question I asked my kids, "What's right with them?" When truth is the standard, anything that isn't means we're not walking in the light and therefore is sin. Our reaction to this line of thinking either affirms or condemns us. If we were to take a moment of introspection and identify all the gray areas of life that we openly or tacitly approve, and compare it to God's standard: "*come out from their midst and be separate,*"[758] it would be a real eye-opener and should drive us to our knees in humble repentance. Paul also told the Corinthians, "*Do not be deceived, bad company corrupts good morals.*"[759]

I guess we should ask ourselves at this point if we're happy just getting our ticket to heaven punched or do we want to please God and show our gratitude by our lives? Everybody knows Psalm 23, "*The Lord is my shepherd...*" but Psalm 24 addresses today's topic, "*Who may ascend into the hill of the Lord? And who may stand in His holy place? **He who has clean hands and a pure heart, who has not lifted up his soul to falsehood** and has not sworn deceitfully. He shall receive a blessing from the Lord and righteousness from the God of his salvation.*"[760]

Father, I've been so complacent for so long, it's hard to even recognize the areas where I fall short of Your holy standard. You call it sin. Forgive me for presuming on Your grace and open my eyes to stay on Your path regardless of the allure of shiny things around me. In Jesus' name. **Amen**

757 John 8:44
758 II Cor. 6:17
759 I Cor. 15:33
760 Psalm 24:3-5 emphasis mine

Purity is attacked by the evil world system

"You adulteresses, do you not know that friendship with the world is hostility toward God? Therefore whoever wishes to be a friend of the world makes himself an enemy of God." James 4:4

Satan hates Jesus Christ. You say duh. But think of the implications if you are a friend of God (like Abraham[761]). Jesus said, "*If the world hates you, know that it has hated Me before it hated you.*"[762] If we are walking in the light (see yesterday's thoughts) in fellowship with Jesus and it shows in our lives, we have a target on our backs for Satan's attacks. Righteous living does not keep us from trials (see Job chap. 1). In fact, we are to *expect* them.[763] Trying to keep a low profile doesn't help either. Satan already knew about Job when God brought him up in the conversation.[764] With today's communications devices, we are an open book. That's why it's so important for us to rightly represent the truth,[765] so our actions support our words. Paul talks about his discipline in making his body his slave so that after preaching to others, he wouldn't be disqualified.[766]

James has harsh language for us today. This is another "frog in the pot"[767] example. In Bible times, stoning was the punishment for adultery (for both parties).[768] Today, it's barely a blip on our radar. But compare what God's Word says, "*Flee immorality...your body is a temple of the Holy Spirit...you are not your own...therefore glorify God in your body.*"[769]

I can't overemphasize the value of purity to God. His *Word* is pure.[770] His *Wisdom* is pure.[771] The *streets of heaven* are pure...gold.[772] We will be clothed in *white garments*.[773] Men, we're soldiers in God's army. What's the purpose of an army? To fight. We have all the armor we need.[774] The end game is in sight. All we need is to stay in the battle and not desert when times get tough. Jesus warned us of this, "*...in the world you have tribulation...but take courage, I have overcome the world.*"[775]

Lord, it's so easy to become discouraged fighting against evil. Keep me mindful that I'm on the winning side and not to be discouraged. **Amen**

761 James 2:23
762 John 15:18
763 I Pet. 4:12
764 Job 1:9-11
765 II Tim. 2:15
766 I Cor. 9:27
767 Week 32-Friday
768 Lev. 20:10
769 I Cor. 6:18-20
770 Psalm 12:6
771 James 3:17
772 Rev. 21:21
773 Rev. 3:5
774 Eph. 6:10-17
775 John 16:33

Purity is THE goal THE standard

"Blessed are the pure in heart for they shall see God." Matt. 5:8

Ever think about the purity of things that come out of the ground? The purer, the better. How about diamonds and the cut, color, carat, and clarity? Or gold; 24K gold is more expensive because it's purer—not mixed with other metals. Then there's oil—sweet crude is highly desirable because of its low sulfur content. But how about the purity of the *One* who came out of the ground—the Lord Jesus Christ—on Resurrection Day? He lived the perfect standard of holiness and set the example we are to strive for.

What is it about standards that we cringe from? Is it because we know we can't keep them and "good enough" becomes our standard? In week 31-Thursday, we talked about standards of *obedience*. Today, *purity* is our focus. Why do standards change? One reason could be that, through knowledge or experience, we have something better to aim for. And that could be good. Another could be society changes and things are now acceptable that weren't yesterday. The problem with that thinking is as society adopts a new normal, it's always worse than the previous normal. Consider the slippery slope of the abortion movement.

It's comforting to know that there is one standard that never changes—God's. No matter what society thinks or does with "normal," God will have the final word. Listen to the finality of Psalm 2: "*The kings of the earth take their stand and the rulers take counsel together against the Lord and against His Anointed...He who sits in the heavens laughs, the Lord scoffs at them.*"[776]

This week we've talked about God's command for purity in His family and how purity applies to our thinking as well as our actions. We also saw that it pleases and honors God and leaves no guilt or regrets in our lives. We were reminded that God's Word is black and white, and we are not to walk in the gray areas. Lastly, we saw how wanting to live pure lives makes us a target for evildoers. I told you Sunday this would be a tough week. But if you're still with me, then praise God for your desire to walk in holiness and purity. The fight is still raging all around us. May I encourage you in the Lord to hang tough? Get one or more guys you trust to meet for mutual building up of each other. Most importantly, remember God's promise in today's verse...**we will see God.**

Lord God, this study has convicted me of just how far I have compromised my walk with you. Forgive me for missing the mark so badly in the area of purity. Strengthen my commitment to walk in the light of Your Word, to view women as fellow heirs of Your grace, and to set a better example for my family of purity. May I grow in my relationship to You and have a boldness to talk openly of forgiveness in Christ with anybody who will listen. In His name, **Amen**.

776 Psalm 2:2, 4

Righteousness can't be bought...by us, but there is a cost.

"...you were not redeemed with perishable things like silver or gold.." I Pet.1:18

The Bible has nearly 1,200 references to the word righteous or righteousness, holy or holiness. And that doesn't even count any other synonyms. So, my conclusion is it must be important to God. We're going to explore, albeit only at a high level, some of the facets of righteousness this week and why it's so important.

Let's start with the most important reason: God commands it. "*You shall be holy for I the Lord your God am holy.*"[777] What does it mean to be holy or righteous? It means we are called to a different standard. Different from the world. Different than how we lived before we met Christ. It means a life borne out of gratitude for God's indescribable gift (of Jesus).[778] As we work our way through this week, we'll visit these and more.

Many people, even in the church, look at righteousness as a limitation, a warden, a wet blanket intended to take all the fun out of life. That view couldn't be farther from the truth. On the contrary, righteousness opens up the very doors of heaven. We have to re-examine our definition of "fun." The Bible admits that sin can be pleasurable...for a season.[779] But, even though the world has created instant everything, when were they right about *eternal* anything? I admit, I like and am often drawn to shiny things. But if I have, through practice, learned to filter everything through the lens of scripture, then "good" things won't get in the way of "best" things.

How would you feel if you were an 11th hour (5 PM) worker? (see the parable in Matt. 20:1-16) You didn't know it when you started, but you got paid the same as the guys who started early that morning (6 AM). Would you be grateful to the boss? Would you feel special? The Kingdom of heaven is *exactly* that. If you come to Christ late in life (it's never *too* late until you're dead), you get the exact same thing—Heaven and life with Jesus forever—as those who have known and served God for decades. Get your mind around that for a minute. But, it comes with a price. The price is humility; knowing there is NOTHING we can do to save ourselves and earn righteousness. By humbly believing what Jesus did on the cross (died to pay for my sin), we are *given* righteousness. Keep reading...

Lord God, it sounds too good to be true, that You will forgive me just because I believe that Jesus died in my place. Open my eyes and heart to know the truth. **Amen**

777 Lev. 19:2
778 II Cor. 9:15
779 Heb.11:25

Week 36 Monday

Righteousness is credited to God's kids.

"But to the one who does not work, but believes in Him who justifies the ungodly, his faith is ***credited*** *as* ***righteousness****." Rom. 4:5*

We all know the difference between a credit and a debit. Credits = money in; debits = money out. The more credits we have, the easier it is to meet our budget. You *do* have a budget, don't you?

You know the parable of the servant who owed 10,000 talents (literally a zillion dollars) and couldn't pay.[780] That's an unimaginable amount (debit). Guess what? The king forgave him the entire amount (credit). The parable starts out, "*...the kingdom of heaven may be compared to a king who wished to settle accounts with his slaves.*"[781] Today's topic is exactly what this parable is teaching. Righteousness (credit) is a ***free*** gift from God, a credit on our sin-account. By the way, it's an account ***we*** can ***never*** reduce, let alone pay off by our own work. God's credit covers ***all*** our sins, past, present, and future. Talk about a no-brainer deal.

But some who are reading this will still doubt that this offer applies to them. Jesus said, "*the one who comes to Me I will certainly not cast out.*"[782] Sounds like a promise to me. There is no exclusion here based on how young or old you are, what color your skin, or how many or how bad your sins are...nothing. There is only one way to get this credit. Again, Jesus said, "*I am* ***the*** *way* ***the*** *truth and* ***the*** *life, no one comes to the Father but through Me.*"[783] The cost? You must realize that *your* sin (even if you think it's not that bad) has separated you from a holy God. Hear what God thinks of your "good deeds": "*All our righteous deeds are like a filthy garment.*"[784] So, you want in on this? Good. After you recognize your sin and separation from God and accept that you can't do anything on your own to make it right, the next step is so simple, many will say something like "no way." Way! Believe what Jesus said about Himself: that He died in *your* place so you could hang out with Him at *His* place (Heaven)...**forever**. Confess your sin in prayer to God (no middleman required) and then rejoice that your sins are forgiven...forever. Now for the good part: "*If you confess with your mouth Jesus as Lord, and believe in your heart that God raised Him from the dead, you* ***will be saved****.*"[785] "*He who has the Son has the life; he who does not have the Son of God does not have the life. These things I have written...so that you* ***may know*** *that you have* ***eternal life****.*"[786]

Heavenly Father, thank You. **Amen**

780 Matt. 18:23-35
781 Matt. 18:23
782 John 6:37
783 John 14:6 (emphasis added)
784 Isa. 64:6
785 Rom. 10:9 (emphasis added)
786 I John 5:12, 13 (emphasis added)

Righteousness is our response to God for His grace.

"Therefore, since we receive a kingdom which cannot be shaken, let us show gratitude, by which we may offer to God an acceptable service with reverence and awe;" Heb. 12:28

Remember when mom used to say, "Now Johnny, what is the correct response?" when Aunt Emmy gave you a present? Whether you liked it or not, you knew a kiss on Auntie's cheek and a thank you was what was expected.

Today's verse talks about gratitude and acceptable service. We generally understand gratitude, but what is acceptable service? For our purposes, I'll define it as *righteous living.* Pretty much everything we do can be summed up in the word living. But *how* we live depends on the adjective, righteous. When we consider yesterday's session and remember the immeasurable debt that God forgave through Jesus, how can we not be overwhelmed with gratitude and *want to* live our lives to please the one to whom we owe everything? If that's not our goal, our heart's desire, then we need to "*Test yourselves to see if you are in the faith; examine yourselves!*"[787]

Was there a time when you gave a nice present, an expensive present, and you got a grunt of recognition, maybe a mumbled thanks? Didn't feel too good, did it? You know, God is our Father, and He's given us a priceless gift that I'm sure we won't fully understand until we get home. But meanwhile, we can show our gratitude by right(eous) living. What does that look like? Space doesn't allow a lengthy discussion, but some key points are appropriate.

Home is where it starts. Your wife and kids need you to exhibit the Godly character traits of love, joy, peace, patience, kindness, goodness, self-control, you know, the fruits of the Spirit.[788] I know; it's hard. You just want to come home and unwind as if you're the only one who could have one of those days. If you don't think your family does too, think again. No matter how tired or beaten down or discouraged you are, you're still the one the others look to for their support, their encouragement. Man up. Take care of business at home.

The next major impact area in your life is your work world. Do not make the mistake of trying to compartmentalize your faith, family, and job. It doesn't matter if you're a stock clerk or a CEO; you're a man of God in all endeavors. "*Be on the alert, stand firm in the faith, act like men, be strong.*"[789]

Tomorrow, we'll talk about raising the bar.

Lord God, most of the time, I don't feel righteous. I feel guilty over my repetitive sin and ashamed to have to keep coming to You time and time again for the same things. Help me to really know your forgiveness. In Jesus' name. **Amen.**

787 II Cor. 13:5
788 Gal. 5:22
789 I Cor. 16:13

Righteousness demands we live by a higher standard.

"The righteous shall live by faith." Hab. 2:4

Imagine the most elaborate home you can in Beverly Hills or Saudi Arabia, no expense spared, no finishing touch too extravagant. Everything of the finest quality that money and imagination can conceive. You'd want to live in a house like that, wouldn't you? Well, I've got great news for you. The house God has planned for us makes your imagined house look like the city dump by comparison. This is an example of a higher standard. Jesus told His disciples (and us), *"I go to prepare a place for you..."* [790]... *"a house not made with hands, eternal in the heavens."* [791] Think about the Creator of everything, mountains, seas, stars, to name a few, and the magnificence visible to all.[792] If He is creating our future home, with a higher standard than earthly homes, I can't wait to see it.

A righteous life, by definition, requires a higher standard. Here are just a few examples:

> *"Treat others the same way you want them to treat you."* [793]
> *"If anyone wants to be first, he shall be last of all and servant of all."* [794]
> *"Do nothing from selfishness or empty conceit, but with humility of mind regard one another as more important than yourselves."* [795]

And there are many more. How different the world would be if Christians applied just these three. But we must start somewhere. Men, righteous living is not for sissies. And it's not a life we can live in our own power. Today's verse from Habakkuk gives us a clue. First, where does faith come from? It's a gift from God.[796] And just what is faith? *"Faith is the assurance of things hoped for, the conviction of things not seen."* [797] In a nutshell, we believe God's Word and act on it, knowing that the character of God is truth. Remember, the *results* of our actions, our lives, are not our responsibility—it's God's. So, don't watch the scoreboard; just do the next right(eous) thing.

Holy God, the more I see of Your requirements for a righteous life, the more I know I can't do it by myself. Keep me close and hungry for Your Word and Your ways. In Jesus' name, **Amen**.

790 John 14:2
791 II Cor. 5:1
792 Rom. 1:19, 20
793 Luke 6:31
794 Mark 9:35
795 Phil. 2:3
796 I Cor. 12:9
797 Heb. 11:1

Righteousness is proven through obedience.

"Do you not know that when you present yourselves to someone as slaves for obedience, you are slaves of the one whom you obey, either of sin resulting in death, or of obedience resulting in righteousness?" Rom. 6:16

We've all tried to pick just the right color from a palette for a room in our house. Usually, it involves more than one trip to the hardware store and more than one "discussion" with our wife. Current styles are all about grays and whites and blacks. Today, God's Word makes our color choice simple: the outer darkness[798] (the result of sin) or the white robes of righteousness.[799]

When King Saul tried to rationalize to Samuel his and Israel's disobedience in the battle against the Amalekites by saying, "*...the people took some spoil...to sacrifice to the Lord your God at Gilgal*",[800] Samuel called him out on it and said, "*...behold, to obey is better than sacrifice...*"[801] It cost Saul his kingdom.

Let's try a "little" test. Using today's color chart, what color would you call a little lie? Tradition calls it white, but is it? In Paul's rebuke to the Galatians (chap. 5), he says, "*You were running well; who hindered you from **obeying** the truth?...a little leaven leavens the whole lump.*"[802] How'd you do?

Here's another example to show how much God hates lying and disobedience. When the church was first formed right after Jesus' resurrection, people were selling their stuff and bringing the money to be used for others' needs. A married couple sold some property and decided to keep some of the money for themselves while letting everyone think it was the whole amount. Peter called them out on it. [803] It cost them their lives. They died instantly upon hearing Peter's rebuke.

Little lies are a chink in our armor of righteousness that our enemy can exploit to our detriment. An overgrown garden starts with a single weed left untreated. A lightbulb is either on or off. A woman is either pregnant or she's not. You're either a Ford or Chevy man. You get the point. These examples accept no middle ground. So why would God tolerate anything less than true and full obedience? Righteousness cannot exist apart from it. And it *is* a life or death decision. Are you in or out?

Lord God, the world has dulled my sense of right and wrong and truth. I know it's because I spend more time there than in Your Word, which *is* truth. Create in me a consistent desire to know You on a deeper level and to take Your warnings seriously. In Christ's name, **Amen**.

798 Matt. 25:30
799 Rev. 7:9, 14
800 I Sam. 15:20, 21
801 I Sam. 15:22
802 Gal. 5:7, 9
803 Acts 5:1-11

Righteousness opens the door for effective prayer.

"...The effective prayer of a righteous man can accomplish much." James 5:16

When you think of open doors, what mental picture do you get? Rubber pads to step on, electric eyes, other automatic devices, and, of course, doormen—nearly a thing of the past. But what's beyond that open door? How about words like invitation, welcome, linger, relax? Today's verse implies all that and much more because it is a promise from God Himself. Notice that through prayer, we can "accomplish much." How's *your* prayer life? Are you accomplishing much? Or do you need some encouragement? As with many of God's promises, this one comes with a condition: *a righteous man.* No surprise there, since we've been talking about this all week.

By now, I trust that you've grasped some of the significance, the seriousness, the blessings of righteousness. And this one I've saved until now. Let's go back to your mental picture and let me suggest God's slant on His open door. 1. We're all welcome. 2. Many things are NOT required to enter: No middleman. No fancy words or lengthy phrases, just what's on our hearts. No special clothing or paraphernalia. No memorized mantras, practiced platitudes, or syrupy supplications. 3. No time limits. We can stay for as long or as short as we need/want to. 4. We can express a full range of emotions: e.g., love, anger, fear. 5. We can come back as often as we want. 6. There's no age requirement. 7. There's no strict protocols to get in the way of us talking to "dad."

The open door I'm talking about is the very door to God's throne room. He invites us (*"Come to me all...and I will give you rest"* [804]). He hears us (*"The Lord hears when I call to Him."* [805]). He answers us (*"Ask and it will be given to you..."* [806]).

What about the one condition, the key to open the door: *a righteous man*? Hopefully, we understand that we are and we aren't righteous (come back tomorrow). God has granted us righteous standing because of Jesus. This is not something that we can boast about because we didn't do anything to earn or deserve it.[807] It's a little like the will your grandpa left. In it, you were to receive everything he had. But until you claim it, you're just as poor as before. The Christian walk is exactly like that. God has named you in His will and Jesus died that you could claim eternity. Don't let lack of knowledge, or pride or anything rob you of that.

Father, I want to believe all you've said. I want to come to You, talk to You, hang out with You, love you. But so many things pull me away. Open my eyes and ears to the truth that is only in Jesus. In His name, **Amen**.

804 Matt. 11:28
805 Psalm 4:3
806 Matt. 7:7
807 I Cor. 4:7

Righteousness is both an event and a journey.

"...walk in a manner worthy of the calling with which you have been called, with all humility and gentleness, with patience, showing tolerance for one another in love, being diligent to preserve the unity of the Spirit in the bond of peace." Eph. 4:1-3

Have you ever heard the saying, "The journey is the destination"? I used to think it was sort of dumb until I started taking short 2- or 3-day trips on the back of a motorcycle. Riding through Colorado, which has some of the most beautiful country in the world, with fresh air blowing in your face, is the *reason* for the trip as much or more than where you end up. Today's wrap up is like that. Righteousness is both a once-for-all-time *event* that comes when we believe in Jesus. But it's also a lifetime *journey*—the "religious" term is sanctification—that moves us *practically* to the point we are *positionally*. Thanks to God's mercy, when we put our faith in Jesus, we are immediately granted forgiveness of all our sins, a reservation in heaven,[808] sealed by the Holy Spirit,[809] and imputed righteousness (see Monday). We have settled *the most important question* we'll ever face: "What will you do with Jesus?"[810]

As we learned Wednesday, "*The righteous shall live by faith.*" Now that we're trusting in Jesus, we don't have to worry about the future, the bumps in the road (the Bible calls them trials[811]), or our "results." All of that is in God's hands.[812] And He does with us what's best for us and brings Him the most glory. But, and here's the proof in the pudding, God compares us to branches, and He expects fruit and prunes us to produce more.[813] In the same verse, He also says, "*Every branch that does not bear fruit, He takes away.*"[814] It is crystal clear in Paul's comments to the Romans that just because we're saved, and heaven is assured, we are not to "*...continue in sin so that grace may increase.*"[815] On the contrary, we prove our love and commitment to Christ through our works: "*faith without works is dead.*"[816] And this should be our focus as long as we have breath. "*Whether you eat or drink or whatever you do, do all to the glory of God.*"[817] We are certainly blessed along the journey, but the destination is clearly worth it.

Father, the journey can seem long and hard. Give me endurance so I can finish well, produce fruit, and hear "well done." In Jesus' name, **Amen**.

808 John 14:2
809 Eph. 4:30
810 Josh. 24:15
811 Jas. 1:2
812 Psa. 2:4; Prov. 21:1; Psa. 146:9
813 John 15:2
814 Ibid. implied, in judgment
815 Rom. 6:1, 2, 15
816 Jas.2:26
817 I Cor. 10:31

Self-Control remembers that God has my circumstances.

*"But I say, walk by the Spirit, and you **will not** carry out the desire of the flesh."*
Gal. 5:16 (emphasis added)

Whenever we commit to doing something God's way, you can bet our enemy is waiting in the weeds to set his traps. This week as we work to improve our self-control, we will be tempted again and again.

Whether you're struggling with anger issues, eating problems, sexual temptations, or something else, know this: God has the answers and the power to help you become victorious. Our verse has a great promise today. *Will not* is a strong assurance of God's intent and desire for us.

Let's start with the big picture, and during the week, we'll drill down to some specifics. The issue is C.O.N.T.R.O.L. and who has it. Everybody wants it. We want it. The Spirit of God wants it. Satan wants it. But each has a different agenda. We want it because of pride. Satan wants it to destroy us.[818] Only the Spirit has our good in mind.[819]

We need to realize one thing. "*...our struggle is not against flesh and blood, but against... the spiritual forces of wickedness in the heavenly places.*"[820] Don't be fooled. There are only two camps in the war for control. As a child of the King, we're in the winning camp. The father of lies[821] would have you believe that's not true. Remember his ploy in the Garden of Eden? He asked Eve, "*Indeed, has God said...*"[822] Casting doubt on the truth of God's Word is one of his favorite tricks. The verse I used to prove that the Spirit has only our good in mind says, "*And we **know** that God **causes ALL** things to work together for good **to those who love God**.*"[823] Can we believe that ALL things, even those that don't seem good, work for our good? We can if we know the God behind it.

What's it mean to "walk by the Spirit"? The simplistic answer is on the bracelets that I haven't seen lately: WWJD. What Would Jesus Do? One question to ask ourselves is, "Why am I (re)acting this way?" Is it because someone did me wrong? Real or perceived, at that moment, the answer is, I'm not trusting God to have my six. Whatever this was, it's covered by ALL. Don't misunderstand me. I'm far from perfect and still struggle with this one too. But I know I'm moving in the right direction. How about you?

Holy Lord, I have a problem in this area. I'm quick to speak, quick to judge, slow to apply correction to myself. I'm guilty of wanting what I want, whether it's what you want for me or not. Help me to walk by Your Spirit and win the battle over the flesh. In Christ's name, **Amen**.

---

818 John 10:10
819 Rom. 8:28
820 Eph. 6:2
821 John 8:44
822 Gen. 3:1
823 Rom. 8:28 (emphasis added)

Self-control overcomes temptations.

"No temptation has overtaken you but such as is common to man; and God is faithful, who will not allow you to be tempted beyond what you are able, but with the temptation will provide the way of escape also, so that you will be able to endure it." I Cor. 10:13

Everything God created was "very good."[824] But master deceiver that he is, Satan corrupts everything God has made. We've looked at this before (Week 21-Tuesday) but consider all things beautiful (music, women, scenery). Who made them that way? Then consider the perversion. Who did that? Music was intended for God's glory and to lift our hearts in praise and worship. Worldly music is anything but God-honoring and worshipful. Yet it permeates our existence. You can't even greet folks on the street anymore because they've got stuff attached to their ears and they can't hear you. And, be honest with me guys, if you're reading this book, it's because you want to be closer to Jesus and live a life that pleases Him. How does fantasizing over scantily clad women further our goals? We're on a slippery slope, and standards of decency, once common, are now rare to non-existent. Haven't we seen and heard enough? Have you noticed over the past several years that your favorite TV shows have increasingly introduced more nudity, the homosexual agenda, and foul language peppered throughout? "Pervasive language" is the warning in Redbox on many R-rated movies.

If temptations didn't appeal to our lusts and desires, they wouldn't be temptations. No matter how good they look, you could never tempt me with a plate of cucumbers and tomatoes. Make it anything dark chocolate and raspberry, and it's a different story. To exercise self-control in the face of temptations, the first step is to *recognize* that we are being tempted. Then, RUN…*away from* youthful lusts and *to* righteousness.[825] Sometimes, all we need is an accountability partner, another guy we trust with our deepest secrets. It's like sponsors in AA. You know you're weakening, so you call your sponsor. Why doesn't Christianity offer that?

What about the temptation to become angry? Where does that come from? Usually, it's because someone has stepped on my "rights." Or they haven't met my expectations. And we don't even have to think about it, we immediately just speak harshly, or yell, or strike out at the object of our anger—usually someone we are closest to. Others wouldn't put up with it and might strike back. Sad. Pray for a quiet spirit. Don't set unreasonable expectations. Offer the grace to others you expect…from them and from God.

God, I confess that often I don't want to overcome temptations. I want to give in…to eating, anger, 2nd and lingering looks. My spirit wants to be victorious, but my flesh is oh so weak. Help me want to win this sin battle. For Christ's sake and in His name, **Amen**.

824 Gen.1:31
825 II Tim. 2:22

Self-control and discipline are inseparable.

"All things are lawful for me, but not all things are profitable. All things are lawful for me, but I will not be mastered by anything." I Cor. 6:12

Reinforcement. It's said that if you do something for 30 days, it becomes a habit. Our minds often go to the dark side and think of habits as bad; drinking habits, smoking habits, eating habits, pornography habits, etc. And these are a result of lack of self-control, lack of discipline, lack of want-to. They also grow because of poor or no goal setting, nothing powerful enough to encourage change. It's also said that until the pain of continuing (anything) becomes greater than the pain (discipline) of change, no change will occur. But habits can be good too: study habits, work habits, time-in-the-Word habits. There's a pattern here. Good habits require discipline. Bad habits often are our default and require no discipline, no self-control.

One of the best things I've found to help me is a Christian buddy who thinks like me and keeps me pointed in the right direction. The opposite is true too. The Bible says, "***Do not be deceived**: "Bad company corrupts good morals.""*[826] The Bible also says, "***Do not be deceived**, God is not mocked; for whatever a man sows, this he will also reap.*"[827] Why a warning about deception? Because it's so easy for us to compromise. A little lie here, a little fudging on our expense report there, a little time spent with wrong friends, and soon we've convinced ourselves that a) it's ok because nobody was hurt and b) I'm capable of making my own choices. Just who do you think is fanning that flame of *deception*? Yep, you've got it, the deceiver himself.[828]

God's warnings are exactly from the same heart that *you* warn *your* kids: Don't play in the street. Don't run with scissors. Don't text while driving. It's because He loves us and wants us to avoid unnecessary pain and heartache. Our actions have consequences. Maybe not immediately, but sin is a slippery slope. Solomon tells us, "*Before destruction, the heart of man is haughty, but humility goes before honor.*"[829] Do you want to avoid deception and destruction? Get off the slope. "*Do not be conformed to this world, but be transformed by the renewing of your mind...*"[830] "*Let the Word of Christ richly dwell within you...*"[831] "*All discipline for the moment seems not to be joyful, but...yields the peaceful fruit of righteousness.*"[832]

Today, is your pain (bad habits) the kind that leads to destruction, or the kind (discipline) that yields righteousness? The choice is yours.

Father, I struggle and I'm embarrassed over my habits. Grant me the "want to" to overcome them and enjoy Your peace. In Jesus' name, **Amen**.

---

826 I Cor. 15:33
827 Gal. 6:7
828 II John 1:7
829 Prov. 18:12
830 Rom. 12:2
831 Col. 3:16
832 Heb. 12:11

Self-control bridles my tongue.

"And the tongue is a fire...which defiles the entire body..." Jas. 3:6

"Even a fool, when he keeps silent, is considered wise..." Prov. 17:28

Why did you say that? What were you thinking? Often, we wish we could grab the word we just spoke and pull it back, ruing our inability to just shut up. James tells us today that our speech "defiles" the entire body. What does that really mean? Pollutes, contaminates, profanes, violates, betrays, dirties, rats out. Sometimes it helps to look at the opposite for clarity: sanctify.

It's said that actions speak louder than words. But we destroy with our words what we'd never do to someone physically. Why are we so quick to respond with a biting retort? I believe it's largely because we are not "*regarding one another as more important than ourselves.*"[833] As we looked at yesterday, WE are number one, and we haven't built the habit of humbly taking a backseat on anything. Pity. Abraham Lincoln or Mark Twain had a comment on Solomon's wisdom: "It is better to remain silent and be thought a fool, than to speak and remove all doubt." Much of what we say in the heat of the moment is pure folly, intended to make us feel better and put the other person "in their place." Just exactly what *is* their place?

James tells us, "*But **no one can tame the tongue**; it is a restless evil and full of deadly poison.*"[834] Jesus said, "*The **good man** out of the **good treasure of his heart** brings forth what is good; and the **evil man** out of the **evil treasure** brings forth what is evil; for his **mouth speaks from that which fills his heart**.*"[835] So, no one can tame the tongue. But it doesn't speak in a vacuum; it speaks from what is in the treasure chest of our heart. And, therein is the answer: Fill the heart with good things. I'm not talking about feel-good stuff. I'm talking about truth. The Psalmist tells us, "*the sum of Your word is truth.*"[836] If our heart is full of truth, 1) there's no room for error, false doctrine, jealousy, bitterness, etc. and 2) that's what comes out when we open our mouth. Proverbs helps us, "*If you have been foolish...put your hand on your mouth.*"[837] In today's vernacular, shut up. Good: Think before you speak. Better: Pray before you speak. Best: Don't speak...unless it follows Paul's admonition: "*Let no unwholesome word proceed from your mouth, but only such a word as is good for edification according to the need of the moment, so that it will give grace to those who hear.*"[838]

God, it feels good in the moment to crush someone with my words. I know that doesn't honor You. Forgive me. Give me a love for Your Word, so when I speak, it is truth that gives grace. In Christ's name, **Amen**.

833 Phil. 2:3
834 Jas. 3:8 (emphasis added)
835 Luke 6:45 (emphasis added)
836 Psa. 119:160
837 Prov. 30:32
838 Eph. 4:29

Self-control says no to too much of anything.

"...let us also lay aside every encumbrance and the sin which so easily entangles us, and let us run with endurance the race that is set before us..." Hebrews 12:1

Distractions come in all forms. Some are visual, some aromatic, some audible, many are imaginary. Today's verse is about goals and focus. With so many shiny objects pulling us in a direction different from our goal (i.e., *the race that is set before us),* it's no wonder we wander. Consider a literal race in which we allow ourselves to be distracted. At best, we'd finish last. At worst, we'd never finish. Silly example? Of course. But sometimes hyperbole makes the best points.

I'm assuming we all *want to* finish the race; to hear "*well done, good and faithful servant.*" [839] But here's where the distractions attack. And mostly they're subtle. A little more of this, a little longer at that, and we look up and have just wasted an hour, a day, even a life. Self-control sets limits. The writer of Hebrews encourages us to "*lay aside **every** encumbrance...*" Many things in our lives are, by themselves, good and fun and profitable. But Satan would have us focus on the *good* in life and never grow into the *best.*

So, what exactly is "the race"? When we came to Christ, we became new creatures[840] with new attitudes, new futures, new requirements. What constitutes "encumbrances"? Jesus told His disciples, "*If your right hand causes you to stumble, cut it off and throw it from you; for it is better for you to lose one of the parts of your body, than for your whole body to go into hell.*" [841] He was not advocating self-mutilation but simply emphasizing the deadly effects of sin and the drastic measures to keep it at bay. The race is simply our life in Christ until He calls us home. OK, if "good" isn't good enough, what is "best?" Jesus answered it this way, "*Heaven and earth will pass away, but My words will not pass away.*" [842] If we really understood the claim Christ has on our lives because of the price He paid for our salvation and our eternal future, the shiny things we spend so much time on would become as tarnished, rusting heaps of scrap by comparison, and we'd spend much more time getting to know something and Someone that will never pass away or change.[843]

God's Word is eternal. Spend some time memorizing key verses that can help throughout the day. Pray the prayer of the Psalmist in 119:38:

"[**Father]** establish Your Word to Your servant, as that which produces reverence for You." **Amen**.

839 Luke 19:17
840 II Cor. 5:17
841 Matt. 5:30
842 Matt.24:35; Mark 13:31; Luke 21:33
843 Heb. 13:8

Self-control models Godliness.

"... I discipline my body and make it my slave, so that, after I have preached to others, I myself will not be disqualified." I Cor. 9:27

Don't you just want to grab some politicians and shake them while exhorting them to "practice what you preach"? I can't think of many things worse than hypocrisy. As a boy, I used to hear my dad say, "Do as I say, not as I do." Hated it.

I've heard many times from people I share Jesus with that the church is filled with hypocrites. I'm tempted to say that there's always room for one more, but that doesn't move the conversation in the right direction. The sad fact is that they're right. Pews are filled with professing Christians who aren't the same Monday through Saturday as they are on Sunday. Why? There are many possibilities, but they all boil down to excuses—attempts at justifying a non-defensible position. If we claim the name of Christ, we are commanded to live differently (*...come out from their midst and be separate...).*[844] When we don't, it raises doubts about our commitment. But worse, it erects roadblocks to others seeing Christ in us and wanting the thing that makes us different.

When Jesus told His disciples to "follow me," He laid out a pretty grim picture of the cost of discipleship: "*If anyone wishes to come after Me, he must **deny** himself, and **take up his cross daily** and follow Me.*" [845] Hopefully, when you were introduced to Christ, you got both sides of God's plan; the blessings and future hope of eternity where there is no mourning, crying, or pain,[846] and the side reserved for those who don't follow Christ (*weeping and gnashing of teeth*).[847]

So how does self-control enter into this? The answer presupposes that we are truly saved and want our lives to display the gift of God we received. We must be **alert** to our surroundings, our behavior, our speech, and know that others are watching. We must be **aware** that our enemy's goal is to destroy our testimony.[848] Most importantly, our **focus** needs to be on "the prize"[849] of faithfully following Christ. Brothers, don't let your circumstances deplete your joy. Don't succumb to momentary temptations and the world's substitute for true happiness. Remember, it takes a lifetime to develop a Godly reputation, but only a split second to destroy it. Don't hinder God's plan to use you in someone else's path to Christ.

Heavenly Father, help me remember that eternity is a long, long time. Teach me to stay focused on Your ways, Your truth, Your plans that include me in someone else's life. In Christ's name. **Amen**

---

844 II Cor. 6:14-18
845 Luke 9:23 (emphasis added)
846 Rev. 21:4
847 Luke 13:24-28
848 I Pet. 5:8
849 Phil. 3:12-16

Self-control promotes peace.

"Blessed are the peacemakers..." Matt. 5:9

Today's news is filled with false hopes that ceasefires and formal peace talks will actually accomplish anything to change men's hearts. But we who know Jesus know different. Because of the evil in men's hearts, true peace *cannot* be experienced until the *Lord of peace*[850] Himself is on the throne, both of individual man now and the entire world during the coming millennium.[851]

What's the connection between self-control and peace? Ask yourself, "What is the opposite of peace?" James gives us the answer. "W*hat is the source of quarrels and conflicts among you? Is not the source your pleasures that wage war in your members? You lust and do not have; so you commit murder. You are envious and cannot obtain; so you fight and quarrel...*" [852] If we can (self) control our desires and envy, then quarrels and conflicts will cease. If we can practice Paul's admonition to the Philippians ("*...regard one another as more important than yourselves; do not merely look out for your own personal interests, but also for the interests of others...*"[853]), the result will be peace, in your heart and between brothers.

So, looking at the world scene, we've got a long way to go, and it seems an impossible dream. Frankly, without Christ, it is. But Jesus told His disciples (and us) to "*...make disciples of all nations...*"[854] If we can't control our own quarrels and conflicts because our attitudes and desires are wrong, how can we expect those with whom we share the gospel to control theirs?

I'm not suggesting that we have to be perfect before we tell others where to find lasting peace. Then nobody would ever open their mouth. But I am suggesting that we need a self-examination of where we are and where we're going. If there's not growth in our self-control, it's time for serious introspection...and penitent prayer. Yesterday, we talked about hypocrisy. Today, when we open our mouth to share Christ, let's have something that people can see working in our lives that makes us different, and Christ attractive.

Lord God, this week has been tough because I don't want to admit how self-centered I am. Help change my desires to line up with Yours and let me see the eternal value of putting others first. Let me (and others) see progress in my self-control, and may it be lasting through the power of Your Holy Spirit. God, You are faithful, and Your promises are true. May that be my Rock when things don't work like I expect. In Christ's name. **Amen.**

850 II Thess. 3:16
851 Rev. 20:4
852 James 4:1, 2
853 Phil. 2:3, 4
854 Matt. 28:19

Steadfast men are unwavering in their commitments.

"Therefore, my beloved brethren, be steadfast, immovable, always abounding in the work of the Lord, knowing that your toil is not in vain in the Lord." I Cor. 15:58

What do God, wife, family, and employer have in common? They are, in order of the list, worthy of our commitment. When we say "yes" to God, it's forever. "I do" is too. So is family. As long as we're taking a paycheck, our employer deserves our commitment.

This week, we're talking about being steadfast. It's not a common word, so a few synonyms may help, faithful, dedicated, single-minded, immovable, focused, wholehearted.

"When the going gets tough, the tough get going" has been attributed to both Knute Rockne and Joseph Kennedy. Can we still see evidence of those who live by that saying? Or do we more often find those who are likely to say, "When the going gets tough, I'm done"? What happened to the men in our society? Even Christian men. Paul told the Corinthian men, "*Be on the alert, stand firm in the faith, act like men, be strong.*"[855] Without becoming too political, I believe that the women's lib movement and the feminization of men have impacted our society and the church to the point of men confusing the leadership role God assigned[856] and allowing women to fill the vacuum left by men who abdicated their responsibility. You see it in churches (e.g., women in pulpits and roles as elders) and in homes (e.g., leading family devotions and spiritual education). Shame on us, men.

Of course, this presumes we are committed to something. What are you committed to today? If our priorities are in order, our first commitment is to the God who loves us, saved us, prepared a future home in heaven for us, and promised to come back and get us. If this describes you, well done. Then the other commitments should fall into place as we obey the orders found in God's Handbook. If this is not quite where you're at, don't get discouraged. Our God is a God of 2^{nd,} 3^{rd,} 10^{th,} and an infinite number of reboots. Go to Him in prayer. Pour out your heart in humility and repentance. Re-commit to doing things His way. Then expect to be attacked by the enemy of righteousness. He hates when we desire and strive to get and stay close to Jesus. Hang in there. It's eternally worth it.

Father, I confess that I often take the easy path, not the committed one. I get weary of the battle and lose focus on the goal. Thank You for the reminder that my commitment to You is not in vain, that You've got a plan for me now and for eternity. Help me stay faithful until You call me home and to eagerly expect that call. In Jesus' name, **Amen**.

855 I Cor. 16:13
856 I Cor. 11:3

Steadfast men follow the right goals.

"He who is steadfast in righteousness will attain to life, and he who pursues evil will bring about his own death." Prov. 11:24

It's been said that if you don't know where you're going, any road will get you there. The implication, when coupled with today's verse, is that being steadfast in the wrong thing can lead to disaster. For example, you can believe as steadfastly as you want about how the law of gravity doesn't apply to you. But… So, let's get right to the point. We've got God's handbook—the Owner's manual, if you will—that helps us set the right goals, helps us focus on those goals, and empowers us to reach them. So, what are we waiting for?

I know; life gets in the way. There are too many shiny things to draw our attention. But I submit that our focus is wrong. We're comparing the wrong things. All we know is time: minutes, days, decades. But time is a created thing, not eternal. And because it's all we know, it's what we focus on. How much can I get done in x amount of time? When we focus on what we know (time) and not on what we don't know (eternity), the important thing (eternity) seems dim and far away. As such, it fades into the background of our consciousness, and we go days, sometimes weeks, without giving our future with God much thought. But God warns us over and over that "*You do not know what your life will be like tomorrow. You are just a **vapor** that appears for a little while and then vanishes away.*"[857] And again, "*Do not fret because of evildoers, be not envious toward wrongdoers. For they will wither quickly like the grass and fade like the green herb. Trust in the Lord and do good; dwell in the land and cultivate faithfulness.*"[858] How long is eternity? Think about a 10K hike to take a drop of water and dump it in an empty Pacific Ocean. Then walk back to get another drop. Do this until the ocean is full. When that's done, eternity is just getting started.

God wants us to focus on eternity: "*Set your mind on things above where Christ is, not on things on the earth.*"[859] The problem in our society is we live for the "now." We have grown to expect instant gratification, nothing delayed for us; and we deserve it. *Bah.* That's why we're in so much debt that can never be paid. And that's a perfect segue back to today's verse. Simple. Righteousness produces life. Evil produces death. I'm calling us to make the same decision Joshua asked of the Israelites: "*…choose this day whom you will serve…as for me and my house, we will serve the Lord.*"[860]

Our Father, we're only here for a breath, and we don't understand eternity. Plant in our hearts a knowledge of and yearning for heaven where we'll be with You forever. Help us focus on You so You can produce in us the righteousness You promised because we love Your Son, Jesus. In His name, **Amen**.

857 Jas. 4:14
858 Psa. 37: 2, 3
859 Col. 3:2
860 Josh. 24:15

Steadfast men stick with it.

"Therefore, since we have so great a cloud of witnesses surrounding us, let us also lay aside every encumbrance and the sin which so easily entangles us, and let us run with endurance the race that is set before us." Hebrews 12:1

In the 60s, Elvis had a song titled *Stuck on You* in which the line "I'm gonna stick like glue because I'm stuck on you" was repeated several times. That's the gist of today's discussion: sticking with it. Sunday, we discussed commitments. Today looks at a different slant.

How many of us have (multiple?) projects around the house that remain in various stages of incomplete? Me too. Discipline is another word for *steadfast*, seeing whatever we start through to completion. Sometimes, we (I) just get bored and find some other interest. But God encourages us to focus and to get rid of "*the sin which so easily entangles us.*" Notice the verse says, "*...the race that is set before us.*" We don't all have the same race to run. Some are on the front line. Many are in support roles. The body (of Christ) is made up of lots of different parts [861] all working together. The key is **working** together. It's said that the Christian life is a marathon, not a sprint. How do we maintain the endurance to keep running (working) when we're physically tired, beat down by trials, and entangled by nagging sin? A good place to start is in Paul's letter to the Romans: "*...be transformed by the renewing of your mind, so that you may prove what the will of God is, that which is good and acceptable and perfect.*"[862]

Today, we hear about all kinds of renewal, urban renewal, water cleanup projects, and the like. But God invites us to spiritual renewal. How? It starts in our minds: First, a thought, then an act, then a habit, then a way of life, finally a destiny. Every ultimate result begins with a single thought. I'm gonna do this. I want more of that. Think about it.

What's keeping us from running our race? Is it laziness? Or fear? Or Insecurity? Or lack of knowledge? God's Word has answers to all of them. That's why He tells us to renew our minds because **everything** starts there. Is there anything in your life that you're "stuck like glue" to? The handbook reminds us, "*Whatever you do, do your work heartily, as for the Lord rather than for men.*" [863]

Lord God, today help me want to be stuck like glue to You and the race You designed specifically for me. I ask for endurance, renewal of my mind to line up with Your thinking and confidence that You have equipped me to successfully complete it. When you call me home, I want to hear "well done." In Christ's name, **Amen**.

---

861 I Cor. 12:14-26
862 Rom. 12:2
863 Col. 3:23

Steadfast men are alert to error.

"You therefore, beloved, knowing this beforehand, be on your guard so that you are not carried away by the ***error of unprincipled men*** *and fall from your own steadfastness, but grow in the grace and knowledge of our Lord and Savior Jesus Christ." II Pet. 3:17, 18*

Fake news. It's the latest buzzword and euphemism for lies. Where does it come from? Ultimately, it's the father of lies—Satan.[864] But he uses "unprincipled men" who have an agenda of evil. Proverbs 2 is filled with wonderful promises for the man who pursues God's wisdom and "treasures" His commandments.[865] Here is just a taste of the breadth of them: Discover the knowledge of God (v.5); gain wisdom (v.6, 7, 10); discern righteousness and justice (v.9); deliver you from the way of evil, from the man who speaks perverse things (v.12); deliver you from the adulteress (v.16).

I try not to be political, but sometimes I just can't help it. Today's verse perfectly describes a part of our political arena: men with an evil agenda. God is calling His men to a higher standard that permeates our lives 24/7, not just a casual Sunday stroll. We must understand we're at war for the souls of men and our enemy is cunning, sneaky and, yes... he lies. So how do we prepare for combat? First, we have to recognize that we are in a battle, not against flesh and blood, but the very powers of darkness.[866] Next, we must "put on" the full armor of God: truth, righteousness, the gospel of peace, the shield of faith, the helmet of salvation, and the sword of the Spirit.[867] Finally, we must be strong in the Lord so that we can stand firm against the schemes of the devil.[868]

Standing firm is another way of saying steadfast. We can prepare for battle all we want, but if we're not actively ***in*** the battle, what good is all our preparation? None of us is on God's bench; we're all first-stringers. The truth allows us to *be on our guard* by recognizing anything false and dismissing it or debating it, not to prove that we are right but with an eye toward sharing the gospel. Trying to prove we are right is the kind of pride that repels others like the same poles on two magnets. Our mission, our battle is simply one beggar telling another beggar where the bread (of life) is. It's time to suit up and "*grow in the grace and knowledge of our Lord and Savior, Jesus Christ.*"

Heavenly Father, I look at the sin-laden world and the falsehoods everywhere and get discouraged. Remind me today that it's all within Your plan, and none of it surprises You. Help me be a team player on Your team. In Christ's name, **Amen**.

864 John 8:44
865 Prov. 2:1
866 Eph. 6:12
867 Eph. 6:11, 13-17
868 Eph. 6:10, 11

Steadfast men are not distracted by earthly things.

"Brethren, follow my example, and observe those who walk according to the pattern you have in us. For many… are enemies of Christ… whose end is destruction… who set their minds on earthly things." Phil. 3:17-19

Yesterday, we discussed being alert to—and not distracted by—error; error in teaching, error in thought and attitudes. Today, I want to share some thoughts about the error of being distracted by earthly things. You've heard the saying, "all that glitters is not gold." Remember that Satan is no dummy. He has been observing mankind for millennia. He won't tempt us with shiny things that have no appeal. I own a smartphone, but it's three or four generations older than the current ones. I'm too cheap to spend over $1,000 on a phone that does a lot of things I don't want or need. So, when the latest gizmo is released, I'll look and be amazed, but I won't be moved to buy one. But there are things I'm tempted by that I have to be on guard against buying or even desiring…more power tools, for example.

Paul warns us against setting our minds on earthly things "*because you have died and your life is hidden with Christ in God.*"[869] It would be like being on a football team and wearing the opponent's jersey. We're on "Team Jesus," and we need to fly His colors. Satan would have us wear anything that takes our focus off our mission: "*be on the alert, stand firm in the faith, act like men, be strong.*"[870] The dictionary defines focus as "*a central point, as of attraction, attention, or activity.*"[871] There are so many things that tug at us for our focus, jobs, family, hobbies, trips, pleasure, etc. Don't get me wrong. There's nothing wrong with any of those…as long as they don't become idols and take the place of Christ. "*Seek **first** His kingdom and His righteousness and all these things will be added to you.*"[872] None of those things require us to leave our Christianity at the door. We're 24/7 followers of Jesus Christ. His Spirit lives in us. How can we leave Him at the door? Jesus told us, "*I came that (you) may have life, and have it abundantly.*"[873] As a father, you don't take toys from your kids and send them to their rooms when they obey you. Why would God do that to His kids?[874] Answer: He doesn't. We may feel separated from Him because we've been lured by the glitter. It happens. Don't wallow in it and believe that God can't or won't welcome you back any time you choose to return. He will! Isn't that great news?

Lord Jesus, I have a hard time staying focused on Your call on my life. Show me the folly of "all that glitters" and prod me onto Your path when I stray. **Amen**

869 Col. 3:2
870 I Cor. 16:13
871 Dictionary.com
872 Matt. 6:33 emphasis added
873 John 10:10
874 Matt. 7:11

Steadfast men press on.

"I press on toward the goal for the prize of the upward call of God in Christ Jesus"
Phil. 3:14

"Nothing in the world can take the place of Persistence. Talent will not; nothing is more common than unsuccessful men with talent. Genius will not; unrewarded genius is almost a proverb. Education will not; the world is full of educated derelicts."[875] Unfortunately, Coolidge only had part of the answer correct. He attributed success to persistence and determination, calling them omnipotent—not to the God who controls all.

This week, we've batted around the ideas of having right goals, sticking to them, and not being distracted by error or glitter. We've looked at how easy it is to lose focus and become discouraged by our weaknesses. So, persistence and determination *are* important. But not the be-all and end-all. Today, Paul brings our focus back to what really matters: the prize of being "*in Christ Jesus.*" When we apply these two to the right goal, we have the formula for overcoming any and all obstacles on our way to the prize. James tells us, "*Consider it all joy my brethren when you encounter various trials...*"[876] Really? Yes, because he had his eye on the prize: perfection (in Christ). I'm sure many of us have questioned James' wisdom as we were in the middle of our personal trials (serious accidents, death of a child, loss of a job, etc.). I know I did. But, "*...God is faithful, who will not allow you to be tempted beyond what you are able, but...will provide the way of escape...*"[877]

What goal(s) are we chasing today? You know, Satan always tries to get us off on rabbit trails; to keep us from growing in our steadfast commitment to Christ. He will throw every "good (looking)" thing our way to keep us from the "best" God has to offer. Good is the enemy of best. The problem with us is that "best" usually takes longer than "good." And we grow weary of the struggle. As always, Jesus has the answer, "*Come to me, all who are weary... and I will give you rest.*"[878] And again, "*Let us not lose heart in doing good, for in due time we will reap if we do not grow weary.*"[879] The key is "due time." God's not ours. Remember the goal, the prize. Remember, God is faithful. Remember the promised rest. Remember, we're not alone.[880]

Holy God, the prize seems so clear when I'm in Your Word. But then the world invades my space and clamors for attention. Remind me of Your faithfulness, Your promises, Your future, and strengthen my resolve to keep pressing on toward the goal. In Jesus' name, **Amen.**

875 Calvin Coolidge, 30th President of the United States
876 Jas. 1:2
877 I Cor. 10:13
878 Matt. 11:28
879 Gal. 6:9
880 Deut. 31:6

Steadfast men have hope.

"...constantly bearing in mind your work of faith and labor of love and ***steadfastness of hope*** *in our Lord Jesus Christ..." I Thes. 1:3*

Being a steadfast man is challenging. But today's word is HOPE. I can't think of another thing that is so powerful, so promising, so purposeful as hope. How dark it must be for those who have none. Jesus' disciples must have experienced despair before He told them, "*...in the world you will have tribulation, but take courage; I have overcome the world.*" [881] Take courage. That's a word for us today. We certainly know some of the tribulation Jesus talked about. It seems like things can't get any worse. But they always do... until God's clock runs out and He calls, "everybody out of the pool."

We are so impatient and judgmental and usually use ourselves as the standard to which everyone should aspire. Hah. In today's verse, Paul praises the Thessalonians for their "work" of faith and "labor" of love. Doesn't sound like they were slackers, does it? How are we doing in our work and labor in Christ? If God continues to grant us breath, then be assured, He's not done with us yet. Can it be said of us, we are "steadfast in hope"? I hope so. (Sorry, I couldn't resist)

Think of the things in our future that God has promised to those who trust His Son: A place for you (John 14:3); I will come again (John 14:3); no more tears, death, mourning, crying, pain (Rev. 21:4); In God's presence forever (Psalm 41:12). If that doesn't stir hope beyond what we experience with our five senses...well, you get my drift.

Don't ever give up. Press on. Have the right goal. Focus on "the Prize." Commit. Stay away from the glitter. Be alert to error. Do these things, and upon arrival in heaven, you will surely hear, "Well done, good and faithful servant."

Father, I get so excited when I remember all that You have in store for me and all Your children. May I never lose sight of that future or grow dim in my hope for Christ's return. But also, may I not get so focused on the future that I forget or fall into complacency about the present and the souls around me that don't share my hope in Jesus. Keep me alert to both error and opportunity to share Your truth and see others come to know You. Thank You for writing my name in Your Book of Life and for Your continued mercy and grace, which I so desperately need each day. May I walk faithfully in the path You've laid out for me. In Jesus' name, **Amen**.

881 John 16:33

Teachable men are humble.

"Therefore, putting aside all filthiness and all that remains of wickedness, ***in humility*** *receive the word implanted, which is able to save your souls." James 1:21*

Can we agree that most learning requires humility? Some come the hard way, and those lessons tend to stay with us because they're expensive or hurtful. But even then, we are humbled by them. So, it would seem we can choose; we can go into learning with humility or come out of it with humility.

Can we also agree that "receiving the word implanted" is the most important teaching we can pursue? God's Word is the source of truth, and the only 100% reliable and trustworthy book in existence. The reason is simple. All other books are written by man and are man's opinions or interpretations. The Bible was written by God Himself, using men inspired by the Holy Spirit. And we know that God cannot lie.[882]

Having said that, there is another side to learning. There has to be a teacher. I know many of us think we have a corner on knowledge, at least in certain areas, and aren't as open as we should be to examination of our strongly held beliefs. I remember reading years ago about a man climbing the ladder of success, determined to get to the top. He did. But he hadn't done things God's way and discovered his ladder was leaning against the wrong building. For those of us who aspire to teach in church, I remind us of God's warning: "*Let not many of you become teachers, my brethren, knowing that as such we will incur a stricter judgment.*" [883] Why does God add such a warning? Simple. He jealously guards the truth. Last week we learned about the error of unprincipled men,[884] men who would lead us astray from following Christ. The only way to spot the false teachers is to have the truth stored up in our minds.[885] It's like having a loaded gun when the burglar comes. An unloaded gun is worthless for protection. A Bible that sits on a shelf is worthless against the schemes of Satan.[886]

The first step in problem-solving is recognizing there is one. The first step in being teachable is being humble and knowing we can learn something from everybody we meet; not with an attitude of "what could *you* teach *me*? This week will change you…if you let it, if you approach it with humility.

Our Father, I've always struggled with pride and thought I could do things my way because I'm smarter than the average bear. But Your Word doesn't pull punches. I'm guilty of the sin of pride, and only Jesus' blood can take care of it. Thank you for the forgiveness that is mine in Christ. Help me this week to see my sin and put it to death. I want to be teachable and open to Your truth. In Christ's name, **Amen**.

882 Tit. 1:2
883 James 3:1
884 II Pet. 3:17 (Week 38 – Wednesday)
885 Rom. 12:2
886 II Cor. 2:11; Eph. 6:11

Teachable men study to know the truth.

"For Ezra had set his heart to study the law of the Lord and to practice it, and to teach His statutes and ordinances in Israel." Ezra 7:10

I'm sure we all know those who love to flaunt their knowledge. All they want to do is talk, preferably with a large audience. They are not interested in your ideas or opinions. They just want to show how much they know compared to you. They are described by Solomon, "*A fool does not delight in understanding, but only in revealing his own mind.*"[887] Jesus knew them too and called them out every chance He got.[888]

That's the negative side. Timothy gives us the positive, "*Be diligent to present yourself approved to God as a workman who does not need to be ashamed, accurately handling the word of truth.*"[889] And he goes on to tell us why, "*But avoid worldly and empty chatter, for it will lead to further ungodliness,*"[890] It seems a simple question, but why do we want to know the truth? Jesus said, "*If you continue in My word...you will know the truth and the truth will set you free.*"[891] Free from what? Sin, guilt, ungodliness, unprincipled men, adulteresses, the list goes on. But a big one for me is I don't have to be ashamed before God because I "accurately handle the word of truth." It's not a pride thing. It's about accountability to the God before whom I will someday stand and give account. Also, why would anyone want to believe and live a lie? "Fool" says it all. The key is "***continue*** in My word."

It's ironic. But the more I know, the more I know I don't know. And that alone is humbling. That's true on the spiritual level too. The closer I get to God by reading, studying, memorizing His word, the farther away from His standard of righteousness I realize I am. It could be discouraging if I didn't do what Ezra did—study, practice, teach... and trust God's promises. Don't you find that when you have to teach, even if it's confined to your own family, you study more so you know your subject? That's the point of today's talk. If we're going to live lives that attract others to Jesus in us, we must have it together and have something that's different from the world's teaching.

Take away for today: Study. For your own benefit and those around you who depend on you for direction. See you tomorrow.

God, I want to study and practice Your Word, but life pulls at me from so many directions. Help me see the value of prioritizing these demands and make my relationship to You my number one priority. Open my mind and heart to be teachable and to treat Your Word as a hidden treasure that pays huge dividends now and for eternity. In Jesus' name, **Amen**.

---

887 Prov. 18:2
888 Matt. 23:27
889 II Tim 2:15
890 II Tim 2:16
891 John 8:32

Teachable men repent early.

"When He killed them, then they sought Him, and returned and searched diligently for God" Ps. 78:34

The Israelites were a stubborn bunch. Probably a lot like many of us. They tried God's patience to the point of forcing Him to "*...kill some of their stoutest ones, and subdued the choice men of Israel.*"[892] Why does it often take harsh measures, sometimes extreme measures, to get our attention? It's because we have bought the world's lie, hook, line, and sinker, that macho is better than meek. He-man is better than humble-man. I warned you Sunday that this week would change you. How are you doing with that?

Let's be clear. God doesn't punish us (we who know Jesus) because He's angry or had enough of our rebellion. He does it because He loves us.[893] As parents, we can understand that a little. Sometimes we punish our kids out of anger. But generally, it's because they've misbehaved or did something dangerous. As adults, we can see down the future to probable outcomes of leaving bad behavior unchecked. God perfectly sees, knows, and controls the future, and He wants to protect us from the consequences of following the wrong path. "*Do not enter the path of the wicked and do not proceed in the way of evil men. The way of the wicked is like darkness; they do not know over what they stumble.*"[894] God does not want His children stumbling in darkness. On the contrary, "*But the path of the righteous is like the light of dawn, that shines brighter and brighter until the full day.*"[895] Sounds like a choice to me. Darkness and stumbling or brightly lit path.

It seems to me that if we focused on the consequences of our behavior, being teachable would be a no-brainer. We'd learn from those who have gone before about the side of God that's not often spoken of: His righteous anger. We would understand the fear of God. Sure, there's the reverence side of fear. But God is someone to be afraid of. Consider these descriptions: *"vengeance, anger, wrath,"*[896] *"retribution, day of calamity,"*[897] *"judgment by fire, those slain by the Lord will be many,"*[898] "*It is a terrifying thing to fall into the hands of the living God.*"[899] I'm not trying to scare you into teachability; just make sure you see both sides of the issue. God's anger and wrath will be poured out without hesitation when Jesus returns. "*...for the great day of their wrath has come, and who is able to stand?*"[900]

Lord God, I want to serve You because I love You, not because I'm afraid of You. Teach me to walk humbly with You. In Christ's name, **Amen**.

---

892 Psa. 78:31
893 Heb. 12:6
894 Prov. 4:14, 19
895 Prov. 4:18
896 Ezek. 25:14
897 Deut. 32:35
898 Isa. 55:16
899 Heb. 10:31
900 Rev. 6:17

Teachable men learn from nature.

*"For since the creation of the world, His invisible attributes, His eternal power and divine nature, have been **clearly** seen, being understood through what has been made so that they are without excuse..." Rom. 1:20*

Have you ever looked at a sunset, a tree, a flower, or a furry critter and marveled at God's imagination and awesome creative power? The attention to detail. The intricate and often delicate design. What are the odds of that just happening? Evolving. From what? About a bazillion to one...like, uh, never. Being teachable means we can learn from experience, surroundings, others. But unless we attribute the lessons to our ultimate teacher—the Holy Spirit—we're apt to come to wrong conclusions.

Our first thought when we hear the word nature is likely to be about rocks and weather and animals. But man has a nature too. The Bible refers to two types of man: natural man and spiritual man. "*Natural man does not accept the things of the Spirit of God, for they are foolishness to him...*"[901] Sometimes our learning is of what *not* to do. We need to surround ourselves with like-minded individuals that point us to the path of righteousness. *"Do not be deceived; Bad company corrupts good morals."*[902] Remember, the path to destruction is broad and *many* are on it.[903]

Spiritual man does not include most people who call themselves spiritual. For example, those who "commune with nature," those who worship trees or animals. No, spiritual man is one who follows the only spirit who matters: The Holy Spirit. Scripture warns of unclean spirits, evil spirits, deceitful spirits, all of which are spirits of demons.[904] We're told to "*test the spirits to see whether they are from God,*"[905] Our nature, created in the image of God, is naturally curious, and Satan will use that to draw us into all kinds of "spiritual" foolishness. Stick with what we've covered this week. The *only* source of truth that we stake our eternal future on is the Word of God. Everything else isn't.

According to today's verse, we are without excuse. God won't accept any reason which, in our minds, justifies or validates why we didn't take Him seriously. The seven words most often used by non-teachable men are, But I've always done it that way. Today, enjoy nature; God created it for our enjoyment. But let it build praise in your heart for the creator, not the created.

Father, Your creation is a marvel. May it remind me of Your power and authority and spawn praise for allowing me to enjoy it. Keep me focused on You and Your plan and purpose for me. Teach me today. In Christ's name, **Amen**.

---

901 I Cor. 2:14
902 I Cor. 15:33
903 Matt. 7:13
904 Matt. 10:1; Mark 1:27; Luke 4:36; Rev. 16:4
905 I Jn. 4:1

Teachable men are discerning.

"But solid food is for the mature, who because of practice have their senses trained to discern good and evil." Heb. 5:14

Solid food is like calculus vs. two plus two; sirloin steak vs. pureed peas; scripture meditation and memorization vs. the funny paper. Discernment comes through maturity and practice. Practice of what? Giving up our own way and walking daily in the path of righteousness[906] that we talked about Tuesday. Being teachable means being alert to our surroundings, to false teaching, to wrong attitudes (in ourselves), to needs in others, and much more. Being discerning means applying the truth we learn in the Bible to the previous list and recognizing quickly if *I* need an adjustment or if I need to do something for someone else. We don't have the prerogative to coast through life and let "Larry" do it. We will someday be called to give an account of what we did with what God gave us.[907]

Training our senses to discern good and evil implies that we know the difference. In our society, lines are blurring, standards are becoming lax to the point of fading into the ether. Civility? What's that? Even in the church, God's Word apparently doesn't require the kind of obedience of years gone by. But this is exactly what our training, our teaching, is meant to recognize. We can't be afraid to take a stand for good vs. evil, righteousness vs. ungodliness. Even when it seems nobody else in our circle is. When we stand before God, He won't ask us about Larry. Just to clarify from "the Bible", "*Jesus Christ is the same yesterday and today and forever. Do not be carried away be varied and strange teachings.*" [908]

Paul reminds us in Romans 12 not to be conformed to this world but to be transformed by the renewing of our minds. The dictionary defines transformed as a change in condition, nature, or character; to convert.[909] Paul is not encouraging us to become more like the world so they will like us and listen to us. If we're like them, with the same message they have, why should they listen to us? On the contrary, he goes on to write, "*...so that you may prove what the will of God is, that which is good and acceptable and perfect.*" [910] Did you catch that? We are to "prove" to an unbelieving world that only God's way is GOOD, ACCEPTABLE, and PERFECT.

Men, I hope this teaching is resonating with your spirits. The hour is late. The Marine Corps is looking for a few good men. God looks for one: "*I searched for a man who would...stand in the gap before Me...but I found no one.*"[911] May that not be said of us.

Father, I desire to be that man. Teach me. In Christ's name, **Amen**.

---

906 Prov. 4:18
907 Rom. 14:12
908 Heb. 13:8, 9
909 Dictionary.com
910 Rom. 12:2
911 Ezek. 22:30

Week 39 Friday

Teachable men learn to be content.

"Not that I speak from want, for I have learned to be content in whatever circumstances I am. I know...humble means...I know...prosperity...I have learned the secret of being filled and going hungry..." Phil. 4:11, 12

Everybody loves a secret. It portends a shortcut to some hidden treasure, be it riches, knowledge, or juicy gossip. Paul tells us he learned the secret of contentment. How do *we* learn it? Paul suffered but kept his focus on eternity; he considered his suffering to be "*...momentary, light affliction...producing for us an eternal weight of glory far beyond all comparison." (II Cor. 4:17)* With beatings, stoning, and shipwrecks, Paul calls his trials "momentary" and "light affliction." I'd hate to think what he considered a severe trial. But the "secret" comes in the next verse: "*I can do all things through Him [Christ] who strengthens me." (Phil. 4:13)* And the great news is, it's not really a secret. Anybody can know it. The Greek word translated "I can do" means "to be strong" (physically, not spiritually). Isaiah said it this way, "*He gives strength to the weary...those who wait for the Lord will gain new strength...they will run and not get tired, they will walk and not become weary." (Isa. 40: 29, 31)* This is a promise to those who walk humbly with God. (Micah 6:8)

Because Paul "saw" eternity in his future, he could confidently say that the glory of eternity was "far beyond all comparison." Think about this: The Lord of all creation has gone to "*prepare a place for you." (John 14:2)* I've seen some pretty fabulous homes constructed by phenomenal craftsmen. I can't even begin to imagine how glorious heaven will be, what with streets paved with pure gold. (Rev. 21:21)

So how does all this fit into contentment? Contentment doesn't just happen. Many at both ends of the financial spectrum are not content. The poor want more. The rich want more. But Paul cautioned Timothy, "*If we have food and covering, with these we shall be content. But those who want to get rich fall into temptation... For the **love** of money is a root of all sorts of evil..." (I Tim. 6:8, 9)*. We are tempted when we are "enticed by our own lust" (James 1:14). It's like any other sin, and Satan constantly whispers in our ear, "it's ok. Nobody will know. Just this once." We must control it, or it will control us. It takes practice. It takes getting knocked down and back up, over and over and over. Sooner or later, the pain of not changing becomes greater than the pain of change and, you got it... we become teachable. Do you have more than food and covering? Good. Tomorrow, the taught becomes the teacher.

Our Father, I confess that often I'm not content. I look at what others have and feel sorry for myself. Forgive me. I have Jesus and eternity with You. Teach me that I don't need anything else to be content. God, may I never stop being teachable. In Christ's name, **Amen**.

Teachable men become teachers.

"These words, which I am commanding you today, shall be on your heart. You shall teach them diligently to your sons and shall talk of them when you sit in your house and when you walk by the way and when you lie down and when you rise up." Deut. 6:6, 7

"Go therefore and make disciples of all the nations, baptizing them in the name of the Father and the Son and the Holy Spirit, teaching them to observe all that I commanded you; and lo, I am with you always, even to the end of the age." Matt. 28:19, 20

It's been said that more learning is caught than taught. And today's wrap-up for the week assigns your homework...for the rest of your life. The first *command* above lays out God's strategy for passing on to our children the faith we have. Talk it. Live it. Everywhere. Our kids are always watching us to see if what we say lines up with what we do.

The second *command* is to evangelize the world. Jesus told His disciples (and us) to teach what we've been taught. For a good roadmap of how to do this in detail, check out Operation Timothy (OperationTimothy.com). This is a mentoring program designed to pass our faith to the next generation.

This week, we've looked at some of the elements that go into a teachable man. Humility is the starting point. No learning comes apart from it. Next comes studying to know the truth. All learning is not equally important; only the truth found in God's Word lasts forever. We were encouraged to repent early, so God's lessons wouldn't have to be at the end of a big stick. Discernment was next; being able to spot, hopefully at a distance, the difference between good and evil. Finally, we discussed learning to be content. God's Word is so full of promises, encouragement, maps to successful living. For example: "*...the Lord knows how to rescue the godly from temptation." (II Pet. 2:9)* If we trust God when things are good or bad, then contentment will sneak up on us, and suddenly...we're content and we don't know when it happened.

You'll notice that today's verses are both commands, meaning they're not optional. I've heard many men ask, "How do I know God's will?" It's really simple. In today's verses alone, there are two statements defining some of it: Teach your children and make disciples. Couldn't be plainer. The only question is, are we really interested in *His* will, or are we still in the "let Larry do it" stage? My prayer for us is that we continue to be teachable so that the Lord can grow us into the men He designed us to be. How about it? Are you with me?

Lord Jesus, You have exposed my pride this week. Forgive me. I want to be the man you created me to be, but I'm so full of excuses. I think the truth is that I'm scared to commit to You fully. Open my heart to see Your heart and desire You above everything. **Amen**.

Thankful men are humble.

"...so that in us you may learn not to exceed what is written, so that no one of you will become arrogant in behalf of one against the other. For who regards you as superior? What do you have that you did not receive? And if you did receive it, why do you boast as if you had not received it?" I Cor. 4:7

Are you beginning to see a pattern here? The man of God is humble. Have you ever thought about just what being thankful means? We all say thanks—to God and others—for stuff. But do we ever consider the giver over the gift? James tells us, "*Every good thing given and every perfect gift is from above, coming down from the Father of lights,"* [912] Paul tells us in today's verse that we have received everything we have. Sure, we work and earn money to buy things. But where did the talent to work and earn come from? Have we ever considered how worthy we are to receive gifts from God? I submit it's a humbling experience to realize we only deserve God's wrath and condemnation, yet He lavishes blessing after blessing, gift upon gift, just because He loves us. How do we know? "*He who did not spare His own Son, but delivered Him over for us all, how will He not also with Him freely give us all things?"* [913]

Think of your role as a parent. Why do you give to your children? There are many reasons. Keep them warm, fed, safe. And the list could go on. But isn't the driving force behind it your love for them? Of course it is. And so it is with God. But here's the big difference. God loves us despite how we treat Him. We can't make Him love us any less... or any more regardless of what we do. We don't earn heaven or hell by our deeds. In fact, we don't earn it at all.[914] We *choose* it by putting or not putting our faith in Christ's gift on the cross and the unfathomable cost for Him to offer us a *second-birth* day.

My hope is that by the time we finish this week, we will have a deeper understanding of thankfulness. And in the future, when we say thanks, we'll consider the giver.

Lord God, You are the giver of every perfect gift. And You give to me just because You love me and want to. Because of You, I have everything I need and then some. Thank You. Father, I know I don't totally grasp the extent of Your love that cost You Your Son...for me. Don't let me drift into complacency or a glib thanks, but help me comprehend more fully the depth You went to so that I could be with You for eternity. In Christ's name, **Amen**.

912 Jas. 1:17
913 Rom. 8:32
914 Eph. 2:9

Thankful men reflect God's goodness.

"The Lord is my shepherd…surely goodness and lovingkindness will follow me all the days of my life, and I will dwell in the house of the lord forever." Ps. 23:1, 6

The moon has no inherent light. It reflects the sun. In like manner, we have no inherent goodness in ourselves;[915] we are to reflect the *Son*—the goodness of God—to a world in darkness. Many of us probably memorized this psalm as youngsters. I wonder how often we go back to it and parse the words for deeper meaning. For example, *shepherd.* You know how dumb sheep are. What more could we ask than to be part of God's flock? To be cared for, protected from the wolves of this world. And how about "guides me"? The world is an evil place. But our Shepherd hasn't left us without a map to righteousness. And what better companion in the valley of the shadow of death? He has overcome all enemies that would hurt us.

So how does all that impact our ability and willingness to reflect God's goodness? When we recognize all that God has done for us, there's no excuse for being glum. Our very countenance should beam from the joy within. As an icebreaker, I've used the question, "Are you as happy as you look?" with both smiling and frowning folks. Just "salting the oats" (you know, leading a horse to water…) for a conversation about Jesus.

To reflect something, we must be exposed to it and immersed in it. We are exposed to God's goodness every day regardless of whether we recognize it. Every breath we take is a result of God's goodness. And that's only the beginning; all nature shouts glory to the creator. Paul wrote that "*unrighteous men who suppress the truth about God, know about Him from nature but do not honor Him or give thanks and they became futile*[916] *in their speculations; so they are without excuse.*"[917]

Look at an example of how God values our thanks to Him and the consequences when we don't. God had just delivered the Israelites from slavery in Egypt. Moses was on Mt. Sinai receiving the 10 commandments. The Israelites became impatient and prevailed on Aaron to "*make us a god who will go before us.*"[918] So, because they went from amazing deliverance to idolatry in a few short weeks and grumbled and complained, rather than joyfully giving thanks for all God had just done for them, God killed 3,000 of them.[919] "*It is good to give thanks to the Lord and sing praises…*"[920]

Father, we benefit daily from Your goodness. Make us quick to see that, and may our lives show the real You to others. In Christ's name, **Amen**.

---

915 Gen. 6:5
916 Romans 1:21
incapable of producing any useful result
917 Rom. 1:18-23 (my paraphrase)
918 Ex. 32:1 Read the whole chapter for the rest of the story of God's anger and the surprise ending.
919 Ex. 32:28
920 Ps. 92:1

Thankful men understand the gravity of their sin.

"For he who does wrong will receive the consequences of the wrong which he has done, and that without partiality." Col. 3:25

Lady Justice—a woman holding a scale—is said to be blind. That's because the law is supposed to be applied equally across all accused. Doesn't always happen. Money, prejudice, power can affect decisions in the court. Today, Paul tells us that there are consequences for wrongdoing. God has no blindfold because He has perfect and complete knowledge and He set the standards. When we know Jesus as our Savior, it's because we understand that we've done wrong—sinned—and we deserve the punishment God outlined (death).[921] Further, we understand that Jesus took our death penalty on Himself so that through faith in Him, we could live forever with Him in heaven. That doesn't mean that consequences were waived and Paul misspoke. On the contrary. God's law, which will never pass away,[922] had to be fulfilled. That's why, when we understand our sin and its deserved consequences, we should be on our knees thanking God for His mercy that "saved a wretch like me."[923]

The best illustration of this is in Jesus' parable of the slave who owed ten thousand talents (an unfathomable sum, literally an infinite number) and pled with the king to whom he owed the debt to have mercy "*...have patience with me and I will repay you everything.*" [924] The king did and forgave the entire debt. That should have generated overflowing thanksgiving in the slave's heart, but no. Read Matthew 18:23-35 for the sad ending and warning to us about how serious God is that we show gratitude for what He has done.

It's fitting as I write this, Thanksgiving is only two days away. My wife reminded me of some of the great discussions we've had about God's goodness around the Thanksgiving table. This year, because I'm immersed in this week's topic, I plan to try and steer it to a deeper level. For example, rather than ask "what are you thankful for?" ask "to whom are you thankful...and why?"

A little offbeat, but fitting, I woke last night, and my back itched. I thanked God for my fingernails. Then I went into silent praise for His amazing design of my body. Just following orders, "*In everything give thanks; for this is God's will for you in Christ Jesus.*" [925]

Lord, I don't want to be like the ungrateful slave. Help me truly understand how large my debt was that You totally forgave through Jesus and give You thanks for all eternity. In His name, **Amen**.

921 Rom. 6:23
922 Matt. 24:35; Mark 13:31; Luke 21:33
923 *Amazing Grace* John Newton, 1725-1807
924 Matt. 18:26
925 I. Thes. 5:18

Thankful men do not whine or complain.

"Do all things without grumbling or disputing; so that you will prove yourselves to be blameless and innocent, children of God above reproach in the midst of a crooked and perverse generation, among whom you appear as lights in the world..."
Phil. 2:14, 15

Ever want to be the star of the show, the one in the limelight? Guess what? You are whether you want to or not. Paul says we appear as lights in the world. Remember the moon in Monday's discussion? Truth is, we aren't lights; we're reflectors. The question is, do we have anything worth reflecting? People are watching our actions and *re*actions.

The older I get, the more I see intolerance rampant in the world. I'm not talking about racial intolerance. I mean all the petty little things which have to do with inconsiderate drivers, people in public everywhere demanding their space, their rights, their importance. And whining or complaining when they don't get it. I admit, sometimes their attitude rubs off on me and I whine.

One of the things that helps me stay thankful, even through trial-filled circumstances, is remembering (from yesterday) all my selfish, whining, and complaining that God nailed to Jesus' cross. Yes, sometimes I fail because I think I deserve to whine "just a little" and/or get irritated because somebody stepped on my "rights." God says, "think again." I have to go back to Sunday's verse (I Cor. 4:7) and ask myself what right do I have to anything! For example, doing things my way (we're told to regard others more important than ourselves [926]), consideration from others (expecting *from them* what I may not be willing to give *to them*), a safe following margin on the freeway? I find when my thoughts are on God's glory, of Himself and His creation, it's hard to whine about anything. In Week 33-Friday, I quoted a line from *Maranatha Singers,* "He makes all things beautiful in His time." Things that I don't find beautiful now—things that irritate me—just haven't reached their time yet. Or maybe, it's me that hasn't reached my "beautiful time" yet. Hmmm. By the way, that discussion was on patience. Ouch.

If I'm a reflector, I want to be the brightest one I can be. That means my thankfulness has to outshine my whining because people *are* watching. My motive is not to please people, but to please my audience of one. The byproduct of that is a reflector people will be drawn to. When we replace our grumbling and disputing with thanksgiving, God says we're above reproach, not guilty, cleared of all accusations from the crooked and perverse around us.

Lord God, You know what it's like to live among the crooked and perverse; it can be discouraging if I let it, if I take my eyes off You. Your creative power is on display all around. Help me focus on that and give thanks for what I have in Your Son, not on what I don't have from the world. In His name, **Amen**.

926 Phil. 2:3

Thankful men are prepared for the future.

"I will give thanks to You, O Lord my God, with all my heart, and will glorify Your name forever." Ps. 86:12

There's only one place to give thanks to God *forever*: heaven. There's only one reason to give thanks to God forever: because we're *there*. There's only one way to get there: Jesus. [927] I could stop here and that would be a complete message for today. What peace what joy we experience because our future is secure. Jesus promised to come back for us. [928] "What a day, glorious day that will be." [929]

There is coming a day,
When no heartaches shall come,
No more clouds in the sky,
No more tears to dim the eye,
All is peace forever more,
On that happy golden shore,
What a day, glorious day that will be.

Chorus

There'll be no sorrow there,
No more burdens to bear,
No more sickness, no pain,
No more parting over there;
And forever I will be,
With the One who died for me,
What a day, glorious day that will be.

Chorus:
What a day that will be,
When my Jesus I shall see,
And I look upon His face,
The One who saved me by His grace;
When He takes me by the hand,
And leads me through the Promised Land,
What a day, glorious day that will be.

Father, the anticipation of thinking about spending eternity in Your presence is like Christmas Eve times infinity. Keep polishing my rough edges so I won't be ashamed to stand before You and my Savior. In His name, **Amen**

927 John 14:6
928 John 14:3
929 *What A Day That Will Be* lyrics © Ben Speer Music

Thankful men are not arrogant or discontent

"...in the last days...men will be lovers of self, lovers of money, boastful, arrogant... ungrateful...avoid such men as these." *II Tim.3:1-5*

Arrogance is the spawn of ignorance, i.e., wrong thinking about your abilities and accomplishments vis a vis how you got to where you are. Paul had a first-class pedigree.[930] But he didn't flaunt it; in fact, he counted it all as loss when compared to the "surpassing value" of knowing Christ.[931] Thankfulness and arrogance are mutually exclusive; they can't fill the same space. A thankful man recognizes his acquisitions and accomplishments as gifts from a gracious God. As such, there's not one thing we can do to earn God's favor. It's all Him. The arrogant man doesn't recognize God as the giver of every gift.[932] He smugly believes *he* is all that.

We've seen in the last couple of days what God thinks about grumbling, complaining, arrogance. Moses and Aaron learned the hard way. Not only did Moses disobey God and hit the rock instead of speaking to it like God had told him, he proudly asked the Israelites if they wanted *him* to bring forth water for them.[933] It cost both of them entry into the Promised Land. Don't fall into thinking that just because God doesn't zap us immediately when our arrogance and discontent offend Him that He really isn't offended. Just remember Moses. Also consider Nebuchadnezzar, the great king of Babylon. Daniel interpreted Neb's dream and warned him that if he didn't abandon his sins and recognize that all rule and authority belongs to God, he would be like an animal for seven years—until he realized that truly God was ruler of all. Exactly 12 months later...it happened.[934] One year can lull us into thinking God has forgotten or forgone our punishment. Not. God doesn't forget the bad or good we've done. But here's our hope: We don't have to live with the guilt of our past sins, or the pride borne of man's praise for our deeds (which, by the way, is sin too). Jesus is God's answer to both.

Understand that even our best day isn't enough to sway God's planned punishment for sin. But Jesus is. I sound like a broken record, but there is *only one way* to God: His Son, Jesus Christ.[935] Being thankful for what Jesus did for us is the key to defeating arrogance (pride) and discontentment. If we have food and clothing, we are to be content.[936] And thank God for trials as well as blessings.[937]

Father, I know everything I am and have is because of Your plan for my life. Often I forget that and think highly of myself. Forgive me. I want to be content. I don't want to be arrogant. Make me more like Jesus. **Amen**

---

930 Phil. 3:5, 6
931 Phil 3:7, 8
932 Jas. 1:17
933 Num. 20:10
934 Dan. 4:29-33
935 John 14:6
936 I Tim. 6:8
937 Jas. 1:2

Thankful men know whom they are thanking…personally.

*"Therefore I will give thanks to **You**, O Lord, among the nations. And I will sing praises to **Your** name." II Sam. 22:50*

If you ask the man on the street if he is thankful, 99 out of 100 will be able to tell you something they are thankful for. But ask them whom they are thankful to, and most will not have a good answer. It'll be a general feeling, a warm and fuzzy when something has gone their way. But today's verse is different. The "therefore" is there because of all that has just gone before. David recounts, for 49 verses, all that the Lord has done for him. So his automatic response is to give thanks and sing praise to *his* God. The same God who delivered him countless times. The same God who said of him, "*I have found David…a man after my heart.*"[938]

For those of us who are in Christ, there's no hesitation when it comes to knowing to whom we owe thanks. Our sins are forgiven.[939] New blessings every morning.[940] Jesus coming back for us.[941] Only one place this all comes from: God's heart. THE God. The one and only. When we think of whom we're thanking, it should prompt us to think more of the giver than the gift because He even knows who we are. God only gives us things for our good AND His glory.[942] And He doesn't have to do any of it. I think sometimes we feel like God owes *us* something instead of the other way around. You ever feel that way? You know, when you've been kind or patient or generous or you name it. Well, the Bible says that our righteous deeds are as "filthy garments."[943] That should be enough to keep our pride in check. But not usually. It keeps whispering to us how good we are and how much we're doing for God. When we have those thoughts, alarm bells should be clanging in our ears. God will not share His glory with anyone.[944] Look out when we want to take credit for what God alone has done.[945]

Our prayers should be filled with thanks and praise; more time spent on that than on what else we want God to do for us. Don't get me wrong. It's ok to ask for salvation for others, for success in business, for kinder hearts. We just need to keep it all in proportion.

Jesus told His disciples not to rejoice that demons were subject to them in His name but to rejoice that their names were recorded in heaven.[946] Think about that and you'll have no problem with being thankful.

Lord, You've done it all…for me. Thank You doesn't begin to cover it but it's all I've got. Thank You, forever. In Christ's name, **Amen**.

938 Acts 13:22
939 Acts 10:43
940 Lam. 3:22, 23
941 John 14:3
942 Ps.84:11
943 Isa.64:6
944 Isa. 42:8, 11
945 I Cor. 3:7
946 Luke 10:20

Trustworthy/Truthful men DO NOT lie.

"...a trustworthy witness WILL NOT lie..." Prov. 14:5 (emphasis added)

"He who conceals hatred has lying lips." Prov. 10:18

"Do you promise to tell the truth, the whole truth and nothing but the truth, so help you God?" Familiar words even if we've never been asked them. As I ponder this subject, our country is in the middle of an impeachment trial of President Donald Trump. I am saddened at the state of our society in which pure hatred has replaced the oath of office for many House members and Senators and seems to have been conveniently shelved, along with the commitment to *serve* those who elected them.

In the list of seven things the Lord hates, two deal with lying: "*...a lying tongue*" and "*a false witness who utters lies...*"[947] To add further emphasis to the Lord's attitude toward liars, hear this: "*A worthless person, a wicked man, is the one who walks with a perverse mouth...who continually devises evil, who spreads strife...his calamity will come suddenly.*"[948]

I believe we are on a slippery slope leading to destruction. Wherever we look, there is hatred, bigotry, and selfishness that manifests in church, shopping mall, movie theater shootings, and bombings. Respect for law enforcement has deteriorated to a dangerous level. How should the man of God react to all this? I believe it starts with a commitment to the truth, such things as not compromising our (God's) standards, rightly representing His Word in our lives and to others, and keeping our promises even when it hurts.

One thing I need to remember, and maybe some of you are in the same boat, is to not use the truth as a club for the purpose of venting on anyone. The Bible is clear, "*...with gentleness correcting those who are in opposition, if perhaps God may grant them repentance leading to the knowledge of the truth,*"[949] And, "*A gentle answer turns away wrath, but a harsh word stirs up anger.*"[950] Let's remember, it's God's truth, and we are Christ's ambassadors.[951] Jesus was not afraid to confront the lost and hypocrites of His day, and we should do the same with boldness because truth is on our side. We are to be filled with the fruit of the Holy Spirit: "*Love, joy, peace, patience, kindness, goodness, faithfulness, gentleness, self-control...*"[952]

Heavenly Father, sometimes I get angry at the lunacy of the world and forget that most likely, they're lost and on their way to destruction. I ask You to replace that anger with a heart for their souls and a desire to pray that they would come to know You before it's too late. In Christ's name, **Amen**.

947 Prov. 6:16-19
948 Prov. 6:12-15
949 II Tim. 2:25
950 Prov. 15:1
951 II Cor. 5:20
952 Gal. 5:22, 23

Trustworthy/Truthful men keep their word, even to their own detriment.

"Oh Lord, who may abide in Your tent? Who may dwell on Your holy hill? He (who) swears to his own hurt and does not change…" Ps. 15:1, 4

King Solomon, writing on behalf of God, said, "*When you make a vow to God, do not be late in paying it; for He takes no delight in fools. Pay what you vow.*"[953] A vow is a promise. We make wedding vows "'til death do us part." Unfortunately, today's version is more like, "'til I'm tired of you or find somebody better." According to God, you're a fool if you vow and break it. Strong language, but it frames the seriousness God ascribes to keeping our word. Why do you think people lie? I believe there are two main reasons. First, to achieve some real or imagined advantage over someone. Second, to avoid consequences for bad behavior. Rather than lying, the best way to avoid consequences for bad behavior is to avoid bad behavior in the first place. God's ways are not our ways.[954] God's laws are black and white; there's no gray area, no fudging, no such thing as a "white" lie. A lie is a lie. Men cheat on their wives. They lie. Men cheat on their taxes. They lie. Men steal. They lie. You getting the drift? Avoid the behavior. Avoid the lie.

Take the example of a sports player who signs a multi-year contract—a promise, a vow—and after one spectacular year, he wants to renegotiate for more money. He is not a trustworthy man. Now, there are many who would encourage him to break his word by saying things like, "You deserve it. Without you, the team wouldn't be in the playoffs." But what does God say? Fool! Sorry, my job is to tell you the truth. What you do with it is up to you. We'll get to compromising later in the week. As men of God, our standard is much different and higher than the world's. We can represent our Savior honestly by our lives and bring glory to Him. Or we can represent Him dishonorably by our lives and bring shame to His name. The choice is ours. Our focus, our goal is what will determine glory or shame. We either believe God means what He says, or we don't. In a book by Andrew Murray, in the very first chapter, he says, "Nothing dishonored and grieved Him (God) so much as unbelief."[955] As God's children, we disappoint God through our limited faith. It's the one thing that seemed to exasperate Jesus in His disciples more than anything else.[956] I encourage you to think before you vow. God is watching.

Lord God, no excuses. I have sinned by lying and breaking promises. Forgive me. Help me keep my eyes on Your standard, not the world's. **Amen**

---

953 Eccl.5:4

954 Isa. 55:8

955 *The Two Covenants and the Second Blessing*, ©2014 Ichthus Publications

956 Matt. 6:30; 8:26; 14:31; 16:18; 17:20

Trustworthy/Truthful men don't worry about a "hot mic."

"...in your bedchamber do not curse a king, and in you sleeping rooms do not curse a rich man, for a bird of the heavens will carry the sound and the winged creature will make the matter known." Eccl. 10:20

"...be sure your sin will find you out." Num. 32:23

Mar 26,2012*, President Obama was overheard on a hot mic telling President Dmitri Medvedev of Russia he would have "more flexibility" to negotiate with Putin after the election.*

In today's tech-savvy world, any smartphone can capture audio and video with clarity. This overheard event created quite a stir. And just as in consequences for bad conduct, the way to avoid "hot mic" situations is never to say anything about anybody you wouldn't say to their face. Not easy. The coffee breaks. The smoke breaks. The ball games. So many opportunities to "share." King Solomon said, "*he who is trustworthy conceals a matter.*"[957] And that includes opinions that are intended to do harm.

My question for us today is this: Do we have or want a reputation of being trustworthy and truthful? A reputation can take a lifetime to build, but only a moment—one instance—to destroy.

When my kids were little, they knew the punishment would be more severe if they lied about it. We always hear about God's love, grace, and mercy. And thankfully, He is all those things. We don't often hear about His wrath, His judgment, the things He hates. On Sunday, we learned just how much He hates lying and liars, two of the big seven. So, we may never be on national TV, but what consequence would you face if you told a coworker how stupid you think the boss is, and it got back to him? Or, you're the boss and hear through the grapevine that one of your employees thinks you're stupid. Mercy or judgment?

Realize that every time we break this commandment ("*thou shalt not bear false witness*"[958]), we test the Lord with something He hates. Are you a Christian? Yes, you're forgiven. But why do you presume on God's goodness and risk damaging your testimony? Make a commitment to always speak the truth, no matter the audience.

Father, remind me often that no matter the audience, You're always listening and watching, to bless me for sure, but also to correct and reprove. Thank You that You know my name. In Christ, **Amen**.

957 Prov. 11:13
958 Ex. 20:16

Trustworthy/Truthful men don't bend scripture for their own benefit.

"Be diligent to present yourself approved to God as a workman who does not need to be ashamed, accurately handling the word of truth." II Tim. 2:15

God is jealous.[959] For His glory. For His name. For His Word. We do well to remember that when we take verses out of context and apply them to a teaching not intended in the original. For example, "*For I know the plans that I have for you, declares the Lord, plans for welfare and not for calamity to give you a future and a hope.*"[960] This promise was specifically to the Israelites during 70 years of exile in Babylon. Many "teachers" today use this verse to say things like, "God wants you to be rich" or "God wants you to be healthy," and it's usually followed up with a plea for money. This is not to say that God doesn't, in a general sense, want those things for us. But to teach that it is for everyone always is not "*accurately handling the word of truth.*" Remember James' warning, "*Let not many of you become teachers, my brethren, knowing that as such we will incur a stricter judgment.*"[961] If we are to teach from God's Word, we better be sure that what we're teaching is right, is truth, and is for everybody.

So, today's discussion is not intended to discourage you from teaching. Just encouraging you to have right motives and approach God's Word with humility and awe. Humility, knowing that the Creator of the universe has trusted us with His character, His heart, His desire that all men come to know the truth.[962] Awe, in that God is always part of the audience to whom we speak, and He's grading us on how we handle His Word.

Being trustworthy in the world sets us apart from the majority ("*Many a man proclaims his own loyalty, but who can find a trustworthy man?*")[963] But being trustworthy in God's eyes puts a whole different value on us. Wouldn't it be great to be a man… "*after God's heart*"[964] and "*whose heart is completely His?*"[965] The good news is that we can. Today's verse gives the answer: Be diligent (be faithful, be disciplined in and by the word, don't lie), and we will be "*approved to God as a workman who does not need to be ashamed.*" Okay, workmen. It's time to punch in.

God, give me wisdom to understand Your Word and to live by it and teach it faithfully in truth and humility. In Jesus' name, **Amen**.

959 Exo. 20:5; Deut. 4:24
960 Jer. 29:11
961 Jas. 3:1
962 I Tim. 2:4
963 Prov. 20:6
964 I Sam. 13:34; Acts 13:22
965 II Chron. 16:9

Trustworthy/Truthful men do not compromise the truth.

"Lying lips are an abomination to the Lord, but those who deal faithfully are His delight." Prov.12:22

The dictionary defines compromise as "a settlement of differences by mutual concessions."[966] That often works fine in the workplace or at home in a disagreement with our wives about new furniture or where to eat dinner. But not so much when truth is at stake. The Apostle Paul says, "*our struggle is not against flesh and blood, but…rulers… powers…world forces of this darkness…spiritual forces of wickedness.*" [967] One of Satan's favorite tools—especially when he knows an outright lie won't work—is to get us to compromise. We discussed this Monday. No lies, no fudging, no gray areas when it comes to the truth.

Why are we so often eager to vacate the high ground of truth to wallow in the muck of half-truths and lies propagated by those empowered by what Paul warned against? It could be we feel alone, outnumbered, outsmarted. And, in our own power, that may be true. But, fellow soldiers, we don't fight in our own power. We represent almighty God, the Creator, the author of truth. Rather than seeking the approval of men, we need to remember whose army we're in…and that the battle is already won. We don't have to give account to the world, only to God.

What are some hard to recognize compromises we routinely make? How about speed limits? Are they mere suggestions? Or movies with language and sex? Or pornography (because it's not hurting anyone)? Or taking a little longer for lunch? Or speaking up when others profane God's name or His truth? The reason these might be hard to recognize is we've become accustomed to them over time (the frog in the pot syndrome) and consider them normal. And we want to be liked, to be accepted. But what does God say? "*Do not be bound together with unbelievers…*"[968] and "*…come out from their midst and be separate.*"[969]

Men, our lives are to be different from the world. If we're not, why would anyone want Christ? Our verse today tells us to "deal faithfully" and we will "delight" the Lord. What better stamp of approval could we ask for? I'll close with this. Are we only concerned with delighting ourselves with temporary pleasures, or is our focus a little more long-range?

Father, when I consider Your standard, I realize how far short I fall in meeting it. I confess that sometimes I don't even want to meet it because compromise is comfortable and I'm lazy. Help me to focus on the end of the road, not the potholes along the way. In Christ's name, **Amen**.

966 dictionary.com
967 Eph.6:12
968 II Cor. 6:14
969 II Cor. 6:17

Trustworthy/Truthful men can handle the church's money.

"Now he (Judas) said this, not because he was concerned about the poor but because he was a thief, and as he had the money box, he used to pilfer what was put into it." John 12:6

One of the easiest temptations to fall into is mishandling money. Stealing is obvious, but so is paying too much, being open to bribes, etc. Pilfer is an interesting word. It means stealing, especially in small quantities. So, did Judas pilfer because there wasn't a way to hide larger sums? Or maybe there wasn't that much in the money box to begin with and more would have been missed. Whichever, he was a thief…and untrustworthy. Aside from betraying Jesus, being a thief is all we know about Judas. But how did John know about it to include it in his gospel? Hmmm. Something to think about when we think we're so clever in *our* sin and nobody knows.

In today's church, especially the larger ones, a lot of money flows through the coffers. But my question is how much of it gets invested in ministry and missions rather than bigger paychecks, bigger buildings and bigger…wait for it…jets? There *will* be an accounting, and it's not the IRS. Keep in mind our topic of the week: Trustworthy and Truthful. Character qualities God *highly* values. Malachi has a question for money managers in churches: "*Will a man rob God?*" and God's position: "*You are cursed with a curse, for you are robbing Me.*"[970] Protection for the man of God is in accountability, two or three trustworthy men who share in managing God's money in a church setting. Two signers on checks. Two (or more) counters of offerings. Simple checks and balances that trustworthy men should embrace.

The words money, riches, and wealth are used nearly 300 times in the Bible. Frequency is a strong indicator of importance (to God). What a man does to get money, how he spends and invests it, and how generous he is with it says volumes about whether it is an idol. And we know what God thinks about idols. Not all of us will ever be called upon to handle God's money in a church. But isn't all money God's? And aren't we accountable for how we treat it? If you have a problem in this area, please don't wait for disaster to strike. There are several good Christian programs to help get our arms around it. Start by confessing the problem to our Father, who will abundantly pardon.[971] Then find another man who is trustworthy to be an accountability partner. The measure of a man is not in how big his bank account is but in how loosely he holds onto it, whatever the size.

Lord God, it all belongs to you, and I'm just a manager. Give me wisdom to manage whatever you give me according to Your plans. Thank You that Your blessings are new every morning. Great is Your faithfulness. In Christ's name, **Amen**.

---

970 Mal. 3:8, 9
971 Isa. 55:7

Trustworthy/Truthful men love and defend the truth.

"...but I give an opinion as one who by the mercy of the Lord is trustworthy."
I Cor. 7:25

When we open our mouths, what comes out? The psalmist said, *"(the wicked) have closed their unfeeling heart, with their mouth they speak proudly."*[972] Jesus said, *"for the mouth speaks out of that which fills the heart."*[973] To paraphrase, Jesus also said, *"good treasure (in the heart) begets good words; evil treasure begets evil words."*[974] Do you ever wonder why so much hatred and lying spews from certain politicians or co-workers? Sadly, it exposes what is truly in their hearts. Proverbs tells us, *"When he (a whisperer, v22) speaks graciously, do not believe him, for there are seven abominations in his heart."*[975] The dictionary defines abominable as repugnantly hateful; detestable; loathsome. It belies their lostness and should cause us sorrow that they don't know Jesus; It should cause us to pray for their salvation.

So, I'll ask again. When we open our mouths, what comes out? Paul was arguably one of the greatest preachers in the Bible. But look what he says in today's verse: *"by the mercy of the Lord."* That's humility. His opinions were trustworthy *because* of God's mercy, and that's what filled his heart. Are our opinions backed up by God's mercy, or are they filled with wrong motives (e.g., revenge, jealousy, etc.) or wrong goals like one-upmanship?

On Thursday, we talked about compromise when someone profanes our God. This should fill us with righteous anger for God's name and His holiness, and it should be hard for us to keep quiet. We are marked as trustworthy by our lifestyle as well as our words. By what we take a stand for. By what we defend. Think back over this week's ideas and remember who's watching and keeping score. Wednesday, we were reminded to be diligent (i.e., faithful and disciplined). How are we doing when confronted by enemies of our Savior?

I encourage us to guard our tongues, and if we are prone to give opinions, especially when not invited to, wait on the Holy Spirit for the proper openings. And when we open our mouths, let's be sure that our hearts are filled with good treasure.

Heavenly Father, fill my heart with good treasure—truth—from Your Word so that when I open my mouth, it's Your opinion that comes out. Give me boldness to speak up, to defend Your truth and You to an unbelieving world so desperate, so in bondage by Satan and his lies. May I, like Paul, realize it's only because of Your mercy that I can claim trustworthiness. Thank You for trusting me with Your reputation. In Christ, **Amen.**

---

972 Ps. 17:10
973 Matt. 12:34
974 Luke 6:45
975 Prov. 26:25

Understanding men walk by the Spirit and have the mind of Christ.

"But a natural man does not accept the things of the Spirit of God, for they are foolishness to him and he cannot understand them because they are spiritually appraised." I Cor. 2:14

As a believer in the Lord Jesus Christ, I'm often surprised, sometimes dumbfounded, at how really simple things seem to escape the understanding of many people. For example, many folks don't accept that life begins at conception even though at 6 weeks, a baby's heart is beating around 110 times per minute. Again, though everything in creation has design and purpose, implying a designer (we know Him as Creator), people reject that in favor of a statistically impossible alternative, big bang/evolution.

The reason is simple. To accept what *we* know to be true, they would have to acknowledge the Creator. And if a creator exists, He deserves credit, honor, and obedience; terms that prideful man wants nothing to do with. Pity. Someday, they will know the truth. But then it will be too late.

But lest we think more highly of ourselves than we ought, it should humble us to realize that God even knows our name;[976] that He chose us before the world existed,[977] and regardless of our sins, loves us unconditionally. We don't deserve any of it. And in addition to humility, this knowledge should overflow in us with gratitude that our sins are forgiven; they are not held against us, and there is no condemnation because of them.[978]

Do you have family or friends that don't know Jesus? Wouldn't you like to see them in heaven with you? Our time is short. It's time to wake up. Paul tells the Romans, "*…that it is already the hour for you to awaken from sleep; for now salvation is nearer to us than when we believed.*"[979] As I write, the world is embroiled in fighting the coronavirus pandemic. Everywhere people are wondering, "Is this the end?" My response is, "I don't know. Are you ready if it is?" Always a thought provoker. Ready for what, they say. It's a great time to brush up on how to share our faith. The Apostle Peter wrote, "*…always ready to make a defense to everyone who asks you to give an account for the hope that is in you, yet with gentleness and reverence.*"[980] My question for you today is, "Are you ready? Do you know Jesus personally?" Then wake up. You know people who don't.

Father, thank You for choosing and knowing me. May my gratitude to You overflow with compassion for those who don't know You, especially my family and friends. Embolden me to look for opportunities to share Your love with them. In the power of Jesus' name. **Amen**.

---

976 Isa. 43:1
977 Eph. 1:4
978 Rom. 8:1
979 Rom. 13:11
980 I Pet.3:15

Understanding men know the truth and are set free from sin.

"... you will know the truth, and the truth will make you free." Jn. 8:32

Sin enslaves. It digs its claws in and doesn't let go. Once becomes a habit. Things you never saw yourself doing are now chains around your neck. The Gospel has been called the *good* news of Jesus Christ. And it is. Listen to what Paul says to the Romans, *"the law of the spirit of Christ Jesus has set you free from the law of sin and of death."* [981] If that isn't the *best* news we could hear, I don't what else could be.

For men who don't know Jesus as their Savior, this is the truth that you've been looking for; the truth that sets you free. If that's you, even if you didn't know it, find a friend who knows Jesus and let them introduce you.

For those of us who *do* know Jesus but still struggle with chains of addiction, anger, pride, the list can go on, the message is the same—except in the past tense. Jesus *has already* paid the price with His blood for *all* our sins, past, present, and future. The solution is similar: find a friend who knows Jesus and proves it by his lifestyle, not one who just talks the talk, and share your struggles with him. James tells us to *"...confess your sins to one another and pray for one another so that you may be healed. The effective prayer of a righteous man can accomplish much."* [982]

I know, as men, most of us don't like the touchy-feely stuff. And we're prone to be more loner than joiner. But that's a lie from the pit intended to keep us bound.

If you're the one to whom others come for advice and counsel, remember that God's word is a light,[983] not a weapon to beat them with. Make sure your mental storehouse of scripture is filled up and follow Solomon's advice: *"...do not reveal the secret of another."* [984] Having someone place their trust in you to allow them to open up is a privilege earned by a life of humility and service. Remember Christ's words to His disciples, *"...whoever wishes to be first among you shall be slave of all."* [985]

To understand our position in Christ is indeed the most freeing experience I can imagine. As we get closer to the return of Christ for us, our hope should be bursting at the seams, looking forward eagerly to His coming and escorting us to our eternal home. *Maranatha*. Come, Lord Jesus.

Lord God, thank You for allowing me to know and embrace Your truth and the freedom that comes with it. May I show my gratitude through a life of obedience and service as Your ambassador in an evil world. Give me eyes to see the lost and hopeless all around me and the boldness to share what You've given me. In Christ's name. **Amen.**

---

981 Rom. 8:2
982 Jas. 5:16
983 Ps. 119:105
984 Prov. 25:9
985 Mark 10:44

Understanding men seek wise counsel for big decisions.

"A wise man will hear and increase in learning. And a man of understanding will acquire wise counsel." Prov. 1:5

New career? Marriage partner? Buy or rent? A few of the biggest decisions you will make in life. Looking back over a few decades at some of the decisions I've made, thinking I was smarter than the average bear, I realize that I would be much further ahead if I hadn't been so proud to think *I don't need no stinkin' advice.* According to Solomon, that was a very *unwise* period in my life.

I believe the very biggest decision any of us can make, because it affects where we spend eternity, is "what am I going to do with Jesus?" For me, I didn't need counsel to tell me I needed a Savior. God had used a series of events to bring me to my knees, realizing what a mess I had made up to that point. But, praise God. His mercy and compassion flooded me, and that must have been what came out of my eyes. 'Cuz I know real men don't cry. Bah. My past was gone. I had a new slate on which to write the rest of my story.

What decisions are you facing? Are you using your wife as a sounding board? You should; that's the voice of experience talking. Trust me, it's better to ask her opinion beforehand, when she's open. It's much better to hear, "I don't think that's a good idea" than to wait until we've screwed up and hear, "I told you so."

Others are more than willing to share their opinions with you. But, spoiler alert, you have to be wise enough to discern *their* objective. So, if we are to acquire wise counsel as Solomon advises, how do we know we're getting it? There are two primary yardsticks. First, and *most important*, does it line up with scripture? God WILL NOT lead us in a path that doesn't agree with His revealed heart. And ask yourself, "Will this honor God?"[986] Second, does the counselor's life reflect his words? (I can't hear what you're saying, your actions are too loud.) If those two standards are met and what you want doesn't violate your own conscience, do it.

A word of caution. I believe we are living in the last days. I mean the *really* last days. No, I'm not pointing to a specific month, day or year. Because nobody *knows.*[987] *But, we are* to observe the signs and **be ready**.[988] I urge us all to have the gospel of Jesus ready on our lips to anyone we meet who needs to know our Savior.[989]

Lord Jesus, You have warned us repeatedly to wake up, to be ready for Your return. May we stay watchful and alert to false teaching, false counsel, and false friends. Instead, fill us with Your Spirit to discern truth from error. In Your name, **Amen**.

986 I Cor. 10:31
987 Matt. 24:42
988 Matt. 24:3-13
989 II Tim. 4:2

Understanding men can read the signs of the times.

"...and they did not understand until the flood came and took them away; so will the coming of the Son of Man be." Matt. 24:39

Noah was a righteous man, blameless in his time, who walked with God.[990] His neighbors, and the rest of the world not so much. In fact, it was to the point that God said, *"I will blot out man whom I have created from the face of the land...for I am sorry that I have made them."*[991] God gave Noah instructions to build a boat. So, he started to build a boat—sometime *after* his 500th birthday.[992] It took him, give or take, a hundred years to build this boat.[993] Considering the boat was 450 ft. long, 75 ft. wide, and 45 ft. tall,[994] and there were no power saws or cranes, not a bad accomplishment.

Why did God do this? Because the earth was filled with wickedness and violence and "*every intent of the thoughts of his* (man's) *heart was only evil continually.*"[995] Does that sound like the days we're living in? Jesus told the Pharisees and Sadducees, "*...Do you know how to discern the appearance of the sky, but cannot discern the signs of the times?*"[996] And to His disciples, He said, "*...just as happened in the days of Noah, so it will be also in the days of the Son of Man: ...eating...drinking...marrying...until the day that Noah entered the ark, and the flood came and destroyed them all.*"[997]

Noah was an example of righteousness for 100 years while he built the boat. Our society has had preachers of righteousness for decades. But we're still on a slippery slope of sin and depravity with no offramps or U-turns in sight. As I write, the COVID-19 pandemic is sweeping the world. Could this be a wakeup call from God that our time is short? God always gives time for us to repent...until He doesn't. Look at the signs, men. Understand God's plan of salvation for anyone willing to come to Jesus on His terms. If God destroyed the entire earth except for eight people,[998] and He is the same yesterday, today, and forever,[999] what makes us think He won't do it again? He said He will.[1000] Is *your* boat ready for the coming storm?

God, as I look at the wickedness, the pure evil all around and wonder how much more You will tolerate, I'm comforted by Your promise of eternity to all who believe in Christ's death and resurrection on their behalf. **Amen**

---

990 Gen. 6:9
991 Gen. 6:7
992 Gen. 5:32
993 Gen. 7:6
994 Gen. 6:15, A cubit is approx. 18 inches
995 Gen.6:5, 13
996 Matt. 16:3
997 Luke 17:26, 27
998 Gen. 6:18; Gen. 7:13
999 Heb. 13:8
1000 II Pet. 3:10

Understanding men have insight into God's heart and plans.

"Many will be purged, purified and refined, but the wicked will act wickedly; and none of the wicked will understand, but those who have insight will understand."
Dan. 12:10

What do you call somebody who willfully disregards warning signs like slow down, bridge out, high voltage, or thin ice? Foolish? Stupid? Arrogant? There are lots of possibilities. God calls those who disregard *His* warning signs "wicked." And He says they will continue in their wickedness. Today's verse is part of God's vision given to Daniel regarding the end of time.

Yesterday we talked about signs of the times. I believe the evil of men's hearts, the wickedness of their actions, and the increasing disregard for law and order and other's rights is clearly a sign of our times. Where is it on God's timetable? I don't know. But I do know this: it's been prophesied, which means it *will* happen.

Jesus told His disciples, "*Because lawlessness is increased, most people's love will grow cold.*" [1001] Is lawlessness increasing? Is people's love growing cold? The evidence is overwhelming. Riots using the most trivial of excuses. Racial tension. Road rage. Everywhere we look, me, me, me.

Not only are laws being flaunted by criminals, governments aren't enforcing them. Consider San Francisco's Prop 47 (2014), which reduced theft of property under $950 from a felony to a misdemeanor with little to no jail time. Whaaat? Of course, "petty" crimes have increased. Of course, resentment of authority has increased. Reread today's verse, "the **wicked will act wickedly**; and **none** of the wicked **will understand**." It's kind of like, duh. But that's because the man of God *does* understand.

So, where does that leave us? What are we to do about society crumbling all around us? Shrug our shoulders and say, "what can one person (me) do?" NO! First, thank God that none of this has sneaked up on Him. He's still in charge. Second, to the best of your ability, make sure your family knows Jesus. Now is not the time to give up on anybody. Pray for them. Provide a Godly role model. Use the only weapon that has the power to change lives, God's Word. Read it. Memorize it. Meditate on it. It will change you and, as a result, those around you. Finally, be bold in sharing the only map to heaven: Jesus. Get it? Got it? Good.

Father, Your love is amazing that you don't just zap us now and be done. Thank You for Your patience with me, that You kept calling until I finally woke up and heard You. May I have an urgency for the souls of my family and not give up on them while there's still time. In Christ's name. **Amen**

1001 Matt. 24:12

Understanding men know their eternal destiny.

"A man who wanders from the way of understanding will rest in the assembly of the dead." Prov. 21:6

Ever give serious thought to what the "assembly of the dead" is like? I remember the deflection of truth and flippancy by some saying (of hell), "I'll be so busy with friends I won't have time to worry." Sad. The real sadness, however, is that though God has made it abundantly clear with warnings and word pictures, many *choose* to ignore the truth. Consider words like agony, torment, flames,[1002] lake of fire, forever.[1003] Not a picture of happiness and joy.

What exactly is the "way of understanding?" When my son was maybe 3 or 4 years old and we would ask him a question during family devotions, he would invariably say, "Jesus." We chuckled then and, in fact, still get a smile when we think about that. But really, isn't Jesus the answer to most things in life? He *is* the answer to the question above. He said, "*I am **the way** and the truth and the life; no one comes to the Father but through Me.*"[1004]

I guess it's appropriate to ask the question, "Just what is it that we are to understand?" The simple answer is God's plan. And not only is the answer simple, the plan is simple too. God loves you. Your sin separated you from Him. Jesus died for you. Repent and believe. Go to heaven when you die. Many people miss it *because* of its simplicity. They have bought Satan's lie that we can *earn* our way to heaven. You know, Jesus *plus* good works. Jesus *plus* tithing. Jesus *plus*...anything. Understand that is Satan's plan, not God's.

In addition to understanding God's plan, we must understand God's heart as revealed in His Word. God is faithful, cannot lie, loves unconditionally. All that's true, and we can confidently base our hope on it. But God has another side too. He's righteous, hates sin, and will someday (soon, I hope) destroy it **and** sinners. If you take away nothing else this week, take this: judgment is coming. We won't know the day or hour, just like those in Noah's day didn't. But it's as sure in our time as it was in Noah's.

God has given us clear warning signs of impending disaster. When we hear the tornado sirens, we head for the basement. In the L.A. school system in the 50s and 60s, they were called air raid sirens. Didn't even know what an air raid was, but we all got under our desks. We knew that if we didn't act quickly, something bad could happen. Why don't we react to God's "early warning system," otherwise known as the Bible, with the same intensity? Where are you wandering today?

Lord God, You have given us ample preparation time because You love us and want us to spend eternity with You. Open our eyes to the warning signs and prod us as much as necessary to keep us on the right path. **Amen**

1002 Luke 16:23, 24
1003 Rev. 20:10
1004 John14:6, emphasis added

Understanding men are disciplined and teachable.

"He who neglects discipline despises himself, but he who listens to reproof acquires understanding." Prov. 15:32

Solomon predates modern psychology by millennia. But look at the wisdom in his words in the first part of our verse. Today's psychology would likely make this a chicken and egg problem. Does he neglect discipline *because* he despises himself? Or does he despise himself because he neglects discipline?

God has placed within each of us a spirit capable of knowing right and wrong. We call it the conscience. One who neglects discipline is basically lazy. Inherently, when lazy behavior patterns start, before they become habits, we know they're wrong. But for whatever reason, we make the wrong choice. It's been said that it only takes 30 days of doing something for it to become a habit, good or bad. This doesn't have to become a way of life, a destiny. The answer is in the second part of the verse.

What exactly is reproof? It is rebuke, correction, teaching, changing wrong thinking. It boils down to identifying error and attempting to make it right, whether in thinking or actions. And why should I listen to it? What if my reprover is wrong? First, if we don't listen, if we're not open to correction, we go on our way oblivious to our (possible) error. Second, if we allow our pride to put up roadblocks to what may be the truth, not only do we not gain understanding, God labels us "fool." ("*The way of a fool is right in his own eyes, but a wise man is he who listens to counsel.*") [1005]

Ask yourself, "why is discipline so important?" One of the main reasons is that our enemy, the Devil, is always looking for ways to destroy us, our testimony, our joy, anything he can.[1006] And without discipline, we can easily fall into old habits, become lazy and apathetic toward God and His plan for us.

We've talked about warnings this week, and here's one to finish our discussion of understanding. It applies primarily to those who have not turned from their sin and embraced the truth of Jesus Christ. But it's also a good reminder to those of us who may be wavering on the discipline issue: "*See to it that you do not refuse Him who is speaking. For if those did not escape when they refused him who warned them on earth, **much less will we escape who turn away from Him who warns from heaven**.*" [1007]

Father, discipline is hard work, and I can be lazy. Strengthen me in my spirit to stay the course. And, Lord, I think I'm usually right, and it pokes my pride to admit I could be wrong. I know that's a good thing. Give me the gift of humility to accept the message of correction even if I don't like the messenger. In Christ's name, **Amen**.

1005 Prov. 12:15
1006 I Pet. 5:8
1007 Heb. 12:25, emphasis added

Victorious men trust in God, not their own strength.

"A horse is a false hope for victory." Ps. 33:17

Football may be the closest thing we still have to mano a mano combat since the days of the gladiator in Rome. It's brutal, crushing, some even say barbaric. And the endzone celebrations have gone from a mere spike to fully choreographed exhibitions. Yet we watch, even plan our Sundays around "the game." Why? To see strong, athletic men push each other around trying to prove their prowess? Maybe. I confess that I'm right there with you whenever I can catch the Broncos or when the playoffs start. Hopefully, they're one and the same, but not so much recently.

It's almost comical to see how players who've just made a great play strut around like they're all that and a bag of chips, when they should be sharing that glory with their offensive line and usually one key block that breaks them free. But, to get back to my point, the real glory, literally for everything we accomplish because of our talents, belongs to the One who gave us those talents.[1008] And we need to know that when we take credit for and boast about something that God *gave* us, we're on thin ice. The Bible is clear when God says, "*...I will not give my glory to another.*"[1009] He also reminds us that we "*cannot make one hair black or white*"[1010] or add "*a single hour to his life's span.*"[1011]

I was scrolling through Pinterest the other day, looking for inspirational quotes, and came across one I thought apropos to our discussion. A lion, looking fearsome, said, "If size mattered, the elephant would be king of the jungle." Do we feel inadequate to the tasks God has called us to? Good. Then we will be more inclined to trust Him to provide the mission, the strategy, the tactics, and, most importantly, the victory. In my life, when I'm tempted to gloat over some accomplishment, accolade, or award, my pride swells, and before long, I'm very close to God's corrective measures. I pray for God's wisdom and grace to allow me to see that sooner than later. I've been through some of His corrections. Not fun. Today's takeaway? God will provide. We can trust Him even when things look darkest.

Lord God, it's so easy to think that I have earned or deserve anything good and forget that it's You who bless and bless and bless me. Forgive me and keep me close so I don't take credit for what You do in my life. **Amen**.

1008 I Cor. 4:7
1009 Isa. 48:11
1010 Matt. 5:36
1011 Luke 12:25

Victorious men rely on wise counsel, not just their own opinions.

"For by wise guidance you will wage war. And in abundance of counselors there is victory." Prov. 24:6

Fool or wiseman? Solomon said, "*The way of a fool is right in his own eyes, but a wise man is he who listens to counsel.*"[1012]War is a subject that's never too far from our consciousness. Fortunately, not many of us carry the weight of wartime decisions. (A reminder to pray for those who do.) But isn't living in the 21st century kind of like a war? Societal niceties like kindness, patience, courtesy, etc. are gathering speed on a slippery slope. Bars on windows, gangs with no respect for other people's property or laws that protect it, and even younger children with attitudes of disrespect and anger.

It's tempting to go to work, come home and hunker down with our doors locked and guns loaded. The Israelites were a fearful bunch. God had to tell them over a hundred times, "Do not fear." Fear comes when we don't trust God to "have our six." Knowing we're making good decisions that keep us in line with God's plans goes a long way to remove fear.

Aside from God's Word being filled with wisdom, and our prayers for wisdom which God *promises* to answer,[1013] do we have a group of guys who are like-minded and filled with the Holy Spirit that we can depend on for Godly advice? In decision making, the Christian life is more like a small group than a solo performance. Don't forget to include your wife in the decision. Two reasons for that. First, she sees things differently than you and likely will see things you've missed. Secondly, if she's on board with the decision, you can have confidence she'll be right by your side encouraging you when bumps in the road appear. And they will. Also remember, God gave her to you to be a "helper." Why would He call her that if that weren't one of her primary roles?

Failure to seek or heed wise counsel is a sign that we haven't put to death our pride yet. And remember, "*Pride goes before destruction, and a haughty spirit before stumbling.*"[1014] I don't think any of us wants to stumble or be destroyed. The answer is easy. The implementation, not so much. Get "your guys" together and sharpen each other.[1015]

Lord, I know I'm not the sharpest tool in the shed, but my pride keeps me from seeking Your wise counsel. Help me overcome my foolishness. In Christ's name, **Amen.**

1012 Prov. 12:15
1013 Jas. 1:5
1014 Prov. 16:18
1015 Prov. 27:17

Victorious men don't take credit for "wins" that belong to God.

"The horse is prepared for the day of battle, but victory belongs to the Lord." Prov. 21:31

Everybody loves to celebrate a win. The star player. The salesman who just closed a big sale. Even folks who had nothing to do with it, e.g., the fans in the stands. Somehow, taking ownership of another's accomplishments is acceptable in some circles (college alumni, for example). It's called bragging rights or team pride. And is it really harmful? Probably not.

But there is a kind of robbing of honor that God *will not* tolerate. We learned Sunday that God doesn't share His glory with anybody.[1016] How do we (try to) rob God of His glory? One obvious way is often (not always) found in mega-churches where public persona preachers get a lot of publicity and recognition. They are quoted, sought for "how to" advice from other growth-oriented preachers, and spend an inordinate amount of time "grooming their horse."

Those of us in not-so-public occupations or ministries are no less susceptible to the temptation to take credit for stuff we've done. It's OK, as long as we don't start thinking we've done it in a vacuum. Don't force God to remind you that "*everything you have you were given.*"[1017] Sometimes His reminders hurt.

The prophet Micah asks, "*what does the Lord require of you, but to do justice, to love kindness, and to walk humbly with your God?*"[1018] Thought much about the last part of that, walk humbly? In week 30-Tuesday, we talked about "Newness of thinking." We said that every action starts with a thought. If we want to change our actions, we *must* change our thinking. In today's noisy world with earbuds pouring music, helpful hints, or even sermons, it's rare that we take time to ponder. I love that word, ponder. It means to think or consider especially quietly, soberly, and deeply. I find when I ponder, I usually accuse myself of not doing more or better something. It can be painful. Maybe that's why I don't do it more. But my honest goal is to walk humbly with my God. If I do that, I won't take credit for what He's doing in my life. And it also helps me remember that I'm not responsible for results—God is. That doesn't alleviate my responsibility to be faithful in my work and my walk. That's still on me. But knowing God is not judging my results takes a lot of pressure off. Where are you in your pondering today?

Father, it's so tempting to want the credit, the glory for something You've allowed me to accomplish. Forgive me for trying to steal Your Glory for my own benefit. Change my thinking so I change my actions. **Amen.**

1016 Isa. 48:11
1017 I Cor. 4:7
1018 Mic. 6:8

Victorious men work with God's plan, no matter how beaten up or limited in strength, because they know the end of the story—WE WIN!

"A battered reed He will not break off, and a smoldering wick He will not put out, until He leads justice to victory." Matt. 12:20

In the military, a commanding officer has a huge responsibility. They have resources, training, and experience. But they're still the go-to guy for "the plan" that allows for a successful mission. Even if those of us in the trenches don't understand because we don't have all the intel he has, we trust the orders and do our best to carry them out. Sometimes it works, sometimes not.

The Christian life is exactly like that with one exception—God never loses. He knows the end from the beginning.[1019] We can be tired, weary even, but God still uses what we offer. Remember the loaves and fish?[1020] God will take whatever we offer with a willing heart and multiply it to accomplish His plan.

We're blessed to live in America where, for the most part, the wars we've been involved in were to protect the less fortunate. When we put that into a Biblical context, God's heart is that nobody perishes.[1021] And He allows us to play a part in that. Consider missionaries who toil years, maybe decades, without seeing much fruit. But remember yesterday we saw that fruit is not our responsibility[1022]—only faithfulness.

Have you been in the battle a long time and are growing disheartened? I've got GREAT NEWS for you. The Lord's coming back to get us…soon.

Have you *not* been in the battle because you were too busy, too tired, or just didn't know how to get started? I've got GREAT NEWS for you too. It's never too late. Our God is a God of great compassion and will *abundantly* pardon.[1023] Talk to yourself. Remind yourself often that we are on the winning team even when it doesn't seem like it. Re-read Revelation, especially the last three chapters. Maranatha. Come, Lord Jesus.

Lord God, it's easy to get discouraged when I don't see fruit for my labor. Help me to toughen up and remember the long game that You have already won. Thank You that my name was written in Your Book of Life from before I was born. May I not be a drain on Your team, but with Your help, be an encourager to all around me, knowing that You've prepared a place for me to come home to because of Jesus. In His name, **Amen.**

1019 Isa. 46:10
1020 Matt. 15:36-38
1021 Matt. 18:14
1022 I Cor. 3:6
1023 Isa. 55:7

Victorious men know that death is NOT the end

"...death is swallowed up in victory" I Cor. 15:54

Ever find yourself, at the end of a movie, asking, "Is that all there is?" Leaving you wanting more is the sign of a good script, good director, and good actors.

Unfortunately, many people have bought the lie that "death" is all there is; there is no eternal future. If that was the case, I can understand the "if it feels good, do it" mentality. Jesus told a parable about a rich man who was planning to build new warehouses to store his goods. The rich man was talking to himself: "*...take your ease, eat, drink and be merry.*"[1024] But listen to what God says to him in the next verse, "*You fool! This very night your soul is required of you; and now who will own what you have prepared? So is the man who stores up treasure for himself, and is not rich toward God.*"[1025]

Does that mean God is against our success, our prospering? Not at all. God is generous with His provision, just like He's generous with His compassion and lovingkindness. His concern is that prosperity frequently replaces Him as the object of our affection, an idol if you will. And we know what God thinks of idols. In a word: DON'T.

Our verse for today is a huge encouragement and promise for those of us who know the Lord Jesus. Encouragement because it feeds the hope we have for our heavenly home. Promise because we don't have to fear that final foe; we can live in Christ's victory over death and the grave. But let's look at where the rich man went wrong.

The last phrase is our clue, "*...is not rich toward God.*" Jesus told us to "*seek **first** the kingdom of God and all these things will be added unto you.*"[1026] As long as we put God first in all we do and have a right heart attitude toward things, He has no problem trusting us with earthly riches. I suggest one way to not get bogged down in money-making and thing acquisition is to spend more time in the Word, prayer, and fellowship with your accountability team. God promises to provide all we need *IF* we do that first. Sounds like a win-win to me.

True, we all will die unless the Rapture happens first. But it's not the end for us. It's really just the beginning, the portal to eternity. Hallelujah!

Heavenly Father, You have never lied to me about anything. So I'm excited about my future with You. I'd prefer not to go through a painful death, but I know You won't let me do it alone; You'll be right by my side. Thank You for Your plan from eternity past that included me in Your book of life. May my joy overflow so that others are drawn to Jesus. In His name, **Amen.**

1024 Luke 12:19
1025 Luke 12:20, 21
1026 Matt. 6:33

Victorious men know that victory is won...ONLY one way.

"...but thanks be to God, who gives us the victory through our Lord Jesus Christ." I Cor. 15:57

The world is convinced that all roads lead to God: Buddhism, Islam, Hinduism, Mormonism, and the lot. Not true. Jesus said, "*I am **the** way, and **the** truth and **the** life, no one comes to the Father but **through me.**"*[1027] Have you ever wondered why so many people believe Satan's lie about all roads? It's easy:

- *"...they loved approval of men rather than the approval of God." (John 12:43)*
- *"...they loved the wages of unrighteousness." (2 Pet. 2:15)*
- *"...men loved the darkness rather than light because their deeds were evil." (John 3:19)* and
- *"...they exchanged the truth of God for a lie and worshipped and served the creature rather than the Creator." (Rom. 1:25)*

In this section in Romans (1:18-32), we see a slippery slope of sin and depravity. God gives them over...first to ***impurity*** (v24), then to ***degrading passions*** (v26) and finally to a ***depraved mind*** (v28). You don't have to look very far to see the results of a depraved mind. Think about the vitriol and lack of civility toward the President of the United States. There is nothing that justifies or explains this behavior...except Romans 1. And Paul further elaborates to the Thessalonians, "***For this reason,** God will send upon them a deluding influence so that **they will believe what is false.**" (1 Thess. 2:11)* Ask yourself, "What reason?" Paul answers in the next verse, "*in order that they all might be judged who **did not believe the truth** but **took pleasure in wickedness.**"* (v12).

If any of this seems unfair, remember God gives everybody plenty of time to repent and turn to Christ. The reality is that most people (remember the wide and narrow gates Jesus talked about?)[1028] choose the wide gate because they don't want any accountability. That's why evolution hangs around. Because if there is a God, then I've got somebody to answer to. Nope. Not for me. Where are you on God's timetable? If you've turned from sin to Christ and you're not one of those in the above verses, praise God. I'll see you in heaven. If you're still deciding, don't wait. Tomorrow is not promised. Thanks be to God, who *gives* us the victory over death through Jesus. It's all Him. We can't earn it. We surely don't deserve it. Are you in or out?

Lord Jesus, thank You for what you went through for me so that I can go through You to God. It boggles my mind to think that kind of love really exists...and embraces me. Thank You forever. **Amen.**

1027 John 14:6 emphasis added
1028 Matt. 7:13, 14

Victorious men are assured of the future because God said so.

"...I go to prepare a place for you. If I go and prepare a place for you, I will come again and receive you to Myself, that where I am, there you may be also." John 14:2, 3

On Thursday, we saw that death is not the end but a new beginning; in heaven for those of us who trust Jesus, in hell for those who don't. There's no middle ground. Jesus said, "*He who is not **with** me is **against** me.*"[1029] But today, I want to focus on what our future holds.

I love reading through the Psalms. It's a great reminder of the character and attributes of our God. Some that really stand out over and over are His faithfulness, lovingkindness, mercy, and extreme patience. I'm more like Peter, "*how often shall my brother sin against me and I forgive him? Up to seven times?*"[1030] God exercises untold patience, especially with Israel (see Psalm 78). But the trait that we can hang our hat on without question or doubt is God ***cannot*** lie.[1031] So when Jesus said He's getting our place ready then He'll come back for us, it's already happened in His mind in eternity. Doesn't get much better than that.

Consider this. In this world, gold is revered above most other things. Rare gems, perhaps more. In heaven, God uses gold to pave the street.[1032] Makes me wonder what the rest of His building materials will be like. Each of the twelve gates is a single pearl.[1033] Wouldn't want to meet the oyster that produced those. In heaven, there's no more death, mourning, crying, or pain.[1034] How can we not joyously anticipate that day? But look around. The same God who promised this bliss to His children also promised unimaginable destruction to those who haven't believed Christ for forgiveness of their sins. Their future holds everything that heaven doesn't: darkness, mourning, crying, pain, agony. And it ***never*** ends.

For those of us victorious in Christ, this should be a wakeup call to "*go and make disciples of all nations.*"[1035] "All nations" doesn't just mean across the sea. There are those in our neighborhood, our workplace, maybe even in our own family that need the message of the cross. Today, let's share our victory with someone who's on the losing team and doesn't even know it.

Father, it's easy to set my life on cruise control because I know my future. Give me greater compassion for those not yet in the lifeboat. In Christ's name. **Amen.**

1029 Luke 11:23 emphasis added
1030 Matt. 18:21
1031 Tit. 1:2
1032 Rev. 21:21
1033 Ibid.
1034 Rev. 21:4
1035 Matt. 28:19

Men of Wisdom fear the Lord and keep His commandments.

"The fear of the Lord is the beginning of wisdom; a good understanding have all those who do His commandments." Ps. 111:10

The Bible speaks about wisdom as much or more than many other issues. It is often contrasted with fools. There is so much, in fact, we will take two weeks on the topic. We'll talk about the value of wisdom, the benefits of wisdom, what men of wisdom do, and much more.

A good place to start is our verse for today. "*The fear of the Lord…*" Where does wisdom come from? How do I get it? Does it come in one lump sum or small doses? We'll answer all that.

If the beginning of wisdom is the fear of the Lord, what exactly is fear? There are two types of fear with respect to the Lord. First, and this is for those among us who haven't believed God about their spiritual condition and turned to Jesus for forgiveness and salvation. The writer of Hebrews says, "*It is a terrifying thing to fall into the hands of the living God.*" [1036] The God of the Bible is a God of wrath and vengeance. Only a fool wouldn't be afraid of the coming judgment and eternal punishment. The Bible calls that out too, "*The fool says in his heart, there is no God.*" [1037]

For us who *do* know Jesus, our fear is one of reverence, awe, and respect for God's majesty, power, mercy, lovingkindness, and all the things you'd associate with a good father. It draws us *to Him*. It doesn't cause us to run *from Him*. It gives us the desire to know Him, to fellowship with Him, to obey Him. The psalmist said, "*Establish Your word to Your servant as that which produces reverence for You.*" [1038] God's Word *is* the answer, *has* the answers, and, in that, opens His storehouse of wisdom to us.

But there is a key requirement stated in the second half of our verse, "*a good understanding have **all** who **do** His commandments.*" Notice the "all." God's wisdom is offered to everybody, but if we're not committed to *doing* what God requires, we can't expect wisdom and understanding to just magically appear.

I encourage all of us to examine our hearts this week with respect to our commitment to grow in wisdom and the discipline of time in the Word as the means of reaching our goal. In the coming days, we'll talk about another prerequisite to wisdom: humility. Didn't say it would be easy…just worth it.

Lord God, again Your generosity is shown in offering us *Your* wisdom, *Your* understanding in exchange for our obedience. Seems like a good deal to me. Open my heart to hear Your Spirit teach, reprove, correct, and train me in righteousness this week. In Christ's name. **Amen.**

1036 Heb. 10:31
1037 Ps. 53:1
1038 Ps. 119:38

Men of Wisdom know the difference.

"'Do not handle, do not taste, do not touch!'... These are matters which have, to be sure, the appearance of wisdom in self-made religion and self-abasement and severe treatment of the body, but are of ***no value*** *against fleshly indulgence." Col. 2:21, 23*

"Fake news" has become a common criticism of certain political and media factions. One way to discern what's real and what's not is to look behind the words to the motive, the agenda. If that's off, everything that follows will be off. Fortunately, we have the *only* standard of truth that can be relied on in *every* situation—the Bible.

Because God *cannot* lie,[1039] we can base *every* decision on truth we find in scripture. If something appears to have wisdom but it doesn't square 100% with God's Word, dump it. All false religions, no matter how good they sound or how close to Christianity they seem, are from the pit of hell and the father of lies.[1040] Isn't it great that there is still truth? And isn't it great that God has entrusted it to us so we can spread it around?

Since we have the truth, there may be a temptation to flaunt our privilege, our knowledge and condescend to others who are not as "enlightened" as we. And I'm not talking about just those outside the church. Paul warned the Corinthian church, "*... we all have knowledge. Knowledge makes arrogant, but love edifies.*"[1041] He also wrote to Titus, "*avoid foolish controversies and genealogies and strife and disputes about the Law, for they are* ***unprofitable and worthless.***"[1042] Why would anyone be involved in something unprofitable and worthless?

Do you know the difference between Biblical Christianity and the fake news of other religions? Do you know that **all roads don't** lead to God? Only one does.[1043] Do you know that **good deeds don't** earn a ticket to heaven? Only faith in Jesus Christ's death and resurrection do.[1044] Do you know that **wisdom and humility** go hand in hand?[1045] If you can't answer yes to these four questions, go back to yesterday's discussion on the fear of the Lord. If you can, you're on the right track. Stick with me. Lots more ahead.

Heavenly Father, sometimes Your way seems hard and restrictive, and the permissiveness of other religions is attractive. May I not wander from Your path and lose my way. Thank You for providing the lamp for my feet and light for my path. Shine it on anything fake ahead. In Jesus' name. **Amen**

1039 Tit. 1:2
1040 John 8:44
1041 I Cor. 8:1
1042 Tit. 3:9, emphasis added
1043 Jn. 14:6
1044 Eph. 2:8, 9
1045 Prov. 11:2

Men of Wisdom know where to go to get more.

"But if any of you lacks wisdom, let him ask of God who gives to all generously and without reproach and it will be given to him. But he must ask in faith without any doubting…" Jas. 1:5, 6

Running out of materials on a job site is irritating, wastes time, and cuts into your profit. Fortunately, in most big cities, Lowe's or Home Depot is close and usually has what you need.

Do you ever hit a wall in your walk with the Lord? Feel like you just don't know what to do next? Sometimes that's exactly where God wants us, because when we've exhausted our own supply of strength, wisdom and any of the fruits of the Spirit (love, joy, peace, etc.), we're forced to come back to the faithful source of whatever we lack. Today's verse gives us hope. I know I don't have all the wisdom I'll ever need, and I suspect few of us do.

That's why God's promise to "give generously" encourages me. Now, here's the kicker. Sometimes God's messenger to deliver the wisdom we need isn't what (or who) we expect. Not often do we get a call from a friend saying, "God told me to call you and tell you…" But I bet you'd get wise counsel from your wife if you give her a chance. I know I do. I wish I'd started listening to her more and earlier in our marriage.

There are two things we need to know about wisdom. First, God will NEVER contradict His written Word. So if you feel you're being told something that goes against scripture, guess who's behind it? Paul wrote to the Romans, "*…do not be conformed to this world, but be transformed by the renewing of your mind.*" [1046] That means we need to read up, memorize up and meditate up in our scripture time so we can spot doctrinal error before it digs its claws into us.

Second, we need to *expect* God to answer our prayer for wisdom. James says if we doubt, we'll get coal in our stocking—nothing. Why? "*…without faith it is impossible to please* [God]*)* [1047] James says we're like "*the surf of the sea, driven and tossed by the wind*" [1048] and that we're "*double minded…unstable in all our ways.*" [1049] Reminds me of a pinball machine. The ball gets batted by the flipper and caroms off various bumpers until it falls in the hole; no well-defined path.

If that's where you find yourself today, take a minute right now and confess to God your drifting. Then, knowing God's promise **to you** is true, ask and expect Him to give you wisdom for exactly your circumstances. He will.

God, Your Word is so encouraging. Give me the discipline to daily spend time in it so I get to know You better. That alone will increase my faith to ask You for the wisdom I need. Thank You. In Jesus' name. **Amen.**

1046 Rom. 12:2
1047 Heb. 11:6
1048 Jas. 1:6
1049 Jas. 1:8

Men of Wisdom are directed and led by God.

"I have directed you in the way of wisdom; I have led you in upright paths." Prov. 4:11

For those of us who have hunted or backpacked in unfamiliar territory, one of the most important tools we carry is a GPS or map. It shows exactly where we want to end up and how to get there. Sometimes there is more than one way, and we have to decide between shorter, steeper, more scenic, etc.

I'm thankful that the choice we have to make in our pilgrimage to heaven is not between different paths, but between "do we choose *the* path or no path at all." Of course, the world shows us many different paths, and they're all labeled "heaven." The problem is that they don't lead to the one true God, Creator of all things. How do I know that? Simple. Their paths aren't labeled "Jesus." They might be labeled "Jesus + good works" or "Jesus + baptism" or "Jesus + *anything.*" But if it's not just Jesus, it's a dead-end...literally (and eternally).

Solomon, in writing the Proverbs, has more to say about wisdom than any other book of the Bible. Ask yourself, "What is the (primary) goal of wisdom?"

The Bible says that wisdom is better than gold, silver, and jewels, and *nothing* we desire compares with it. That makes it pretty valuable. But why? I believe that God doesn't take us home to heaven as soon as we're saved because He has work for us to do. What work? Jesus told His disciples to *"go...make disciples of all nations."* [1050] I believe God chose wisdom as our primary tool for soul winning. *"The fruit of the righteous is a tree of life and he who is wise wins souls."* [1051]

More people are led to saving faith in Jesus Christ by the witness of one other person than by sitting in church pews. I'm not diminishing Biblical preaching. It's just not as personal. And salvation is a personal thing.

If we follow God's directions, we'll never hear the word "recalculating." He doesn't make mistakes or get thrown off course by unexpected events. Everything is working according to His plan from the beginning. And it's comforting to know that He sees the end from the beginning.[1052]

Are you in "the way of wisdom and upright paths" today? Do you need to recalculate your GPS?

Lord God, I feel like I'm bombarded with choices and paths and maps, and I get overwhelmed. Draw me back into Your truth and nudge me when I get off the only path that leads to You. In Christ's name, **Amen.**

1050 Matt. 28:19
1051 Prov. 11:30
1052 Isa. 46:10

Men of Wisdom are humble.

"When pride comes, then comes dishonor; but with the humble is wisdom." Prov. 11:2

A favorite verse that I refer to often when I think I'm all that and a bag of chips is, "*For who regards you as superior? What do you have that you did not receive? And if you did receive it, why do you boast as if you had not received it?*" [1053]This comes in the middle of Paul's correcting the Corinthian church's thinking and arguing.

No matter how pretty the package it comes in, none of us eagerly looks forward to someone else correcting us. Where we land on God's maturity scale is determined by how we receive it. Do we get indignant, defensive, combative? Think to ourselves, "Who are you to correct me?" Or do we realize we lost our "bag of chips" some time back?

If we remember that God uses messengers we probably wouldn't choose and view the correction as coming from a loving Father, it won't be as hard a pill to swallow and will go down easier.

Wisdom is learned. God uses lessons of life to teach us. And as with all learning, it begins with our recognition that we really don't know everything. That, in itself, is humbling, especially when we want to present a picture of someone who has it all together. Today's verse juxtaposes wisdom with dishonor. Sometimes it helps to ask ourselves, "what's the alternative?" to assess whether the cost is worth it.

I don't imagine any of us wants to wear the badge of dishonor. Even if humility for humility's sake isn't enough to motivate us, dreading the negativity accompanying such a badge should be enough to keep us on the path and out of the weeds.

Note the coupling of humility and wisdom. There's a potential for trouble ahead if we allow the enemy of our soul to whisper, "You're becoming *so* wise." Come back tomorrow for the "rest of the story."

Lord God, sometimes Your path seems hard. But it's only because I've bought the world's lies that I deserve it all. Remind me that what I deserve is condemnation for sin and eternal separation from You. But because of Your great love and mercy and Jesus' death and resurrection **for me**, I get to be with You forever in heaven. Thank You. In Christ's name, **Amen.**

1053 I Cor. 4:7

Men of Wisdom let their deeds speak for them.

"The Son of Man came eating and drinking, and they say, 'Behold a gluttonous man and a drunkard, a friend of tax collectors and sinners!' Yet wisdom is vindicated by her deeds." Matt. 11:19

We've all heard the saying, "the best revenge is success." While it may be tempting and allow us to strut and puff our chests, it's terrible advice. As men of God, we need to remember that revenge belongs to God,[1054] and He promises to act on our behalf. Could we have a better advocate?

If anyone ever had a reason to boast, it was Jesus. Nobody had ever turned water to wine, walked on water, healed everyone who came to Him, and brought the dead back to life. But not once while Jesus was on earth did He defend Himself when wrongly accused. About the closest He came was in today's verse, "*wisdom is vindicated by her deeds.*"

Maintaining a persona and character of humility is harder the more we are in public view. And if we've had any success, our enemy whispers in our ear how amazing we are. Whether it's about the good we're doing, the wisdom which others flock to hear, or comparison to others in the same arena, if we aren't current with God, there's a strong chance we'll start to believe it. And if we don't catch it immediately, it will start to change us. We'll forget where our success comes from, lose our spirit of gratitude to God and others, and get back on the slippery slope of pride.

Our success will almost surely bring accusations of wrongdoing from those who resent us or are jealous of us. This book is written to point us to Jesus, our example. What did He do when He was wrongly accused? Pretty much nothing. Even in our verse today, He's not defending Himself to His accusers. He's talking to the crowd and simply stating a fact. Wisdom is not vindicated by lengthy debate or argument. It is vindicated by what it does. It's hard to argue with the results of good decisions and wise choices.

The enemy's temptation often works because we like the praise of men, the accolades, the recognition. We forget where it all comes from (see yesterday's opening) and that our goal is to please the "audience of one."

If our deeds are truly the result of God's wisdom dwelling in us, we can be confident that He is accurately recording them in His books and that two things will happen. *We* will be rewarded, and those who oppose us will get what's coming to them too. Remember, brothers, God has our six.

Father, thank You for Jesus' example of letting His deeds speak for Him. Keep me conscious of that same goal in my life. Strengthen me in Your Word so I don't succumb to Satan's false flattery and feed my pride. In Christ's name, **Amen.**

1054 Deut. 32:35, 36

Men of Wisdom do not boast of their wisdom.

"...professing to be wise, they became fools." Rom. 1:22

We see it everywhere. "Expert" witnesses. "The last word" on this or that. The "chief" whatever on the news channels. All of it appeals to our egos.

Today's verse is in a paragraph in Romans that starts out, "*For the wrath of God is revealed from heaven against...men who suppress the truth.*" [1055] If you haven't read this section lately, do so. It's a sobering section of what awaits those who think they know more than the One who created all things.

Without trying to be political, there is so much going on in the world today that begs to be used as an example of men professing to be wise. I'll just grab a couple. Fossil fuel. Global warming and coastal flooding. Consider fossil fuel and ask yourself, how did decaying material (or dinosaurs) work their way to a depth of over 6 miles into the earth's crust? According to *Science News for Students*, what we're burning today began 300 million years ago. If you believe the Bible, the earth is less than 10,000 years old. Do a Google search on "abiotic oil or abiogenic petroleum origin." Strike one.

How about global warming and coastal flooding? Over 15 years ago, Al Gore predicted the rise of the global sea level of 20 feet, flooding coastal areas and creating 100,000,000 refugees. It's too bad he didn't know his Bible. In Proverbs 8, wisdom is personified as possessed by God "*at the beginning of His way, before His works of old.*" [1056] In verse 29, wisdom speaking, "*When He set for the sea its boundary so that the water would not transgress His command...*" Just to state the obvious, God is in control of the sea level, not self-proclaimed experts...on any subject. Swing and a miss.

I used to kid my wife and say, "People who think they know everything really irritate those of us who do." That was before I got a good case of the "humbles." But I digress.

True wisdom, plain and simple, **is a gift from God.** If what man thinks of as wisdom didn't come from God, it is worldly. The Bible is clear, "*This wisdom is not that which comes down from above, but is earthly, natural, demonic.*" [1057] So all the so-called wisdom that gets foisted on us today by the experts may seem legitimate, coming from people with titles. But weigh it against what God has said. Game, set, match.

Heavenly Father, Your Word gives me everything I need to survive in an unrighteous and evil world. Don't let me become discouraged by what I see but keep me faithful to what I know from Your Word. In Jesus' name. **Amen**.

1055 Rom. 1:18
1056 Prov. 8:22
1057 Jas. 3:15

Men of Wisdom have something money can't buy.

"Wisdom is better than jewels; and all desirable things cannot compare with her."
Prov. 8:11

One credit card company spent millions on ads touting experience as "priceless." But today's verse gives us the true definition of priceless. Think of expensive, valuable stuff: gold, silver, luxury cars, boats, etc. They are in the "all desirable things" category. Wisdom is better. And it's free.

When God says something more than once, it's good to pay attention. Along with today's verse, Solomon adds, "*How much better it is to get wisdom than gold! And to get understanding is to be chosen above silver.*"[1058] This verse carries a little twist. It appears we have a choice, gold and silver (the world's value system) or wisdom. That is always God's way. He never forces us to love, trust, or obey Him. And if we had an eternal perspective on things that will survive the Day of the Lord, our choice would be a no-brainer. "All desirable things" will be gone. Only the treasures we've laid up in heaven remain.[1059] I've never seen a hearse towing a U-Haul trailer.

In the middle of a warning about the last days, James rebukes the rich for living as if Jesus isn't coming back. He says, "*Your gold and silver have rusted; and their rust will be a witness against you...*"[1060] James is not condemning them for *being* rich but for misusing their wealth.

Not only is wisdom priceless, but *everything* God gives us is free. Was there a price tag on your Salvation?[1061] How about your daily blessings that are new every morning?[1062] Now, just because *we* didn't pay anything doesn't mean there was no cost. It cost Jesus everything, including a painful brutal death endured of His own free will because He wants us with Him and knew we could never pay the price. Wow.

When I think of how long eternity is compared with my life on earth, it's not even a drop in the ocean by comparison. I'd like to think that I can say with Paul, "*But whatever things were gain to me, those things I have counted as loss for the sake of Christ. More than that, I count all things to be loss in view of the surpassing value of knowing Christ Jesus my Lord, for whom I have suffered the loss of all things, and count them but rubbish so that I may gain Christ...*"[1063] Now that's something money can't buy.

Lord Jesus, may I never forget that though my future is free to me, it cost You everything. Thank You just doesn't seem to cover it, but it's all I've got. Thank You. **Amen.**

1058 Prov. 16:16
1059 Matt. 6:19-21
1060 Jas. 5:3
1061 Eph. 2:8, 9
1062 Lam. 3:23
1063 Phil. 3:7, 8

Men of Wisdom take God at His Word.

"The testimony of the Lord is sure, making wise the simple." Ps. 19:7

We've all heard it, "fool me once, shame on you, fool me twice, shame on me." In today's world, where it seems many have an agenda and lying to accomplish it is par for the course, isn't it reassuring to know that God doesn't, in fact cannot, lie?[1064]

We make appointments, we expect them to be kept. It would be great if everybody operated on *Lombardy time.* The great Green Bay Packers coach used to tell his players, "If you're five minutes early, you're already 10 minutes late."

Of course, there can be delays, unexpected traffic; the babysitter was late. But the person who depends on you to be on time suffers when you don't leave time for a flat tire or a spilled cup of coffee. It's considered rude to make others wait on you. I know this is old-school thinking. But when did consideration for others go out of style?

One of the things I love most about God is He says what He means and means what He says. He doesn't toy with us. Today's verse makes that as clear as can be. What He says He'll do, He will. Period.

For those of us in Christ, this should be comforting. It means the hope we have in Christ's return to take us home should be unwavering. But it also means that for those who don't know Jesus, they should be fearful of their future. Just as God's promise for the redeemed is true, so is His promise of judgment and an eternity of torment and agony for the unsaved. [1065]

In addition to being sure, God's Word "*makes wise the simple.*" We don't have to be a Ph.D. candidate or Rhodes Scholar to understand the Bible. In fact, Jesus told His disciples to…"*let the children alone…for the kingdom of heaven belongs to such as these.*"[1066] He wasn't saying that only children get in, but that often our "knowledge" can keep us from seeing the truth.

One has only to look around to see that once-held standards are becoming passé—a thing of the past. Thank God His Word lasts forever.[1067] God entrusts His Word to faithful men who will neither add to nor subtract from it.[1068] Woe to the preacher who compromises in this area.

Father, thank You for Your faithfulness, Your integrity and the truth of Your Word that gives me hope in my future, faith to endure, and a standard that never changes. May I be "*diligent…as a workman…accurately handling the word of truth.*" In Christ's name, **Amen.**

1064 Tit. 1:2
1065 Luke 16:23, 24
1066 Matt. 19:14
1067 Ps. 119:89
1068 Rev. 22:18, 19

Men of Wisdom choose friends of like mind.

"He who walks with wise men will be wise, but the companion of fools will suffer harm." Prov. 13:20

What do you look for in a friend? Somebody who shares your interest in cars, sports, literature? Remember when mom used to say, "Now, Johnny, I don't want you playing with Spike, he'll get you in trouble?" Did you listen? I know I didn't. Because I thought Spike was cool, and I wanted to be cool too. I didn't understand a mother's love and her years-honed wisdom wanting to protect me from danger. Who knew?

We still have a "parent" who loves us with an infinite love and doesn't only suspect the future, He knows it, He planned it, and He warns us. Are we mature enough to listen? What might some consequences be of rejecting His warnings?

Our verse gives us the broad scope: we **will** suffer harm if we hang out with fools. What is it about fools (who say there's no God)[1069] that attracts us? Do we still think they're cool and want to be cool? Do they seem to have more fun, less restraints? Admittedly, God's ways are not the world's ways. And the Bible even acknowledges the pleasures of sin.[1070] But if you read the rest of the verse, it also says "passing" as in transitory, no lasting value.

Righteousness, which is what we're called to, is, by definition, a higher standard. And it is the only lifestyle that promises eternal rewards: "*The wicked earns deceptive wages, but he who sows righteousness gets a true reward.*" [1071] If we don't already have an eternal perspective, we're running out of time. Paul tells the Roman church, "wake up…the night is almost gone, and the day is near. Therefore let us lay aside the deeds of darkness and put on the armor of light."[1072]

As men, we sometimes feel we don't need a lot of friends; we are just fine alone. Not true. Proverbs observes, "*Iron sharpens iron, so one man sharpens another.*" [1073] The presumption is that both men desire the accountability, the honing that scripture brings and the faithful wounds of a friend.[1074]

If you're discussing sports, the weather, politics, or other insignificant issues and not the weightier matters of spiritual life and death, perhaps another look at today's verse to determine which applies to you is in order.

Lord God, life is brief, and we have one chance to get it right. Give me wisdom to choose my friends well, those who point me to You. **Amen.**

1069 Ps. 14:1
1070 Heb. 11:25
1071 Prov. 11:18
1072 Rom. 13: 11, 12
1073 Prov. 27:17
1074 Prov. 27:6

Men of Wisdom are in a different league than fools.

"Doing wickedness is like sport to a fool and so is wisdom to a man of understanding." Prov. 10:23

Today's verse begs a comparison between T-ball and the bigs. I remember when my son played T-ball. Anything you can imagine happening, did. Batters stopped halfway to first to tie their shoe. Outfielders either sat down and played in the grass or were distracted by butterflies. Fielders didn't know where to throw the ball, so they carried it to...wherever. It was a hoot. But there's always the parent who takes himself too seriously and expects little Johnny to be scouted by somebody.

Obviously, the actions of T-ballers would never be tolerated even at the next level of play and would result in immediate removal and a trip to the nuthouse if tried in the majors.

Allow some comparisons. "*The wise will inherit honor but fools display dishonor.*"[1075] "*A wise man is cautious and turns away from evil, but a fool is arrogant and careless.*"[1076] "*The tongue of the wise make knowledge acceptable, but the mouth of fools spouts folly.*"[1077] There are over 180 references to fool or a derivative in scripture. And often, it is contrasted with wise or wisdom. Review just these three: honor vs. dishonor, cautious vs. careless, knowledge acceptable vs. folly. I know which camp I want to be in.

There appears to be no middle ground. We're either a fool, denying the God who made us, or we're wise, recognizing God's claim on us in Christ. The problem is fools don't know they're fools. They fight against all wisdom.[1078] They don't want to listen to wisdom and truth. They only want to talk.[1079]

God takes no delight in fools,[1080] but He *does* delight in "the blameless in their walk,"[1081] "those who deal faithfully,"[1082] and "the prayer of the upright."[1083] I find it amazing that God even knows my name, let alone that my actions can delight Him.

All sports have rules. You don't play by them, you're out. God's ballgame has rules. It's our choice to play by them or not. Are you in or out?

Father, when I understand that I don't even qualify for Your team apart from Jesus, I'm grateful You picked me to be in the game. May I do all I can to delight You and bring glory to the uniform. In Jesus' name, **Amen.**

1075 Prov. 3:35
1076 Prov. 14:16
1077 Prov. 15:2
1078 Prov. 18:1
1079 Prov. 18:2
1080 Eccl. 5:4
1081 Prov 11:20
1082 Prov. 12:22
1083 Prov. 15:8

Men of Wisdom are careful of their path.

"Watch the path of your feet and all your ways will be established. Do not turn to the right nor to the left; turn your foot from evil." Prov. 4:26, 27

When I was young, my family camped most years in Yosemite. One of my favorite things to do was climb the big rocks in the riverbeds and jump from rock to rock. I was a lot more surefooted then and don't ever remember missing a step or turning an ankle. Not so much the case anymore.

Today's verse is filled with promise. Who of us doesn't want our ways to be established? God's command is not political. He's not saying keep to the middle of the road. It sounds a little like Yogi Berra, "When you come to a fork in the road, take it."

Seriously, God is warning us to head the other way when evil approaches. The presumption is that we're wise enough to recognize evil even in attractive packaging. In other verses, God warns us to *flee* youthful lusts, immorality, idolatry, and *pursue* righteousness, godliness, faith, and love. We're not just to run *from* something, we're to run *toward* something else.

Another reason we are to watch our path is others are watching us. Our family, our neighbors, our co-workers, and anybody we've shared Christ with. Their yardstick? Are we genuine; does our faith make us different from the world? I hope so. Otherwise, what's the point? If Christ hasn't made an observable change in us, if we're indistinguishable from the world, why would that be attractive to anyone else?

Our path is narrow, and there are not many others on it.[1084] Staying on it requires alertness, discipline, and light. There are detours, wider paths that are easier, and paths with more company along the way. The psalmist identifies the light we need, "*Your word is a lamp to my feet and a light to my path.*"[1085] Two types of light; one for the next step and one for the path ahead. Both are found in God's Word. I can't stress enough the importance of storing it up in our hearts. Like any good warrior, our weapons need to be in good condition…and close. When God describes the armor we are to put on, the *only* offensive weapon we have is the sword of the Spirit, the Word of God.[1086] All other parts of our armor (truth, righteousness, peace, faith, salvation) are defensive.

Satan will tell you you're on the wrong path because everybody else is "over there." Turn your foot…and run.

Lord, You have defined the path and given me the map of Your Word. Keep me alert to anything that would sidetrack me. In Christ, **Amen.**

1084 Matt. 7:13, 14
1085 Ps. 119:105
1086 Eph. 6:17

Men of Wisdom control their emotions.

"A fool always loses his temper but a wise man holds it back." Prov. 29:11

It starts small. Just a little irritation. Your wife burned your toast. Your neighbor's dog won't shut up. Some jerk cuts you off in traffic. They pile on, irritation after irritation. Most irritants are beyond our control and seem to come at the worst time. Before long, we're angry. And that doesn't honor God, "*The anger of man does not achieve the righteousness of God.*"[1087]

People annoy us, irritate us, make us angry. Why? Do they do it intentionally? Probably not. Usually it's because they're not thinking…at all, let alone about us. No, it says more about us than them. We have expectations. And in most cases, we have no right to expect courtesy, thoughtfulness, the common social norms of days gone by, from others. We live in a fallen world.

Annoyance leads to irritation, irritation to anger, anger sometimes to rage. As soon as I recognize it, I need to examine why. Is it them or me? Both are sin, and I need to confess it and ask for forgiveness, then ask the Holy Spirit to give me patience and love for the person who stirred those emotions. Then, let it go.

All our actions begin with a thought. No matter how quickly, we thought it before we did it. A simple solution? Change your thinking, change your actions. Easy to say, hard to do. God says, "*renew your mind.*"[1088] "*The heart of the wise instructs his mouth and adds persuasiveness to his lips.*"[1089]

What are some other emotions a wise man needs to keep in check? Desire, jealousy, bitterness, to name a few. What's the secret to success in this area? One, we need to check our gratitude level for what we *do have,* **not** focus on what *we don't have.* Two, don't compare ourselves with others. We may be a 1-talent man. God doesn't expect or demand the same results as the 5-talent man. Three, remember who we're working for; it takes pressure off *our* success and focuses on God's glory, "W*hether, then, you eat or drink or whatever you do, do all to the glory of God.*"[1090]

Wednesday, we talked about being compared to a fool. The Bible says a lot about it, I suggest doing a personal study on the topic. Here's a good place to start: Prov. 1:7; Prov. 10:14; Prov. 26:12; I Cor. 1:18, 25. If your blood pressure is up, maybe you don't need a med, just more control.

Father, my anger does not honor you and causes problems for me. I bear Your name, and people are watching to see if You are real in my life. Remind me before I act in a way that discredits my witness. In Christ, **Amen.**

1087 Jas. 1:20
1088 Rom. 12:2
1089 Prov. 16:23
1090 I Cor. 10:31

Men of Wisdom are preparing their gift to God.

"So teach us to number our days, that we may present to You a heart of wisdom."
Ps. 90:12

Ironic that wisdom is a gift *from* God, and also our gift *to* God. But isn't that just like Him, to provide everything we need to serve and worship Him, like the ram caught in the bush when Abraham was going to sacrifice Isaac,[1091] or the coin in the mouth of the fish for Jesus and Peter's taxes?[1092]

What do you give to the person who has everything? Think about that in terms of earthly friends or family. One more pair of socks? Another tie? A gift certificate to their favorite restaurant?

Now put it into a heavenly perspective. What do you give to the One who literally has and created everything when He says, "*...every beast of the forest is Mine, the cattle on a thousand hills...everything that moves in the field is Mine. If I were hungry I would not tell you, for the world is Mine, and all it contains."*[1093] Now that's a challenge of creativity for us.

What does it mean to number our days? The MacArthur Study Bible says, "Evaluate the use of time in light of the brevity of life." According to Psalm 139:16, our days were numbered in God's book before we were born. We are told to "*be ready for the Son of Man is coming at an hour that you do not expect."*[1094] All that should lead to the conclusion that we don't know "the day." If we knew guests were coming, we'd clean the house. If a test were tomorrow, we'd cram tonight. Do we not take God's warning to be ready seriously? We don't want to be like the five foolish virgins who weren't ready and couldn't get in.[1095]

It seems fitting as we conclude our two weeks on wisdom and all the facets we've look at, knowing we've just scratched the surface and there's so much more that God has for us, that we remember God's promise. *"But if any of you lacks wisdom, let him ask of God, who gives to all generously and without reproach, and it will be given to him."*[1096] Remember also the two caveats James gives us: we must ask in faith with no doubting[1097] and with the right motives.[1098] Let's make sure our "gift" is ready for presentation.

Lord God, Your ways continue to amaze me. I have nothing to offer You and I deserve nothing from You, yet You've covered both in your love and mercy. I'm ready only because of Jesus. Thank You. In His name, **Amen.**

1091 Gen. 22:13
1092 Matt. 17:27
1093 Ps. 50:10-12
1094 Luke 12:40
1095 Matt. 25:2, 11, 12
1096 Jas. 1:5
1097 Jas. 1:6
1098 Jas. 4:3

Men who worship God are getting ready...

"For this reason also, God highly exalted Him, and bestowed on Him the name [Jesus] which is above every name, so that at the name of Jesus ***every knee will bow****, of those who are in heaven and on earth and under the earth, and that* ***every tongue will confess*** *that Jesus Christ is Lord, to the glory of God the Father." Phil. 2:9-11*

Think about the prep that goes into an appearance by the President of the United States or another head of state. The details would boggle the average person's mind. There's security, transportation, lodging, meals with different dietary restrictions. The list goes on and on. And this is for anywhere from only a few dozen to multiple thousands. Or consider the anticipation and excitement over a concert of your favorite rock star. The preparation can happen because you have advance notice, sometimes well in advance.

Now consider the advance notice God has given the world to be ready for the return of Christ for His church. Not including the Old Testament prophets, just from what came out of Jesus' own mouth, it's been over 2 millennia.[1099] So why does the world go about their business like nothing will change? The short answer is *unbelief.* Peter nailed it when he called out the mockers of his day, "*...in the last days mockers will come with their mocking, following after their own lusts, and saying, 'Where is the promise of His coming? For ever since the fathers fell asleep, all continues just as it was from the beginning of creation."*[1100] That's like the people of Noah's day saying, "because there's never been a worldwide flood..."

Men, we need to stay alert. God's formula seems to be warn us, warn us again, then repeat. Those who are surprised when the trumpet blows[1101] will have nobody to blame but themselves. They are the mockers of our day.

Worship has many facets which we'll touch on this week. But two of them are in today's verse, the bent knee and the confessing tongue. This might be a good place to ask ourselves, just exactly what is worship? The dictionary definition is general but still a good start: deferential respect, such as a bow or curtsy, acknowledgment of another's superiority or importance. To that I add, "who deserves it because He is God." This will be a week of praise, prayer, anticipation, all elements in our worship. Dust off your kneepads.

Oh God, You alone are worthy of my worship. My heart overflows with thanksgiving for Your holiness, faithfulness, mercy, and love for me. Fill me with excitement and anticipation for Jesus' return, and may I never waiver in my faithfulness to You. Thank You for my home in heaven. In the superior name of Jesus, **Amen.**

1099 John 14:3
1100 II Pet. 3:3, 4
1101 I Thes. 4:16

Men who worship God don't do it to be seen by man.

"But the tax collector, standing some distance away, was even unwilling to lift up his eyes to heaven, but was beating his breast, saying, 'God be merciful to me, the sinner!'" Luke 18:13, 14

There are all styles of worship. I don't mind the beat of drums or the variety of instruments, and I'm not wedded to the organ and piano. But what I do love is the depth of message in the old hymns that I wish I could hear more of. I can never make it all the way through "*How Great Thou Art*" without getting a little misty and choked up. Consider the following words:

"And when I think that God His Son not sparing
Sent Him to die, I scarce can take it in
That on the Cross, my burden gladly bearing
He bled and died to take away my sin.
When Christ shall come with shout of acclamation
And take me home, what joy shall fill my heart
Then I shall bow with humble adoration
And there proclaim, my God how great thou art." [1102]

It's the gospel and hope of heaven in two short verses. Sometimes after a good hymn sing, I don't need preaching. I have experienced what Paul calls *"...singing and making melody with your heart to the Lord."* [1103]

I believe there are two primary ways to worship, either alone or with somebody. I'm not trying to be cute. We can worship anywhere at any time and with anyone (or no one). Time and place don't matter. The only thing that matters is our heart attitude. Are we there to honor the Lord or to impress somebody else?

Heaven will be a wonderful mixture of all things that glorify God, honor Christ, and express gratitude for our salvation. Think of how often we use the word *awesome* to describe mundane things, an awesome car, a touchdown catch, a favorite restaurant. What about sunsets, waterfalls, the birth of a baby? God *is* awesome. God *does* awesome.

If we're not in a mindset of worship today, we need to ask ourselves why not. Are we thankful for salvation? You know, don't you, there won't be denominational schisms in heaven? We will be one body praising one God. Hopefully, we're not so set in our ways that we cannot adapt. We should check our own heart attitudes and not worry about others. Last I checked, God was still the judge.

Father, old habits die hard, and so do old traditions. May I be open to all kinds of worship so long as You are the object of it. Remove any tendency to judge anyone because they're different than me. In Christ's name, **Amen.**

1102 Carl Boberg (1859–1940)
1103 Eph. 5:19

Men who worship God focus on the object of their worship.

"Worship the Lord with reverence...rejoice with trembling." Ps. 2:11

You've heard of *idle* gossip and *idol* worship, but have you ever heard of *idle worship*? We are a society of sound bites, *instant* messaging and ADD (Attention Deficit Disorder). I think the worst punishment for many a Millennial would be to make them sit by themselves with no phone, tablet, or computer. They wouldn't know what to do. And it's partly our fault. We haven't trained them to be silent...and think.

The Psalmist today reminds us that worship is to be done reverently. That has several implications. One, no distractions. God is worthy of our *full* attention. We are not to look around and see what dress Mary is wearing or think of our plans for after church until after church. Two, not by rote. I grew up in a church that repeated the same liturgy every week. I can't remember ever really thinking about the words I voiced. Three, remember what a privilege it is to be in God's presence. Even though Esther was queen, she couldn't approach the king unless he extended the golden scepter, the sign of invitation.[1104] God has graciously invited us to come "*while He may be found.*"[1105]

I think the most important implication is to understand who God is in all His majesty, holiness, and power. If we get that right and realize we have nothing to offer as expressed by the hymn Rock of Ages, "nothing in my hands I bring, simply to Thy cross I cling..." we should get the rest right.

Yesterday, we talked about the word *awesome.* Awesome is the God of eternity knowing *my* name,[1106] preparing a place in heaven *for me,*[1107] not holding *my* sin against me[1108] so I *can* come into His presence any time anywhere. He promises to answer.[1109]

Reverence means with the right heart attitude. *Open the Eyes of My Heart*[1110] has the lyric, *"I want to see You...to see You high and lifted up shinin' in the light of Your glory."* That's what we can bring as our offering.

O Holy God, You truly are worthy of all worship and praise. Thank You for opening my eyes to who You are and all You've done for me. May I come to You in reverence knowing that I'm *not* worthy...except for Christ's sacrifice for *me.* In His name, **Amen.**

1104 Est. 8:4
1105 Isa. 55:6
1106 Isa. 43:1
1107 John 14:2, 3
1108 Ps. 103:12
1109 Ps. 86:7
1110 lyrics by Paul Baloche recorded by Michael W. Smith, Mercy Me and others.

Men who worship the true God know God's love.

"You shall not worship them [idols] or serve them; for I, the Lord your God, am a jealous God, visiting the iniquity of the fathers on the children, on the third and the fourth generations of those who hate Me, but showing lovingkindness to thousands, to those who ***love Me*** *and* ***keep My commandments.****" Ex. 20:5, 6 (emphasis added)*

Our worship is important to God. He set out the guidelines, the promises, and the warnings. We have such short memories, and becoming sidetracked is so common there's even a one-word description: *squirrel.* It originated with dog walking. A squirrel would almost certainly cause the dog to forget everything else he was doing and focus on it.

We're not so different. What are some of our "squirrels"? Money, possessions, titles, any shiny thing. All can become idols. God's choice of words indicates if we let idols come between Him and us, we *hate* Him. How do we prove our love to Him? Obedience. "*Samuel said, 'Has the Lord as much delight in burnt offerings and sacrifices as in obeying the voice of the Lord? Behold, to obey is better than sacrifice…'"* [1111]

When someone asks, "How do I know the will of the Lord?" My reaction is they must not be in the Word much, because God's general will is very clear. *"You shall love the Lord your God with all your heart, with all your soul, with all your mind and with all your strength."* [1112] There's also a list of ten, eight of which start out "you shall not." But even more basic than that is you must first be a child of God, a friend of Jesus.[1113] If you are, you have the very spirit of God living in you. Jesus talking, *"…the Holy Spirit…will teach you all things, and bring to your remembrance all that I said to you."* [1114] You can't remember something you haven't read, memorized, and meditated on. You want to know God's will? You have to read it. God does not change anything in the Bible to fit the times. Man is the one who has done that.

On a practical note, questions like what house to buy, what job to take, and others can be answered by asking yourself and your wife does it violate any of God's principals? Will it hinder my walk with the Lord in any way (work overtime to pay for, less time with family, etc.)? If you can answer no to these questions, then do whatever you want and expect God to shower you with His love.

Father, thank You for including me in those to whom You show lovingkindness. Keep me from anything that I would worship instead of You. Give me a deeper love for Your Word and a desire to store it in my heart so I have something to remember when temptation comes. In Jesus' name, **Amen.**

1111 I Sam. 15:22
1112 Mark 12:30
1113 John 15:15
1114 John 14:26

Men who worship God do it in the right place at the right time.

"When the burnt offering began, the song to the Lord also began with trumpets... While the whole assembly worshiped, the singers also sang and the trumpets sounded; all this continued until the burnt offering was finished." II Chron. 29:27, 28

Lest you misinterpret today's title, there *is* a time for *corporate* worship, and we, as believers, are to partake. The writer to the Hebrews clearly says, *"...not forsaking our own assembling together, as is the habit of some..."* [1115] But it's not the only time and place. When we consider some of the things that constitute worship, i.e., prayer, praise, thanksgiving, this can and should be done at all times and in all places. Words like "continually,"[1116] "without ceasing,"[1117] "at all times,"[1118] give us a clue as to God's thinking on the where and when of worship.

To rightly worship God, we first need to know Him, have faith in Him, and expect His blessings. Hebrews tells us, *"And without faith it is impossible to please Him, for he who comes to God must believe that He is and that He is a rewarder of those who seek Him."* [1119] The gist of this verse is that God is *not* pleased with those who don't acknowledge Him. It's not His fault; He has put it into the heart of man to know Him: *"...because that which is known about God is evident within them; for God made it evident to them."* [1120]

Two things emerge for us who know God. First, He is pleased with us. But only because we put our faith in His son, not for anything intrinsic in us. And second, He promises "rewards" to those who seek Him. I don't know if rewards include tangible things while we're still on earth, but I know I want whatever it is ("lovingkindness... compassions...new every morning"[1121]), and when Christ returns for us, they will have burned up anyway. Eternal rewards are what I'm looking for: *"Behold I am coming quickly, and My reward is with Me, to render to every man according to what he has done."* [1122]

Rewards are a byproduct of our worship, not an end in themselves. True worship comes from a grateful heart and a humble heart, recognizing we don't deserve anything but God's wrath. It's the only response appropriate when we remember God's generosity, Christ's death, and our future.

Father, may I not let the cares of today sidetrack me from a worshiping heart at all times. Fill me with gratitude for You, not just any rewards You have planned for me. In Christ's name, **Amen.**

1115 Heb. 10:25
1116 Heb. 13:15
1117 I Thess. 5:17
1118 Ps. 34:1
1119 Heb. 11:6
1120 Rom. 1:19
1121 Lam. 3:22, 23
1122 Rev. 22:12

Men who worship God dress the part.

"Worship the Lord in holy attire, tremble before Him all the earth." Ps. 96:9

What is holy attire? Is it fine or formal clothing? Is it clothing of a specified kind? Is it symbolic or for sacred service? Maybe. And that was certainly true in the Old Testament. But then what do you do with the verse that says, "*...for God sees not as man sees, for man looks at the outward appearance, but the Lord looks at the heart.*"[1123] In fact, judging a man by his clothing is a potential temptation to sin. Listen to James, "*...and you pay special attention to the one who is wearing the fine clothes, and say, 'You sit here in a good place,' and you say to the poor man, 'You stand over there, or sit down by my footstool.'*"[1124] God does not care about our clothes; He cares about our hearts. We can wear our "Sunday best" out of respect, but it can be a source of pride.

So, what is holy attire? Isaiah answers that "*I will rejoice greatly in the Lord, my soul will exult in my God; for He has clothed me with garments of salvation, He has wrapped me with a robe of righteousness.*"[1125] Salvation and righteousness are garments for proper worship. And did you notice, God provides both of them? Again, nothing we do deserves either of them. We are only *considered* righteous; we only have the *gift* of salvation because we trust in the Lord Jesus Christ for forgiveness of our sin and adoption into God's family. Can you think of a better reason to worship the true God?

It's Sunday morning. You're ready to walk out the door for church. Your wife says, "You're not wearing that, are you?" Forgot to check the mirror again, did you?

Is there a mirror we can check to make sure our "clothing" is on properly, is not wrinkled or stained before we worship? Yes, for sure. It's the only thing that gives us a true picture of our condition before a holy God. It's the mirror of God's Word—the Bible—God's love letter to His children.

Paul tells the Corinthians, "*Test yourselves to see if you are in the faith; examine yourselves!*"[1126] He also warns us to examine ourselves before taking the Lord's supper.[1127]

We would hardly go to a meeting with anyone of importance without checking ourselves in a mirror. We dare not come into God's presence without our proper clothing, either. Time to get dressed.

Lord God, You amaze me. You never demand anything of me that You haven't provided. Help me keep my robes clean so I'm always ready to meet You. In my Savior's name, **Amen.**

1123 I Sam. 16:7
1124 Jas. 2:3
1125 Isa. 61:10
1126 II Cor. 13:5
1127 I Cor. 11:28

Men who worship God eagerly anticipate the future.

"But I am hard-pressed from both directions, having the desire to depart and be with Christ, for that is ***very much better****;" Phil. 1:23*

Henceforth. What a great word, filled with promise, hope, future rewards. Paul tells Timothy, "*Henceforth there is laid up for me a crown of righteousness which the Lord, the righteous judge, shall give me at that day; and not to me only but unto all them also who love His appearing.*" [1128] Paul was clearly one of the most ill-treated-because-of-the-gospel men in the Bible. It's no wonder he wanted to go home. There are days, thank God not anything like Paul, that going home seems sooo appealing to me too.

It's not that life for me is bad. Sure I've had bad experiences like most people. But I have a great wife that puts up with me. I live in a great place (Colorado Springs). I have good health. God provides daily everything I need, and a lot more. But my times of worship here whet my appetite for what I know it'll be like when I get there. I've been called a Biblical singer; you know, the one who makes a joyful noise unto the Lord. But there, we'll all have perfect pitch, know the words, and not care that it goes past noon.

This week we've just skimmed some of the aspects of what worship is all about. Time and place, right object, right response, right "clothing." And all that is necessary to understand Who we worship, why we worship, when and where we worship. But the bottom line is this: Do we worship? We can know all about something without actually doing it.

My challenge to us this week is to identify anything that impedes or keeps us from being the worshipers God desires. Jesus told the woman at the well, *"But an hour is coming, and now is, when the true worshipers will worship the Father in spirit and truth; for such people the Father seeks to be His worshipers."* [1129]

Don't let anything, whether family, job, recreation, general busyness, keep you from worship. It'll be one of the highlights of heaven. And we want it to feel natural. Remember, we're like Abraham, "*...they desire a better country, that is, a heavenly one.*" [1130] And it's coming soon.

Lord God, You, only, are worthy of my worship. You, only, are holy. Forgive me for so often taking Your blessings, Your faithfulness for granted and not responding with overflowing gratitude in humble, heartfelt worship. Grow the desire of my heart to praise You, honor You in all I do, and look forward to Your upward call. May I be alert and ready when You do. **Amen.**

1128 II Tim. 4:8 KJV
1129 John 4:23
1130 Heb. 11:16

Men of God follow Christ's eXample.

"Beloved, do not imitate what is evil, but what is good. The one who does good is of God; the one who does evil has not seen God." III Jn. 1:11

There are many role models we could follow. A lot of them are public figures: sports stars, movie stars, business leaders, politicians. Then there's those closer to home: parents, older siblings, schoolteachers. But even those we think have led an exemplary life can let us down; consider Bill Cosby. When I was younger, I thought he was a comedic genius. I remember parroting his "Noah" sketch. To this day, I can still hear his sound effects of Noah's saw and Noah's conversation with God. The Bible warns us, *"...be sure your sin will find you out."* [1131] What we do in darkness is not hidden.[1132]

We have a lot of role models in the Bible to choose from. Abraham was a friend of God,[1133] David was "...a man after my heart,"[1134] Paul wrote much of the New Testament. Yet look at their track record: Abraham was a liar.[1135] David was an adulterer and murderer.[1136] Paul tortured and killed Christians.[1137] So even the best of the best of men... are sinners. But isn't that what Jesus is all about, second chances?

That's why the only role model that will *never* let us down, *never* disappoint us, *never* lie to us or lead us astray is the Lord Jesus Christ. Peter says, *"for you have been called for this purpose, since Christ also suffered for you, leaving you an example for you to follow in His steps,"* [1138] Now there's a motivational thought. I'm all in to follow Him to heaven, but suffering?

Brothers, everything we've been talking about in this book, it's all tied together. It starts and ends with humility. If we're to follow Christ's footsteps, listen to this, *"He humbled Himself by becoming obedient to the point of death, even death on a cross."* [1139] We must be humble to admit we need a Savior. We must be humble to take orders, to learn, to model Christlikeness. But there is coming a day when God will exalt us.[1140] Don't count on it being this side of heaven.

Lord God, thank You for providing the perfect role model for me to copy. May I just follow Christ's lead and not try to take over, thinking I've got a better way. Help me not to aspire to man's praise, only Yours. In Christ's name. **Amen.**

1131 Num. 32:23
1132 Ps. 139:12
1133 Jas. 2:23
1134 Acts 13:22
1135 Gen. 20:2
1136 II Sam. 11:4, 15
1137 Acts 8:1
1138 I Pet. 2:21
1139 Phil.2:8
1140 I Pet. 5:6

Men of God lead by eXample.

"Let no one look down on your youthfulness, but rather in speech, conduct, love, faith and purity, show yourself an example of those who believe." I Tim. 4:12

In this book, we've talked about pleasing the audience of One. But in reality, everyone's watching us to see if our lives, our actions add credibility to our words or if we're just another hypocrite. I don't know about you, but I find hypocrisy and deception detestable. For example, take politicians who enact laws and then exempt themselves. I imagine God hates it too. In fact, it's covered in His list of seven.[1141]

Speech and conduct, two things observable by everyone. Love, faith and purity are more on display to those who know us well but should empower our speech and conduct. Paul tells his Ephesian audience, "*Let no unwholesome word proceed from your mouth, but only such a word as is good for edification according to the need of the moment, so that it will give grace to those who hear.*"[1142] Ever stop to think that edification and grace can come out of your mouth? It's automatic if our motives and focus are right and on others rather than ourselves. When you arise in the morning, do you ask yourself, "Who can I edify and give grace to today?" Wouldn't that be a great way to start our day?

Who comes to mind when you think about who could be following your example? Your kids? Wife? Co-workers? Neighbors? Lots of possibilities. Does it make you proud or worry you? Kinda scary if we think about it. Can't say this. Can't do that. Can't go there. Have to drive the speed limit. (Ouch) I suggest that's totally the wrong attitude. Much better to respond to the privilege of God's trusting us to faithfully carry His message with a happy heart, knowing God wouldn't *trust us* if He didn't also *equip us* and *expect from us*, success. Burden or blessing? That's the question.

The last part of today's verse puts on us an extra load. We are to represent the *entire* church of God—those who believe—to an unbelieving world. I've been told by many people that "I won't do business with anybody who has a 'fish' on their business card." That's a terrible rap, but unfortunately, I've been burned too by people claiming Christ. How sad for the church. How sad that must make God, that His trust in us might not be warranted. That hurts my heart to think I could be, and sometimes am for sure, one who disappoints the One who has done so much for me.

Lord God, many times I'm saddened by my own conduct and words, especially because people are watching and know I claim Jesus as Savior. Forgive me for not being a better example of what Your children should be in Word and conduct. Thanks for a second chance…again. In His name, **Amen.**

1141 Prov. 6:16-19
1142 Eph. 4:29

Men of God are aware of bad eXamples and avoid them.

"Do not be deceived: 'Bad company corrupts good morals.'" I Cor. 15:33

The Bible is filled with examples of how to live; some godly, some not so much. As we saw Sunday, even the "godly" examples have their warts.

Paul talks about "bad company." The Bible has several lists of them. Here are some things that define bad company: the way of evil men,[1143] worldly and empty chatter,[1144] and the ultimate list of lists, "*for men will be lovers of self, lovers of money, boastful, arrogant, revilers, disobedient to parents, ungrateful, unholy, unloving, irreconcilable, malicious gossips, without self-control, brutal, haters of good, treacherous, reckless, conceited, lovers of pleasure rather than lovers of God, holding to a form of godliness, although they have denied its power; AVOID SUCH MEN AS THESE.*"[1145]

Lest you think this list only applies to unbelievers, hear what Paul says earlier in this letter, "*I wrote you in my letter not to associate with immoral people; I did not at all mean with the immoral people of this world, or with the covetous and swindlers, or with idolaters, for then you would have to go out of the world. But actually, I wrote to you not to associate with any so-called brother if he is an immoral person, or covetous, or an idolater, or a reviler, or a drunkard, or a swindler—not even to eat with such a one.*"[1146]

Do we have bad examples sitting in the pew with us? Probably. Are we a bad example to others sitting in the pew with us? Maybe. God's standard is impossibly high for us to attain in our own strength. That's the whole reason for the cross—to provide ONE way for us to reach His standard.

Re-read the last part of the 2nd paragraph: "holding to a form of godliness." That pretty much describes *every* religion except Christianity. We don't have a *form* of religion; we have the real deal. Jesus said He is the *only way* to the Father.[1147] All other paths, even though they're labeled "heaven," don't lead there. We shouldn't be surprised. The father of lies[1148] is pulling the strings on ALL religions that claim anything except Jesus Christ as the way to heaven. That includes the ones that are "Jesus plus anything—good works, baptism...*anything!*

We ARE an example to others whether we want to be or not. Let's not be included in the wrong list.

Heavenly Father, I get frustrated when I know I've not been a good example because I've sinned. Forgive me. Thank You for always hearing my prayer and granting forgiveness, no matter how many times I come for the same thing. Restore me to fellowship with You. In Jesus' name, **Amen.**

1143 Prov. 4:15
1144 I Tim 6:20
1145 II Tim. 3:2 (emphasis added)
1146 I Cor. 5:9-11
1147 John 14:6
1148 John 8:44

Men of God leave a good eXample as a legacy.

"And Joseph her husband, being a righteous man and not wanting to disgrace her, planned to send her away secretly." [1149]

We don't know much about Joseph, Mary's husband, except he was a carpenter[1150] and a righteous man. After Mary and Joseph returned to Jerusalem to find their son,[1151] we don't hear anything else about Joseph. What a legacy for the few verses we do have. He was a **righteous** man. If people say that about me, I will have been a success in this life. I've made money and done "stuff." But really, who cares? Being righteous carries all kinds of implications. First, let me be clear, any righteousness I have was imputed to me when I believed in Jesus as my Savior. The Bible doesn't pull any punches, *"...all our righteous deeds are like a filthy garment."* [1152]

Who are some that might care about our legacy? And just what is a legacy anyway? If there's a sizable estate involved, even distant relatives you never hear from will care. From a worldly perspective, a legacy is a gift via a will of money, property, or other valuable asset. Or, it can be something transmitted or received from an ancestor or predecessor. I want to focus on something we can all leave to our heirs that has nothing to do with assets: a good example.

This book is about character and, for the most part, character is a choice. We choose to be honest, not dishonest. We choose truth over lies, diligence over sloth, kindness instead of cruelty. You get the picture. In addition to a choice, character, it's said, is caught, not taught. How do you catch something? You're exposed to it. What kind of character are you exposing to those around you? Is it something they avoid through social distancing or is it an irresistible force?

Your wife, kids, and grandkids are those most impacted by your legacy. And it will live on after you're gone. How long it will live on is a result of how much is caught and passed to the next generation. And, be aware, it takes a lifetime to build, stone upon stone, a legacy worth emulating. But it only takes an instant to destroy. Think about that next time temptation flirts with you. Say to temptation what Jesus said to Peter when Peter tried to rebuke Him, *"Get behind me Satan; for you are not setting your mind on God's interests, but man's."* [1153] *"A good name is to be more desired than great wealth."* [1154]

Lord God, I want my legacy to be that of a righteous man. Call me out when I sin and damage it. Grant me humility to take Your correction, knowing the results could have eternal implications in someone's life. In Christ. **Amen.**

1149 Matt. 1:19
1150 Matt. 13:55
1151 Luke 2:45
1152 Isa. 64:6
1153 Mark 8:33
1154 Prov. 22:1

Men of God are never too old or young to be an eXample.

*"**Older men** are to be temperate, dignified, sensible, sound in faith, in love, in perseverance. 6. Likewise urge the **young men** to be sensible; 7. in all things show yourself to be an example of good deeds, with purity in doctrine, dignified, sound in speech which is beyond reproach…" Tit. 2:2, 6, 7*

We all have peer groups. Young men don't want to hang around a bunch of old geezers, and us geezers don't understand a lot of what fires young people's jets. It's OK. Each group could learn (and benefit) from the other if we'd take the time and not pre-judge.

As I get older, and I assume it's this way with most older guys, I find it harder to adopt new ideas and new ways of doing things. I like to think it's because I've already found the best way. But that's arrogant. Besides, it stifles my learning, and I still like to learn new things.

When I look at the list in today's verse, two things stand out for both young and old: be sensible; sound faith and pure doctrine. Sensible has the tone of practical, full of common sense, logical, in accordance with wisdom, likely to be of benefit. Notice they are *not* things we *do*. They are things we *are*. What we are, who we are, automatically comes out in what we do. Jesus told Peter, "*…the things that proceed out of the mouth come from the heart, and those defile the man.*" [1155]

All actions begin with a thought. What if we thought more about the example we are setting? What would I change? What would I do more of? It all goes back to who's watching. Someday we will stand before God and give account for why we didn't care more about the details, why we let our pride stand in the way of self-initiated change. Trust me, changing myself is far less painful than waiting for God to do it. *"For those whom the Lord loves He disciplines, and He **scourges** every son whom He receives."*[1156]

In our discussion Monday, Paul told Timothy, "*Let no one look down on your youthfulness…*" [1157] Age is not the deciding factor in whether or not we can be a good example. Jesus made it clear to His disciples not to get in the way of children coming to Him, "*…for the kingdom of God belongs to such as these.*" [1158] Heart attitude and motive are what make one a good example or bad. Don't let yourself think that because you're too young or too old, you can't display God's standard, Jesus' example for all to see…even if nobody else around you is doing it. *"Be on the alert, stand firm in the faith, act like men, be strong."* [1159]

Father, I am full of excuses why I can't be a good example. The truth is, they are just excuses. Fill me anew with Your Spirit that I may have confidence in my salvation and live accordingly. In Jesus' name, **Amen.**

1155 Matt.15:18
1156 Heb.12:6
1157 I Tim. 4:12
1158 Luke 18:16
1159 I Cor. 16:13

Men of God encourage others to follow their eXample.

"Be imitators of me, just as I am of Christ." I Cor. 11:1

At first glance, this sounds boastful, proud, arrogant. But it's exactly the opposite. It takes a lot of humility to be transparent enough to put all our words and actions on display for scrutiny even to the point of judgment. It also puts a burden on us to **make sure we have something to imitate**; namely, whether we're following Christ in manner and motive. Meditate on the following verses:

- *"For I gave you an example that you also should* ***do as I did to you."*** *John 13:15* (Jesus to His disciples after washing their feet)
- *"Brethren, join in* ***following my example****, and* ***observe those who walk according to the pattern*** *you have in us." Phil. 3:17* (Paul to the Philippian church)
- *"The Lord was with Jehoshaphat because he* ***followed the example*** *of his father David's earlier days" II Chron. 17:3* (God's blessing for obedience)
- *"Do not* ***imitate*** *what is evil, but* ***what is good****." 3 John 1:11*
- *"But it shall come about,* ***if you do not obey*** *the Lord your God...you will be an* ***example of terror*** *to all the kingdoms of the earth." Deut. 28:15, 25*

We've talked about good examples and bad ones. We don't really need any bad examples; we do enough bad things on our own. What we need more is Christlike examples—people willing to obey what the Bible says, whether they like it or not; people who trust God in everything He sends into their lives (joys or trials), whether they understand it or not.

God often used just one man to accomplish His plan; He never formed a committee. Consider Joseph, sold into slavery by jealous brothers yet led the world to prepare for a great famine, and this, after being wrongly imprisoned for attacking Pharaoh's wife. Or how about John the Baptist? He wandered the desert alone preaching the coming of Christ, eating bugs and wearing burlap bags. But what did Jesus say about him? "*Among those born of women there has not arisen anyone greater than John.*"[1160] Then he was beheaded.

The Lord is on constant watch throughout the earth to find those whose heart is completely His, catch this...to support them.[1161] If you're looking to build a following, Facebook's not the place. *You* concentrate on improving your obedience. *God* will provide those He wants to follow your lead.

Lord, I am thankful You provided an example, in Jesus, of what You expect from your sons. May I have the courage to be one man You can count on to trust You, whatever You allow my way. In Christ's name, **Amen.**

1160 Matt.11:11
1161 II Chron. 16:9

Men of God (elders/pastors) have a unique opportunity to be an eXample.

"...shepherd the flock of God among you, exercising oversight not under compulsion, but voluntarily, according to the will of God; and not for sordid gain, but with eagerness; nor yet as lording it over those allotted to your charge, but proving to be examples to the flock." I Pet. 5, 2, 3

It's a travesty that in some churches today, the "face" of the church is a captivating speaker, able to take false teaching and make it alluring. But below the surface lies a heart of self-promotion and greed. James warns that those who would teach, "*will incur a stricter judgment.*" [1162] Jesus also warned, "*whoever causes one of these little ones who believe in Me to stumble, it would be better for him to have a heavy millstone hung around his neck, and to be drowned in the depth of the sea.*" [1163] Yet even with these warnings, false teachers seem drawn, like a moth to a flame, to pulpits across the country, deceived and deceiving as many as possible.

We've been warned this would happen. Peter says they will "*secretly introduce destructive heresies, bringing swift destruction upon themselves.*" And he goes on to say that **many** will follow their sensuality and the way of the truth will be maligned; and in their **greed** they will exploit you with false words.[1164] We know who is ultimately behind their charade, and the widespread nature of this evil is one more sign we're living in the last days.

I'm assuming the majority reading this are not pastors or elders. So what's our responsibility? Exercise wisdom in choosing a church home. Don't pick on the basis of proximity or convenience. God gives discernment that we can choose wisely. Be like the Bereans, test what is said against scripture. God doesn't change, and His Word means the same today as when it was written millennia ago. Make sure what comes out of the mouth of the teacher perfectly lines up with God's Word, 100%, the standard for a prophet. Pray your pastors don't succumb to the temptations of popularity and growth.

To you who are pastors/elders, I encourage you to take *very* seriously God's warnings. Surround yourself with a small group of godly men, proven by their lifestyle, and be transparent and accountable to them. Above all, "*humble yourselves under the mighty hand of God, that He may exalt you at the proper time.*" [1165] "*Do not reject the discipline of the Lord or loathe His reproof, for whom the Lord loves He reproves.*" [1166]

Father, I know Satan is ramping up his evil tricks, trying to deceive as many as he can. Keep me grounded in Your Word so I know truth and can spot lies quickly. Protect my pastor and elders from alluring deception. In Christ's name, **Amen.**

1162 Jas. 3:1
1163 Matt.18:6
1164 II Pet. 2:1-3
1165 I Pet. 5:6
1166 Prov. 3:11-12

Men of God are Zealous for God's name.

"I am the Lord, that is My name; I will not give My glory to another, nor My praise to graven images." Isa. 42:8 "You shall not take the name of the Lord your God in vain, for the Lord will not leave him unpunished who takes His name in vain." Exo. 20:7

What's in a name? Shakespeare tries to downplay Romeo's name in Juliet's mind by penning the famous quote, "a rose by any other name would smell as sweet." But the reality is that names do matter.

There are many baby names books on the market. Some parents give much thought to picking one. Others, not so much. But names are important to God. In Bible times, names had much more meaning and purpose than we ascribe to them today. In Genesis, God changed the names of Abram, Sarai, and Jacob to Abraham, Sarah, and Israel. Look at the names of God that identify different characteristics, for example, El-Elyon (God Most High), El-Shaddai (God Almighty), and 10 Jehovah-somethings. Or how about how God describes Himself in His conversation with Moses: "*Thus you shall say to the sons of Israel, I AM has sent me to you.*"?[1167]

Why is God so protective of His name? It's because names are the embodiment of who we are. Consider the following names: Billy Graham, Adolph Hitler, Mohammed Ali, Snow White. You immediately get a mental picture of everything that goes with these names. You wouldn't get the same picture if you heard the name William Graham, or Mo Ali. Reputation is inextricably linked to a name. Think of how quickly someone like Bill Cosby, who used to be the shining example of clean comedy, lost his rep. There are many other examples.

Why do you think Satan says Buddha and Allah are gods? Because he is a deceiver and does everything in his power to degrade and demean God's preeminence and superiority. If he can get people to believe that the *One God* is the same as *all gods*, he scores. He is also behind using God's name to curse and blaspheme, "*My name is continually blasphemed all day long.*"[1168]

And on that last point, as men of God, we should be guardians of God's name. Even if we're the last (Christian) man standing in a gathering of non-Christians and someone takes the Lord's name in vain, we should, politely, ask that they not use God's name in their cursing. It's a poor substitute for a good vocabulary.

Lord God, You only are holy and deserving of all honor and glory. The world doesn't know You and has no respect for Your name. I ask for boldness to defend Your name when confronted with those taking it in vain. May I represent You faithfully so others will be drawn *to* You, not repelled because of me. In Christ's name, **Amen.**

1167 Exo. 3:14
1168 Isa. 52:5

Men of God are Zealous for God's glory.

"For My own sake, for My own sake, I will act; for how can My name be profaned? And My glory I will not give to another." Isa. 48:11

We are blessed to see glorious sunsets and sunrises. We see an inkling of God's glory in lightning storms, a soaring eagle, a roaring sea, a hummingbird, good music with full orchestra and choir. But none of this compares with what Ezekiel saw in his vision, "*...a throne like lapus lazuli...as the appearance of the rainbow in the clouds on a rainy day... such was the appearance of the likeness of the glory of the Lord. And when I saw it, I fell on my face.*"[1169] When Moses asked to see God's glory, God said, "*I Myself will make all My goodness pass before you...[but] You cannot see My face, for no man can see Me and live!*"[1170] When John, in Revelation 1:12-17, saw the glory of the Lord, he "*fell at His feet like a dead man.*"

You've probably struggled a time or two finding the perfect gift for the man "who has everything." With that in mind, what can we possibly give to God? You may be surprised to find that we (believers) were created for God's glory.[1171] What? How? It's a mind-blowing concept that God gets glory from us. It's not in our clothes, from our jobs or even our good deeds. It's because we believe the message His Son came to deliver: **"***I am the way and the truth and the life, no one comes to the Father but through Me.*"[1172]

Take a minute and try to wrap your head around this thought. I bring glory to God just by believing in Jesus Christ as my Savior. Nothing else added. Of course, once we are saved and our future is assured, we *will* honor God through our obedience. When we showcase, by our lives, what Jesus did for us and what He offers to do for others, that brings glory to Him.

If that doesn't put a new focus on what we should be all about, check your pulse. When we realize the difference between heaven and hell and know that we deserve hell but are heading to heaven, how can we not, as Paul says, "*Whether, then, you eat or drink or whatever you do,* ***do all to the glory of God.***"[1173] It doesn't make sense (from the world's perspective) that we who have, literally, nothing to offer the creator God, can give Him glory. But then, when was the world right about anything? Read the Bible.

Time is short. Rejoice that your name is written in God's book of life[1174] and make the moments count for eternity, yours and someone else's.

Father, sometimes it's hard for me to grasp Your ways. But I believe You. May my focus be to bring glory to You in whatever I do. **Amen.**

1169 Ezek. 1:26, 28 (read Ezekiel 1 for a fuller description)
1170 Exo. 33:19, 20
1171 Isa. 43:7
1172 John 14:6
1173 I Cor. 10:31 – emphasis added
1174 Luke 10:20

Men of God are Zealous for God's Word.

"Your word is a lamp to my feet and a light to my path." Ps. 119:105

In the automotive world, there is an ongoing debate over Halogen, Xenon and LED headlights. Cost vs. performance. I like driving at night less and less, partly because oncoming traffic's headlights keep getting brighter. That's good for the driver of *that* car. Not so much for drivers of other cars.

I'm sure we've all been camping at some time. And it can get dark between your tent and the facility. You often need to alternate your light between close and farther away, so you don't trip or get lost.

Today's verse is, metaphorically speaking, without equal. We're not talking about literal light from some type of lantern. The psalmist talks about two types of illumination, one for the *next* step and another for the *ultimate* steps. Knowing where you're going is different than seeing what you're about to trip over. God's Word provides for both.

Our zeal for God's Word will increase our zeal for God Himself. "*Establish your word to your servant as that which produces reverence for You.*"[1175] If we neglect our daily Bible reading, how can we expect to have any zeal for the God who wrote it? If we're struggling with carving out time to read, we should ask ourselves why. Is it because the Bible is hard to understand? Find a different translation. Make sure it's a translation, not just a paraphrase. I like the New American Standard Bible.

Is daily reading just not a priority? Are we too busy, distracted, or just lazy? If so, it implies a one-way relationship. God did and continues to do His part in caring for us and providing all our needs, "*And my God will supply all your needs according to His riches in glory in Christ Jesus.*"[1176] What are we doing to show our gratitude? Our faith? Our dependence?

Let's say you have a $500,000 debt that you try and try to repay. But something always comes up, so your payment is late or short. And let's say you have an uncle you didn't know about who pays that debt for you. Is there anything you wouldn't do to show your thankfulness? And keep doing it.

How big is your debt of sin? Do you still owe it? Or was it paid by your "uncle"? Maybe, just maybe, you're still under the weight of unpaid sin. The Bible says, "*So if the Son makes you free, you will be free indeed.*"[1177] To know that we will avoid hell is the **best news** we could ever hear. And it should compel us to the Word, which *will* produce reverence for our God. Check your dipstick. If your love of the Word is down a quart or two, don't wait 'til you start hearing noises.

God, I can always find something to do besides reading and studying Your Word. But that doesn't help me know You better. Today, may I find renewed desire for Your truth on which to build my life. Thank You. In Christ, **Amen.**

1175 Ps. 119:38
1176 Phil. 4:19
1177 John 8:36

Men of God are Zealous for God's house.

"And He found in the temple those who were selling ... and the money changers... And He...drove them all out of the temple...and He poured out the coins of the money changers and overturned their tables...and He said...'stop making My Father's house a place of business.'" Jn. 2:14-16

For the record, I am not casting stones; I am not against anyone in the church making an honest buck. Emphasis on honest. Sadly, many of the wealthiest preachers today aren't. Paul was clear in his condemnation of those who "*want to distort the gospel of Christ.*"[1178] Here is a quote from *Beliefnet, Inc.* about one Texas preacher, "[He] says that he aims to focus more on the goodness of God and on living an obedient life **rather than on sin**. He says that he tries to teach biblical principles in a simple way, emphasizing the **power of love and a positive attitude**." (emphasis added). When did the gospel eliminate a discussion about sin and humility and repentance?

To be sure, God *is* good and holy and righteous, but He also *cannot* and won't abide sin. To not present that side of God is tickling ears and preaching a god not defined in the Bible. Jesus didn't mince words when He drove the money changers from the temple because they weren't there for the purpose of the temple—worshiping God. If He were on earth today, He'd have a full-time job chasing the money changers. The "*pastor / elder who rules well, is worthy of double honor.*"[1179] While that is true, he must also be **above reproach** and **free from the love of money**.[1180]

God's house is for worship. But worship is so much more than what we do in a building on Sunday. Yes, it includes music and preaching, but it's not just a one-hour event; it's a lifestyle that involves "*spirit and truth.*"[1181] For many churchgoers, worship is one of the most misunderstood concepts in the church today. They think it's what happens once a week when they meet **at** "the church." It is that. But if you stop there, you miss 90% of what worship is. It's a "persistent inclination of your heart and mind toward the majesty and glory of the Lord. It's not a momentary event, but a full-time, nonstop activity borne out in faithful praise, prayer, service, and study of God's truth."[1182]

God's house is not a building. Neither is the church. Our body is a temple of the Holy Spirit, who is in us.[1183] Are we a prayer and praise fountain, bubbling over into other lives? That's zeal for God's house. You with me?

Father, I confess, often I let the cares of this world bog me down, and I don't feel like praying or praising You. Rekindle the fire of Your Spirit in me that I may bubble over into my sphere of influence. In Jesus' name, **Amen.**

1178 Gal. 1:7
1179 I Tim.5:17
1180 I Tim. 3:2, 3
1181 Jn. 4:24
1182 John MacArthur letter, May 28, 2020
1183 I Cor. 6:19

Men of God are Zealous for God's people.

"For even as the body is one and yet has many members, and all the members of the body, though they are many, are one body, so also is Christ." I Cor. 12:12

You ever play on a company softball team? Or root for your hometown footballers? Did you like everybody on the team, the coaches? You may not, but I bet you didn't boo them. Why? Because you all wore the same uniform. The military branches have a good-natured rivalry, but when push comes to shove, we all wear the same flag.

Wouldn't it be wonderful if, as brothers in the Lord, we all supported each other regardless of style? We all have the same commanding officer. Instead, we divide over trivial things. As long as we have the basics right, "the 5 solas"—Scripture Alone, Grace Alone, Christ Alone, Faith Alone, the Glory of God Alone—we should be able to live with differences of style and preference. "John" worked for me years ago. He was a disciplined, buttoned-down ex-Army Captain and got frustrated with certain management decisions. His favorite expression was, "Why are we pole-vaulting over rabbit turds?" The church often focuses too much on secondary and tertiary issues.

The godly man's role in the church is to lead it, doing everything to make sure its reputation is above reproach and to take care of the spiritual and moral health of the members. All the petty bickering, jealousy, and pride has no place in the family of God. It's been said that if you don't care who gets the credit, a lot more gets done. Only a few have been gifted for the limelight. The rest of us need to use our gifts to support the whole.[1184] After all, we will spend eternity with each other. Might as well learn how now.

What about the parts of the family we never see? The ones who sacrifice comfort, indoor plumbing, Redbox, and Netflix and live in remote parts of the world? Are we supporting them with prayer? With finances? Care packages? When I was in the Army, I used to love getting a box from home. It often meant homemade cookies. Family. We don't always like our siblings. But God doesn't make mistakes in placement. If we valued our gift(s) rather than grousing about why someone else has the one(s) we wanted, we'd be a lot happier and content. Don't question God's reasoning. "*But one and the same Spirit works all these things, distributing to each one individually* ***just as He wills.***"[1185]

Let's look out for each other. If we all do that, we'll have more than one looking out for us.

Holy God, forgive me for questioning Your choices that impact me. May I be content to follow orders *even when I don't understand.* Grow my faith to trust You when I can't see the next step. In Christ's name, **Amen.**

1184 Read all of I Cor. 12 for a thorough understanding
1185 I Cor. 12:11 emphasis added

Men of God are Zealous for God's message.

"Your word I have treasured in my heart that I may not sin against You." Ps. 119:11

Be honest with me. Do you read the owner's manual before you tackle toys, tools, or furniture assembly? I do, usually after I have leftover parts. We have an owner's manual written by the Spirit of God Himself and "*profitable for teaching, for reproof, for correction, for training in righteousness;* ***so that*** *the man of God may be adequate, equipped for every good work.*"[1186]

Have you ever noticed all the "so thats" in Scripture? God *always* has a purpose behind everything He does. Even in today's verse, the "so" is implied; **so that** I may not sin. The psalmist knew that time in the Word was the only way to know God and know what pleases Him.

There are many parts to God's "message" to us. There's history, poetry, wisdom, and more. I just finished reading Genesis, and I'm encouraged that God still blessed, sometimes exorbitantly, the scoundrels we read of. Abraham lied ("she's my sister"), Jacob deceived ("I *am* Esau"), and there are many more examples. But if we boil it down to its essence, the Bible is an autobiography of God, past, present, and future. It is true cover to cover because God *cannot* lie.[1187] And it's the *only* resource we need to prepare us to live righteously in this world *and* the next. John 3:16 has been called the Gospel in a nutshell: "*For God so loved the world, that He gave His only begotten son, that whoever believes in Him shall not perish, but have eternal life.*" That's God's heart; He loves sinners and paid for our sin Himself.

I don't know how many tens of thousands of sermons are preached every Sunday. But I do know this. Not all of them come from the Bible. Many are just opinions of the speaker that promote a personal agenda. Beware, you who preach and teach, that when you're speaking for God, it's what He would say—what He has said—in His Word. The Bible warns that a stricter judgment is incurred by Bible teachers.[1188] Why? Because God is jealous for His truth. In Moses' song, speaking of the Israelites, he says, "*They made Him jealous with strange gods; with abominations* ***they provoked Him to anger.***"[1189] We don't want to incur God's anger.

How does zeal for God's message increase? First, read it, study it, memorize it. Second, apply it in daily living. Third, share it and watch lives change. There's nothing more satisfying than seeing a new convert to Christ.

Heavenly Father, Your Word is complete and has everything I need to know You, trust You, love You. May I not keep it to myself but share it everywhere I go by my life and my speech. In Jesus' name, **Amen.**

1186 II Tim. 3:16 emphasis added
1187 Tit. 1:2
1188 Jas. 3:1
1189 Deut. 32:16 emphasis added

Men of God are Zealous for God's work.

"We must work the works of Him who sent Me as long as it is day; night is coming when no one can work." Jn. 9:4

From 1959 to 1963, a TV show, Dobie Gillis, had a beatnik character named Maynard. Every time he heard the word "work," he screeched it in echo. We all laughed. But not funny is the fact that since then, for the most part, television sitcoms have portrayed men as bumbling idiots, bigots, or lazy.

That's sad because work is a gift from God. Adam was assigned to "*cultivate and keep*"[1190] the garden—*before the fall.* It was only after Adam and Eve sinned that God cursed the ground, "*...in toil you will eat of it...both thorns and thistles it shall grow for you...by the sweat of your face you will eat bread...*"[1191]

Men were created to work. In Paul's instructions to Timothy, he says, "*But if anyone does not provide for his own, and especially for those of his household, he has denied the faith and is worse than an unbeliever.*"[1192]

So what are the works of Him who sent Me [Jesus]? Jesus' last command before leaving planet earth was, "*Go...make disciples...teach...*"[1193] That is still our "work." Further, in our verse today, there's a sense of urgency. Paul reinforces that to the Ephesian church, "*...making the most of your time, because the days are evil.*"[1194] And again to the Colossian church, "*Conduct yourselves with wisdom toward outsiders, making the most of the opportunity.*"[1195]

This book has been about focus. The world offers more and more shiny things to distract us from God's work. Don't misunderstand. I'm not saying we should all be in full-time ministry jobs. Then where would the Christian influence be in factories, grocery stores, schools? But what I am saying is we should view the workplace as *our* mission field. You say, "But I'm only one man." Very often, God only needs one man whose heart is completely His to strongly support.[1196]

I want to encourage us to take seriously the role God has assigned. He appointed us to lead our families, to represent Him to them, and advocate for them to Him. Beyond that, we are to be leaders in the church; to make sure the Word is preached in truth and any heresy is squelched. That's our job. You in?

Lord, I am energized when I have a goal, something of value to fill my time. May mine be the same as Yours. Keep me on the narrow path with my eye on the prize of Your upward call in Christ. In His name, **Amen.**

1190 Gen. 2:15
1191 Gen. 3:17-19
1192 I Tim. 5:8
1193 Matt. 28:19, 20
1194 Eph. 5:16
1195 Col. 4:5
1196 II Chron. 16:9

Week 49 Promises For Me - Introduction

As we approach the end of our time together, I've been praying about how to wrap up a book on character. I believe God answered my prayer by giving me several things that showcase His character. The next four weeks will be just that. When I think of God's character, it's hard to choose one attribute that's more important than the others. So I've chosen one that is at least very practical, if not the most practical: God CANNOT lie.

The implications of this are huge. In this world, everybody lies. Many do it to gain an advantage. Some do it to not hurt others' feelings. I've been burned because I want to trust people, and I'd rather that than approach people expecting them to lie to me.

So why is the fact that God cannot lie so important? The biggest reason is that we can trust our eternal future to Him. He doesn't play games. He says what He means and means what He says. He doesn't toy with us to see how much we can handle. Can you imagine God calling Jesus over and saying, "Hey, watch this, Son. Let's see how much Bob can take"?

I wrote this book with only Scripture to support what I've written. If I didn't believe what God said in His Word, this book would have no validity, being just my opinions.

With that said, the first of these weeks is given to a handful of God's promises that we can take to the bank (see chart below). They are true for all time and all people. Again, how do you pick seven promises from so many? I tried to zero in on ones that, whether you know Jesus Christ or not, will encourage you, convict you, and bring you to saving faith in Him.

I hope you've gotten as much out of reading these daily truths as I have out of writing them. If you don't remember anything else from this book, remember this: Character counts. And Christ's character is the *only model* with eternal ramifications.

Sunday	*Gratitude*
Monday	*Comfort*
Tuesday	*Revenge*
Wednesday	*Fear*
Thursday	*Hope for Christ's return*
Friday	*Hope for heaven*
Saturday	*Hope for rewards*

Men of God are GRATEFUL for forgiveness of their sins.

"Bless the Lord, O my soul, and forget none of His benefits; who ***pardons all your iniquities****...As far as the east is from the west, so far has* ***He removed our transgressions from us****."* *Ps. 103:2, 3, 12*

"For I will be merciful to their iniquities, and I will ***remember their sins no more****."* *Heb. 8:12*

"If we confess our sins, ***He is faithful*** *and righteous to forgive us our sins and to* ***cleanse us from all unrighteousness****."* *I Jn. 1:9*

I don't know about you, but I'm glad God is not like me. I may offer forgiveness to someone who has wronged me, and it may or may not have stipulations. But apart from God, sometimes it's hard for me to forget it ever happened and restore the relationship to pre-violation conditions. Our verses today promise that when we confess, God forgives AND forgets. It is as if we never did it, a clean slate.

The problem is us. Because we usually can't forget, we think God remembers our sin. So the next time we do the same thing, we hesitate to take it to Him...again. That's a lie from the pit to keep us in a broken relationship with our Father. God chastises the wicked for that kind of thinking, "*...you thought I was just like you.*"[1197] It's great news that He isn't.

In thinking about God's promises, this ranks near the top of my list. Guilt is like a sack of rocks being carried by my soul, a heaviness that affects my whole being. When God, through His mercy, takes my sack and not only empties it but burns the evidence, I have no other option but to rejoice and praise Him for His mercy and patience and love.

Notice the completeness in today's verses: pardons *all*, remembers no more, cleanse us from *all*. I'm sure I won't really understand all the implications of my being forgiven until I get to heaven. But I know this. I didn't do anything to earn or deserve it, and yet, here I am, on my way with a paid-in-full ticket given to me personally by Jesus. How can I not be filled with gratitude and anticipation for the trip?

Merciful God, forgive me for trying to fit You into my mold. Help me understand that all means all, and no more means just that. Your faithfulness is what allows me to trust You and believe You for my position in Christ and my future with You. Spirit, fill me with a desire to share this great news with anybody who will listen so that they, too, can dump their sack and grasp the depth of what a relationship with Jesus gives them. In His name, **Amen.**

1197 Ps. 50:21

Men of God are COMFORTED by God's presence.

"Make sure that your character is free from the love of money, being content with what you have; for He Himself has said, 'I ***will never desert you, nor will I ever forsake you****, so that we confidently say, 'The Lord is my helper, I will not be afraid. What will man do to me?'" Heb. 13:5, 6*

When we think of ourselves as macho, he-man, and self-reliant, comforted doesn't quite fit the mold. But ask yourself, "Why do I take an air mattress camping?" Why do I buy a car with A/C, power windows, and seats? Face it. We like comfort…in a physical sense. We probably don't give a lot of thought to emotional comfort. After all, we're men. And men aren't supposed to show emotion. Hogwash.

None of us can be a true loner. We all need somebody sometime. Solomon said, "*Two are better than one because they have a good return for their labor. For if either of them falls, the one will lift up his companion. But woe to the one who falls when there is not another to lift him up.*"[1198] I don't believe he was speaking just in the physical sense. We experience betrayal, disappointment, loneliness, and if we don't have a listening ear to talk to, it can lead to depression and other addictive behavior. Jesus knew the need, and when He sent out the seventy, He sent them in twos.[1199]

Today's verse is a strong reminder that, though we can't see Jesus, He's working on our behalf; He promised He would, and that's where our faith comes in. Listen to a promise relative to our giving, "*…I will rebuke the devourer for you, so that it will not destroy the fruits of the ground.*"[1200] And another, "*…He always lives to make intercession for them* [those who draw near to God through Christ]."[1201] Think about these for a minute. Why would Jesus need to rebuke the devourer? Can we agree that Satan is bent on doing anything he can to discourage and defeat us, including destroying the work of our hands? And who would you rather have praying for you than Jesus?

This is another example of our old enemy, pride, telling us we don't need anybody (especially to ask directions from). Lies, lies from the pit. If we consider that every promise God made was to address a need He knew we'd have, and realize it was for our benefit, we'd be more open to admit our need for comfort. Isn't that one of the last things Jesus told His disciples, that He would send the Comforter to them?[1202] They needed Him. We still do.

Lord God, we tend to remember all the false wisdom of the world over the years, like real men don't cry. I know that's not true. Tears are a gift from You. Thank You for the comfort You provide when I am man enough to admit my need. In my Savior's name, **Amen.**

1198 Eccl. 4:9, 10
1199 Luke 10:1
1200 Mal. 3:11
1201 Heb. 7:25
1202 John 16:7

Men of God are freed of anger by God's REVENGE.

"Never take your own revenge, beloved, but leave room for the wrath of God, for it is written, 'Vengeance is Mine, I ***WILL*** *repay,' says the Lord." Rom. 12:19*

This may seem like a strange topic for a week on God's promises. But stick with me. Doesn't it seem like the bad guys always get away with *stuff*? And doesn't that just chap your hide? Praying for my enemies is not always the first thing I think of. Many times I don't think of it at all.

God's reasoning, I believe, has two sides. First, He will mete out the exact punishment that is *fair,* no more, no less. Second, and this is for our benefit, He knows that if we take revenge ourselves, we end up with a sack of guilt to carry around. We would be more apt to accept this command if God's timing were NOW. We've been cheated, wounded, defrauded, and we're angry. We want to *see* the punishment, the consequences.

The problem is me. When I struggle to let God do what only God does (revenge), it shows my heart isn't right. We're told to love our enemies and pray for those who persecute us, not to do whatever it takes to get even.[1203] Here's the tough one. No amount of anger or self-righteousness on our part justifies our disobeying the word *never.* We just need to trust God. He always has our six.

We've noted several times in this book that God *cannot* lie.[1204] Therefore, when He says, "I will," He will. End of story. The interesting thing about today's verse is that we are told to "*leave room for the* ***wrath*** *of God.*" If every time someone in the Bible fell down when encountering just an angel, and that usually wasn't to punish but to announce something from God, think of encountering God in His wrath. Not a place (or person) I want to be.

I think we get the message. God tells us clearly, "don't do it." Why did I include this promise as one of my favorites? Partly because it shows God is in control of everything and doesn't miss even the little things that are unfair to His kids. And He will deal with them in His time and His way. Also, it takes a huge burden off us that, if left to ourselves, we might destroy our testimony or, worse, do something really stupid that ends us in jail. When someone takes advantage of us, we're to turn the other cheek. Take the step of faith and give it to God. He'll do a much better job of revenge than we ever could. And then pray for the perp's soul.

Jesus, You were the ultimate example of turning the other cheek because You never lost sight of Your mission. Keep reminding me that it's not about me, it's about Your path *for* me and that You have gone before to make that path clear. Give me the discipline to stay the course for Your glory, not mine. In Your name, **Amen.**

1203 Matt. 5:44
1204 Tit. 1:2

Men of God have no need to FEAR.

"In God, whose word I praise, In God I have put my trust; I shall not be afraid. What can ***mere man*** *do to me?" Ps. 56:4 (emphasis added)*

Fight or flight. We've all heard these two options when faced with danger. But for the man of God, there's a third option—faith. There are over 100 forms of "do not fear" in scripture. When training animals, repetition is critical. We're called sheep for a reason. Maybe after 100 times of telling us not to be afraid, God's point will find its target.

What is the opposite of fear? It could be a lot of things like confidence, complacency, or indifference. I like to think it's peace. Fear brings angst, agitation, worry, nervousness, and other bad stuff. But if we have peace, none of that can grab hold. Jesus told His disciples, "*These things I have spoken to you, so that* ***in Me*** *you may have peace. In the world you have tribulation, but take courage; I have overcome the world.*"[1205]

Today's verse reminds us we're on the winning team. We're told, "*Do not fear those who kill the body but are unable to kill the soul; but rather fear Him who is able to destroy both soul and body in hell.*"[1206] What's the worst that man can do to us? Kill us? Didn't Paul say that it is "*very much better to depart and be with Christ?*"[1207] "*If God is for us, who is against us?*"[1208]

Having said all that, we still have an enemy who hates Jesus and, by extension, all who follow Him. So we need to be armored up and alert for battle. It won't be a frontal attack. He's sneaky and will do all in his power to catch us off guard. He knows he can't steal our salvation—it's absolutely secure—[1209] but he'll try to put us on injured reserve and out of the game of sharing Christ with others.

One way to preemptively fight back is to look up all the instances of "do not be afraid" and "do not fear" and pick a handful of the ones you particularly like and **memorize** them. Quoting scripture (the sword of the Spirit) is our only offensive weapon. All other parts of the armor of God are defensive and designed to keep us above reproach, e.g., truth, righteousness, the gospel of peace, the shield of faith, and the helmet of salvation.[1210] And remember, it doesn't do any good to have our armor on and sit on the bench. Get in the game.

Lord God, again Your promises encourage me to trust You and not my circumstances. You alone are truth and faithfulness. Help me to sharpen my sword by storing Your Word in my heart so I'm always ready for battle. In the all-powerful name of Jesus, **Amen.**

1205 John 16:33 (emphasis added)
1206 Matt. 10:28
1207 Phil. 1:23
1208 Rom. 8:31
1209 Eph. 4:30; John 10:28
1210 Eph. 6:13-17

Men of God have hope for Christ's return.

"In My Father's house are many dwelling places; ***if it were not so, I would have told you****; for I go to prepare a place for* ***you****. If I go and prepare a place for you,* ***I will come again*** *and receive you to Myself, that where I am, there you may be also." Jn. 14:2, 3 (emphasis added)*

Where to start? I get so excited over this promise, we'll take the next three days to look at it. Let's start at the beginning. JESUS IS COMING BACK FOR ME. What else is there to know? If it were a regular trip, I'd already have my bag packed and ticket bought.

You've probably heard someone say, "I've got good news and bad news. Which do you want first?" Read the verses again; there is NO BAD NEWS here. Jesus said He would tell us if there were. Hallelujah!

I realize some of you reading this may not be excited about Jesus' return. Could be several reasons. You're young and feel you have a lot of life ahead of you. I suggest there are two things wrong with that thinking. First, you don't know the day you will die. Second, no matter how bright your future looks, it can't compare with what God has in store for us.

There might be another reason too. You may not be ready to meet God face to face; you're not sure what happens after you die. "*...it is appointed for men to die once and after this comes judgment.*"[1211] Judgment. That can be a scary word...unless. Unless what? Unless your sin has already been judged at the cross by Jesus' death and resurrection.

Let's review. 1. There is a God. He is holy and hates sin (I Peter 1:16). 2. Your sin separated you from Him and earned the death penalty (Rom. 6:23). 3. God loves *you* so much He sent Jesus to die *in your place*, to pay the penalty you could never pay on your own. (Jn. 3:16) 4. Good works, good attitudes, and good deeds *can't* solve your problem. You must believe that Jesus (alone) is THE ONLY WAY back to God and trust that His death *on your behalf* erased *your* debt (Eph. 2:8,9). 5. Tell God you're sorry (repent) for your sin, and you want to turn your life around (Rom. 10:9). 6. Believe that God has forgiven you and restored you to fellowship with Him (I John 5:13). 7. Tell everyone what has just happened to you. 8. Spend time daily reading the Bible and talking to God (prayer).

"*Hope does not disappoint, because the love of God has been poured out within our hearts...*"[1212] More tomorrow.

Holy God, my future with You is assured because of Jesus' death, and because You said so. May that prospect light a fire of excitement in me to not fear the unknown but to embrace it with eager anticipation. May it also cause me to share this good news with all I meet. In Jesus' name, **Amen.**

1211 Heb. 9:27
1212 Rom. 5:5

Week 49 Friday – Promises For Me

Men of God have hope of heaven.

"...I go to prepare a place for you." Jn. 14:2

This world has much beauty and grandeur for us to enjoy both in the macro and micro sense. Who in their right mind could not believe in a Creator when confronted with the complexities of living and inanimate objects? A house does not create itself; it requires an architect and a contractor. Many architects are identifiable through some signature design elements in their projects. Likewise, an observable design in all of nature demands an intelligent designer. God's signature is on all of it.

Paul lays it out clearly in Romans, "*...that which is known about God* ***is evident*** *within them; for God made it evident to them. For since the creation of the world His invisible attributes, His eternal power and divine nature, have been* ***clearly seen****, being understood through what has been made.*"[1213]

The 2nd law of thermodynamics says (in layman's terms) everything moves from order to chaos, *never* from chaos to order. Big Bang? Fake news on the Big Screen. Consider a jigsaw puzzle in the box. Now open it and pour the pieces on a table. How many times would you have to do that for all the pieces to fall into just the right place, even in a child's puzzle of a dozen pieces? How about just one piece landing correctly? Not gonna happen.

We're told in Proverbs, "*It is the glory of God to conceal a matter, but the glory of kings is to search out a matter.*"[1214] In this world, man continues to discover new things God has hidden in His creation for our enjoyment, our benefit, and the realization of His awesomeness. Many scientists have come to know God through the recognition of the designer behind the design. Things in nature don't just happen. They happen because God designed them that way.

So, all that is just background for what we have to look forward to. Admittedly, I have no secret or advance knowledge of the exact plans or design of heaven. But I do know the architect. And, from what He designed just to be our home away from home, and what little we *do* know of heaven (streets of gold, amazing colors, angels, etc.), it's going to be fantastic, awesome, amazing, and any other superlatives you can conjure up.

He's coming back. He's prepared a new home. Tomorrow, the environment and the rewards.

Father, Your creation continues to amaze me by the detail, the function, and the beauty. I know heaven is beyond my comprehension, but I can't wait to see more of Your wisdom and creative power in what You have prepared. May I continue strong and ready for Your timing and the upward call. In Christ's name, **Amen.**

1213 Rom. 1:19, 20 (emphasis added)

1214 Prov. 25:2

Men of God have hope of reward.

"Behold, I am coming quickly, and my reward is with Me, to render to every man according to what he has done." Rev. 22:12

Everybody likes to get presents; the younger we are, the more we like to get. But as I get older, the giver rather than the gift is more important to me. Just the fact that somebody thought of me means more to me than gifts.

When I think about our future home, some of the things I really look forward to are not gifts in the usual sense of the word, but rather part of the environmental package. The Bible tells us there will be no lying, stealing, tears, pain, sorrow, or death. I can't wait.

One of the consequences of living in a sin-cursed world is having to deal with selfish, greedy liars. When I was young, I'm sure people lied. But there seemed to be a morality that is sorely missing in the 21st century. It's hard to imagine a society where none of that exists. Heaven is that society.

Aside from the environment where sin doesn't exist, what else do we have to look forward to? The Bible gives us a general sense when it talks about crowns: of righteousness (II Tim. 4:8), of life (Jas. 1:12), of glory (I Pet. 5:4). In Bible times, crowns were a sign of royalty, position, and wealth. They were made of gold and jewels and probably weighed enough to give me a headache.

We're also told, "*Do not store up for yourselves treasures on earth…store up for yourselves treasures in heaven*"[1215] What does that mean? It means we can't take it with us. But as one wag said, "Yeah, but we can send it on ahead." I have to confess, I don't know exactly what treasures we'll have in heaven. But I know using our resources here on earth (money, time, etc.) to advance God's kingdom is what adds to our treasure chest there. And really, when you think about it, whatever it is was planned by our Father for His kids. It doesn't get better than that.

When Jesus comes with His reward, will it include a "*Well done good and faithful slave*" or a "*depart from Me, I never knew you*"? For me, anything above just being with Him for eternity is icing on the cake. Now don't get me wrong; I love cream cheese icing on a carrot cake my daughter makes, but how do you top hanging with Jesus…forever?

The bottom line to these last three days is Jesus is coming back for me, for us, and whatever heaven will be like, we know it will be perfection, planned and executed by the God of Creation Himself. If you can't get excited about that, call the paramedics, you're circling the drain.

Lord Jesus, You promised to come back for me. I am sooo looking forward to that day. I know it's only Your mercy that includes me in Your book. Thank You for knowing my name and choosing me. **Amen.**

1215 Matt. 6:19, 20

Week 50 The Word of God—Introduction

The book you are reading is not a seminary text of Greek and Hebrew languages. But even so, my firm belief is that God wrote His book—the Bible—in simple enough language that everyday Joes like me can understand it. Yes, there's poetry in which some of the nuances of the original language escape me; and, yes, there's prophetic, apocalyptic symbolism in it too that can be hard to visualize and understand. But remember, the writers of Ezekiel and Revelation especially were trying to describe something that was millennia in their future, and they had no concept of modern technology as a frame of reference.

The Bible is the Owner's manual given to teach us how we're supposed to run and let us know what to do when we go "chugga chugga" instead of whir. You'll recall from the daily readings that every point I make is based solely on Scripture. Occasionally, I'll quote someone or something else, but it's only to flesh out the narrative. It's been said that the Bible is God's letter to his family, and when non-Christians complain about it being a difficult, hard to understand book, that's what they get for reading other people's mail. As believers, we have the author—the Holy Spirit—living in us to help us grasp His truth. He wants us to know it, to live it, to love it, and to share it.

Let's agree on one thing. The Bible is true, cover to cover. If that isn't so, there's no reason to read any of it. There may be hard parts we don't particularly want to hear, but those are probably the areas we need to spend more time in. Many modern preachers have a propensity to teach only about God's love, patience, and mercy, you know, all the *good* stuff. The truth is that God *is* all those things. But He is also just, wrathful, vengeful, and demanding.

As the second of "the Final Four" chapters, I have tried to highlight a handful of the reasons we can have confidence in God's Word. It is, in essence, His character rolled into one document so that we can know Him and Jesus Christ, who made this all possible. It is a 66-book promise that I hope you love, live by, and personalize. It was, after all, written for you.

Sunday	*The Word is... Inerrant and Infallible*
Monday	*The Word is... Sufficient*
Tuesday	*The Word is... Complete*
Wednesday	*The Word is... Effective*
Thursday	*The Word is... Our Link to know God*
Friday	*The Word is... Everlasting*
Saturday	*The Word is... Relevant for today*

The Word of God is...Inerrant and Infallible

"The sum of Your word is truth, and ***every one*** *of Your righteous ordinances is* ***everlasting****." Ps. 119:160 [emphasis added]*

In last week's introduction, we noted that God *cannot* lie. There are two means God uses to communicate with us: speaking and writing. God's written Word is just as veracious as His spoken Word. The test of a true prophet of God is 100% accuracy. When we say the Bible is *inerrant* and *infallible*, it means all historical events reported, all future events predicted, and all promises are "Rock" solid. They *did* happen or *will* happen. It's rare that God speaks audibly to men now since the Bible was completed. So we have to "hear" God speak to us in His Word.

Critics of the Bible try to debunk things that point to God's omnipotence (all-powerful) or omniscience (all-knowing), things like six literal days of creation, a world-wide flood, and miracles. When they refer to an earth that is billions of years old, they do so because a) they're ignorant of the interaction and dependency of various parts of the creation, and b) they don't want the accountability of a Creator. If there really is a God who did all this, then He has the absolute right to write the rules governing His creation (including us). Besides, science has proof of "some worldwide cataclysmic event" because of the various earth strata which contain evidence of such. Ask yourself, "How else did seashells get distributed to the tops of mountains?"

Other critics say the Bible is out of date, that what was once applicable no longer is. But the Bible says, "*Jesus Christ is the same yesterday and today and forever.*" [1216] Technology has certainly changed society and made life easier, albeit not always better. Has man's heart gotten better? The Bible says in God's own words of the wickedness of man, "*...every intent of the thoughts of his heart was only evil continually.*"[1217] And that is only six chapters into Genesis. We've had half a dozen millennia since then. No. Man's heart has not gotten better. Man needs Jesus.

Because of the perfect and precise fulfillment of prophecy that has already occurred, we have confidence that those that still await fulfillment will, in God's timing, also be precisely fulfilled. Reread Week 49 – Thursday for an encouraging prophetic promise about Christ's return for His church. The Bible is NEVER wrong. As such, we stake our eternal future on the gospel message found there. Jesus died for my sin and yours. Don't let that fact fall on deaf ears. It's crunch time. If you already know Jesus, someone you know doesn't. Share the everlasting truth with them.

Father, You gave us the only road map we need to get to heaven—Your Word. Help us treasure it above all earthly possessions as the only thing we can bring with us when You call us home. In Jesus' name, **Amen.**

1216 Heb. 13:8

1217 Gen. 6:5

The Word of God is…Sufficient

"All Scripture is inspired by God and profitable for teaching, for reproof, for correction, for training in righteousness; so that the man of God may be adequate, equipped for every good work." II Tim. 3:16

Libraries are great storehouses of knowledge of all kinds of stuff. The Library of Congress has over 16 million books. Local libraries, a lot fewer. The Bible incorporates everything God knew we would need to know Him, teach our children, correct false doctrine, and live righteous lives. Not one of the 16 million (except their copies of the Bible itself) can claim that, even in the area of child-rearing.

I'm so glad I raised my kids in a time before electronic toys and communication became ubiquitous. Have you ever read some of the drivel put out by so-called experts? Don't spank, they say. The Bible says, "*The rod and reproof give wisdom, but a child who gets his own way brings shame to his mother.*"[1218] You can sure see the ones today who had poor parenting. It's discouraging that there are so many of them.

The Bible is filled with history, strategy for war, poetry, love stories, drama, wisdom, scoundrels, and of course, mercy, grace, forgiveness, and best of all, hope. And none of it is fiction. All true, front to back.

Today's verse has a phrase that caught my attention some time ago. It frequently appears in Scripture: so that. God doesn't do anything in a vacuum. Everything has a purpose. Look at today's purpose: we are to be equipped for every good work…adequately. Kinda takes away all the excuses, doesn't it? Don't feel qualified? Your time in the Bible is probably behind schedule.

Let's look at the first part of the verse, "*All Scripture is inspired by God.*" What does that mean? It means that the Holy Spirit gave the 40 writers, spread over 1,500 years, the exact thoughts to put to paper. Since man's heart hasn't changed since creation, Scripture is just as fresh, just as powerful to change lives today as when it was written thousands of years ago.

Sin is still sin. The only way to forgiveness is still through faith in Jesus Christ's atonement. Nothing else satisfies the holy requirement of God that sin demands death. God knew we couldn't pay the price ourselves. That's why the free gift of God (salvation through faith in Christ), though not free to Him, is such an indescribable gift. How could anybody who has the humility to admit that they are a sinner and deserve death, not understand the price paid and the value imputed to them totally free of charge. No matter how many good works we amass, they're as filthy rags before God.[1219]

And how do we know all this? It's in the Bible.

God, help me realize that looking anywhere beside Your Word will not lead me to the truth I need to order my life according to Your plan. Thank You for opening my eyes to see what really matters. In Christ, **Amen.**

1218 Prov. 29:15
1219 Isa. 64:6

The Word of God is...Complete

"You shall not add to the word which I am commanding you, nor take away from it, that you may keep the commandments of the Lord your God which I command you." Deut. 4:2

There are religious sects, most notably the Mormon church, that publish a "companion" book (The Book of Mormon) that, in their church, is considered inspired just like the Bible. It is not. This is not the venue in which to dissect all that's wrong with this group. But just to suffice for our point, God is as jealous for His Word as He is for His name.

In addition to today's verse, Revelation has a dire warning, "*I testify to everyone who hears the words of the prophecy of this book: if anyone adds to them, God will add to him the plagues which are written in this book; and if anyone takes away from the words of the book of this prophecy, God will take away his part from the tree of life and from the holy city, which are written in this book.*"[1220]

To me, "not add...nor take away" is about as plain an instruction as you can get. And why would you want to anyway? We learned yesterday that the Bible is sufficient. But let's get practical. Psalm 19 has six specific things that the Bible is and what each does. It also gives a "value" statement and promise:

1. The **law** of the Lord is **perfect**, restoring the soul
2. The **testimony** of the Lord is **sure**, making wise the simple
3. The **precepts** of the Lord are **right**, rejoicing the heart
4. The **commandment** of the Lord is **pure**, enlightening the eyes
5. The **fear** of the Lord is **clean**, enduring forever
6. The **judgments** of the Lord are **true**; they are righteous altogether

Value: "They are **more desirable than gold**, yes, than much fine gold; **sweeter also than honey** and the drippings of the honeycomb."

Promise: "Moreover, by them, **Your servant is warned**; in keeping them there is **great reward**. (Psalm 19:7-11)

These sure sound like qualities we can count on—stake our lives and future on—without hesitation. But we have to go one step further. In Psalm 119, the psalmist asks a rhetoric question and then answers it: "v. *9 How can a young man keep his way pure? By keeping it according to Your word. v. 11 Your word I have treasured in my heart, that I may not sin against You.*" Our challenge today: Do we treasure God's Word? Do we store it in our hearts? A book this valuable shouldn't just sit on the shelf. Dig in. There's plenty for everyone.

Lord, You designed Your Word to be all that I need to know You, Your will while I'm on earth, and Your plan for my future. May it be to me more desirable than gold, my all-in-one, go-to resource for living in a sin-cursed world. Thank You. **Amen**.

1220 Rev. 22:18, 19

The Word of God is...Effective

"For the word of God is living and active and sharper than any two-edged sword, and piercing as far as the division of soul and spirit, of both joints and marrow, and able to judge the thoughts and intentions of the heart." Heb. 4:12 "So will My word be which goes forth from My mouth; it will not return to Me empty, without accomplishing what I desire, and without succeeding in the matter for which I sent it." Isa. 55:11

What comes to mind when you think of the word "effective?" Medicine? Cramming for a test? Cleaning products? Isn't the only thing that matters, with anything you buy for a particular purpose, does it work? In advertising, it's strictly a numbers game. A mail campaign is considered successful with a 1% to 2% response rate. Anything above that is a home run.

Remember the old "Got Milk" campaign? It ran for nearly 20 years and gained great popularity, so much so that many copycats tried to adapt it to their product. But it didn't stop the decline of per capita milk consumption. A case study in ineffectiveness.

God says His Word works. It judges our innermost thoughts and motives. It *always* succeeds for the purpose He sent it. This should be the key takeaway for those of us involved in spreading the gospel. Paul was a great model of this. He told the Corinthian church, "*I determined to know nothing among you except Jesus Christ, and Him crucified.*"[1221] No emotional pitches. No sales gimmicks. Like Jack Webb's character in *Dragnet* used to say, "Just the facts ma'am." We went over the facts of the gospel in Week 49, Thursday. It would be a good thing to memorize and have in your arsenal.

What is the effectiveness of the Word? It introduces us to God. It paints, with detailed strokes, a picture of God's love, mercy, faithfulness, and sacrifice. It identifies sin and leads men to repent. It provides hope for our future. And much more.

The good news for us is that we can do what we can to be effective. We can take public speaking classes, memorize different outlines for presenting the gospel, and go door-knocking to share. But we're not accountable for results. Spoiler alert: It's the Word that has the power, not us. If we're faithful to go, God will cause the increase.[1222] Even Moses tried to bargain with God when God wanted to send him to Pharaoh. He said, "*I have never been eloquent...I am slow of speech and slow of tongue.*"[1223] Read the whole story in Exodus 3 and 4. Moses went. You know the rest. Don't be concerned if you're not a polished orator. Let the Word out, and it will do its job.

Father, Your Word is powerful. Grant me boldness to speak it to those who need to know You and then get out of the way and let it work. May my pride not hinder Your Spirit's activity in other's lives. In Jesus' name, **Amen.**

1221 I Cor. 2:2
1222 I Cor. 3:6
1223 Exo.4:10

The Word of God is...Our Link to Know God

"Establish Your word to Your servant as that which produces reverence for You." Ps. 19:38

What kind of a father would God be if He just left us to fend for ourselves? We hear of fathers abandoning their children all the time. Life gets tough. The kids are out of control. The pasture looks greener elsewhere. It's a sad consequence of sin. But thankfully someday, hopefully soon, that will all be behind us. Until then, our Father has promised to take care of us and provide for us. There are conditions.

In my house, we have house rules. God has house rules too. There are ten of them and most start with "thou shall not." And just like at my house, if you obey the rules, things go better. Same with God. He is not capricious or arbitrary. He treats all His kids the same, and He expects the same obedience from all of us. Little brother doesn't get away with more (sin) than big sis.

Many of us didn't have the best, or in some cases, any relationship with our earthly father. No role models. God knew that and made it possible for us to know Him. Like with any relationship, it takes time and commitment. The key is in today's verse. We've got to be in the Word to really know God.

God wants a relationship with us. That's why He created us in the first place, so we could experience His glory in eternity. Not because He's an egomaniac and wants little robots worshipping Him, but because He wants to share it with us. That's why He gave us the Bible, so we could get to know Him, respond to His love and mercy for us, and pass it on.

Many of you *are* fathers. Many of you *had* good fathers. Isn't it true that we would do anything for our kids? Why? Because we want them to think highly of us? No. Because we love them. We were created in God's image—with a built-in father's love for our kids.

Some of you may say, "Yeah, but Jesus came and said, '*he who has seen me has seen the Father.*'"[1224] That's true. He said that. But what is one of Jesus' names? Remember this verse, "*In the beginning was the Word, and the Word was with God, and the Word was God...and the Word became flesh and dwelt among us, and we saw His glory.*"[1225] So we have the speaking Word and the written word, double-dipping, so to speak. Maybe because some of us are visual learners, and some have to read and ponder. Isn't God amazing?

No matter what kind of learner you are, you can know God. If you don't know Him and want to, find a good **Bible-believing** church in your area, and talk to the Pastor. Or you can email me (address in the front of the book).

Father, what a wonderful, personal name: Father. Thank You for choosing me to be part of Your forever family. Thanks too for Your Word, which shows me Your heart, Your patience, love, mercy, and so much more. May I show my gratitude by time in it to know You better. In Christ, **Amen.**

1224 Jn. 14:9
1225 Jn. 1:1, 14

The Word of God is...Everlasting

"Heaven and earth will pass away, but My words will not pass away." Mark 13:31

On my dining room table, I have a Bible published in 1884. The leather is cracked in several places and coming off the spine. Some of the extra pages in the front have water damage. But all from Genesis through Revelation is still in good shape. We rarely open it because it may cause more damage. Isn't it interesting how much value is placed on relics, antiquities, and old cars? I wish I still had my '58 Impala and '68 427 Vette. But, just a memory.

It's hard for us to picture anything lasting forever. That's because of the curse of sin this world is under and the law of entropy (the general trend of the universe toward death and disorder). Not so, God's Word. It will not pass away...or change. Can you name one other thing that can claim that?

Jesus is "the Word made flesh," eternal—without beginning, without end. Therefore, the Word is everlasting. With only time and this world as comparisons, how do we comprehend love, joy, peace that never ends?

Not only is God's Word everlasting, it's also *the only pure source of truth* on the planet. The Word said, "*I am **the** way and **the** truth...*,"[1226] not **a** way or **a** truth. Pretty bold claim unless you're God. That's a critical criterion—literally life and death—for something we're committing our eternity to. When you compare other religions to the iron-clad, rock-solid Word of God, you find many things that just don't measure up. They all smack of man's (sinful) desires, e.g., 70 virgins, killing infidels, heaven through good works. When you know God's Word, it's easy to pick out the error. If you don't know the Word, there's no telling what wrong path you may be on.

But as long as you have breath, it's not too late to come to the truth. I believe the fact that you're reading this is God's divine appointment for you. The thing about truth is it never changes. Society changes. Morals change. But sin is still sin, and the truth about it is still the truth. Sin causes death,[1227] spiritual for sure and sometimes physical. Don't wait another day; the end is getting closer when it *will* be too late. "*...it is appointed for men to die once and after this comes judgment.*"[1228] If you don't know Jesus and want to, in the back of this book is a step by step plan to meet Him and trust Him for forgiveness and salvation.

If you do know Jesus, praise God. Thank Him your eternity is secure.[1229] You want to be a wise man? "*He who is wise wins souls.*"[1230] Get busy.

Lord, thank You; your Word anchors my soul, my future. **Amen.**

1226 Jn. 14:6
1227 Rom. 6:23
1228 Heb. 9:27
1229 Jn. 10:29
1230 Prov. 11:30

The Word of God is...Relevant for Today

"...while we look not at the things which are seen, but at the things which are not seen; for the things which are seen are temporal, but the things which are not seen are eternal." II Cor. 4:18

Can we agree that we are all eternal beings? One place or the other, we will all live forever. How long is that? Can we say in general, man lives 70 or 80 years? Is that even a drop in the ocean compared to eternity? With that in mind, ponder these words from C.T. Studd: Only one life, 'twill soon be past, only what's done for Christ will last. [1231]

Today's verse wraps this week in a bow of reality and relevance. What we see will be burned up;[1232] what we can't see (yet) is what's real. Paul could say this with confidence, having been to the third heaven.[1233] Likewise, can you even imagine what must have gone through Elisha's mind when, while he and Elijah were "*going along and talking...a chariot of fire and horses of fire separated the two of them and Elijah went up by a whirlwind to heaven.*[1234] Not something you see every day.

The reason God's Word is relevant today is simple; man's heart hasn't changed since the garden, except maybe to get worse. Also, the devil has strategies to tempt us that continue to work. Why should he change them? Have you ever heard the phrase, "some things never change?" It's usually said in a derogatory way about someone who has a bad attitude. It would be nice if morals never changed. But because they're written in the hearts of sinful man, and society is on a slippery slope of allowing more and more decadence, they are amended (by society) to accommodate the sinful behavior.

When Jesus' disciples asked Him about the end of the age, He foresaw the lawlessness we see today in rioting and looting and said because of it, most people's love will grow cold.[1235] Look around. America has never seen such "in your face" evil, with many in charge doing nothing about it.

Our response to the wickedness all around us should be twofold. First, we should get on our knees and thank God for the confidence that His Word gives us regarding our future and that He is still in control. Second, because the time is short and many still need the gospel message, that should be a priority for us, especially for those in our families that have heard the message over and over and still haven't humbled themselves and come to Jesus.

What are we doing today that will last and be seen beyond the veil?

Father, thank You that neither You nor Your Word changes. And because sin is still sin, Your Word is as timely a solution for sin today as when You wrote it. May I treasure it in my heart because it's true. In Christ, **Amen**.

1231 Charles Thomas Studd 12/2/1860 – 7/16/1931
1232 II Pet. 3:10
1233 II Cor. 12:2
1234 II Kings 2:11
1235 Matt. 24:12

Favorite Verses—Introduction

I'm sure all the verses in the Bible are God's favorites. But there are a number of verses that, over the years, have guided me, pushed me to grow in my faith, and encouraged me to keep going even when things looked dark. I started out thinking I would just do one week on this. But as I began listing my favorites, I couldn't pick just seven.

My prayer as I share them with you, and give you a little peek into my journey, is that God will use these last two weeks to encourage you and give you hope that no matter where you are today, you don't have to stay there. In fact, one of the verses deals with just that...all things are new.

I have written this book with men in mind, but women have provided incredibly positive feedback too. Some have been about the insight it has given them into their man's makeup. Others have told me it hits them where they live too. I am encouraged by that, but what fires my jets is that throughout the writing process, I have been encouraged by the Spirit of God Himself, sometimes in the Word as I'm looking for just the right text, sometimes by His providing an idea when I hit the wall and can't think of the next sentence.

What I've included in the next two weeks of favorite verses is exactly that—verses that have been my companions, some for years, some very recently. My wedding verse is one of the days (nearly 50 years). Another was a great comfort when my 27-year old son was killed (16 years). Some remind me of the greatness of God and draw me into a spirit of worship. Some point my heart to heaven, while many show God's faithfulness until I get there.

You've probably got your own favorites. I hope so. Maybe after reading this section, you'll be prompted to capture your thoughts as a reminder of the God we serve, the God who gives us hope, the God without whose mercy and grace we're forever lost. Sometimes it's easier to share our inner self in the written word rather than orally. Give it a try.

When my kids were little, my wife and I used to motivate them with $.10 for each Bible verse they memorized. I'm sure the little bandits of today would negotiate for more. Whatever the price, it's worth it.

"And without faith, it is impossible to please Him, for he who come to God must believe that He is and that He is a rewarder of those who seek Him." Hebrews 11:6

Week 51 Sunday – Favorite Verses

"In the beginning, God..." Gen. 1:1

What else do I need to know? The way to look at this verse is to conclude that beginning means time as we know it. God was already there. When I try to comprehend that, I always go down a black hole. So I don't go. One thing I learned early in my Christian life was to believe the whole Bible or none of it. I chose the whole. It doesn't make sense to pick and choose sections of Scripture that support my beliefs and reject those that contradict me. Some don't think that way. The problem with that is they are trying to be God. Sorry, there's only one.

The rest of Genesis is a fascinating story of man and his innate sinfulness, including murder (the third person on earth killed the fourth person on earth)[1236] and deceit ("*she is my sister*").[1237] But as a backdrop to all of man's sin and treachery is God's goodness. As early as the very first sin, God informed man of His plan for salvation.[1238] It only took about 1600 years to go from creation to the flood—destruction of everybody on earth except eight people.

In Genesis, we also get a small glimpse of God's ability as a master planner. Joseph was sold into slavery by his brothers over fifteen years before the famine that would bring them to Egypt, where Joseph, as the second-highest ruler in the land,[1239] had a little fun with their grain sacks. Read the whole story in Genesis 42. I believe that orchestrating all the events required to make things appear coincidental is as big a miracle as healing the blind or making the lame walk. No one but God could pull it off. Was it coincidental that the caravan just happened to be passing while Joseph was in the pit? The first of many?

Why is this a favorite verse? With any good story—and the Bible is a true story—you have to have a powerful opening. The first verse tells us this is going to be a story about God. The rest of the verse, "*created the heavens and the earth*" says power (the act of creation) like nothing else could.

In every one of the sixty-six books, God is either the primary character or controlling things behind the scenes. We see His majesty, His omnipotence, His omniscience; we learn of His infinite love, infinite mercy and grace, and His infinite patience with sinful man. And though we don't know it when we open the Bible and read the first verse, each chapter reveals more and more of His character and points us unwaveringly to the cross.

Almighty God, Your character oozes from every page in Your story. May I have a greater appreciation as I seek to know You deeper while reading, meditating, and memorizing it. Thank You that Your message of the cross and salvation through Jesus couldn't be plainer, and You have opened my eyes to the truth contained from cover to cover. In Jesus' name, **Amen.**

1236 Gen. 4:1, 2, 8
1237 Gen. 12:12, 13
1238 Gen. 3:15
1239 Gen. 41:40

Week 51 Monday – Favorite Verses

"Bless the Lord, O my soul! O Lord my God, You are very great; You are clothed with splendor and majesty, covering Yourself with light as with a cloak, ***stretching*** *out heaven like a tent curtain." Ps. 104:1, 2*

One of the things I look forward to in heaven is seeing God's majesty, His glory up close and personal. There are so many verses that paint a glimpse of it, but words fall short of doing it justice. For example, today's verse. What else could you say except "You are very great?" Maybe add a very, very? I'm not proposing changing Scripture, just pointing out how limiting our vocabulary is to describe something indescribable. John, in Revelation, had the same issue.

But, be that as it may, we have enough to imagine with words like splendor and majesty. Then add a covering of light. Wow. For us in Colorado, the summer light shows with the lightning storms against the night sky are beautiful, awesome in power, and a reminder of the God who controls the weather. As amazing as they are, they can't compare to what awaits those who are forgiven in Christ.

Don't you get excited just thinking about seeing God face to face? Paul says, "*…to depart and be with Christ, for that is very much better.*"[1240] It's probably because most of my life is in the rearview mirror, but I am more and more drawn to thinking about heaven, what it will be like, what I'll do there, and what will the reunion with my two kids who preceded me be like.

I know many who read this are younger than I., But this morning, while reading Colossians, God prompted me to add this verse, "*Set your mind on the things above not on the things that are on earth.*"[1241] I believe there are several reasons for this. One, heaven is permanent, the earth is not. Two, we're told to lay up treasures in heaven, not on earth.[1242] Three, focusing on things above keeps us on the narrow path; we're not as susceptible to shiny objects on a different path. Fourth, Paul wrote to Timothy, "*godliness is profitable for all things, since it holds promise for the present life and also for the life to come.*"[1243]

For sure, this life offers much in the way of family, friends, accomplishment, and more. You want to experience it all. Your bucket list is long and challenging. And heaven seems a long way in your future. I'm not trying to discourage you from any of that. But may I suggest a verse to help you make life decisions: "*Whether, then, you eat or drink or whatever you do, do* ***all*** *to the glory of God.*"[1244]

Lord God, Your splendor and majesty exceeds my comprehension, but what I do see causes me to eagerly look forward to our meeting. Help me stay on the narrow path and finish the work You have for me while on earth. **Amen.**

1240 Phil. 1:23
1241 Col. 3:2
1242 Matt. 6:19, 20
1243 I Tim. 4:8
1244 I Cor. 10:31

Week 51 Tuesday – Favorite Verses

"The Lord's lovingkindnesses indeed never cease, for His compassions never fail. They are new every morning. Great is Your faithfulness. 'The Lord is my portion' says my soul, 'therefore I have hope in Him.'" Lam. 3:22-24

The Christian life is built on hope. The Bible tells us, "*...faith is the **assurance** of things hoped for.*"[1245] This verse hits my top ten because it's filled with God's character, a promise for each day, and the confidence I will get what I need (my portion).

Life can have a way of dealing bad cards. People get sick. They die. Finding someone to trust can be a challenge. Jobs come and go. Income can be less come, more go. All levels of government test our resolve to subject ourselves to them.[1246] That's why today's verse is important to our sanity. We're told that God is faithful. Reminds me of Romans 3:4, "*...let God be found true, though every man be found a liar...*"

Hope that is based on wishful thinking isn't hope at all. It's fantasy. How many hope to win the lottery? How many win? But today's verse has a key word: therefore. It means based on all that has just been said, the following is true. So I hope *because* of the Lord's lovingkindnesses, His compassions, and His faithfulness. That places my hope on pretty solid ground.

"Because" is a cousin to therefore. Listen to Paul's encouragement to the Roman Christians. It fits perfectly, "*...tribulation brings about perseverance; and perseverance, proven character; and proven character, hope; and hope does not disappoint, **because** the love of God has been poured out within our hearts through the Holy Spirit who was given to us.*"[1247]

I'm a firm believer that words have meaning, except when I use them to try and make a point during a "discussion" with my wife, words like always and never preceded by the word you. Enough said. But God doesn't hype His Word. He says exactly what He means. Take the word never, for example. His lovingkindnesses **never** cease, His compassions **never** fail. New each day. Never means it ain't gonna happen; not today, not tomorrow, not ever. Remembering that, now that's the way to start a day.

Ever ask yourself, "What is my portion?" (And are there seconds?) When I came across this verse, it hit me between the eyes. A portion can be part of the total or, as in today's case, it ***is*** the total. It's not part of the Lord, it's all of Him. Imputed to me. My allotment. **Never** to be taken away. Hallelujah! Come, Lord Jesus.

Lord, I get excited when Your truth jumps off the page at me. Thank You for Your character, which fills me with hope IN YOU...every morning. I often feel like a kid at Christmas anticipating Your return. May I remain faithful to Your calling and purpose for my life until You come. In Your name, **Amen.**

1245 Heb. 11:1 [emphasis added]
1246 Rom. 13:1
1247 Rom. 5:3-5 [emphasis added]

Week 51 Wednesday – Favorite Verses

"But seek first the kingdom of God and His righteousness and all these things will be added to you." Matt. 6:33

This has been my wife's and my life verse for our marriage. We were both saved when we married, Lin when she was thirteen, I at twenty-two just after separation from the U.S. Army. We met at Bible School in Los Angeles and the rest is history, five decades of it. We came from quite different backgrounds. I grew up in Southern Cal with the beach scene and hot rods. She was raised in Minnesota with mid-western values (and accents). It was good that we didn't meet before I knew the Lord; she wouldn't have had anything to do with me. All God's timing. My life did a complete one-eighty when I met Jesus.

Aside from being our wedding verse, this verse is a favorite because it reminds us to keep things in perspective. In the sermon on the mount, Jesus addresses the crowd's concern over food, drink, and clothing. He assures His listeners that, "*your heavenly Father knows that you need all these things.*"[1248] And what newly married couple isn't concerned about them? But He goes on to say that if we put God first and seek His righteousness, i.e., salvation, God will provide all we need, "*according to His riches in glory in Christ Jesus.*"[1249]

Lin and I have had, what I would judge, more than our share of trials and tragedies. Two of our four kids are waiting for us in heaven. We have been cheated out of a large sum of money. I spent nearly three years recuperating from a motorcycle accident that I didn't cause with no job to go back to. And I could go on and bore you. I say that to say this, God is still on His throne, and He doesn't make mistakes either in content or timing. Tomorrow, the sequel.

On balance sheets, your assets and liabilities equal out. That's why they call it a *balance* sheet. On God's balance sheet, for those of us in Christ, there is only one asset, salvation, and it was placed there by God, and no liabilities; they were deleted at the cross. For those who don't know Christ, the term for their balance sheet is *bankrupt.* No amount of assets (good deeds) can offset the liability of sin. But cheer up. Just like there are companies that will represent you to the tax judge, there is an advocate, Jesus Christ the righteous,[1250] who will represent you before the Judge of the universe.

A good strategy when called for an audit is to approach it humbly, recognizing the auditor has all the power to be lenient or make your life miserable. The same advice goes when approaching God. You *must* come in humility, confessing your sin, and believing that Jesus Christ is the only one to clear your slate. Do that, and "all these things will be added to you."

Father, may I have Your perspective on the things that matter. May the needs of food, drink, and clothing not displace my seeking Your kingdom first. Thank You for providing everything I need every day. In Jesus' name, **Amen.**

1248 Matt. 6:32
1249 Phil. 4:19
1250 I Jn. 2:1

Week 51 Thursday – Favorite Verses

"And we know that God causes all things to work together for good to those who love God, to those who are called according to His purpose." Rom. 8:28

Yesterday, I touched briefly on some of our trials. A little more detail today. Sixteen years ago, my 27-year old son was killed in a motorcycle accident. Thankfully, he knew Jesus as his Savior. The reason today's verse is special is it was one of my son's favorite verses. The picture at the left is of a laminated bookmark I made to give to funeral attendees (over 500).

Hopefully, you can read the small print and see the verse quoted at the bottom. It still brings a tear to my eye even as I write about this. My (our) faith in God is the only thing that got Lin and me through this time. As David said when his son died, "*I will go to him, but he will not return to me.*"[1251] Another reason I look forward to heaven.

Having experienced this once before with our 1-year old daughter, we never thought we'd have to bury a second child. In our grief, we had questions. But not once did we blame God, nor did it shake our faith that He knew what He was doing. The psalmist said, "*...in Your book were all written the days that were ordained for me, when as yet there was not one of them.*"[1252] If I believe the Bible and I do, I have to say this was Dan's appointment to meet God.

Now, there's a qualifier in this verse. And the verse is often misquoted. It is not "all things work together for good." Somehow that negates God's involvement. No, it says, "*God causes* all things to work together for good." But it doesn't stop there. Not all things *are* good. And on their own, they don't somehow magically turn out good. You have to include, "to those who love God, who are called according to His purpose." Death and tragedy are everywhere. It's the consequence of sin. But God's children are not alone to grieve through the difficulty. The Holy Spirit, also known as the *Comforter,* who lives in us, supernaturally empowers us to survive whatever God allows to cross our path. Satan's desire to destroy us is no match for God's power in us. "*Greater is He who is in you than he who is in the world.*"[1253] God is still and always in control. Let's act like we really believe that. Anything less takes away from His glory

Father of Mercy, I trust You for my eternity. But I also trust You for my day-to-day. I know Satan wants to destroy, but You have limited his influence. Thanks for Your power in me to resist him. In Jesus' powerful name, **Amen.**

1251 II Sam. 12:23
1252 Ps. 139:16
1253 I Jn. 4:4

Week 51 Friday – Favorite Verses

"Therefore, if anyone is in Christ, he is a new creature; the old things passed away; behold, new things have come." II Cor. 5:17

I don't know what your background is like, but I've had my share of false starts, missteps along the way, and wrong attitudes to accompany the trip. That's why this verse is special; it reminds me that my old self is dead. I am new from the ground up. Let that sink in. God doesn't just shave a little here a little there from the old model with a little Bondo® and a touch of paint. New. That describes everybody who is "in Christ."

The world will tell you that you can become new on your own, usually with a little help from this product or that diet. We may be able to adjust what our outer man looks like, but apart from the Holy Spirit, we can't do anything about our inner man. That is strictly God's domain. And here's a big problem that keeps people from Christ. We think we can hide our inner man from the world (maybe) and from God (never). Our inner man always gives us away. The Bible says, "*The good man out of the good treasure of his heart brings forth what is good; and the evil man out of the evil treasure brings forth what is evil; for his mouth speaks from that which fills his heart.*"[1254] Watch people's reactions when they're off guard. Their heart will rat them out.

Modern medicine is amazing. We can get new knees, new teeth, a lot of new parts. Some can be slightly used, like kidneys and hearts. Many of these transplants can extend our life. But without Christ, it's just more of the same. In Christ, the old things passed away. They're dead. It may not seem like it when we continue some of our sin habits. The process of putting these habits to death is called sanctification—moving toward righteousness. God imputes Christ's righteousness to us *positionally*, but *practically* we won't be there until we get our new bodies in heaven. Don't be discouraged; the trip is exciting and definitely worth it.

We all like new things, new cars, new houses, new clothes. And often, our focus is on the acquisition of these "shiny objects." What would the church be like today if Christ's body were focused on their new "creatureness" instead of clinging to the world's ways? How would that change our commitment to build each other up and minister to the lost? Remember, all these shiny things are going to burn up anyway. The proof is in the pudding. We're told to examine ourselves to "*see if you are in the faith.*"[1255] What are we looking for? New things (attitudes, desires, habits, etc.) How's your list doing?

Creator God, not only did you create man in Your image, but after the fall, You re-create him (me) and put me on the path to righteousness. Thank You for making the way to You and heaven clearly marked "Jesus." May I focus on the new me, concentrate on the activities that keep me on the path, and not let the shiny objects distract me from the finish line. In Jesus name, **Amen.**

1254 Luke 6:45
1255 II Cor. 3:5

Week 51 Saturday – Favorite Verses

"I can do all things through Him who strengthens me." Phil. 4:13

Self-help books and videos are everywhere. "For three easy payments of $49.95, you can change your life. But wait, there's more." These tactics have got to work, or advertisers would quit using them. There must be a lot of dummies because you can find just about any "Blank" for Dummies you want. I believe one reason these books are so successful is that our public schools fail to prepare kids for real life. Where are the shop classes that teach basic electrical, woodworking, and auto familiarization? When was the last time a clerk counted your change to you? I wonder if they even could without the cash register telling them how much you get. I'm amazed at the answers I can find using Siri on my iPhone. The downside is we lose the ability to do our own research.

Today's verse has the sense of stamina, strength to deal with whatever comes our way, whether prosperity or want. It's not a license to watch and wait for Christ to do something. It's been said that God can't steer a ship anchored in the harbor. The little word "do" is a clue, an exhortation and encouragement to put down the Xbox controls and work your plan.

This is a good spot to plug a parenting tip. One of the best things parents can do for their kids is talk with them. You are the adult they look to, the one from whom acceptance and approval are most important. Use this time to encourage them to stretch, to reach higher, to become the best (whatever) they can be. Reinforce optimism. Negative reinforcement, e.g., "Don't you ever pay attention?" has the opposite effect. Don't let your frustrations influence your conversation with them. And *always* include Jesus in your talks. If it seems natural coming from you, it will be natural to them too. Big responsibility, dads. Don't leave it all to mom. Remember, *you can do all things through Him...*

You may not have mechanical skills and not know where to begin on a home project your wife would like to do. A good place to start is by thinking that if *someone* can do it, *I* can do it. Today's verse says, "all things." Obviously, it doesn't mean brain surgery in your garage. Start small. Little victories can be addictive. Take another step. Then another. Pray for guidance and expect answers. Don't be too proud to ask for help.

The thing about the Bible is every word is true. God wouldn't tell us we can if we really can't. So who do you think is telling us we can't? Yep, you got it. Anything he can do to keep us from believing what the Bible says and acting on it, he'll do. Don't fall for it. Learn from *The Little Engine That Could.*[1256]

Lord Jesus, thank You for the strength and encouragement You provide. Help me remember it when I get down. You haven't abandoned me so I know I can finish what I start. Show me the projects that have Your stamp of approval. In Your powerful name, Jesus, **Amen.**

1256 Watty Piper c1930

Week 52 Sunday – Favorite Verses

"How blessed is the man who does not walk in the counsel of the wicked, nor stand in the path of sinners, nor sit in the seat of the scoffers! But his delight is in the law of the Lord, and in His law he meditates day and night. He will be like a tree firmly planted by streams of water, which yields its fruit in its season and its leaf does not wither; and in whatever he does, he prospers. The wicked are not so…" Ps. 1:1-4a"

If you ever needed a reason to embrace God's Word, don't look any further. Compare and contrast is a technique used to support a point in debate, public speaking, or writing. Here, the Holy Spirit uses it to encourage the man of God by contrasting the haves and have nots of the godly man vis-à-vis the wicked man. The godly man is blessed…if he doesn't hang around or take advice from the wicked, sinners, or scoffers, but takes delight and meditates in God's Word. You'll have to read the rest of verses 4-6 to get the full picture of the "not so." Spoiler alert. It's not good.

Contrast the outcome of the one who is blessed by God with the not so much. One is like a productive, solid tree nourished by streams of water, bearing fruit regularly and not withering. The other is like chaff (seed coverings and other debris separated from the seed in threshing, comparatively worthless). One prospers in whatever he does. The other perishes.

The reason so many are in the "wicked" camp is they have been blinded to the truth. They have heard the gospel and rejected it, or they tell themselves they can decide later they are too busy with idols of self-gratification and apathy. Romans 1:18-32 describes their downward spiral into depravity. I think some of the scariest words in the Bible are, "God gave them over." You'll see this three times in these verses. Men rejected God. The result? God rejected them and "gave them over" first to impurity, next to degrading passions, finally to a depraved mind.

I'm so thankful God has been patient with me on my journey to sanctification, I sometimes feel like the Hebrews being chastised for not growing in their faith and needing milk, not solid food.[1257]

There are many parts of Scripture that compare or contrast the wicked with the godly. It would be a great study to solidify your belief and provide a well-stocked arsenal to combat the accusations of the evil one. Remember Jesus' encounter with Satan? What was His only weapon? Each response started with "it is written." [1258] The Devil gave it his best shot but couldn't fight the Word. Take your stand in the Word and be prepared. You'll have a target on your back.

Lord Jesus, thank You for the example of how to battle the enemy. The sword of the Spirit—the Word of God—is the only effective weapon I have. May I delight and meditate in Your Word, so I'm fully armed for war. In Your name, **Amen.**

1257 Heb. 5:12
1258 Matt. 4:4, 7, 10

"For I am not ashamed of the gospel, for it is the power of God for salvation to everyone who believes, to the Jew first and also to the Greek." Rom. 1:16

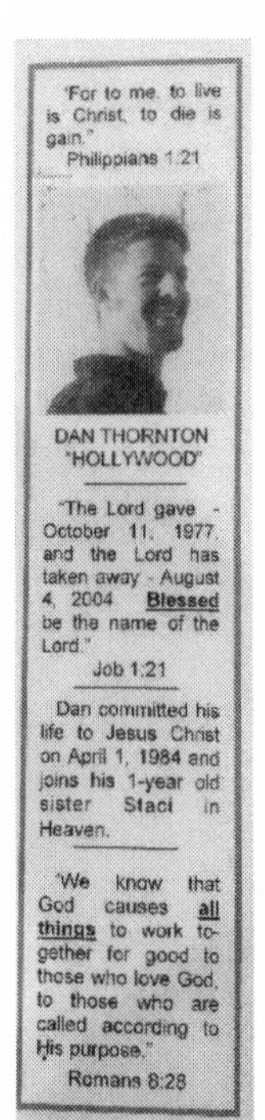

"For to me, to live is Christ, to die is gain."
Philippians 1:21

DAN THORNTON
"HOLLYWOOD"

"The Lord gave - October 11, 1977, and the Lord has taken away - August 4, 2004. **Blessed** be the name of the Lord."
Job 1:21

Dan committed his life to Jesus Christ on April 1, 1984 and joins his 1-year old sister Staci in Heaven.

"We know that God causes **all things** to work together for good to those who love God, to those who are called according to His purpose."
Romans 8:28

You ever think about why we feel shame? I believe it's because we're so caught up in what everybody thinks about us. Truth is, not many people think about us, except to maybe pass judgment on some perceived arbitrary standard we don't meet. Why do we care? Aren't we to be more concerned with the audience of One?

We are told, "*...**always** be ready to make a defense to everyone who asks you to give an account for the hope that is in you.*"[1259] In this country, we don't have to fear beheading or torture for speaking our faith...yet. Not the same in other parts of the world. I wonder if the American church would be more pure, more powerful, more attractive if openly confessing Christ was potentially dangerous for believers.

Yesterday, we saw how Jesus dealt with Satan's temptations. He quoted Scripture to him. Today, we see why it worked. The gospel is called here "the power of God." What better example do we have than creation itself, *spoken* into existence by God. Now *that's* power.

The real power, the power we can't see, is the Holy Spirit using His Word to change lives, to bring a dead soul back to life and add one more voice to the heavenly worship team. We have a part in that when we share the truth of the gospel with another person. It's the power of God in the Word that changes people, not our eloquence, our sales ability, or the bling we wear. Humility, not showy performances, is what draws people to listen to the life-changing message.

Are you ashamed of anything today? Maybe some physical characteristic that someone in the past has made fun of? Just consider their immaturity and thank God for the special mark of ownership He placed on you. Remember that, every time you're tempted to wish you were different. Remember, too, that "*...man looks at the outward appearance, but the Lord looks at the heart.*"[1260] If our heart is right, if we've found peace in Jesus, our inner beauty overshadows any perceived deficiency you think you have on the outside. Let the mirror of God's Word highlight your best feature—your heart.

Father, Your Word is so encouraging and gives me hope that, because my heart is right with You, my warts don't matter to anyone who matters. Besides, You're responsible for my outward appearance, not me. Thank You for the fact that my appearance won't keep me out of heaven. In Christ's name, **Amen.**

1259 I Pet. 3:15 [emphasis added]
1260 I Sam. 16:7

Week 52 Tuesday– Favorite Verses

"Seek the Lord while He may be found; call upon Him while He is near. Let the wicked forsake his way and the unrighteous man his thoughts; and let him return to the Lord, and He will have compassion on him, and to our God, for He will abundantly pardon. 'For My thoughts are not your thoughts, nor are your ways my ways,' declares the Lord. 'For as the heavens are higher than the earth, so are My ways higher than your ways and My thoughts than your thoughts.'" Isa. 55:6-9.

We've all received invitations to special events like weddings, retirement parties, or grand openings of one thing or another. Today's invitation has life-changing implications. We probably haven't been the guest of honor at many gatherings and maybe wouldn't even be missed if we weren't there. But God's invitation is up close and personal. It's got our name on it, not in gold leaf, but indelibly marked with the blood of Christ.

God is calling the wicked and the unrighteous to turn **from** their ways and thoughts and turn **to** the Lord, who promises compassion and pardon. Once in a while we read of someone convicted of a crime and sentenced to life in prison. Recently, I read of one man who had served twenty years and was released because of a wrong conviction. Can you imagine how he felt? He was free.

Likewise, God's compassion and pardon make us free; we are freed from our sin, and God imputes Christ's righteousness to us. The difference is that we are all guilty. There is no wrong conviction. "*For all have sinned and fall short of the glory of God.*"[1261] And there is no lenient sentencing. "*The wages of sin is death...*"[1262] It may be hard to understand how God can forgive our death sentence. But He explains it in our verse. "*My ways are higher than your ways.*" Besides, the sentence of death *was* carried out, just not by us. That's the good news of the gospel; Jesus Christ died in our place. All we have to do is forsake our wicked ways and unrighteous thoughts and return to the Lord.

My wife is a coupon guru. We're always eating with a BOGO offer (buy one get one). Most all of them have expiration dates in the small print. God's offer is not a BOGO; in fact it is totally free, doesn't cost a dime. There is an expiration date, though. "*...while He may be found...while He is near.*" I don't know when that is. It could be the day you die or sometime sooner. I *do* know the Bible says, "*...it is appointed for men to die once and after this comes judgment.*"[1263] If you're one who's waiting for tomorrow, don't. God **will** have compassion; He **will** pardon. "Seek" and "forsake" are action verbs. Make it happen...today.

Lord, thank You for the promise of compassion and pardon. Help me trust You even though I don't understand how You could love and forgive me. I want, I need to be free of my sin. I come to You in Jesus' name. **Amen.**

1261 Rom. 3:23
1262 Rom. 6:23
1263 Heb. 9:27

Week 52 Wednesday– Favorite Verses

"...you were sealed in Him with the Holy Spirit of promise, who is given as a pledge of our inheritance..." Eph. 1:13, 14

Though this verse alludes to our inheritance, something we should all be interested in, it's about assurance. A pledge is a promise, an oath, a commitment. In courts, we swear to tell the truth, though I wonder how many do, even under the threat of perjury. We used to pledge allegiance to our flag in school and other public settings. Not so much anymore.

This verse is a favorite because of the assurance of my place in heaven. When I see the word sealed, I think of the seven seals in Revelation. Nobody but the Lamb could open them.[1264] I have been sealed and am waiting for the Lamb to come get me and receive my inheritance. This verse is like having two passwords to get into my bank account. "Pledge" and "sealed," as if with God, one weren't enough.

I'm sure the devil knows this verse. He probably knows them all. And just like when he tempted Jesus after 40 days and tried to misuse Scripture to trick the Lord, he does the same to us, hoping we're not as armed as we should be. Consider his tactic in the garden. He questioned God's command, "*Did God really say...*"[1265] Apparently Eve didn't know exactly what God had said, since she elaborated by adding, "*or touch it*" to the command not to eat.

We are secure in our salvation, as evidenced by today's verse and others. But that doesn't stop Satan from trying to either discourage us or make us wildly successful, anything to sideline us and keep us from Jesus' charge, "*...you shall be My witnesses...*"[1266]

Assurance begets confidence. If we're flagging in our confidence, it could be we're striving in our own strength. Get back to basics. The rest of the verse in the paragraph above says, "*...you will receive power when the Holy Spirit has come upon you...*" God's power. The Holy Spirit's power. If we're in a right relationship with Jesus, we have the Holy Spirit (and His power) living in us. If we can grasp the implication of that, nothing should stand in the way of doing our job. We're saved. We're sealed. And delivery is on its way.

Father, Your Word is full of assurance, for Your faithfulness, our future, and Your power in us to finish strong. May I embrace the knowledge of Your Word so that I'm equipped and confident for any battle ahead. In Jesus' name, **Amen.**

1264 Rev. 5:5
1265 Gen. 3:1
1266 Acts 1:8

Week 52 Thursday– Favorite Verses

"...to obtain an inheritance which is imperishable and undefiled and will not fade away, reserved in heaven for you..." I Pet. 1:4

Yesterday, we skimmed over our inheritance. Today is its day, and we're continuing to look at it in view of its reality. Many of us have had parents die and leave us an inheritance, sometimes a large one, sometimes next to nothing. But we get the picture. We know that an inheritance is something somebody else earned that we benefit from. Our heavenly inheritance is exactly that. Something Jesus earned and is sharing with us.

Everybody knows about Fort Knox. It is often referred to as the "gold standard" of security. But even at that, it doesn't compare with the security of heaven: imperishable (won't ever be devalued), undefiled (by thieves or embezzlers), will not fade away (no moths or rust), and reserved...for you.

You ever make a reservation at a popular restaurant, only to get there and be told there's a 2-hour wait, or worse, they don't have it at all? We're told a) we *have* an inheritance, b) it's *permanent*, c) it's got *our name* on it. That sounds like a guarantee to me.

When my kids were little, we used to open one present on Christmas Eve; the rest had to wait 'til the next morning. We never had a problem getting them out of bed on that morning. I wonder if we'll get all of our inheritance when we get there or if it'll be spread out over eternity.

What exactly is our inheritance? I can only answer in general terms:

Eternal Life	*Luke 18:18*
A blessing	*I Pet. 3:9*
Promises	*Heb. 6:12*
Honor	*Prov. 3:5*
Good	*Prov 28:10*
The earth (meek)	*Matt. 5:5*
The land	*Ps. 37:29*

Whatever it is, remember we don't deserve anything. It's only and all because of our Father's great love and compassion which He chose to freely give to all who believe in *the work* Jesus did on the cross...alone.

What can we bring to God as a thank you for all He's done? The prophet Micah answers that for us, "*He has told you, O man, what is good; and what does the Lord require of you but to **do justice**, to **love kindness**, and to **walk humbly** with your God.*"[1267]

Father, I have much to look forward to in heaven. Eternity with You is all I need. But because of Your nature, You've prepared things beyond my imagination to bless me with. Thank You for the assurance in Your Word that gives me confidence to stay in the fight for souls. In Christ's name, **Amen.**

1267 Mic. 6:8

Week 52 Friday – Favorite Verses

"Your commandments make me wiser than my enemies, for they are ever mine. I have more insight than all my teachers, for Your testimonies are my meditation. I understand more than the aged, because I have observed Your precepts." Ps. 119:98-100

In these three verses, the little word "for" can also be translated "because." All wisdom, knowledge, and truth belong to the Lord. And even God's foolishness is wiser than man.[1268] The psalmist attributes his wisdom, insight, and understanding all to God's Word because he spends time in it. Because he loves it. There's a huge takeaway for us in these verses. You want wisdom and understanding? Read, meditate, and practice God's Word.

Many cultures honor their aging population for their supposed wisdom. Keeping God's precepts (commands) gives us more understanding than they. Please understand, I am not putting down older folk (I am one). I'm just putting into perspective what God's Word says. God's wisdom *always* trumps man's.

Don't confuse knowledge with wisdom. The world is full of people with lots of knowledge but no common sense. "*...Knowledge makes arrogant, but love edifies.*"[1269] Knowledge is a good thing to have.[1270] But without the wisdom of how and when to use it, it's "noisy gong or a clanging cymbal."[1271]

This book has been all about God's Word. In addition to the daily verse, there's a reason I've used over 1000 Biblical references throughout, many of which are used in several character qualities. As we saw in the verse of the day in Week 50—Wednesday, God's Word is **active** and **effective**. My goal has been to get you excited about the practicality of God's Word in your everyday life, to get you to see it as more than a text for a Sunday sermon, something that can guide your day, help you make right decisions, remind you of what you have waiting for you, and much more. It's been a labor of love for me, sometimes heavy on the labor, sometimes the love.

I hope you have gotten something from these pages that reinforces or rekindles *your* love for God and His Word, something that can make a difference in your life to the people who are watching, who know of your testimony. If it has, I'd love to hear from you. Email me at the address in the front of the book.

Lord God, thank You for providing the instruction manual that introduced me to You, that paints a picture of Your awesomeness, and that gives me hope for each day and for eternity. May Your Word be deeply rooted in my heart, so I don't sin against You, so I have a filter for my mouth, and when I do speak, it edifies and gives grace to those who hear. In Jesus' name, **Amen.**

1268 I Cor. 1:25
1269 I Cor. 8:1
1270 Prov. 19:2
1271 I Cor. 13:1

"He who testifies to these things says, 'Yes, I am coming quickly.' Amen. Come, Lord Jesus." Rev. 22:20

I've saved the best for last. What do we do when guests are coming? We tidy up, put clean sheets on the bed, stock up the cupboards and fridge. In a word, prepare. Why? So we're ready and not caught off guard. We do the same when catching a plane. The irony is we *know* the schedule, and yet sometimes still have to rush to not miss our flight.

Jesus said He was coming quickly…2,000 years ago. Not our timetable, His. You know, a day is as a thousand years, etc. So, on His clock, it's only been a couple days. I'm sure every generation since His ascension thought they were living in the time when He would return. I know I do.

Looking at the long timeline, what's our lesson? First, He'll come when ***He's*** ready, when "*…the fullness of the Gentiles has come in.*"[1272] Second, ***we*** must be ready; it's going to happen in the twinkling of an eye.[1273] There will be no warning. One second, we'll be going about our business, the next, we'll be with the Lord in the air.[1274]

How do we get ready when we don't know His ETA? The practical answer is we live in a state of readiness, not assuming we have another day, another hour. The spiritual answer is we make sure our relationship to Christ is real, that we've seen changes (remember, we're *new* creatures) and have fruit to prove we've been changed. Then we go about our business as usual.

I am not a prophet, nor do I claim any special knowledge regarding when Christ will return. I can only read what Scripture says about it. Jesus let the Pharisees and Sadducees have it when they asked Him for a sign, and He said, "*Do you know how to discern the appearance of the sky, but cannot discern the signs of the times?*"[1275] The times we are living in certainly point to something on a worldwide scale that hasn't happened before. Does that mean the end is near? I don't know. I hope so.

And that's what we have to cling to: HOPE. Jesus said He's coming quickly. We've already seen it's been 2,000 years. Other than chronological time, the other meaning of quickly is like a surprise attack. Nobody knows when, but readiness assures success. In this case, if we're ready, if we have been saved through Christ's blood, we won't miss our flight. Hope to see you there.

Lord Jesus, this is such good news it's hard not to be excited with anticipation of Your return. Thank You for the salvation You bought for me with Your blood. I'm ready when You are. Come, Lord Jesus. **Amen.**

1272 Rom: 11:25
1273 I Cor. 15:52
1274 I Thess. 4:17
1275 Matt. 16:3

Steps to Salvation

"He [God] says, 'At the acceptable time I listened to you, and on the day of salvation I helped you.' Behold, now is 'the acceptable time,' behold, now is 'the day of salvation.'" II Cor. 6:2

If you're reading this, I believe God is calling you to Himself. He wants a relationship with you, wants to fellowship with you for eternity. There is no magic formula, no special words to recite, and no number of "things" you can do to bring about this relationship. **God has done it all** through His son, Jesus Christ.

The following steps are intended to help you understand your situation, from God's perspective, and open your eyes to the truth of Jesus' words, "*I am **the** way and **the** truth and **the** life, **no one** comes to the Father but through Me.*"[1276] There is a sample prayer at the end that, if you are truly repentant, you can offer to God. The specific words aren't important; it's the humility in your heart that God looks at.

1. There is a God. He is holy and hates sin. "*You shall be holy, for I am holy.*" I Peter 1:16.

2. Your sin separated you from God and deserves death.
"*For **all** have sinned and **fall short** of the glory of God*" Rom. 3:23
"*For **the wages of sin is death**, but the **free gift** of God is **eternal life** in Christ Jesus our Lord.*" Rom. 6:23.

3. God loves ***you*** so much He sent Jesus to earth to die ***in your place***, to pay the penalty you could never pay on your own.
"*For God **so loved** the world that **He gave** His only begotten Son, that **whoever believes** in Him shall not perish, but have eternal life.*" Jn. 3:16

4. Good works, good attitudes, and good deeds ***can't*** solve your sin problem. You must believe that Jesus is THE ***ONLY*** WAY back to God, and trust that His death *on your behalf* erased *your* debt.
"*For **by grace** you have been **saved** through faith; and that **not of yourselves**, it is the **gift of God; not as a result of works**, so that no one may boast.*" Eph. 2:8,9.

5. Tell God you're sorry for your sin (repent) and you want to turn your life around.
"*...if you confess with your mouth Jesus as Lord, and believe in your heart that God raised Him from the dead, **you will be saved;***" Rom. 10:9.

6. Believe that God has forgiven you and restored you to fellowship with Him.
"T*herefore there is now **no condemnation** for those who are in Christ Jesus.*" Rom. 8:1
"*If we confess our sins, **He is faithful** and righteous **to forgive** us our sins and to cleanse us from **all** unrighteousness.*" I Jn. 1:9

1276 Jn. 14:6

> "*These things I have written to you who believe in the name of the Son of God, so that* ***you may know*** *that* ***you have eternal life.***" I Jn. 5:13

The devil will try to tell you that nothing happened, that you're still the same worthless sinner you always were. Don't believe his lies. But you will know because you (and everybody else) will see a change in your attitudes, your desires, and you may even be drawn to different companions.

Jesus told a parable about a sower and four different results from the same seed. Only one of four took root and grew. Make sure you see the results of a changed life. If nothing changes and lasts, come back to this list and examine yourself to see if it was real. Read the whole story about the sower and seeds in Luke 8:4-8.

7. Tell everyone what has just happened to you.
   You Believe in Jesus Christ as your Savior
   You are a child of God
   Your sins are forgiven
   Your relationship with God has been restored
   Your eternity in heaven is guaranteed
8. Find a **Bible-believing** church and **become involved** with fellowship and service. Ask the pastor about believer's baptism and plan for this outward display of the inward change that has taken place.
9. Spend time daily reading the Bible and talking to God (prayer).

Lord God, I confess that I am a sinner and my sin has separated me from You, and there's nothing I can do on my own to change that. I believe that Jesus came to earth and died on the cross for my sin and that He is the only way back to You. I repent and want to receive Your free gift of salvation in Jesus. Thank You for hearing my prayer. **Amen.**

Reference	Week	Page
Acts 1:8	52	364
Acts 10:43	40	280
Acts 13:22	27	186
Acts 13:22	40	280
Acts 13:22	41	284
Acts 13:22	47	323
Acts 17:11	2	8
Acts 2:39	30	207
Acts 5:1-11	22	153
Acts 5:1-11	36	250
Acts 5:3-10	31	215
Acts 6:8	4	25
Acts 8:1	47	323
Acts 8:1-3; 9:1, 2	26	179
Col. 2:13, 14	26	181
Col. 3:1	26	177
Col. 3:12	18	124
Col. 3:12-14	26	179
Col. 3:16	37	255
Col. 3:2	3	18
Col. 3:2	17	119
Col. 3:2	23	161
Col. 3:2	38	261
Col. 3:2	38	264
Col. 3:2	51	355
Col. 3:23	38	262
Col. 3:23, 24	15	104
Col. 3:5	20	137
Col. 4:5	48	336
Dan 9:23	9	58
Dan. 3:24, 25	34	236
Dan. 4:29-33	40	279
Dan. 4:30	25	175
Dan. 6:10	9	58
Deut. 24:16	32	224

Reference	Week	Page
Deut. 30:19	30	205
Deut. 31:6	7	45
Deut. 31:6	38	265
Deut. 32:16	48	335
Deut. 32:35	16	107
Deut. 32:35	24	168
Deut. 32:35	26	178
Deut. 32:35	29	199
Deut. 32:35	39	269
Deut. 32:35, 36	44	307
Deut. 4:24	41	284
Deut. 5:29	20	135
Deut. 6:6, 7	5	35
Deut. 6:6, 7	23	158
Deut. 7:9	32	221
Deut. 8:17, 18	8	50
Deut. 8:18	18	123
Deut. 8:3	21	145
Eccl. 4:9, 10	49	339
Eccl. 4:9-12	4	26
Eccl. 4:9-12	15	100
Eccl. 4:9-12	34	235
Eccl. 5:4	22	149
Eccl. 5:4	41	282
Eccl. 5:4	45	312
Eph. 1:13	34	238
Eph. 1:3	35	241
Eph. 1:4	33	231
Eph. 1:4	42	288
Eph. 2:10	3	15
Eph. 2:10	30	204
Eph. 2:8, 9	29	202
Eph. 2:8, 9	30	204
Eph. 2:8, 9	44	303
Eph. 2:8, 9	45	309
Eph. 2:9	40	274

Reference	Week	Page
Eph. 3:16-19	26	181
Eph. 4:14	32	221
Eph. 4:29	21	145
Eph. 4:29	37	256
Eph. 4:29	47	324
Eph. 4:30	36	252
Eph. 4:30	49	341
Eph. 5:1	18	122
Eph. 5:16	48	336
Eph. 5:18	24	162
Eph. 5:19	46	317
Eph. 5:2	25	171
Eph. 5:20	1	7
Eph. 5:28, 29	31	213
Eph. 5:4	21	145
Eph. 5:6	11	76
Eph. 6:10, 11	38	263
Eph. 6:10-17	30	209
Eph. 6:10-17	35	244
Eph. 6:11	39	267
Eph. 6:11, 13-17	38	263
Eph. 6:11-13	22	148
Eph. 6:12	15	103
Eph. 6:12	30	207
Eph. 6:12	32	221
Eph. 6:12	38	263
Eph. 6:12	41	285
Eph. 6:13-17	49	341
Eph. 6:14-17	12	83
Eph. 6:14-18	32	222
Eph. 6:17	2	9
Eph. 6:17	25	172
Eph. 6:17	45	313
Eph. 6:2	37	253
Est. 8:4	46	318
Ex. 20:14	2	12

Reference	Week	Page
Exo. 20:15	2	12
Exo. 20:16	41	283
Exo. 20:3	0	-1
Exo. 20:5	41	284
Exo. 3:14	48	330
Exo. 32:1	40	275
Exo. 32:28	40	275
Exo. 33:19, 20	48	331
Exo.4:10	50	349
Exod. 4:14	4	25
Ezek. 1:26, 28	48	331
Ezek. 22:30	30	209
Ezek. 22:30	39	271
Ezek. 25:14	39	269
Ezek. 36:26	5	30
Gal. 1:6-10	2	14
Gal. 1:7	48	333
Gal. 4:6	32	222
Gal. 5:16	13	86
Gal. 5:16	24	162
Gal. 5:16	24	168
Gal. 5:16	26	182
Gal. 5:16	35	242
Gal. 5:22	19	132
Gal. 5:22	24	162
Gal. 5:22	36	248
Gal. 5:22, 23	41	281
Gal. 5:7, 9	36	250
Gal. 6:4	33	228
Gal. 6:7	22	153
Gal. 6:7	35	239
Gal. 6:7	37	255
Gal. 6:9	28	196
Gal. 6:9	38	265
Gal.6:7	24	163
Gen. 1:26	6	41

Reference	Week	Page
Gen. 1:31	30	208
Gen. 12:1	4	25
Gen. 12:12, 13	51	354
Gen. 2:15	48	336
Gen. 2:18	13	90
Gen. 20:2	47	323
Gen. 22:13	45	315
Gen. 3:1	18	126
Gen. 3:1	28	195
Gen. 3:1	33	225
Gen. 3:1	37	253
Gen. 3:1	52	364
Gen. 3:12, 13	30	206
Gen. 3:15	51	354
Gen. 3:17, 18	30	208
Gen. 3:17-19	48	336
Gen. 4:1, 2, 8	51	354
Gen. 41	9	63
Gen. 41:40	51	354
Gen. 5:32	42	291
Gen. 6:15	42	291
Gen. 6:18	42	291
Gen. 6:5	20	138
Gen. 6:5	40	275
Gen. 6:5	50	346
Gen. 6:7, 9	42	291
Gen. 7:13	42	291
Gen. 7:6	42	291
Gen. 9:15	30	208
Gen.1:31	37	254
Gen.41:40:43	25	173
Gen.6:5, 13	42	291
Hab. 2:3	33	231
Heb. 10:17	26	178
Heb. 10:24	20	137
Heb. 10:24, 25	4	25

Reference	Week	Page
Heb. 10:25	28	196
Heb. 10:25	46	320
Heb. 10:26, 27	31	213
Heb. 10:31	39	269
Heb. 10:31	44	302
Heb. 11:1	36	249
Heb. 11:1	51	356
Heb. 11:16	30	205
Heb. 11:16	46	322
Heb. 11:25	36	246
Heb. 11:25	45	311
Heb. 11:6	5	35
Heb. 11:6	44	304
Heb. 11:6	46	320
Heb. 11:9, 10	16	109
Heb. 12:10	28	193
Heb. 12:10	31	211
Heb. 12:11	30	21
Heb. 12:11	34	236
Heb. 12:11	37	255
Heb. 12:15	12	82
Heb. 12:15	24	164
Heb. 12:15	24	168
Heb. 12:2	34	233
Heb. 12:25	42	294
Heb. 12:3	34	238
Heb. 12:4	31	217
Heb. 12:5, 6	23	159
Heb. 12:6	23	156
Heb. 12:6	24	164
Heb. 12:6	28	193
Heb. 12:6	39	269
Heb. 12:6	47	327
Heb. 13:15	46	320
Heb. 13:5	15	101
Heb. 13:5	17	118

Reference	Week	Page
Heb. 13:5	23	155
Heb. 13:5	23	161
Heb. 13:5	29	201
Heb. 13:5	34	236
Heb. 13:5	34	238
Heb. 13:8	9	57
Heb. 13:8	18	122
Heb. 13:8	37	257
Heb. 13:8	42	291
Heb. 13:8	50	346
Heb. 13:8, 9	39	271
Heb. 2:10	35	241
Heb. 2:9	35	241
Heb. 4:12	11	74
Heb. 5:12	52	361
Heb. 5:8	31	213
Heb. 7:25	49	339
Heb. 9:27	30	205
Heb. 9:27	49	342
Heb. 9:27	50	351
Heb. 9:27	52	363
I Chron. 28:9	32	220
I Cor. 1:20	29	200
I Cor. 1:25	52	366
I Cor. 10:12	1	5
I Cor. 10:13	2	13
I Cor. 10:13	2	14
I Cor. 10:13	8	50
I Cor. 10:13	8	54
I Cor. 10:13	18	123
I Cor. 10:13	21	142
I Cor. 10:13	23	155
I Cor. 10:13	32	221
I Cor. 10:13	34	236
I Cor. 10:13	38	265
I Cor. 10:31	21	146

Reference	Week	Page
I Cor. 10:31	30	206
I Cor. 10:31	31	212
I Cor. 10:31	34	232
I Cor. 10:31	34	237
I Cor. 10:31	36	252
I Cor. 10:31	42	290
I Cor. 10:31	45	314
I Cor. 10:31	48	331
I Cor. 10:31	51	355
I Cor. 10:4	32	224
I Cor. 11:1	18	122
I Cor. 11:28	46	321
I Cor. 11:3	38	260
I Cor. 12:11	20	139
I Cor. 12:11	48	334
I Cor. 12:14-26	38	262
I Cor. 12:26	33	227
I Cor. 12:28	33	227
I Cor. 12:4	3	18
I Cor. 12:9	36	249
I Cor. 13:1	52	366
I Cor. 13:11	28	189
I Cor. 13:4	24	162
I Cor. 14:33	12	81
I Cor. 15:19	31	215
I Cor. 15:19	34	237
I Cor. 15:33	32	222
I Cor. 15:33	35	243
I Cor. 15:33	37	255
I Cor. 15:33	39	270
I Cor. 15:52	52	367
I Cor. 16:13	25	169
I Cor. 16:13	30	207
I Cor. 16:13	36	248
I Cor. 16:13	38	260
I Cor. 16:13	38	264

Reference	Week	Page
I Cor. 16:13	47	327
I Cor. 2:14	39	270
I Cor. 2:2	19	130
I Cor. 2:2	50	349
I Cor. 2:9	23	157
I Cor. 2:9	30	208
I Cor. 2:9	30	209
I Cor. 2:9	36	249
I Cor. 3:11	5	33
I Cor. 3:11-15	20	139
I Cor. 3:12-15	27	184
I Cor. 3:6	43	298
I Cor. 3:6	50	349
I Cor. 3:7	24	166
I Cor. 3:7	40	280
I Cor. 4:6	12	81
I Cor. 4:7	1	7
I Cor. 4:7	6	37
I Cor. 4:7	12	82
I Cor. 4:7	21	141
I Cor. 4:7	21	146
I Cor. 4:7	25	174
I Cor. 4:7	25	175
I Cor. 4:7	30	210
I Cor. 4:7	36	251
I Cor. 4:7	43	295
I Cor. 4:7	43	297
I Cor. 4:7	44	306
I Cor. 5:9-11	47	325
I Cor. 6:12	35	241
I Cor. 6:18-20	35	244
I Cor. 6:19	48	333
I Cor. 6:19,20	1	4
I Cor. 6:20	30	206
I Cor. 8:1	34	232
I Cor. 8:1	44	303

Reference	Week	Page
I Cor. 8:1	52	366
I Cor. 9:24	34	233
I Cor. 9:24-26	5	35
I Cor. 9:27	35	244
I Cor.11:1	25	170
I Jn. 1:7	32	223
I Jn. 1:8	32	223
I Jn. 2:1	51	357
I Jn. 2:15	28	193
I Jn. 4:1	39	270
I Jn. 4:4	51	358
I Jn. 5:12, 13	36	247
I John 1:9	21	142
I Kin. 15:3	16	111
I Kin. 19:11,12	2	9
I Kings 4:30, 31	34	235
I Pet. 2:19, 20	33	227
I Pet. 2:21	33	229
I Pet. 2:21	47	323
I Pet. 3:15	4	25
I Pet. 3:15	6	38
I Pet. 3:15	42	288
I Pet. 3:15	52	362
I Pet. 3:4	18	126
I Pet. 3:7	13	90
I Pet. 3:7	26	177
I Pet. 3:9	29	198
I Pet. 4:12	35	244
I Pet. 4:8	26	178
I Pet. 4:8	26	182
I Pet. 5:5	20	136
I Pet. 5:5	33	228
I Pet. 5:6	20	134
I Pet. 5:6	25	169
I Pet. 5:6	25	173
I Pet. 5:6	47	323

Reference	Week	Page
I Pet. 5:6	47	329
I Pet. 5:7	6	36
I Pet. 5:7	7	46
I Pet. 5:7	23	155
I Pet. 5:8	28	191
I Pet. 5:8	29	203
I Pet. 5:8	30	207
I Pet. 5:8	37	258
I Pet. 5:8	42	294
I Sam. 13:14	16	111
I Sam. 13:34	41	284
I Sam. 15:20, 21	36	250
I Sam. 15:22	7	43
I Sam. 15:22	36	250
I Sam. 15:22	46	319
I Sam. 15:23	31	213
I Sam. 15:29	30	210
I Sam. 16:7	8	53
I Sam. 16:7	20	135
I Sam. 16:7	46	321
I Sam. 16:7	52	362
I Sam. 17:36	16	111
I Sam. 18-20	27	189
I Thes. 4:16	46	316
I Thes. 4:17	52	367
I Thes. 5:17	46	320
I Thes. 5:18	40	276
I Thess. 2:5-7	18	121
I Thess. 4:1	9	59
I Thess. 5:17	1	7
I Tim 6:4-10	18	123
I Tim. 2:4	41	284
I Tim. 3:2, 3	48	333
I Tim. 4:12	35	242
I Tim. 4:12	47	327
I Tim. 4:8	51	355

Reference	Week	Page
I Tim. 5:17	48	333
I Tim. 5:22	4	28
I Tim. 5:8	48	336
I Tim. 6:10	8	56
I Tim. 6:20	47	325
I Tim. 6:7	27	186
I Tim. 6:8	17	113
I Tim. 6:8	40	279
I Tim. 6:9	27	186
II Chr. 16:9	2	12
II Chron. 15:7	18	123
II Chron. 15:7	29	199
II Chron. 16:9	7	48
II Chron. 16:9	14	95
II Chron. 16:9	25	171
II Chron. 16:9	31	215
II Chron. 16:9	33	225
II Chron. 16:9	34	232
II Chron. 16:9	34	238
II Chron. 16:9	41	284
II Chron. 16:9	47	328
II Chron. 16:9	48	336
II Cor. 11:14	4	27
II Cor. 11:14, 15	12	81
II Cor. 12:2	50	352
II Cor. 13:5	23	160
II Cor. 13:5	26	180
II Cor. 13:5	33	229
II Cor. 13:5	36	248
II Cor. 13:5	46	321
II Cor. 2:11	39	267
II Cor. 3:5	51	359
II Cor. 5:1	36	249
II Cor. 5:10	27	184
II Cor. 5:17	23	160
II Cor. 5:17	30	206

Reference	Week	Page
II Cor. 5:17	35	241
II Cor. 5:17	37	257
II Cor. 5:20	4	25
II Cor. 5:20	29	198
II Cor. 5:20	41	281
II Cor. 5:5	8	56
II Cor. 6:14	41	285
II Cor. 6:14-18	37	258
II Cor. 6:17	21	144
II Cor. 6:17	35	243
II Cor. 6:17	41	285
II Cor. 6:2	33	231
II Cor. 7:10	16	110
II Cor. 9:15	26	181
II Cor. 9:15	36	246
II Jn. 1:7	37	255
II Kin. 6:17	12	81
II Kings 2:11	50	352
II Pet. 2:1-3	47	329
II Pet. 3:10	42	291
II Pet. 3:10	50	352
II Pet. 3:11	32	218
II Pet. 3:17	29	203
II Pet. 3:17	39	267
II Pet. 3:18	28	190
II Pet. 3:3	31	216
II Pet. 3:3, 4	46	316
II Pet. 3:8	33	231
II Pet. 3:9	14	93
II Pet. 3:9	22	153
II Pet. 3:9	25	173
II Pet. 3:9	25	175
II Pet. 3:9	33	231
II Sam. 11:4, 15	47	323
II Sam. 12:22, 23	29	203
II Sam. 12:23	51	358

Reference	Week	Page
II Sam. 9:3-7	27	189
II Thes. 1:4	34	238
II Thes. 2:11, 12	7	44
II Thes. 3:13	28	196
II Thes. 3:16	37	259
II Tim. 2:15	23	160
II Tim. 2:15	28	190
II Tim. 2:15	35	244
II Tim. 2:15	39	268
II Tim. 2:16	39	268
II Tim. 2:22	37	254
II Tim. 2:25	41	281
II Tim. 2:3	15	103
II Tim. 2:4	5	29
II Tim. 2:5	34	233
II Tim. 3:13-17	28	195
II Tim. 3:1-5	24	167
II Tim. 3:16	12	80
II Tim. 3:16	13	88
II Tim. 3:16	35	241
II Tim. 3:16	48	335
II Tim. 3:2	47	325
II Tim. 3:2-5	31	216
II Tim. 3:2-5	32	224
II Tim. 4:2	42	290
II Tim. 4:8	46	322
II Tim.4:2	23	160
Isa. 1:18	5	34
Isa. 1:18	33	225
Isa. 1:19	33	225
Isa. 42:8	25	175
Isa. 42:8	30	210
Isa. 42:8, 11	40	280
Isa. 43:1	17	117
Isa. 43:1	20	135
Isa. 43:1	42	288

Reference	Week	Page
Isa. 43:1	46	318
Isa. 43:7	48	331
Isa. 46:10	43	298
Isa. 46:10	44	305
Isa. 48:11	43	295
Isa. 48:11	43	297
Isa. 51:7	2	9
Isa. 51:7	30	21
Isa. 52:5	48	330
Isa. 53:10	35	241
Isa. 55:16	39	269
Isa. 55:6	46	318
Isa. 55:7	41	286
Isa. 55:7	43	298
Isa. 55:8	41	282
Isa. 6:5-7	18	125
Isa. 6:8	30	209
Isa. 61:1	26	179
Isa. 61:10	46	321
Isa. 61:1-3	11	76
Isa. 64:6	5	34
Isa. 64:6	36	247
Isa. 64:6	47	326
Isa. 64:6	50	347
Isa.64:6	40	280
Jas. 1:13	29	201
Jas. 1:17	1	7
Jas. 1:17	9	57
Jas. 1:17	12	82
Jas. 1:17	16	107
Jas. 1:17	19	131
Jas. 1:17	29	201
Jas. 1:17	40	274
Jas. 1:17	40	279
Jas. 1:2	20	137
Jas. 1:2	23	157

Reference	Week	Page
Jas. 1:2	34	233
Jas. 1:2	34	236
Jas. 1:2	36	252
Jas. 1:2	38	265
Jas. 1:2	40	279
Jas. 1:20	45	314
Jas. 1:2-4	8	51
Jas. 1:2-4	8	52
Jas. 1:2-4	34	236
Jas. 1:5	29	200
Jas. 1:5	43	296
Jas. 1:5	45	315
Jas. 1:6	44	304
Jas. 1:6	45	315
Jas. 1:8	44	304
Jas. 2:13	29	201
Jas. 2:23	35	244
Jas. 2:23	47	323
Jas. 2:3	46	321
Jas. 3:1	39	267
Jas. 3:1	41	284
Jas. 3:1	47	329
Jas. 3:1	48	335
Jas. 3:15	44	308
Jas. 3:17	35	244
Jas. 3:8	37	256
Jas. 4:1, 2	37	259
Jas. 4:14	31	213
Jas. 4:14	31	214
Jas. 4:14	38	261
Jas. 4:2	19	133
Jas. 4:3	19	133
Jas. 4:3	45	315
Jas. 4:4	27	187
Jas. 4:7	4	27
Jas. 4:7	30	207

Reference	Week	Page
Jas. 5:16	42	289
Jas. 5:3	45	309
Jas.1:17	19	128
Jas.2:26	36	252
Jer. 16:17	31	212
Jer. 17:9	25	172
Jer. 17:9	32	223
Jer. 29:11	41	284
Jer. 31:34	16	110
Job 1:3	9	58
Job 1:8, 12	23	159
Job 1:9-11	35	244
Job 13:15	11	77
Job 2:10	16	107
Job 2:10	34	237
Job 2:9	34	237
Job 20:5	32	220
Job 28:24	32	224
Job 31:1	12	79
Job 40:9	18	121
John 1:1, 14	50	350
John 1:5	32	221
John 1:6	4	25
John 10:10	18	121
John 10:10	22	148
John 10:10	37	253
John 10:10	38	264
John 10:28	49	341
John 10:29	28	191
John 10:29	50	351
John 12:43	27	186
John 14:16	31	212
John 14:2	36	249
John 14:2	36	252
John 14:2, 3	23	157
John 14:2, 3	26	181

Reference	Week	Page
John 14:2, 3	46	318
John 14:26	46	319
John 14:3	12	84
John 14:3	40	278
John 14:3	40	280
John 14:3	46	316
John 14:6	0	-1
John 14:6	12	81
John 14:6	14	94
John 14:6	15	105
John 14:6	22	152
John 14:6	23	160
John 14:6	24	164
John 14:6	29	202
John 14:6	36	247
John 14:6	40	278
John 14:6	40	279
John 14:6	42	293
John 14:6	43	300
John 14:6	44	303
John 14:6	47	325
John 14:6	48	331
John 14:6	50	351
John 14:9	50	350
John 15:13	26	176
John 15:15	27	187
John 15:15	28	192
John 15:15	46	319
John 15:18	35	244
John 15:18, 19	7	44
John 15:2	5	34
John 15:2	36	252
John 15:5	5	34
John 16:11	23	155
John 16:13	3	16
John 16:33	2	14

Reference	Week	Page
John 16:33	23	157
John 16:33	24	167
John 16:33	27	189
John 16:33	35	244
John 16:33	39	266
John 16:33	49	341
John 16:7	49	339
John 17:1-26	27	183
John 17:16	27	183
John 17:17, 19	27	183
John 17:5	30	210
John 3:16	32	222
John 3:19	32	218
John 3:19	34	235
John 3:30	3	16
John 3:30	5	32
John 4:23	17	115
John 4:23	46	322
John 4:24	48	333
John 6:37	12	79
John 6:37	36	247
John 8:12	32	218
John 8:32	4	27
John 8:32	9	61
John 8:32	39	268
John 8:36	48	332
John 8:44	2	8
John 8:44	2	13
John 8:44	18	122
John 8:44	28	195
John 8:44	32	220
John 8:44	35	243
John 8:44	37	253
John 8:44	38	263
John 8:44	44	303
John 8:44	47	325

Reference	Week	Page
John 9:5	32	218
Jonah 1:2	4	25
Jos. 3:5	5	30
Josh. 24:15	25	171
Josh. 24:15	36	252
Josh. 24:15	38	261
Josh.24:15	21	147
Jude 21	33	231
Lam. 3:22, 23	8	51
Lam. 3:22, 23	8	52
Lam. 3:22, 23	40	280
Lam. 3:22, 23	46	320
Lam. 3:23	45	309
Lam. 3:25	33	225
Lam. 3:40	19	127
Lev. 19:2	36	246
Lev. 20:10	35	244
Luke 10	26	182
Luke 10:1	49	339
Luke 10:2	18	122
Luke 10:20	40	280
Luke 10:20	48	331
Luke 11:23	29	200
Luke 11:23	43	301
Luke 12:15	29	203
Luke 12:19	43	299
Luke 12:19, 20	34	237
Luke 12:20, 21	43	299
Luke 12:25	43	295
Luke 12:40	45	315
Luke 13:24-28	37	258
Luke 14:33	21	144
Luke 15:17	22	153
Luke 16:23	21	147
Luke 16:23, 24	42	293
Luke 16:23, 24	45	310

Reference	Week	Page
Luke 16:24	32	220
Luke 17:26, 27	42	291
Luke 18:16	47	327
Luke 19:17	27	188
Luke 19:17	34	232
Luke 19:17	37	257
Luke 2:45	47	326
Luke 21:33	37	257
Luke 21:33	40	276
Luke 22:31-34	34	235
Luke 23:42, 43	7	44
Luke 4:36	39	270
Luke 5:26	30	210
Luke 6:31	24	163
Luke 6:31	36	249
Luke 6:45	19	132
Luke 6:45	37	256
Luke 6:45	41	287
Luke 6:45	51	359
Luke 8:15	34	238
Luke 9:23	26	182
Luke 9:23	27	188
Luke 9:23	37	258
Luke 9:26	18	123
Mal. 3:10	1	3
Mal. 3:11	49	339
Mal. 3:16	3	21
Mal. 3:8	17	119
Mal. 3:8, 9	41	286
Mark 1:27	39	270
Mark 10:18	16	107
Mark 10:27	14	98
Mark 10:43	1	6
Mark 10:44	42	289
Mark 12:30	46	319
Mark 12:30, 31	25	174

Reference	Week	Page
Mark 13:31	33	231
Mark 13:31	37	257
Mark 13:31	40	276
Mark 13:37	29	203
Mark 14:3	5	32
Mark 14:53-61	18	125
Mark 15:11-15	16	111
Mark 2:17	10	69
Mark 6:8, 9	7	43
Mark 7:18-23	18	125
Mark 8:33	47	326
Mark 9:35	36	249
Matt 12:34	9	60
Matt. 1:19	47	326
Matt. 10:1	39	270
Matt. 10:28	15	103
Matt. 10:28	23	160
Matt. 10:28	32	221
Matt. 10:28	49	341
Matt. 10:8	17	116
Matt. 11:28	36	251
Matt. 11:28	38	265
Matt. 11:4-6	26	179
Matt. 12:29	30	207
Matt. 12:30	22	154
Matt. 12:33-37	22	154
Matt. 12:34	11	71
Matt. 12:34	24	164
Matt. 12:34	41	287
Matt. 13:41, 42	21	147
Matt. 13:45, 46	21	144
Matt. 13:55	47	326
Matt. 14:31	41	282
Matt. 15:19	5	34
Matt. 15:36-38	43	298
Matt. 16:18	41	282

Reference	Week	Page
Matt. 16:3	42	291
Matt. 16:3	52	367
Matt. 17:1	23	156
Matt. 17:20	41	282
Matt. 17:27	45	315
Matt. 18:14	43	298
Matt. 18:21	43	301
Matt. 18:22-35	26	178
Matt. 18:23	36	247
Matt. 18:23-35	36	247
Matt. 18:24	24	165
Matt. 18:26	40	276
Matt. 18:28	24	165
Matt. 19:14	28	192
Matt. 19:14	45	310
Matt. 20	22	149
Matt. 21:12	18	125
Matt. 22:13	29	199
Matt. 22:21	17	114
Matt. 22:37	3	16
Matt. 22:37-39	15	105
Matt. 23:27	18	125
Matt. 23:27	27	184
Matt. 23:27	39	268
Matt. 23:6	8	53
Matt. 24:12	31	217
Matt. 24:12	42	292
Matt. 24:12	50	352
Matt. 24:3-13	42	290
Matt. 24:35	25	172
Matt. 24:35	27	185
Matt. 24:35	40	276
Matt. 24:42	42	290
Matt. 25: 21, 23	34	238
Matt. 25:1-13	30	205
Matt. 25:16	12	84

Reference	Week	Page
Matt. 25:19	4	22
Matt. 25:19	12	84
Matt. 25:19	28	190
Matt. 25:2, 11, 12	45	315
Matt. 25:21	4	23
Matt. 25:21, 23	30	21
Matt. 25:26	3	19
Matt. 25:26	30	21
Matt. 25:26	32	221
Matt. 25:30	29	199
Matt. 25:30	36	250
Matt. 25:34-40	33	231
Matt. 26:39	5	29
Matt. 26:39	31	215
Matt. 26:56	27	188
Matt. 26:59	22	154
Matt. 27:40	33	225
Matt. 28:17	30	207
Matt. 28:19	30	207
Matt. 28:19	37	259
Matt. 28:19	43	301
Matt. 28:19	44	305
Matt. 28:19, 20	12	83
Matt. 28:19, 20	48	336
Matt. 4:3, 6	33	225
Matt. 4:4	21	145
Matt. 4:4, 7, 10	52	361
Matt. 5:12	29	199
Matt. 5:14-16	32	222
Matt. 5:14-16	34	235
Matt. 5:16	30	206
Matt. 5:16	31	216
Matt. 5:21, 22	29	197
Matt. 5:22	29	198
Matt. 5:28	29	198
Matt. 5:29	22	148

Reference	Week	Page
Matt. 5:30	37	257
Matt. 5:32, 34	29	198
Matt. 5:36	43	295
Matt. 5:37	21	145
Matt. 5:38-41	26	178
Matt. 5:39, 44	29	198
Matt. 5:41	31	211
Matt. 5:41	34	233
Matt. 5:44	7	44
Matt. 5:44	29	199
Matt. 5:44	49	340
Matt. 5:45	32	222
Matt. 6:19, 20	51	355
Matt. 6:19-21	3	21
Matt. 6:19-21	33	231
Matt. 6:19-21	45	309
Matt. 6:20	17	115
Matt. 6:20	24	166
Matt. 6:27	0	-1
Matt. 6:30	41	282
Matt. 6:31-33	33	230
Matt. 6:32	21	142
Matt. 6:32	51	357
Matt. 6:32b, 33	24	168
Matt. 6:33	22	153
Matt. 6:33	33	226
Matt. 6:33	38	264
Matt. 6:33	43	299
Matt. 6:5	26	177
Matt. 6:6	29	199
Matt. 7:11	13	89
Matt. 7:11	19	131
Matt. 7:11	33	226
Matt. 7:11	33	230
Matt. 7:11	38	264
Matt. 7:12	29	201

Reference	Week	Page
Matt. 7:13	32	220
Matt. 7:13	39	270
Matt. 7:13, 14	12	81
Matt. 7:13, 14	18	123
Matt. 7:13, 14	23	160
Matt. 7:13, 14	30	21
Matt. 7:13, 14	31	214
Matt. 7:13, 14	43	300
Matt. 7:13, 14	45	313
Matt. 7:14	31	214
Matt. 7:2	29	198
Matt. 7:21-23	30	205
Matt. 7:22, 23	23	160
Matt. 7:23	4	23
Matt. 7:23	29	202
Matt. 7:5	10	68
Matt. 7:5	32	224
Matt. 7:6	7	44
Matt. 7:7	36	251
Matt. 8:12	21	147
Matt. 8:12	29	199
Matt. 8:26	41	282
Matt. 9:38	19	130
Matt.11:11	47	328
Matt.15:18	47	327
Matt.18:6	47	329
Matt.24:35	37	257
Mic. 6:8	29	197
Mic. 6:8	31	211
Mic. 6:8	31	217
Mic. 6:8	43	297
Mic. 6:8	52	365
Nahum 1:3	26	178
Num. 11:1	19	128
Num. 13:32, 33	11	72
Num. 14:6-10	11	72

Reference	Week	Page
Num. 20:10	40	279
Num. 30:2	27	185
Num. 32:23	32	223
Num. 32:23	47	323
Phil. 1:11	30	21
Phil. 1:23	49	341
Phil. 1:23	51	355
Phil. 2:3	8	53
Phil. 2:3	36	249
Phil. 2:3	37	256
Phil. 2:3	40	277
Phil. 2:3, 4	31	211
Phil. 2:3, 4	37	259
Phil. 2:4	3	17
Phil. 2:6	31	213
Phil. 2:8	33	228
Phil. 3, 13-14	34	233
Phil. 3:12-16	37	258
Phil. 3:13	19	130
Phil. 3:13, 14	21	144
Phil. 3:13, 14	28	196
Phil. 3:13, 14	31	214
Phil. 3:13,14	3	21
Phil. 3:14	12	79
Phil. 3:14	18	123
Phil. 3:14	19	130
Phil. 3:18	29	199
Phil. 3:18-20	8	50
Phil. 3:4-6	28	193
Phil. 3:5, 6	40	279
Phil. 3:7, 8	28	193
Phil. 3:7, 8	34	232
Phil. 3:7, 8	40	279
Phil. 3:7, 8	45	309
Phil. 3:8, 14	23	156
Phil. 4:11	19	131

Reference	Week	Page
Phil. 4:13	17	118
Phil. 4:19	12	83
Phil. 4:19	20	138
Phil. 4:19	48	332
Phil. 4:19	51	357
Phil. 4:4-7	24	164
Phil. 4:7	13	89
Phil.2:8	47	323
Prov. 1:1-7	32	222
Prov. 1:5	28	193
Prov. 11:1	5	35
Prov. 11:13	41	283
Prov. 11:18	45	311
Prov. 11:2	44	303
Prov. 11:20	45	312
Prov. 11:30	5	34
Prov. 11:30	44	305
Prov. 11:30	50	351
Prov. 12:15	42	294
Prov. 12:15	43	296
Prov. 12:22	15	101
Prov. 12:22	45	312
Prov. 14:16	45	312
Prov. 15:1	41	281
Prov. 15:19	28	196
Prov. 15:2	45	312
Prov. 15:33	27	186
Prov. 15:8	45	312
Prov. 16:16	45	309
Prov. 16:18	43	296
Prov. 16:23	45	314
Prov. 16:9	23	159
Prov. 17:22	10	67
Prov. 17:22	12	82
Prov. 17:22	21	143
Prov. 18:1	45	312

Reference	Week	Page
Prov. 18:12	37	255
Prov. 18:2	39	268
Prov. 18:2	45	312
Prov. 19:14	1	4
Prov. 19:14	13	90
Prov. 19:2	34	232
Prov. 19:2	52	366
Prov. 2:1	38	263
Prov. 2:13	27	187
Prov. 2:20	27	187
Prov. 20:11	35	240
Prov. 20:6	41	284
Prov. 21:1	36	252
Prov. 22:1	47	326
Prov. 22:7	17	113
Prov. 22:7	22	151
Prov. 24:17, 18	29	199
Prov. 25:2	49	343
Prov. 25:20	11	74
Prov. 25:21, 22	29	199
Prov. 25:6, 7	25	173
Prov. 25:7	8	53
Prov. 25:9	42	289
Prov. 26:19	21	145
Prov. 26:25	41	287
Prov. 27:17	27	187
Prov. 27:17	43	296
Prov. 27:17	45	311
Prov. 27:6	45	311
Prov. 28:5	32	221
Prov. 29:15	50	347
Prov. 29:23	27	186
Prov. 29:25	30	21
Prov. 3:11-12	47	329
Prov. 3:12	34	236
Prov. 3:35	45	312

Reference	Week	Page
Prov. 3:7	22	148
Prov. 30:32	25	169
Prov. 30:32	37	256
Prov. 4:14, 19	39	269
Prov. 4:15	47	325
Prov. 4:18	39	269
Prov. 4:18	39	271
Prov. 4:19	32	221
Prov. 6:12-15	41	281
Prov. 6:16, 17	16	106
Prov. 6:16, 17	25	175
Prov. 6:16-18	29	197
Prov. 6:16-19	41	281
Prov. 6:16-19	47	324
Prov. 6:17	20	134
Prov. 7:10, 21, 23	32	220
Prov. 8:13	17	118
Prov. 8:22	44	308
Prov. 8:29	30	208
Prov. 9:16-18	32	220
Prov. 9:6	25	169
Ps. 1:1, 2	22	152
Ps. 103:11	26	178
Ps. 103:12	7	49
Ps. 103:12	46	318
Ps. 103:13	34	236
Ps. 103:14	29	200
Ps. 103:19	13	91
Ps. 106:15	17	118
Ps. 106:23	2	12
Ps. 11:4	26	180
Ps. 118:6	7	49
Ps. 119:104	28	196
Ps. 119:105	42	289
Ps. 119:105	45	313
Ps. 119:11	2	8

Reference	Week	Page
Ps. 119:11	28	195
Ps. 119:160	37	256
Ps. 119:38	22	152
Ps. 119:38	29	200
Ps. 119:38	30	207
Ps. 119:38	44	302
Ps. 119:38	48	332
Ps. 119:89	45	310
Ps. 119:9	14	93
Ps. 119:9	35	242
Ps. 119:98-100	28	196
Ps. 12:6	35	244
Ps. 121:4	7	46
Ps. 126:2	21	141
Ps. 127:3	2	11
Ps. 139:12	47	323
Ps. 139:16	0	-1
Ps. 139:16	8	51
Ps. 139:16	8	52
Ps. 139:16	14	94
Ps. 139:16	28	192
Ps. 139:16	51	358
Ps. 14:1	45	311
Ps. 146:9	36	252
Ps. 15:1	27	185
Ps. 16:11	23	155
Ps. 17:10	41	287
Ps. 18:47	29	199
Ps. 2:2, 4	35	245
Ps. 2:4	36	252
Ps. 24:3-5	35	243
Ps. 30:5	23	161
Ps. 32:8	22	153
Ps. 32:8	23	161
Ps. 32:8	31	212
Ps. 33:18	15	105

Reference	Week	Page
Ps. 34:1	46	320
Ps. 34:7	7	46
Ps. 37: 2, 3	38	261
Ps. 37:25	7	47
Ps. 4:3	36	251
Ps. 50:10	33	225
Ps. 50:10-12	45	315
Ps. 50:21	49	338
Ps. 53:1	44	302
Ps. 56:11	15	103
Ps. 56:4	7	49
Ps. 78:31	39	269
Ps. 84:11	40	280
Ps. 86:7	46	318
Ps. 90:12	28	192
Ps. 92:1	40	275
Ps.5:3	13	86
Rev. 16:15	29	203
Rev. 16:21	34	238
Rev. 16:4	39	270
Rev. 2:4	27	187
Rev. 2:4, 5	34	235
Rev. 2:5	4	22
Rev. 20:10	42	293
Rev. 20:10, 15	32	220
Rev. 20:10, 15	32	222
Rev. 20:12	15	105
Rev. 20:12	22	154
Rev. 20:12	32	220
Rev. 20:15	29	202
Rev. 20:1-6	27	189
Rev. 20:4	37	259
Rev. 21:1	30	208
Rev. 21:12	43	301
Rev. 21:21	35	244
Rev. 21:21	43	301

Reference	Week	Page
Rev. 21:4	23	157
Rev. 21:4	37	258
Rev. 21:4	43	301
Rev. 22:12	12	84
Rev. 22:12	46	320
Rev. 22:17	31	214
Rev. 22:18, 19	45	310
Rev. 22:18, 19	50	348
Rev. 22:20	12	80
Rev. 3:10	34	238
Rev. 3:16	5	32
Rev. 3:16	14	98
Rev. 3:16	28	193
Rev. 3:3	33	231
Rev. 3:5	35	244
Rev. 5:5	52	364
Rev. 6:10,11	2	14
Rev. 6:17	39	269
Rev. 7:9, 14	36	250
Rom 12:3	8	53
Rom 8:32	1	4
Rom. 1:18	44	308
Rom. 1:18-23	40	275
Rom. 1:19	12	81
Rom. 1:19	46	320
Rom. 1:19, 20	36	249
Rom. 1:19, 20	49	343
Rom. 1:25	21	143
Rom. 10:10	33	231
Rom. 10:9	33	231
Rom. 10:9	36	247
Rom. 12:15	20	137
Rom. 12:16	3	18
Rom. 12:2	11	76
Rom. 12:2	20	137
Rom. 12:2	30	206

Reference	Week	Page
Rom. 12:2	37	255
Rom. 12:2	38	262
Rom. 12:2	39	267
Rom. 12:2	39	271
Rom. 12:2	44	304
Rom. 12:2	45	314
Rom. 12:3	12	82
Rom. 12:3	25	173
Rom. 13: 11, 12	45	311
Rom. 13:1	23	159
Rom. 13:1	25	175
Rom. 13:1	51	356
Rom. 13:11	28	191
Rom. 13:11	29	203
Rom. 13:11	42	288
Rom. 13:3	31	211
Rom. 13:8	22	151
Rom. 14:12	39	271
Rom. 14:17	4	28
Rom. 15:13	34	238
Rom. 2:1, 3	33	229
Rom. 3:23	5	34
Rom. 3:23	52	363
Rom. 3:4	30	208
Rom. 5:21	33	230
Rom. 5:3-5	34	238
Rom. 5:3-5	51	356
Rom. 5:5	26	180
Rom. 5:5	49	342
Rom. 5:7	31	217
Rom. 5:8	5	34
Rom. 5:8	26	180
Rom. 5:8	26	182
Rom. 5:8	31	217
Rom. 6:1, 2, 15	36	252
Rom. 6:23	40	276

Reference	Week	Page
Rom. 6:23	50	351
Rom. 6:23	52	363
Rom. 7:14-25	16	110
Rom. 7:15	5	34
Rom. 7:19;	24	162
Rom. 8:1	35	241
Rom. 8:1	42	288
Rom. 8:15	18	123
Rom. 8:15	29	202
Rom. 8:15	32	222
Rom. 8:18	11	76
Rom. 8:2	42	289
Rom. 8:28	5	30
Rom. 8:28	5	31
Rom. 8:28	8	56
Rom. 8:28	16	107
Rom. 8:28	19	132
Rom. 8:28	21	142
Rom. 8:28	23	161
Rom. 8:28	37	253
Rom. 8:29	5	35
Rom. 8:29	13	86
Rom. 8:31	49	341
Rom. 8:32	40	274
Rom. 8:37	18	123
Rom: 11:25	52	367
Tit. 1:2	21	142
Tit. 1:2	29	201
Tit. 1:2	32	221
Tit. 1:2	33	230
Tit. 1:2	39	267
Tit. 1:2	43	301
Tit. 1:2	44	303
Tit. 1:2	45	310
Tit. 1:2	48	335
Tit. 1:2	49	340

Reference	Week	Page
Tit. 2:9, 10	26	181
Tit. 3:10	7	44
Tit. 3:9	44	303
Zech. 8:13	6	37